Praise for The Long Depression

"Michael Roberts has established himself as one of the foremost bloggers and theoreticians of classical Marxism. Here he takes on the economic orthodoxy, both Keynesian and neoclassical, as to the causes of the Great Recession and of depressions in capitalism going back to the nineteenth century. [While] 'the new normal' and 'secular stagnation' have be[come] clichés rather than explanations for the slow growth in the world economy since the 2008 crash, Michael Roberts reaches deep into the history of capitalism to set out a Marxist explanation for recent developments."

—**MICK BROOKS**, author of *Capitalist Crisis: Theory and Practice*

"Since the global economic crisis, Michael Roberts's blog has become the indispensable source for those on the left seeking to understand and challenge capitalism. This book presents, with admirable clarity, the ideas drawn from Marxist political economy upon which his analysis rests. Anyone who wants to understand how we ended up here, where we are going, and what we should do about it must read *The Long Depression*."

—**JOSEPH CHOONARA**, author of *Unravelling Capitalism: A Guideto Marxist Political Economy*

"[A] tour de force analysis of the current global economic crisis and the preconditions and prospects for recovery in the years ahead. . . . [Roberts argues] that a full recovery and a return to more prosperous conditions requires an even more severe depression, characterized by widespread bankruptcies, which would devalue capital and restore the rate of profit and would also wipe out much of the debt. He argues that a much better alternative would be to wipe out capitalism and construct a more democratic and egalitarian economy that is not vulnerable to recurring depressions."

—**FRED MOSELEY**, professor of economics, Mount Holyoke College

"With great clarity, Michael Roberts explains capitalism's necessary proneness to profound economic crises and surveys the course of the current and previous depressions. Extensive use of empirical evidence, very accessibly presented, make his own main, Marxist argument and refutations of rival explanations persuasive. This book is at once an engaging read and a powerful political weapon."

—**RICK KUHN**, honorary associate professor at the Australian National University and winner of the 2007 Isaac Deutscher Memorial Prize

"*The Long Depression* is an impressive review of the global economic crisis. Marshalling a wide range of evidence, Michael Roberts counters the facile explanations of establishment commentators and many 'alternative' economists, showing instead how the origins of this crisis, and other historical examples, have clear links to declining capitalist profitability."

—**TONY NORFIELD**, author of *The City: London andthe Global Power of Finance*

The Long Depression

The Long Depression

How It Happened, Why It Happened, and What Happens Next

Michael Roberts

Haymarket Books
Chicago, Illinois

Published by
Haymarket Books
P.O. Box 180165
Chicago, IL 60618
773-583-7884
info@haymarketbooks.org
www.haymarketbooks.org

ISBN: 978-1-60846-468-5

Trade distribution:
In the US, Consortium Book Sales and Distribution, www.cbsd.com
In the UK, Turnaround Publisher Services, www.turnaround-uk.com
In Canada, Publishers Group Canada, www.pgcbooks.ca
In all other countries, Publishers Group Worldwide, www.pgw.com

This book was published with the generous support of the Wallace Action
Fund and Lannan Foundation.

Library of Congress Cataloging in Publication (CIP) Data is available.

Contents

Introduction

Getting Depressed

Recessions are common; depressions are rare. As far as I can tell, there were only two eras in economic history that were widely described as "depressions" at the time: the years of deflation and instability that followed the Panic of 1873 and the years of mass unemployment that followed the financial crisis of 1929–31. Neither the Long Depression of the 19th century nor the Great Depression of the 20th was an era of nonstop decline—on the contrary, both included periods when the economy grew. But these episodes of improvement were never enough to undo the damage from the initial slump, and were followed by relapses. We are now, I fear, in the early stages of a third depression. It will probably look more like the Long Depression than the much more severe Great Depression. But the cost—to the world economy and, above all, to the millions of lives blighted by the absence of jobs—will nonetheless be immense.

—Paul Krugman[1]

Why Did We Miss It?

As the Great Recession unfolded, people asked how it happened and why. In the United Kingdom, we suffer a long-standing monarchy. England had a republic briefly, for only eleven years between 1649 and 1660, after executing the monarch at the time. But now Britain has a queen who has been around a long time. At the height of the crisis in November 2008, she visited the London School of Economics, a major university with a high reputation. She asked the eminent economists bowing before her: why had nobody noticed that the credit crunch was on its way? This caused consternation among the mainstream economics world: even the queen was questioning their skills! Robin Jackson, chief executive and secretary of the British Academy, the prestigious scientific institute, rushed out an official letter in reply, admitting that the great and good in officialdom and mainstream economics did not understand "the risks."[2]

Indeed, before 2007, no official strategist of economic policy forecast any crisis. The mainstream economists in prestigious institutions were no better than government officials in forecasting the Great Recession. Indeed, they were worse, because they really were supposed to know.

The doyen of the neoclassical school, Robert Lucas, confidently claimed back in 2003 that "the central problem of depression-prevention has been solved." Leading Keynesian Olivier Blanchard, former chief economist at the International Monetary Fund (IMF), told us as late as 2008 that "the state of macro is good!"[3] He meant macroeconomics theory as a guide to what is happening in a modern economy.

Forecasting: The Power of the Aggregate

This book offers an ambitious explanation of recent economic events and also, most will say, an overly ambitious forecast or prediction of what is going to happen. Futurology is a popular pastime among authors of "world views." Economic forecasting is a particular nightmare, as the Great Recession proved.[4]

But we cannot throw up our hands in a gesture of failure. As Marx said, we must try to apply scientific methods to looking beneath the surface of things and ascertain the causal processes underneath. By succeeding in that, we can give our conclusions some predictive power. Indeed, prediction is necessary to confirm or falsify our conclusions. It must not be shied away from.

Statistical analysis is much better at forecasting things than "hunches" or human intuition. Everything is not entirely random. Some claimed that the Great Recession was a "random" event, a chance in a billion,[5] as even the most unlikely thing can happen under the law of chance. The example is that it was assumed there were only white swans until Europeans got to Australia and found black ones. It was the "unknown unknown," to quote US President George W. Bush's neo-con Secretary of State Donald Rumsfeld. The most unlikely thing can happen, but you cannot know everything. The Great Recession was one such event that could not have been predicted and therefore bankers, politicians, and above all economists were not at fault. This was the excuse used by bankers when giving evidence to the US Congress and to the UK Parliament.

But modern statistical methods do have predictive power—all is not random. In his book, Nate Silver offers detailed case studies from baseball, elections, climate change, the financial crash, poker, and weather forecasting.[6] Using as much data as possible, statistical techniques can provide degrees of probability.[7] This is the modern form of statistical analysis in what is called the Bayesian approach, named after the eighteenth-century minister Thomas Bayes, who discovered a simple formula for updating probabilities using new data.[8] The essence of the Bayesian approach is to provide a mathematical rule explaining how you should change your existing beliefs in the light of new evidence. In other words, it allows scientists to combine new data with their existing knowledge or expertise.

Bayes's law also shows two other things that are useful to remember in economic analysis. The first is the power of data or facts over theory and models. Neoclassical mainstream economics is not just voodoo economics because it is ideologically biased, an apology for the capitalist mode of production. In making assumptions about individual consumer behavior, about the inherent equilibrium of capitalist production, and so on, it is also based on theoretical models that bear no relation to reality: the known facts or "priors."

In contrast, a scientific approach would aim to test theory against the evidence on a continual basis, not just falsify it (as Karl Popper would have it[9]) but also to strengthen its explanatory power—unless a better explanation of the facts comes along. Isaac Newton's theory of gravity explained very much about the universe and was tested by the evidence, but then Albert Einstein's theory of relativity came along and better explained the facts (or widened our understanding of things that could not be explained by Newton's laws). In this sense, Marxist method is also scientific. Marx begins with concrete phenomena from which he abstracts real forces (as theory) and then returns to the concrete (using facts to show this reality). The reality then strengthens the explanatory power of the theory by modifying it.

The second thing we can glean from the use of Bayes's law is the power of the aggregate. The best economic theory and explanation come from looking at the aggregate, the average, and their outliers. Data based on a few studies or data points provide no explanatory power. That may sound obvious, but it seems that many political pundits were prepared to forecast the result of the last US presidential election based on virtually no aggregated evidence. It's the same with much of economic forecasting. Sure, what happened in the past is no certain guide to what may happen in the future, but aggregated evidence over time is much better than ignoring history.

If economists want to understand the causes of financial and economic crisis, they need to look away from individual behavior or models based on "representative agents" and instead look to the aggregate: from the particular to the general. They need to turn back from deductive a priori reasoning alone toward history, the evidence of the past. History may not be a guide to the future, but speculation without history is even less based in reality. Economists need theories that can be tested by the evidence. In an appendix, I deal at greater length with the failure of Keynesian economic theory to do that.

Mainstream economics does not seem to have any predictive power. "I've been forecasting for 50 years and I had not seen any improvement in our capability of forecasting," said the great maestro, Alan Greenspan.[10] But if we desert data, economists will head into a virtual world.[11] Some have already done so.[12] This book attempts to link theory with data, provide a causal explanation of what has been happening in the world economy since 2007, and make some predictions about what will happen.

Indeed, I made a stab at it my previous book, *The Great Recession*, when I wrote as early as 2005 that "There has not been such a coincidence of cycles since 1991. And this time (unlike 1991), it will be accompanied by the downwave in profitability within the downwave in Kondratiev prices cycle. It is all at the bottom of the hill in 2009–2010! That suggests we can expect a very severe economic slump of a degree not seen since 1980–2 or more."[13] That prediction was not far off, given that the bottom of the Great Recession was in mid-2009.

The Long Depression

The main message of this book is that the major economies of the world (and by that I mean specifically the top seven advanced capitalist economies [G7] and the major so-called emerging economies) are in a long depression.

A *depression* is defined here as when economies are growing at well below their previous rate of output (in total and per capita) and below their long-term average. It also means that levels of employment and investment are well below those peaks and below long-term averages. Above all, it means that the profitability of the capitalist sectors in economies remain, by and large, lower than levels before the start of the depression.

To date, there have been three depressions (as opposed to regular and recurring economic slumps or recessions) in modern capitalism. The first was in the late nineteenth century (1873–97); the second was in the mid twentieth century (1929–39); and now we have one in the early twenty-first century (2008–?). These all started with significant slumps (1873-6; 1929-32; and 2008-9).

Most important, depressions (as opposed to recessions) appear when there is a conjunction of downward phases in cycles of capitalism. Every depression has come when the cycle in clusters of innovation have matured and have become "saturated"; when world production and commodity prices enter a downward phase, namely, that inflation is slowing and turns into deflation; when the cycle of construction and infrastructure investment has slumped; and above all, when the cycle of profitability is in its downward phase. The conjunction of these different cycles only happens every sixty to seventy years. That is why the current Long Depression is so important.

A *long depression* is the best term to use to describe the period through which capitalism is now passing. The Long Depression will be ended by a conjunction of economic outcomes (slump, technological revolution, and a change of economic cycle) or by political action to end or replace the capitalist mode of production. There is no permanent crisis. There is always resolution and new contradictions in the dialectics of history. So the Long Depression will end more like the nineteenth-century depression of 1880–90s ended—with a new upswing in capitalism and globalization.

The nineteenth-century depression ended in the late 1880s and 1890s in the United Kingdom, the United States, and Germany. That is also what happened from 1948 onward in the United States, Europe, and Japan. Eventually this Long Depression will end. But it will take another major slump to create the conditions for sustained recovery (a new "spring" phase for capitalism). The Long Depression still has another stage to go before it will come to an end. We are not there yet—we are still in a period of depression (an economic "winter") that could last another few years or so.

Some of those who accept that there are depressions in capitalism—as opposed to just the cycle of boom and slump alone—reckon that once in the "slough of despond," capitalism can only get out of such a depression by some external events like war or revolution:[14] in other words by the action of human beings "exogenously" on the economic system.

Depressions provoke a social and economic response. The depression of the nineteenth century provoked an imperialist rivalry that eventually led to World War I. The Great Depression of the 1930s led to the rise of fascism and Nazism in Europe, along with revolution and counter-revolution in Spain, militarism in Japan, and the consolidation of totalitarian rule in the Soviet Union that eventually led to a world war as the rising Axis powers threatened the global rule of Anglo-American imperialism.

This book argues that there is no permanent slump in capitalism that cannot be eventually overcome by capital itself. Capitalism has an economic way out if the mass of working people do not gain political power to replace the system. Eventually, through a series of slumps, the profitability of capital can be restored sufficiently to start to make use of any new technical advances and innovation that will have been "clustering" down in the bottom of that deep lake of depression. Capital will resurface for a new period of growth and development, but only after the bankruptcy of many companies, a huge rise in unemployment, and even the physical destruction of things and people in their millions.

The Structure of This Book

This book is not descriptive. There will not be a blow-by-blow account of what has happened economically over the past several years since the global credit crunch began in summer 2007. This book tries to provide an explanation of what has happened, an analysis of the causes, and some hypotheses (even predictions) of what will happen next.

Also, this book is not mainly theoretical, although the different theories presented to explain economic depressions are discussed and criticized on their merits from a Marxist viewpoint. But the critique is mainly based on using empirical evidence. I leave the theoretical debates and, in particular, a theoretical defense of Marx's crisis theory to other authors and another day.[15]

The structure of this book is first to define more clearly the nature of an economic depression as opposed to the regular slumps or recessions (to use the mainstream economics term) that capitalism experiences. To do that, the first chapter considers in detail the causes of capitalist crises from a Marxist point of view. Not every crisis or depression is the same; each has its own characteristics. The most notable feature of the current depression is the role of credit or debt. Never in the history of capitalism has the size and expansion of credit been so great. The collapse in that credit mountain was the trigger for the Great Recession, and the hangover from it is an important factor in the length and depth of the ensuing depression. However, there is an underlying causal framework to crises under capitalism, and the first chapter deals with this.

Chapters 2 and 3 discuss what happened in previous depressions, starting with the long depression in the major economies of Europe and the United States that began in the mid-1870s and lasted until the mid-1890s and defending the view that it was a depression. The chapters on this depression and the Great Depression of the 1930s draw out the similarities and try to define a common cause, which I argue is found in Marx's law of profitability.

Chapter 4 explains how the brief golden age of capitalism after 1945 up to the mid-1960s was followed by a profitability crisis in the major economies. This did not lead to a depression for reasons that will be explained. Instead, it was responded to with a concerted effort on the part of procapitalist governments to restore profitability in what has come to be called the neoliberal period, namely, when capitalist accumulation was "freed" from the interference of government management and when capitalism extended its influence into newly exploited areas of the globe. The chapter shows that the neoliberal period came to an end in the late 1990s as profitability began to decline again, presaging the Great Recession.

Chapter 5 on the Great Recession of 2008–9 describes the abysmal failure of mainstream economics to see it coming or explain what happened. In doing so, the latest fads for an explanation are criticized as inadequate.

The next chapters discuss the specific nature of this depression and its depth and length, followed by a tour of the impact of the Great Recession and the Long Depression on different parts of the global capitalist economy. Starting with the largest, that of the United States, chapters move on to the crisis in Europe, the stagnation in Japan, and the depressing impact on the emerging economies, arguing that these "more vibrant" new economies have not saved global capitalism from the effects of the depression.

The penultimate chapter puts forward the most controversial part of the explanation of this Long Depression: that it is the conjunction of several cycles or waves in capitalism that can be identified, including a much longer global production price cycle, called the Kondratiev. The Long Depression is the "winter" phase of one of the great waves of capitalist production that have lasted sixty to seventy years at a time in the major capitalist economies from about 1780 onward. The waves or cycles break up into four phases or "seasons": spring (economic recovery), summer (crisis and class struggle), autumn (boom and reaction), and winter (slumps and depression). Each season is set by the underlying cycle of profitability: spring is when profitability is on the rise; summer is when it falls; autumn is a period of rise; and finally, winter is a renewed period of decline in profitability. The existence of such a cycle and others is dismissed by most. It is for the reader to judge the arguments.

The final chapter discusses whether capitalism has now reached its use-by date, as many Marxists would argue. It considers the likelihood of the end of the Long Depression—whether capitalism still has opportunities ahead in many parts of the world to exploit labor more and revive its fortunes. It considers the impact, on the one hand, of the revolution in automation, robots, and artificial intelligence that capitalism may take advantage of and, on the other hand, the growing risk of major ecological and environmental calamity brought on by capitalism's rapacious, uncontrolled destruction of natural resources that has led to dangerous climate change.

Capitalism may come out of the Long Depression, but the time until its long-term extinction is getting nearer.

Chapter 1

The Cause of Depressions

The trigger for crisis can be any number of historical accidents such as the subprime mortgage swindle. It is necessary to deal with different levels of causation. The main point here is that capital is drawn into speculative activity when the rate of profit is low, so accident is the manifestation of necessity.

—Mick Brooks[1]

Those who choose to see each such episode as a singular event, as the random appearance of a "black swan" in a hitherto pristine flock, have forgotten the dynamics of the history they seek to explain. And in the process they also conveniently forget that it is the very logic of profit which condemns us to repeat this history.

—Anwar Shaikh[2]

The Nature of Depressions

There have been several depressions (as opposed to regular and recurring economic slumps or recessions) in modern capitalism. The first was in the late nineteenth century (1873–97); the second was in the mid twentieth century (1929–39); and now we have one in the early twenty-first century (2008–?).

Before the 1930s, all economic downturns were commonly called depressions. The term *recession* was coined later to avoid stirring up nasty memories. A recession is technically defined by mainstream economics as two consecutive quarters of contraction in real gross domestic product (GDP) in an economy. According to data compiled by the US National Bureau of Economic Research (NBER), recessions in the US economy on average have lasted about eleven months in the eleven official recessions since 1945. For the period recorded since 1859, recessions average about eighteen months. On average, the gap between each slump has averaged about six years in the postwar period and a little less over all thirty-three cycles, as defined by the NBER (see Table 1.1).[3]

Table 1.1

Business cycle reference dates

		Contraction	Expansion	Cycle	
			Previous	Trough	Peak
		Peak	trough	from	from
Quarterly dates are in parentheses		to	to this	previous	previous
Peak	Trough	trough	peak	trough	peak
....	December 1854 (IV)......	—	—......	—.....	—
June 1857 (II)	December 1858 (IV)......	18	30	48	—
October 1860 (III).......	June 1861 (III)	8	22	30	40
April 1865 (I).............	December 1867 (I)	32	46	78	54
June 1869 (II)	December 1870 (IV)......	18	18	36	50
October 1873 (III).......	March 1879 (I)............	65	34	99	52
March 1882 (I)...........	May 1885 (II)	38	36	74	101
March 1887 (II)	April 1888 (I)	13	22	35	60
July 1890 (III)	May 1891 (II)	10	27	37	40
January 1893 (I)	June 1894 (II)	17	20	37	30
December 1895 (IV)......	June 1897 (II)	18	18	36	35
June 1899 (III)	December 1900 (IV)......	18	24	42	42
September 1902 (IV)......	August 1904 (III).........	23	21	44	39
May 1907 (II)	June 1908 (II)	13	33	46	56
January 1910 (I)	January 1912 (IV)	24	19	43	32
January 1913 (I)	December 1914 (IV)......	23	12	35	36
August 1918 (III)	March 1919 (I)............	7	44	51	67
January 1920 (I)	July 1921 (III)	18	10	28	17
May 1923 (II)	July 1924 (III)	14	22	36	40
October 1926 (III).......	November 1927 (IV)......	13	27	40	41
August 1929 (III)	March 1933 (I)............	43	21	64	34
May 1937 (II)	June 1938 (II)	13	50	63	93
February 1945 (I)........	October 1945 (IV)........	8	80	88	93
November 1948 (IV)......	October 1949 (IV)........	11	37	48	45
July 1953 (II).............	May 1954 (II)	10	45	55	56
August 1957 (III)	April 1958 (II)	8	39	47	49
April 1960 (II)............	February 1961 (I).........	10	24	34	32
December 1969 (IV)......	November 1970 (IV)......	11	106	117	116
November 1973 (IV)......	March 1975 (I)............	16	36	52	47
January 1980 (I)	July 1980 (III)	6	58	64	74
July 1981 (III)	November 1982 (IV)......	16	12	28	18
July 1990 (III)	March 1991 (I)............	8	92	100	108
March 2001 (I)...........	November 2001 (IV)......	8	120	128	128
December 2007 (IV)......	June 2009 (II)	18	73	91	81

Average, all cycles:

1854–2009 (33 cycles).............................		17.5	38.7	56.2	56.4
1854–1919 (16 cycles).............................		21.6	26.6	48.2	48.9
1919–1945 (6 cycles)..............................		18.2	35	53.2	53
1945–2009 (11 cycles)		11.1	58.4	69.5	68.5

A depression has been defined by mainstream economics in two ways. The first is a rather formal rigid standard, namely, that an economy experiences a decline in real GDP that exceeds 10 percent, or suffers a decline that lasts more than three years. Both the late nineteenth-century depression and the Great Depression of the 1930s qualify on both counts, with a fall in real GDP of around 30 percent between 1929 and 1933. Output also fell 13 percent in 1937–38.

Second, it is argued that the difference between a recession and a depression is more than simply one of size or duration. The nature of the downturn matters as well. In the Great Depression, average prices in the United States fell by one-quarter and nominal GDP ended up shrinking by almost half. The worst US recessions before World War II were all associated with banking crises and falling prices. In both 1893–94 and 1907–8 real GDP declined by almost 10 percent; in 1919–21, it fell by 13 percent.

Neither of these definitions does justice to the reality of a depression. A more specific benchmark would be where an economy suffers a major contraction and any recovery is so weak that the trend growth path afterward is never reattained or at least takes several years or even a decade or more.

Think of it schematically. A recession and the ensuing recovery can be V-shaped, as typically in 1974–75; or maybe U-shaped; or even W-shaped as in the double-dip recession of 1980–82. But a depression is really more like a square root sign, which starts with a trend growth rate, drops in the initial deep slump, then makes what looks like a V-shaped recovery, but then levels off on a line that is below the previous trend line (see Figure 1.1). In a depression, precrisis trend growth is not restored for up to ten to fifteen or even twenty years.

With this definition, the Great Depression of the 1930s qualifies as a depression. Although the initial slump from 1929 to 1932 was the deepest in capitalist history so far, it was not the longest-lasting at forty-three months. The initial recession in the first long depression of the late nineteenth century was much longer at sixty-five months from 1873 to 1879. Recovery back to the trend growth rate in the United States was not achieved until 1940 after the Great Depression and not until the 1890s in the earlier depression. In the current Long Depression, the actual initial slump, the Great Recession, lasted only eighteen months, although this was the longest in the postwar period. Trend growth has not been achieved some eight years (nine-ty-six months) after the start of the Great Recession. So in that sense, it is a depression.

Figure 1.1
A Schematic View of Recessions and Depressions

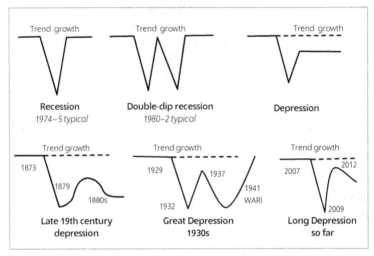

Source: Author

The Theory of Crises

What is the underlying cause of depressions in capitalist economies? I argue that it can be found in Marx's law of the tendency of the rate of profit to fall. Marx reckoned that this law was the most important in political economy. I believe it is logical and consistent and proves the most compelling explanation of the cause of booms and slumps under capitalism and recurrent and regular crises.

Marx starts with a crucial assumption, or prior: that value can only be generated by the exertion of labor. This is a realistic assumption. Factories, equipment, software, and raw materials cannot be put to work unless people (living labor) exert energy to use them. Value cannot be created in an economy without living labor—this implies that a fully robotic world would deliver much useful things, but it would not create value that capitalists could appropriate (see chapter 13 on this).

Marx's law starts with a simple equation. The rate of profit (R) = the surplus value (S) divided by constant capital (C) and variable capital (V). The law says that capitalists are engaged in competition in the marketplace to sell goods and services. If they cannot make a profit, they go bust and must leave the market. They raise profits by getting employees to produce goods or services with a value greater than the cost of production (namely, the cost of employing a workforce; the cost of investing in and using equipment, plant, and technology; and the cost of raw materials). This extra value is the surplus value (S).

Capitalists try to reduce their costs relative to the price they can sell at a profit what their workers produce for them in the market. Increasingly, they must do this by investing in more technology to boost the productivity of the workforce. So Marx's law says that as capitalists accumulate more capital, the value of the equipment, plant, and technology used will rise relative to the amount of labor employed. The value of means of production is called *constant capital* (C), because the means of production cannot add any new value without workers using it. The value of labor power employed is called *variable capital* (V), because the labor employed can produce more value than it consumes in goods and services that workers need to live.

Marx's law says that the ratio of constant capital over variable capital will rise over time. This ratio is called the *organic composition of capital* (C/V). If this rises over time and the rate of surplus value (S/V) is constant, the rate of profit must fall. That is the law of the tendency of the rate of profit to fall as such. But there are countertendencies, the main one being that the rate of surplus value is likely to rise as capitalists use new technology to boost the productivity of labor. However, it will not be possible for the capitalist economy to raise the rate of surplus value (either indefinitely or for any great length of time) more than the increase in the organic composition of capital. Eventually, the law as such will prevail and the rate of profit will start to fall.

This continual process of an upward cycle in profitability—as the rate of surplus value rises faster than the organic composition, in turn replaced by a downward cycle as the "law as such" gains ascendancy—explains the cyclical nature of capitalist accumulation. As the rate of profit falls, at a certain point this causes a fall in total profit, engendering a slump in investment and the economy as a whole. The slump eventually reduces the cost of constant capital of the means of production (through bankruptcies and write-offs of equipment) and variable capital (through unemployment, migration, etc.). Profitability is then restored and the whole "crap" (to use Marx's phrase) starts again.

Currently, profitability in most major economies is still well below the level reached in 2007 and is also below the last peak in profitability of 1997. Thus we are in a downward phase in the cycle of profitability that I argue can be discerned in capitalist economies.[4]

Not Enough Profit: Simple!

Where does this Marxist explanation of crises under capitalism sit in the spectrum of crisis theory? Look at the clever chart in Figure 1.2. Is capitalism subject to *inevitable* (and recurrent) crises? Mainstream neoclassical and Keynesian economics say no. It's chance, bad policy, or some other shock or a technical malfunction that can either be fixed or lived with. If you agree with that, you end up on the very right side of the flow chart. If you agree that crises are inevitable and/or recurring, you head toward the left. As the chart shows, the Marxist school can be subdivided between those who see the cause of capitalist crisis in "overproduction" and/or "underconsumption" or in profitability. If you reckon the latter, then you end up in the very bottom left: "The limit to capital is capital itself."

That's where this author is. *In Marx's view, the most important law of political economy was the tendency of the average rate of profit of capital to fall.*[5] In making this argument, he posits the ultimate cause of capitalist crises in the capitalist production process, specifically in production for profit.

Marx noted that the driving force of capitalism is the relentless search for surplus value. The early phase of capitalism is generally characterized by a drive for increasing extraction of absolute surplus value, that is, increasing the length of the working day and holding the real wage rate constant. In contrast, the later phase is generally characterized by an increase in the extraction of relative surplus value, that is, reducing the social labor time required to produce the consumer basket of the workers and holding constant the length of the working day.

This outcome occurs in the course of labor's struggle against capital, which in particular sets an upper limit to the length of the working day. Thereafter, the search for surplus value primarily takes the form of the drive to increase the productivity of labor.

This drive is at the heart of the enormous technological dynamism of capitalism compared with earlier modes of production. Competition between capitalists induces reductions in the costs of production and thereby increases surplus value for innovative capitalists, frequently via labor-saving technical change. In other words, capitalists increasingly use nonlabor inputs in the course of their efforts to reduce costs of production.

Figure 1.2
Crisis Theory

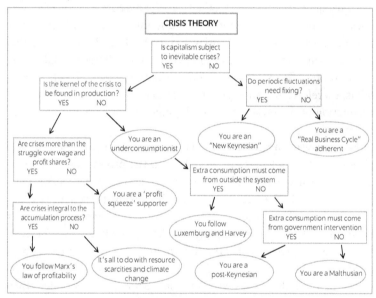

Source: San Francisco Area Marxist Study Group

The contradiction between labor and capital manifests itself not just as a struggle over the division of the value added between wages and profits. This fundamental contradiction also appears as a struggle to control aspects of the production process, like intensity and pace of labor; working conditions relating to safety of workers; break frequency and duration; and pace and direction of technological change. The constant tug-of-war between labor and capital to control aspects of the production process is as old as capitalist social relations.

Therefore mechanization is a potent tool in the hands of the capitalist class for their conflict with labor. A machine, after all, is much easier to dominate than a recalcitrant worker is. Marx highlighted this political dimension of mechanization in his discussion of skilled workers and engineers in England,[6] and it remains valid today. This increasing mechanization of the production process enormously increases the productivity of labor and facilitates the extraction of larger amounts of relative surplus value. The increasing replacement of labor with nonlabor inputs is reflected in a rise of the share of total capital outlays supporting constant capital (the cost of machinery, plant, and technology) in relation to variable capital (the cost of labor power).

Consequently, what Marx called the organic composition of capital rises, and there is a reduction in the amount of labor available for exploitation per unit of capital outlay. If the rate of surplus value remains constant, this rise in the composition of capital will lead to a fall in the rate of profit. "The progressive tendency of the general rate of profit to fall is, therefore, just an expression peculiar to the capitalist mode of production of the progressive development of the social productivity of labour."[7]

Marx's law is framed in terms of tendencies and countertendencies.[8] When new technologies are brought into the production process to increase efficiency, as a rule, assets replace labor and the organic composition rises. So the rate of profit falls. This is the tendency.

Why does Marx argue that the rate of profit tendentially moves downward? To increase their profitability, capitalists must increase their laborers' productivity. The way to do this is by introducing new means of production, which to increase productivity will usually shed labor. Capital-reducing investments could also more productive. They would raise profitability but also free up capital for subsequent investment. After all capital-saving investments have been made, there will be *additional* potential labor-saving ones that the most successful capitals can take advantage of. So the general tendency is still for the organic composition of capital to rise.[9]

Hypothetically, there might be capitalists investing in less efficient and thus lower-productivity means of production, which imply a lower organic composition of capital. But if they persisted in this choice, they would be doomed to bankruptcy. Thus, tendentially, due to the application of new technologies, the number of laborers per unit of capital invested falls, that is, the organic composition rises.[10]

There are also powerful countertendencies to Marx's law. Such countertendencies temporarily dampen or reverse the tendency of the rate of profit to fall. In particular, Marx mentions five countertendencies: (1) the increasing intensity of exploitation of labor, which could increase the rate of surplus value; (2) the relative cheapening of the elements of constant capital; (3) the deviation of the wage rate from the value of labor power; (4) the existence and increase of a relative surplus population; and (5) the cheapening of consumption and capital goods through imports.

In short, Marx's law of profitability goes as follows: as capitalism develops, the amount of constant capital rises in relation to variable capital. Because labor power hired with variable capital is the only part of capital that produces surplus value, the amount of surplus value falls in relation to the cost of the capitalists, and this depresses the rate of profit unless there is a faster increase in the rate of surplus value, among other countertendencies. But the law will assert itself sooner or later as concrete reality.[11]

These countertendencies introduce cyclical trends on the long-term trend of the downward rate of profit: "The operation of these countertendencies transforms the breakdown into a temporary crisis, so that the accumulation process is not something continuous but takes the form of periodic cycles."[12]

Spurred by higher profit rates, hindered by the difficulty to further increase their assets' capacity utilization, and seeing that higher profitability is threatened by rising wages, some capitalists (the innovators) start investing in higher organic composition assets, that is in labor-shedding and productivity-increasing means of production. Constant capital rises and employment falls in terms of percentages. The organic composition rises and the rate of profit falls (while the profitability of the innovators rises). The less efficient capitals cease operating, that is, some capital is destroyed. Production falls. Due to falling employment and falling profitability, both labor's and capital's purchasing power falls.

A crisis or slump in production is necessary to correct and reverse the fall in the rate and eventually the mass of profit.[13] In a period of depression and trough, some capitalists close down. Others can fill the vacant economic space. Production increases. Initially, net fixed investments do not rise. Instead, capitalists increase their assets' capacity utilization. So the means of production's efficiency does not rise, and the numerator in the organic composition of capital does not rise either. Also, due to higher capacity utilization, assets are subject to increased wear and tear, which reduces their value. Finally, the capitalists buy the means of production, raw materials, semi-finished products, and so on of the bankrupt capitalists at deflated prices. Thus the numerator of the organic composition falls. Increased production with unchanged efficiency implies greater employment. So the denominator of the organic composition rises. The organic composition falls on both accounts, and the rate of profit rises. Rising employment increases labor's purchasing power and rising profitability increases that of capital. Both factors facilitate the realization of the greater output.

So the upward profitability cycle generates *from within itself* the downward cycle. This latter, in its turn, generates from within itself the next upward profitability cycle. Given that, as mentioned already, as a rule capitalists must compete by introducing labor-shedding and productivity-increasing means of production (given that they tend to replace labor with assets), the downward cycle is the *tendency* and the upward cycle is the *countertendency*.

Even mainstream economics sometimes recognizes the connection between profit and crises. The connection is investment. Jan Tinbergen concluded that since new investment is usually to obtain higher profits, profit expectations are one of the most important determinants of new investment. Expectations will be based on the experience of past and current profitability.[14] Wesley Mitchell showed that investment behavior is an important component of variations in aggregate demand, so falls in investment are therefore a key element in triggering a crisis.[15]

A strong relationship between profitability and investment has been found in various studies. These studies found that the economic variable that best predicted the level of investment was the overall profitability of the companies, not market valuation of securities or other economic variables.[16]

In a Minority
Yet Marx's law of profitability is not seen by most Marxists as the sole or even main cause of crises under capitalism. The majority view, as Figure 1.2 shows, is that crises are caused by some form of underconsumption by labor and/or overproduction of commodities by capital.

The usual support for the view that Marx had an underconsumption-ist theory of crises comes from a statement that "the ultimate reason for all real crises always remains the poverty and restricted consumption of the masses,"[17] which Paul Sweezy, the Marxist economist most supportive of this view, reckoned was the "most clear cut statement in favour" of that interpretation of Marx.[18] However, elsewhere Marx specifically refutes the argument that underconsumption by labor is the cause of crises, calling the idea no more than a tautology.[19]

Perhaps the most damning refutation of the underconsumption interpretation is the evidence: personal consumption as a share of GDP rose in advanced economies throughout the postwar period and stayed high even during the start of the Great Recession, while profits dropped before the Great Recession and investment plunged. Consumption only fell afterward and was clearly a consequence of the slump.

As for overproduction, Marx explains that overproduction of commodities is really the symptom of the overproduction of capital relative to the surplus value extracted from labor.[20]

Marx's law of profitability has been relegated to the background or dismissed by most Marxists. The reason is partly an accident of history and partly because it is safer to adopt underconsumption or overproduction or divert to financial panics or debt crises as causes. They lend themselves to a "cure" that does not require ending the capitalist mode of production.

It is an accident of history in the sense that the leading Marxists of the late nineteenth century and early twentieth century had not read volume 3 of *Capital* or part 4, called *Theories of Surplus Value*, and had no access to the *Grundrisse* notes. In these publications, Marx's law is spelled out in the clearest fashion as a theory of crises.

In addition, some leading Marxists of the late nineteenth century, like Karl Kautsky, the theoretical head of the Social Democratic Party in Europe, in Germany, specifically adopted an underconsumptionist position. For Rosa Luxemburg and the Bolshevik leaders, Marx's law of profitability was relegated to some long-term tendency for capitalism to reach its use-by date, but not to explain booms and slumps now.[21] The law only came to be used as part of a theory of breakdown or crises with Henryk Grossman in the 1920s.[22]

Indeed, some Marxists now argue that making the law the central cause of recurrent capitalist crises is not "classical Marxism" but an invention of some Anglo-Saxon Marxist economists from the United Kingdom and the United States.[23] Modern Marxist scholars like Michael Heinrich, who has studiously read unpublished notes and papers by Marx, concludes that Marx decided in the 1870s that the law was logically wrong anyway and quietly dropped it.[24]

The law has been under attack by mainstream economists and anti-Marxist socialists from the start. A long line of mainstream economists have disputed Marx's value theory, which is the basis of the law, starting with Austrian economist Bohm-Bawerk through to Von Bortkiewicz and in more recent times, the Marxist Paul Sweezy and the *Monthly Review* school of socialism. Japanese Marxist Nobiru Okishio presented a theorem apparently showing that Marx's law was logically inconsistent from its premises. This led to the so-called neo-Ricardian school of economists, basing themselves on David Ricardo and Piero Sraffa, who announced that Marx's value theory and his law of profitability were dead in the water.[25]

There will be no discussion of these criticisms and refutations of Marx's law here. Suffice it to say that these arguments have been effectively refuted by a number of Marxist economists in recent years.[26] The clearest and most compelling defense of the logical basis of Marx's value theory and the law of profitability has been presented by Andrew Kliman.[27] Kliman provides an interpretation of Marx's writings that offers the best fit to what Marx meant and confirms a logical link between his value theory and the law of profitability with what is called the temporal single state interpretation.[28]

The Evidence

Marx's law may be logically consistent. But does it fit the facts? Well, what do we want to know? Does the rate of profit fall over a long period as the organic composition rises? Does the rate of profit rise when the organic composition falls? Does the rate of profit recover if there is a sharp fall in the organic composition of capital through the destruction of capital?

Esteban Maito presents estimates of the rate of profit on fourteen countries in the long run going back to 1870 (see Figure 1.3). His result shows a clear downward trend in the world rate of profit, although there are periods of partial recovery in both core and peripheral countries. So the behavior of the profit rate confirms the predictions Marx made about the historical trend of the mode of production. There is a secular tendency for the rate of profit to fall under capitalism and Marx's law operates.[29]

The US rate of profit has been falling since the mid-1950s and is well below where it was in 1947.[30] There has been a secular decline. Figure 1.4 irons out shorter fluctuations to show this.[31] Thus the counteracting factors cannot permanently resist the law of the tendency of the rate of profit to fall.

But the US rate of profit has not moved in a straight line. In the US economy as a whole after the war, it was high but decreasing in the so-called Golden Age from 1948 to 1965. Profitability kept falling also from 1965 to 1982.[32] However, in the era of what is called "neoliberalism," from 1982 to 1997, US profitability rose.

The counteracting factors to falling profitability came into play— the greater exploitation of the US workforce (falling wage share[33]), the cheapening of constant capital through new high-tech innovations, the wider exploitation of the labor force elsewhere (globalization), and speculation in unproductive sectors (particularly real estate and finance capital). Between 1982 and 1997, the US rate of profit rose 19 percent (see Figure 1.5), as the rate of surplus value rose nearly 24 percent and the organic composition of capital rose just 6 percent.

Figure 1.3

The Rate of Profit in the "Core" (Advanced Capitalist Economies), %

Source: E. Maito

Figure 1.4
US Rate of Profit (Current Cost Measure), %

Source: BEA, Author's Calculations

Figure 1.5
US Rate of Profit from 1982 to 2012 (%)

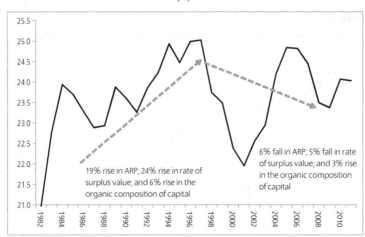

Source: Author's Calculations

So there is a tendency for the rate of profit to fall over a long period of time, and this tendency will overcome any counteracting factors eventually. But for a period, and especially after a major slump that devalues existing capital, counteracting factors can rule—namely, through a rising rate of surplus value, higher profits from overseas, and the cheapening of constant capital through new technology, among other factors. That was the experience of the so-called neoliberal period after the deep slump of 1980–82 to the end of twentieth century.

Even this neoliberal "recovery" period, with the dot-com bubble of the late 1990s and the credit-fueled property boom after 2002, was not able to restore overall profitability back to the high levels of the mid-1960s. The rate of profit peaked in 1997 and the recovery in US profitability during the 2000s and since the Great Recession has not reattained that 1997 peak. The US rate of profit remains below the peak of 1997.

The rate is clearly higher than it was in the early 1980s at its trough. That can be mainly explained by one counteracting factor to the secularly rising organic composition of capital: a rising rate of surplus value since 1982.

The US rate of profit fell 24 percent from 1963 to a trough in 1982, while the organic composition of capital rose 16 percent and the rate of surplus value fell 16 percent. Then the rate of profit rose 15 percent to a peak in 1997, and the organic composition of capital rose 9 percent but was outstripped by the rise in the rate of surplus value of 22 percent. From 1997 to 2008, the rate of profit fell 12 percent while the organic composition of capital rose 22 percent, outstripping the rate of surplus value, up only 2 percent.

All three phases fit Marx's law: when the organic composition of capital rose faster than the rate of surplus value, the rate of profit fell; when the former did not, the rate of profit rose. Over the forty-five years to 2008, the US rate of profit fell secularly by 21 percent *because* the organic composition of capital rose 51 percent, while the rate of surplus value rose just 5 percent. The rise in the organic composition of capital explained 62 percent of the fall in the rate of profit, and there was no significant correlation with any change in the rate of surplus value.[34]

This inverse relationship between the organic composition of capital and the rate of profit that Marx's law predicts is also validated for other capitalist economies. Take that of the United Kingdom.

Between 1963 and 1975, the UK rate of profit fell 28 percent, the organic composition of capital rose 20 percent, and the rate of surplus value fell 19 percent. Between 1975 and 1996, the rate of profit rose 50 percent, while the organic composition of capital rose 17 percent and the rate of surplus value rose 66 percent. Finally, from 1996 to 2008, the rate of profit fell 11 percent, the organic composition of capital rose 16 percent, and the rate of surplus value was flat. All three phases are compatible with Marx's law. Indeed, over the whole period, 1963 to 2008, in the United Kingdom, the organic composition of capital rose 63 percent while the rate of surplus value rose 33 percent, so the rate of profit fell in a secular trend.

Table 1.2 shows the level of the US rate of profit (measured in both historic cost and current cost of capital terms) at the end of certain periods compared to the start (expressed as a fraction of 1). So, for example, in the whole period from 1946 to 2012, the US rate of profit fell 20 percent (from 1.0 to 0.80) in current cost terms and 29 percent (from 1.0 to 0.71) in historic cost terms.

Table 1.2. The Change in the US Rate of Profit 1946–2012 (as fraction of 1)

	1965–82	1982–97	1997–2012	1946–2012	1965–2012	1982–2001	2001–8
Current cost	0.64	1.35	0.99	0.80	0.86	1.24	0.89
Historic cost	0.86	1.12	1.00	0.71	0.96	1.02	0.94

So there has been a secular decline in the US rate of profit from 1946 to 2012 or from 1965 to 2012; with the main decline between the peak of 1965 and the trough of 1982 (however you measure it). There was a rise in the rate between 1982 and 1997 (35 percent under the current cost measure and 12 percent under the historic cost measure). From 1997, the rate has been basically flat. The rate in the trough of the 2008 Great Recession was 11 percent (constant cost) and 6 percent (historic cost) *below* the 2001 trough.

These are my measures. Another Marxist economist has also done a recent analysis.[35] Themis Kalogerakos finds that the US rate of profit, however it is measured, appears to have two main periods: one where a high rate falls from the 1960s to the 1980s, and one where it recovers from the 1980s. He also identifies two subperiods within those two periods. The first is the high and slightly rising rate of profit from 1946 to 1965, then a decline from 1965 to the early 1980s, then a rebound up to 1997 and then, finally, a period of decline from 1997. This matches exactly my own interpretation of the data, first analyzed in 2006.[36]

It seems that however you measure the rate of profit, whether by the broadest or the narrowest measure or in between,[37] the US rate of profit exhibits the described four phases. The average rate of profit (on current cost measures) for the whole period 1946–2012 was 17.99 percent for the broadest measure and 6.03 percent for the narrowest. Between 1946 and 1965, the rate of profit was 11 percent above this average of the broadest measure and 15 percent above for the narrowest. In the neoliberal period from 1982 to 1997, the rate was still 9 percent below the average (broadest) or 18 percent below (narrowest). The average for 1997 to 2011 was still below the overall average by 5 percent (broadest). It was 5 percent higher than the average for the narrowest measure from 1997 to 2011. But in this latest period, the rate in both cases was still below the 1946–65 golden age period by 10 percent and 15 percent, respectively. If historic costs are used, the results are no different. On the broadest measure, the closest to Marx's, the average rate of profit from 1997 to 2011 was 23 percent lower, whereas on the narrowest measure it was 16 percent lower.

Kalogerakos looked not just at the level of profitability but also at the annual change in the US profit rate. Across the whole period from 1946, whatever the version of the rate of profit and whether measured from trough to trough or from peak to peak, the US rate of profit has fallen by about 0.6 percent a year. This confirms that Marx's law has been operating[38]—and was operating just before the Great Recession.[39] So Marx's law of the tendency of the rate of profit to fall over time is thus validated by extensive empirical analysis and is extremely relevant for a theory of crises.

Such is the prima facie case for arguing that Marx's law of profitability is the underlying cause of crises. Profitability has fallen secularly and, despite the neoliberal period, it has not recovered to previous levels in the golden age. Capitalism is under the increased pressure of low profitability and erupts into recurrent crises.

Each Crisis Has a Different Cause (Triggers)

Some Marxists prefer a more eclectic approach. Many argue that each crisis is unique, depending on the particular relationships and alliances forged between workers, business, finance, and the state. How can the Great Recession also be due to the law of profitability when profit rates recovered from the 1980s? Surely, to argue thus is to adopt the dogmatic Anglo-Saxon "monocausal" explanation of crises.[40] These authors prefer to explain the Great Recession as a result of various causes: stagnating wages, or rising mortgage debt and then collapsing housing prices, causing a dramatic fall in consumer spending.

Each crisis of capitalism has its own characteristics. The trigger in 2008 was the huge expansion of fictitious capital that eventually collapsed when real value expansion could no longer sustain it, as the ratio of house prices to household income reached extremes. But such "triggers" are not causes. Behind them is a general cause of crisis: the law of the tendency of the rate of profit to fall.

The crisis of 2008–9, like other crises, has an underlying cause based on the contradictions between accumulation of capital and the tendency of the rate of profit to fall under capitalism. That contradiction arises because the capitalist mode of production is production for value, not for use. Profit is the aim, not production or consumption. Value is created only by the exertion of labor (by brain and brawn). Profit comes from the unpaid value created by labor and appropriated by private owners of the means of production. The underlying contradiction between the accumulation of capital and falling rate of profit (and then a falling mass of profit) is resolved by crisis, which takes the form of collapse in value, both real and fictitious. Indeed, wherever the fictitious expansion of capital has developed most is where the crisis begins—tulips, stock markets, housing debt, corporate debt, banking debt, public debt, and so on. The financial sector is often where the crisis starts, but a problem in the production sector is the cause.

A slump under capitalism begins with a collapse in capitalist investment. The movement in investment is initially driven by movements in profit, not vice versa.[41] In the period leading up to the Great Recession, profits fell for several quarters before the US economy went into a nose dive. US corporate profits peaked in early 2006 (see Figure 1.5) (that's the absolute amount, not the rate of profit, which peaked earlier, as we have seen). From its peak in early 2006, the mass of profits fell until mid-2008, made a limited recovery in early 2009, and then fell to a new low in mid-2009. After that, the recovery in profits began and the previous peak in nominal dollars was surpassed in mid-2010.

What was the reaction of investment to this movement in US profits? When US corporate profit growth started to slow in mid-2005 and then fell in absolute terms in 2006, corporate investment went on growing for a while as companies used up reserves or increased borrowing in the hope that profits would be restored. When that did not happen, investment growth slowed during 2007 and then fell absolutely in 2008, at one point falling at a nearly 20 percent year-on-year rate.

Profits started to recover at the end of 2008, but investment did not follow for a year. It was the same for GDP—it peaked well after profits did and recovered after profits did. The movement of profits leads the movement of investment, not vice versa. Profits were falling well before the credit crunch began. So Marx's law provides an explanation of the crisis of 2001–2, the subsequent recovery of 2002–6, the great 2007–9 slump, and the subsequent recovery.

US corporate profits were falling some two years before the recession began, and investment dropped as a result before GDP contracted. In the recovery, again it was profits that led investment and GDP up.

These conclusions are confirmed by other authors. For example, Tapia Granados found that

> data from 251 quarters of the US economy show that recessions are preceded by declines in profits. Profits stop growing and start falling four or five quarters before a recession. They strongly recover immediately after the recession. Since investment is to a large extent determined by profitability and investment is a major component of demand, the fall in profits leading to a fall in investment, in turn leading to a fall in demand, seems to be a basic mechanism in the causation of recessions.[42]

Sergio Camara Izquierdo also finds that "a significant cyclical decline of the profit rate has substantially preceded the last two recessions . . . the cyclical slump in the rate of profit must be seen as an important precipitating factor in the deepest economic downturn since the 1930s."[43]

There were five recessions or slumps after 1963: 1974–75, 1980–82, 1990–92, 2001, and 2008–9. In each case, the rate of profit peaked at least one year before and on most occasions up to three years before. On each occasion (with the exception of the very mild 2001 recession), a fall in the mass of profit led or coincided with a slump. This is shown clearly for the Great Recession. There was rise in the rate of profit and the mass of profits from 2002 to 2006. But profitability was still in a downward cycle from 1997 and the rate and the mass of profits did start to fall from 2006 onward.

The Role of Credit

That does not mean the financial sector and particularly the size and movement of credit does not play any role in capitalist crises. On the contrary, the growth of credit and fictitious capital (as Marx called speculative investment in stocks, bonds, and other forms of money assets) picks up precisely to compensate for the downward pressure on profitability in the accumulation of real capital.

A fall in the rate of profit promotes speculation. If the capitalists cannot make enough profit producing commodities, they will try making money betting on the stock exchange or buying various other financial instruments. Capitalists experience the falling rate of profit almost simultaneously, so they start to buy these stocks and assets at the same time, driving prices up. But when stock and other financial asset prices are rising everybody wants to buy them—this is the beginning of the bubble, the lines of which we have seen over and over since the tulip crisis of 1637.

If, for example, the speculation takes place in housing, this creates an option for workers to borrow and spend more than they earn (more than the capitalists have laid out as variable capital), and in this way the "realization problem" is solved. Sooner or later, bubbles burst when investors find that the assets are not worth what they are paying for them. The "realization problem" reoccurs in an expanded form compared with before the bubble. Now the workers have to pay back their loans, with interest, so they have to spend less than they earn. The result is even greater overproduction than was avoided temporarily in the first place.

The basic problem is still the falling rate of profit, which depresses investment demand. If the underlying economy were healthy, an imploding bubble need not cause a crisis, or at least only a short one. When workers and capitalists pay interest on their loans, this money does not just disappear—some finance capitalists receive the interest. If the total economy is healthy and the rate of profit is high, then the revenue generated from interest payments will be reinvested in production in some way.

Some Marxists have argued that the credit crunch of 2007 and the ensuing Great Recession is not a classical Marxist crisis of profitability. Marx would have also seen the crisis as financial in cause. It's true that Marx distinguished between different sorts of monetary crisis.[44]

Going further, some argue that the crisis was the product of a brand-new development in capitalism: the globalization of finance capital and its now overwhelming dominance of the capitalist economy. So Marx's law of profitability is no longer relevant. But financial globalization is nothing new. In 1875, banker Karl von Rothschild assigned the banking collapse to "the whole world becoming a city." The interdependence of stock markets and credit with the "real" economy is not new.

It's true that the share of US gross domestic income accruing to finance and insurance rose dramatically from 2.3 percent in 1947 to 7.9 percent in 2006. But as Alan Greenspan said, can we say that the growth of the financial sector was the cause of the Great Recession if it had been expanding for six decades without a crisis of the proportions of 2008?

An artificial and temporary inflation of profits in unproductive sectors of a capitalist economy (like finance) can help sustain the capitalist economy and compensate for a falling rate of profit in productive sectors. Then in a crisis, an increasing share of debtors who cannot finance their debt eventually causes default and the crisis erupts in the financial sector.[45]

Marx's law shows that the capitalist system does not just suffer from a "technical malfunction" in its financial sector but has inherent contradictions in the production sector, namely, the barrier to growth caused by capital itself. What flows from this is that the capitalist system cannot be "repaired" to achieve sustained economic growth without booms and slumps—it must be replaced.

Chapter 2

The Long Depression of the Late Nineteenth Century

It should be clear, then, that the "great depression" of the 1870s is merely a myth—a myth brought about by misinterpretation of the fact that prices in general fell sharply during the entire period.

—Murray Rothbard[1]

In the low level of profits in the last quarter of the century we have an explanation which is powerful enough to explain the retardation of industrial growth in the 1880s and 1890s.

—Arthur C. Lewis[2]

The next few chapters will show that Marx's law can provide the clearest explanation of the depressions of the late nineteenth century, the 1930s and indeed, the current Long Depression that has followed the Great Recession of 2008–9. Moreover, it is a superior explanation than that provided by mainstream economics, both contemporary and historic. Let's start with the depression in the major economies of the 1880s and 1890s.

A Financial Panic?

The long depression of the late nineteenth century started with a financial panic. The panic of 1873 has been described as "the first truly international crisis."[3] It began in central Europe with the collapse of the Vienna stock market in May 1873. Then it spread to the United States on what has been called Black Thursday (September 18) after the failure of the banking house of Cooke and Co. over its investment in the Northern Pacific Railroad.[4]

Cooke's had invested $100,000 in Northern Pacific Railroad, but failed to raise the money in a bond issuance because the railroad boom had come to an end. The railroad boom after the Civil War had culminated in the transcontinental link, achieved in 1869. This was

31

particularly important in that the railroad industry was the largest employer in the US economy (outside of agriculture) and its leading sector.

Cooke's collapse was shortly followed by that of several other major banks. The New York Stock Exchange closed for ten days. The financial crisis returned to Europe, provoking a second panic in Vienna and further failures across Europe before receding.

Some have argued the depression was triggered by the 1870 Franco-Prussian War, which hurt the French economy as France was forced to make large war reparations to Germany. Others have argued that the primary cause of the depression in the United States was the tight monetary policy that the nation followed to get back on the gold standard after the Civil War. The US government was taking money out of circulation to achieve this goal, so there was less available money to facilitate trade. Because of this policy, the price of silver started to fall, causing considerable loss of asset values.

Others concentrate on the speculative nature of financing involving the paper dollar issued to pay for the Civil War and rampant fraud in building the Union Pacific Railroad up to 1869. Both the Union Pacific and the Northern Pacific lines were the focus of the collapse. In the 1870s, Germany had recently reunified and a currency union had been formed in central Europe. In the years leading up to the 1873 crash, new industrial banks such as Deutsche Bank had been formed, and the global bond market was fueling the railroad boom. The ensuing credit squeeze spread globally.

A Credit Squeeze?

Was the cause of the 1873 panic and ensuing long depression really just financial? Monetarists believe that the depression was caused by shortages of gold, which undermined the gold standard, and that the 1848 California gold rush, the 1886 Witwatersrand gold rush in South Africa, and the 1896–99 Klondike gold rush helped alleviate such crises.

The 1873 panic was triggered by the imposition of a new gold standard. The gold standard reduced dollar liquidity, which was then unable to expand with demand, causing a series of economic and monetary contractions that plagued the entire period of the long depression.

The financial panic triggered catastrophic deleveraging in an attempt to sell assets and increase capital reserves. This sell-off led to a the collapse in asset prices and deflation, which in turn prompted financial institutions to sell off more assets, only to increase deflation and strain capital ratios. Irving Fisher, the leading monetarist economist of the 1930s, believed that had governments or private enterprise embarked on efforts to reflate financial markets in the 1870s, the depression would have been less severe.[5]

There Was No Depression!

Economists of the Austrian school deny there was any depression at all. They complain about the characterization of this period as a depression because of conflicting economic statistics that cast doubt on that interpretation. They note that this time period saw a relatively large expansion of industry, railroads, physical output, net national product, and real per capita income.

From 1869 to 1879, US real national product growth rose 6.8 percent per year, with a rise of 4.5 percent per year in real product per capita. According to the Austrian school economics, even the alleged "monetary contraction" never took place, as the money supply was increasing.[6] From 1873 through 1878, before another spurt of monetary expansion, the total supply of bank money rose 13.1 percent or 2.6 percent per year. So there was scarcely a contraction. Although per capita nominal income declined very gradually from 1873 to 1879, that decline was more than offset by a gradual increase over the course of the next seventeen years. Furthermore, real per capita income either stayed approximately constant (1873–80, 1883–85) or rose (1881–82, 1886–96), so that the average consumer appears to have been considerably better off at the end of the "depression" than before.

Studies of other countries, including the United States, Germany, France, and Italy, also reported more markedly positive trends in both nominal and real per capita income figures. Between 1870 and 1890, iron production in the five largest iron-producing countries more than doubled, from 11 million tons to 23 million tons; steel production increased twentyfold (half a million tons to 11 million tons); and railroad development boomed.

In 1877, Robert Giffen[7] found himself countering the "common impression" that a depression of unprecedented severity was in progress. "The common impression," he insisted, "is wrong and the facts are entirely the other way." Despite a drop in Britain's foreign trade and a series of poor harvests, which were serious enough, "the community as a whole," Giffen argued, was "not really poorer by the pricking of all these bladders." In support of his view, he presented statistics showing an upward trend in both per capita taxable incomes and per capita nominal wages commencing in 1880.

Price Deflation

On the other hand, the reason for the rise in real incomes was that prices had collapsed—the price of grain in 1894 was only a third what it had been in 1867, and the price of cotton fell by nearly 50 percent in just the five years from 1872 to 1877, imposing great hardship on farmers and planters. This collapse provoked protectionism in many countries, such as France, Germany, and the United States, while triggering mass emigration from other countries such as Italy, Spain, Austria-Hungary, and Russia. Similarly, while the production of iron doubled between the 1870s and 1890s, the price of iron halved. So as real output rose, prices plummeted. Certainly the impression at the time was of "uniquely persistent deflation"[8] with the British wholesale price index losing close to a third of its value in less than a quarter- of a century. Many thought this "most drastic deflation in the memory of man"[9] was both evidence and cause of what Josiah Stamp called "a chronic depression in trade."[10]

Austrian-school economist Murray Rothbard has dismissed the idea that falling prices constituted a depression.[11] Thus he concluded: "It should be clear, then, that the 'great depression' of the 1870s is merely a myth—a myth brought about by misinterpretation of the fact that prices in general fell sharply during the entire period." A. E. Musson argued similarly.[12] Neoliberal economist George Selgin followed Rothbard in arguing that any fall in prices was due to higher productivity, not a deflationary depression.[13]

The argument that the long depression was really a period of great technological advance was first advanced by David Ames Wells, writing in 1890.[14] He gives an account of the changes in the world economy transitioning into the second Industrial Revolution in which he documents changes in trade, such as triple expansion steam shipping, railroads, the effect of the international telegraph network, and the opening of the Suez Canal. He gives numerous examples of productivity increases in various industries and discusses the problems of excess capacity and market saturation.

Wells noted that deflation only lowered the cost of goods that benefited from improved methods of manufacturing and transportation. Goods produced by craftspeople did not decrease in value, nor did many services, and the cost of labor actually increased. Also, deflation did not occur in countries that did not have modern manufacturing, transportation, and communications.[15]

So the long depression in the 1870s was no such thing. In the words of Rendig Fels: "1873–79 was quite turbulent, but afterward the global economy adjusted to deflation. Those years were among the most beneficial in human history, as the foundations of the modern age."[16]

Revisiting the Revisionism

But is this rosy revisionist view of the long depression really right? It's true that real gross domestic product (GDP) continued to rise between 1873 and 1897, and so did per capita income in real terms. But most countries experienced significantly lower growth rates relative to earlier in the nineteenth century and afterward. Figure 2.1 shows the US data for gross national product (GNP) per capita—clearly showing a slowdown during the 1880s and 1890s.

Figure 2.1

Real US GNP Per Capita 1869–1918 in 2009 Dollars

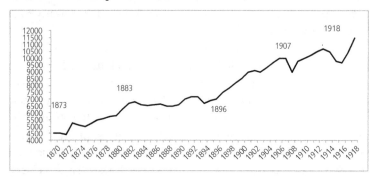

Source: US BEA

The long depression affected different countries at different times and different rates, and some countries accomplished rapid growth over certain periods. Globally, however, the 1870s, 1880s, and 1890s were a period of falling price levels, and rates of economic growth were significantly below the periods preceding and following.[17]

German industrial production growth was 33 percent slower between 1873 and 1890 than between 1850 and 1873. It was 30 percent slower than after 1890 up to World War I. In the United Kingdom it was 45 percent slower than before and 15 percent slower than afterward. The United States was 25 percent slower than before and 12 percent slower than afterward. France was 24 percent slower than before and 52 percent slower than after. Real GDP[18] rose in all countries (except Russia) between 1870 and 1890. But it rose 42 percent in France between 1850 and 1870 compared with just 17 percent from 1870 to 1890. The UK's real GDP rose 57 percent between 1850 and 1870 and 50 percent up to 1890. Germany's rose 61 percent between 1850 and 1870 and 59 percent after.

Evidence for a depression in the United States is most dramatically seen in railroad construction, where the financial panic of 1873 was located. In fact, the post–Civil War boom in rail construction had peaked in 1871, but the decline in production accelerated, going from 6,000 miles' worth in 1872 to just over 4,000 miles' worth in 1873, then plunging to barely over 2,000 miles' worth in 1874 and dropping further to under 2,000 miles in 1875, the bottom. Railroad construction began to recover after 1875, but it did so fitfully and basically remained flat and low during the 1876–78 period, fluctuating around 3,000 miles of construction. Only in 1879 did construction surge again up to 5,000 miles, followed by the biggest surge of all as the 1880s proved to be by far the leading decade of rail construction, followed by a nearly total collapse in the 1890s.

The long depression of the late nineteenth century was not a simple story of economic standstill. Instead, it was—as all future depressions can be characterized under capitalism—a long period where excessive capital stock must be devalued or deleveraged before sustainable faster economic growth can resume. Reinhardt and Rogoff have distinguished crises/recessions that do not involve the entire financial sector from those that do, arguing that the latter involve much longer and slower recoveries. For the US economy they list three such episodes: the 1870s, the 1930s, and today, with the current situation perhaps most resembling the events of the 1870s.[19]

Essentially, a set of innovations in technology and business organization that were made in the late eighteenth and early nineteenth centuries had exhausted their potential to raise productivity and lead to higher growth by the 1860s. This led to overinvestment, much of it unproductive and speculative and achieved by a significant build-up of debt by the early 1870s.

In this sense, Fisher was right. It was a crisis brought about by the realization that many investments were not going to pay enough and the consequent need for sustained deleveraging (paying back or writing off debt). At the same time, there was a burst of technological and organizational innovation. This increased productivity and created many new products but also led to very large adjustments as older industries shrank. There was a shift in the focus of the world economy toward the developing parts of the world, such as Germany and the United States.

The Differences between Britain and the United States

Indeed, the long depression of the nineteenth century began the process of shifting hegemonic economic power from Britain to the United States and Germany. As the comparison data on industrial production show, British industry was depressed between 1873 and 1896, particularly in "basic industries" such as iron, beginning in the 1880s. These troubled sectors of the economy were a source of increased structural unemployment and of "continuous undulations of business people"[20] inspiring calls for "reciprocity" and "fair trade"[21] and provoking various royal and parliamentary inquiries.

As the leading mainstream British economist of the 1920s, Arthur Pigou, pointed out, the irony is that if there ever was a protracted depression at the end of the nineteenth century, it occurred not in the period of the long depression but afterward for Britain: "Whereas during the 20 years before 1896 the trend of general prices had been downward and the rate of real wages had been rising, the reversal of the price trend in the later nineties was accompanied by a check to the upward movement of real wages. Indeed, apart from the shifting of people from lower paid to higher paid occupations, the rate of real wages actually declined between the later nineties and the outbreak of the Great War."[22]

The United Kingdom had the slowest growth of major powers after 1890, hardly faster than in the long depression.[23]

Feinstein has found that net domestic investment as a percentage of national income in the United Kingdom was 4.2 percent in 1857, rising to 6 percent in 1873, and then falling back sharply to 3.4 percent in 1883, before recovering up to 1897.[24] After this, the decline set in and net investment to national income dropped off to 4.3 percent by 1913.[25]

The great economist and historian Arthur Lewis provides the most perceptive account of the relative decline of the UK economy in the long depression and after. Lewis supported the view that there was a long depression in the UK economy between 1870 and 1890. Moreover, he agreed that the UK economy lost ground against all other major industrial powers through to 1913.

British capitalism was a "mature economy" before the 1873 panic, with as much as 37 percent of the workforce engaged in industry and mining by the time of the Great Exhibition of 1851. But a lack of a cheap labor force to boost industry was not the cause of the slowdown in the growth of industrial production after 1873. The cause lay within the heart of capitalist production: investment.

Lewis shows that during the long depression, nominal wages fell, but as prices fell more, real wages stayed up at the expense of profits. He shows that the rate of surplus value in British industry was 74 percent in 1873–83, but then slipped to 69 percent in 1883–89; 66 percent in 1889–99; before recovering to 83 percent in 1899–1907 and 83 percent in 1907–13.[26]

So the 1880s were a very bad time for profits and consequently for capitalist investment. As Lewis puts it,[27] British capitalism suffered badly compared to others. The British share of world trade in manufactures fell from 37 percent in 1883 to 25 percent in 1913, while Germany's rose from 17 percent to 23 percent, and the United States from just 3 percent in 1883 to 11 percent in 1913. British exports of manufactures grew at 2.7 percent a year from 1873 to 1883, but slowed to 1.9 percent a year from 1883 to 1889, while imports accelerated from 3.8 percent a year to 4.5 percent a year. "Britain lost her own market as well as foreign markets."[28]

The Depression and the Business Cycle

Lewis provides definitive proof that there was a long depression.[29] He makes the point, contrary to the revisionists, that there were several recessions during the long depression and they were clearly worse after 1873. Lewis gauged the intensity of these recessions by how long it took for production to return to a level "exceeding that of the preceding peak" growth rate. He found that between 1853 and 1873, it took about three to four years. But between 1873 and 1899, it took six to seven years. He also measured the loss of output in recessions, that is, the difference between actual output and what output would have been if trend growth had been sustained. The waste of potential output was just 1.5 percent from 1853 to 1873 because "recessions were short and mild." From 1873 to 1883, the waste was 4.4 percent; from 1883 to 1899, 6.8 percent; and from 1899 to 1913 5.3 percent, because "after 1873 recessions became quite violent and prolonged." The recessions were longer because Britain (among other countries) was in the grip of a long depression.[30] So the original slump (or financial panic) of 1873 was followed a few years later by another recession (1876) and another (1889) and another (1892). Wastage was thus two to three times greater in the recessions during the long depression.

The long depression in Britain was also characterized by a slump in the construction industry. A construction boom that tried to replace the slowdown in industry eventually turned sour in 1877. Usually, the construction cycle runs for about eighteen years.[31] In the long depression, there was no return to a boom until 1903. As Lewis puts it: "industrial production decelerated. This in turn produced a long depression of building. The building depression reduced industrial production still further."[32] The cause was not to be found in monetary factors, like the gold standard.[33]

The nineteenth-century long depression affected each major capitalist economy at different times and with different degrees of severity. According to Lewis, it was preceded by an international boom from 1866 to 1872 everywhere. Then the business cycle of 1872–83 was fairly international and simultaneous, although "its real core was the US."

Lewis sums up the long depression as follows:

> There was a slackening of aggregate industrial demand in the last quarter of the nineteenth century following the major boom that ended in 1873 . . . the notable severity and prolongation of Juglar recessions. No Juglar recession was equally severe in all countries, different countries prospered in different decades, depending mainly on the timing of the building booms. They thus offset each other to some extent. But the net effect on aggregate industrial production was weakness from 1873 to 1899 in comparison with both the preceding and the succeeding Juglars.[34]

The Real Cause: Falling Profits and Investment

One of the key features of Lewis's analysis is that the cause of the long depression is based on problems in the production sectors of the capitalist economies, even if it was triggered by financial panics. The key cause of the production problem was to be found in the slowing down of business investment. Lewis saw that as caused by a fall in the rate of surplus value in industry. Profits were being squeezed.

Lewis suggests a profit squeeze theory based on international competition keeping prices of production down while wages rose. But a more convincing explanation lies with Marx's law of profitability.[35]

By the beginning of the second half of the nineteenth century, Britain was the leading capitalist power. It had the largest share of world trade, particularly in manufacturing, where it was the global leader in industrial innovation and expansion. It had a large colonial empire and military might to maintain it under Pax Britannica.

The Great Exhibition of 1851 marked the pinnacle of British capitalism's superiority. Through the second half of the nineteenth century, it remained the leading economic, financial, military, and political power. But as Lewis showed, it began to decline relative to the United States, in particular, but also to Europe (France and Germany) in each succeeding decade up to World War I. In that sense, Britain between 1850 and 1914 was in a similar position to the United States between 1970 and now. It was the most important and advanced capitalist state, but its relative superiority was declining.

Marx's analysis of the laws of motion of capital was based primarily on Britain. He lived there, and he used its economic data and events to understand capitalism. So the United Kingdom was the right economy to analyze the validity of his theory of capitalist accumulation and crisis in the late nineteenth century. Unfortunately for Marx and fortunately for us, we now have much better data about the production of value and surplus value, as well as constant and variable capital for the United Kingdom between 1855 and 1914.[36]

If we use data for the period from 1855 to 1914, we can plot the rate of profit in Marxist value terms and other categories, like the organic composition of capital, to see if Marx's law of the tendency of the rate of profit to fall holds for the most advanced capitalist economy of the nineteenth century.

First, the Marxist rate of profit for the UK economy between 1855 and 1914 moved in a cycle of about thirty-plus years from trough to trough, with an up phase from 1855 to 1871. This was a boom period for British capitalism and capitalism globally, with very few recessions, and weak ones at that. After the 1857 international recession passed by, Marx and Engels complained in their writings about this long boom, unlike the period from 1830 to 1848, which had been one of intense class struggle, culminating in the revolutions of 1848.

The up phase of 1855 to 1871 was followed by a down phase from 1871 to 1893. After 1893, we get another up phase in the rate of profit until the start of World War I in 1914, although the peak was reached in about 1900 and there was a (volatile) net decline from 1900 up to the start of the war.

The data confirm Lewis's contention that the rate of surplus value fell during the long depression. There was a steady fall in the rate of surplus value. But the rate of profit varied during the same period (see Figure 2.2).

Figure 2.2

UK Rate of Profit (%) and Rate of Surplus Value, 1855–1915

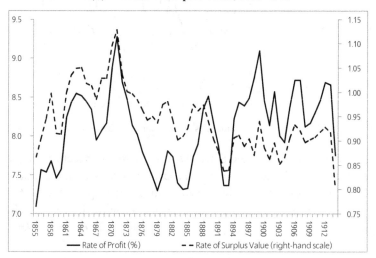

Source: UK Office for National Statistics, Author's Calculations

The data suggest that the main reason for the cycle of profitability under British capitalism between 1855 and 1914 was the movement in the organic composition of capital. There is a significant inverse relationship between the organic composition (OCC) and the rate of profit (ROP) of about 0.4. In other words, when the former goes up (over a period of years), the latter eventually goes down. The OCC stays high right through to the mid-1880s, thus driving down the rate of profit. After the organic composition collapsed, due to the destruction of the value of the means of production during the depression in the mid-1890s, the ROP recovered (see Figure 2.3).

Figure 2.3
UK Rate of Profit (%) and Organic Composition of Capital Ratio (RHS), 1855–1914

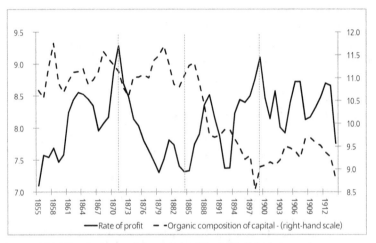

Source: UK Office for National Statistics and Author's Calculations

If we turn to the United States, we find a similar trajectory for the US ROP.[37] The US ROP peaked in the late 1870s, later than that of the United Kingdom. Again, the causal turning point appears to be the OCC, which rose sharply after 1879, driving down the ROP to lows by the late 1880s. The US ROP stayed well below the levels of the 1870s but did recover during the 1890s up to 1906 (see Figure 2.4).

Confirming Lewis's evidence, the rate of capital accumulation (investment) slowed steadily from the late 1870s through the mid-1890s.

A Reality, Not a Myth

The long depression was a reality, not a myth. It was triggered by a major international financial panic ricocheting from Europe to the United States and back. But its main cause was not to be found in the financial sector or due to a squeeze on money supply or a rigid gold standard, as was argued by contemporaries and mainstream economists since then. The cause was in the productive sector of the capitalist economies. Industrial production growth slowed down because capital investment slumped. Capital investment slumped because the profitability of capital took a dive from the early 1870s and stayed low until the mid-1890s. There were a series of recessions and weak recoveries, and different economies experienced various levels of severity and recovery, but all experienced lower growth, lower investment, lower prices, and, above all, lower profitability.

Figure 2.4

US Organic Composition of Capital (OCC) Ratio and Rate of Profit (ROP) Ratio

Source: Dumenil and Levy, Author's Caclulations

Writing in 1967, Lewis finished his analysis by arguing that the long depression of 1873–96 "was a unique event with a unique set of causes . . . our quest thus ends not in a general theory but in a set of historical accidents . . . there is no need for a theory of a fifty year cycle of recurring Kondratiev depression or for any other theory which postulates that the 1873–96 fits into some regular cycle."[38]

This is a surprising conclusion given the Great Depression of the 1930s, just fifty years later and obviously known to Lewis. Now we have the experience of the Great Recession of 2008–9, some eighty years later, and the subsequent depression we are now in. So let us consider the Great Depression of the 1930s and see if we concur with Lewis that each depression has no underlying recurring cause.

Chapter 3

The Great Depression of the Mid-Twentieth Century

The Great Depression was (and in many ways remains) a great puzzle as there were millions of the world's citizens who wanted to consume more housing, food and clothing; and producers by the hundreds of thousands who wanted to manufacture more housing, food and clothing and yet the two sides could not get together. Why? What was preventing these economically improving, mutually beneficial changes taking place? What was it that prevented people from working and producing more? At this moment, the answer remains largely unknown.

—Randall E. Parker[1]

To understand the Great Depression is the Holy Grail of macroeconomics.

—Ben Bernanke[2]

The Trigger for the Depression

The long depression of 1873–97 was originally called the Great Depression. It was seen as a one-off event by even the most perceptive of analysts,[3] although there were hints in the analyses of the Dutch long-wave theorists and the Russian economist Kondratiev that such a depression could reoccur. What we know today as the Great Depression, which started in 1929 and carried on until the beginning of World War II, showed that the long depression of the late nineteenth century was not a unique event in capitalist development and could be repeated. However, mainstream economics has been unable to explain what happened to world economies in the 1930s or why.[4]

At around the beginning of 1928, the US Federal Reserve, worried about financial speculation and inflated stock prices, began raising interest rates. Industrial production turned downward in spring 1929, and overall growth turned negative in the summer. A recession had begun. In the two months leading up to the Wall Street crash, industrial

45

production fell at an annualized rate of 20 percent. When the financial crash came, it was savage, and stunning drops in the stock market followed. By mid-November the market had declined by half.

Despite the stock market collapse that began on October 29, 1929 (known as Black Tuesday), optimism for a recovery persisted for some time. John D. Rockefeller said, "These are days when many are discouraged. In the 93 years of my life, depressions have come and gone. Prosperity has always returned and will again."[5]

Indeed, the stock market turned upward in early 1930, returning to early 1929 levels by April. This was still almost 30 percent below the peak of September 1929. The "real economy" did not recover. Consumers cut back their expenditures by 10 percent; beginning in mid-1930, a severe drought ravaged the agricultural heartland of the United States.

By May 1930, automobile sales had declined to below the levels of 1928. Prices in general began to decline, although wages held steady. Then a deflationary spiral started in 1931. Conditions were worse in farming areas, where commodity prices plunged, and in mining and logging areas, where unemployment was high and there were few other jobs.

The decline in the US economy was the factor that pulled down other countries at first, then internal weaknesses or strengths in each country made conditions worse or better. Frantic attempts to shore up the economies of individual nations through protectionist policies, such as the 1930 Smoot-Hawley Tariff Act and retaliatory tariffs in other countries, exacerbated the collapse in global trade. By late 1930, a steady decline in the world economy had set in, and it did not reach a bottom until 1933.

The fall in US real gross domestic product (GDP) was around 30 percent between 1929 and 1933. The unemployment rate was 3 percent in August 1929; it was 25 percent in March 1933. Industrial production was indexed at 114 in August 1929, it was 54 in March 1933, a 52.6 percent decrease. The United States accounted for one-quarter of the fall in world industrial output. Prices fell 33 percent, and money supply 35 percent. One-third of US banks were closed or taken over.

Excessive Credit, Debt Deflation, or Banking Failure?
What was the cause or causes of the Great Depression? The economic function of a depression is to liquidate failed investments and

businesses that have been made obsolete and unproductive so that these could be redeployed in other sectors of the technologically dynamic economy. If self-adjustment of the economy led to mass bankruptcies, so be it.

This theory came mainly from the Austrian school (Von Mises, Hayek, and Robbins).[6] Their view was that any credit-driven boom ends in a bust. In the wake of the downturn, all manner of policy blunders (monetary, fiscal, and regulatory) caused the Great Depression to be much deeper and longer than it would otherwise have been. The Austrians emphasized that it was not just overinvestment but "malinvestment" (an "intertemporal" allocation of capital at odds with actual saving behavior) that characterizes an artificial boom and leads to a bust.

These liquidationists viewed the events of the Great Depression as an economic penance for the speculative excesses of the 1920s. The depression was the price paid for the misdeeds of the previous decade. Thus we get the infamous quote, in President Herbert Hoover's *Memoirs* from then Treasury Secretary Andrew Mellon: "Liquidate labor, liquidate stocks, liquidate the farmers, liquidate real estate. . . . [The depression] will purge the rottenness out of the system. High costs of living and high living will come down. People will work harder, live a more moral life. Values will be adjusted, and enterprising people will pick up the wrecks from less competent people."[7]

Leading monetarist economist Milton Friedman called this leave-it-alone liquidationism "dangerous nonsense."[8] Monetarists instead argued that the Great Depression was mainly caused by monetary contraction, the consequence of poor policy making by the Federal Reserve system and continued crisis in the banking system. In this view, the Federal Reserve, by not acting, allowed the money supply to shrink by one-third from 1929 to 1933, thereby transforming a normal recession into the Great Depression. Friedman argued that if the Fed had acted, the downward turn in the economy would have been just another recession.

In Friedman's view, the Fed allowed some large public bank failures, which produced panic and widespread runs on local banks and sat idly by while banks collapsed. He claimed that if the Fed had provided emergency lending to these key banks, or simply bought government bonds to provide liquidity and increase the quantity of money after the key banks fell, all the rest of the banks would not have fallen after the large ones did, and the money supply would not have fallen as far and as fast as it did. With significantly less money to go around, businesses could not get new loans and could not get their old loans renewed, forcing many to stop investing. Friedman argues that the Great Depression was a result of bad monetary policy, nothing more.[9]

Leading economist of the Depression era Irving Fisher argued that the predominant factor leading to the Great Depression was overindebtedness and deflation. He tied loose credit to overindebtedness, which fueled speculation and asset bubbles. He outlined several interacting factors under conditions of debt and deflation to create the mechanics of boom to bust. At the time of the 1929 crash, margin requirements for stock market speculation were only 10 percent. Brokerage firms, in other words, would lend $9 for every $1 an investor had deposited. When the market fell, brokers called in loans that could not be paid back.

Fisher argued that banks began to fail as debtors defaulted on debt and depositors attempted to withdraw their deposits en masse, triggering multiple bank runs. Government guarantees and Federal Reserve banking regulations to prevent such panics were ineffective or were not used. Bank failures led to the loss of billions of dollars in assets.

Outstanding debts became heavier because prices and incomes fell by 20–50 percent, but the debts remained at the same dollar amount. After the panic of 1929 and during the first ten months of 1930, 744 US banks failed. (In all, 9,000 banks failed during the 1930s.) By April 1933, around $7 billion in deposits had been frozen in failed banks.

Bank failures snowballed as desperate bankers called in loans, which the borrowers did not have time or money to repay. With future profits looking poor, capital investment and construction slowed or completely ceased. In the face of bad loans and worsening future prospects, the surviving banks became even more conservative in their lending. Banks built up their capital reserves and made fewer loans, which intensified deflationary pressures. A vicious circle developed and the downward spiral accelerated.

The liquidation of debt could not keep up with the fall of prices it caused. The mass effect of the stampede to liquidate increased the value of each dollar owed, relative to the value of declining asset holdings. The very effort of individuals to lessen their burden of debt effectively increased it. Paradoxically, the more the debtors paid, the more they owed. This self-aggravating process turned a recession into the Great Depression.[10]

Do the facts support the idea that bank failures were the key determinant of the depth and duration of the Great Depression? Actually, the earlier recession of 1921 had already significantly decreased the net assets of the banking sector, and the number of banks had declined well before 1929. The modern economics expert of the Great Depression and former Federal Reserve chief Ben Bernanke found that during the three years prior to 1929, the number of banks had reduced more than 3 percent a year, with the largest decrease (3.9 percent) between 1926 and 1927.

So the Great Depression was not initiated in 1930 with a banking crisis and, indeed, until December 1930 there was no significant increase in bank failures. Between 1929 and 1930 bank assets increased by 2.7 percent. What was much more significant was that the real economy had been declining since mid-1929, with industrial production contracting by almost half since mid-1929 through mid-1930, while the unemployment rate tripled from 2.9 percent in 1929 to 8.9 percent in 1930. The real economy deteriorated before the banking crisis took place.[11]

According to Parker and Fackler, it took a combination of causes to account for the actual movements in output over the course of the cycle. Nobody in mainstream economics has a clear answer. Most of the mainstream explanations of the Great Depression were the same as those presented for the long depression of the nineteenth century: a banking crisis, debt deflation, bad monetary policy, credit bubbles, and a rigid gold standard.

The Keynesian Explanation

A new explanation of the Depression came to the fore in the 1930s. It was provided by British economist John Maynard Keynes. He argued that lower aggregate demand in the economy contributed to a massive decline in income and employment. In such a situation, the economy reached equilibrium at lower than average levels of economic activity and with high unemployment.

An increase in output depends on "the amount of purchasing power . . . which is expected to come on the market." Recovery depends on increasing purchasing power. There are, Keynes pointed out, three factors operating to raise purchasing power and output. The first is increased consumer spending out of current income, the second is increased investment by capitalists, and the third is that "public authority must be called in aid to create additional current incomes through the expenditure of borrowed or printed money."[12]

Since the vast majority of consumers are workers, increased consumption expenditure is impossible on the required scale during a period of high unemployment and low wages. Business investment will eventually materialize, but only "after the tide has been turned by the expenditures of public authority."[13] Large-scale government investment in employment-generating public works must come first; only then can private investment be expected to kick in.

A revival of aggregate investment by the capitalist class is necessary to constitute recovery. But investment by an individual capitalist in a severe downturn would be irrational. So each capitalist will defer investment until there is evidence of recovery, that is, evidence that the other capitalists have undertaken productive outlays. So a structural contradiction is in place. If each investor refrains from investment until all the others invest, no capitalist will invest—they will die waiting for the others to come across. In the absence of an external impetus to the private investment system, the depression will be endless. Recovery is only possible, then, if a force external to the private market gets the ball rolling. Enter government to the rescue.

So the collapse in aggregate demand caused the depression. A recovery in demand requires outside intervention, otherwise an economy can stay in depression. The Keynesian explanation, however, suffered from two failings. First, it was not a causal explanation, in the sense that it did not show why aggregate demand should suddenly collapse (see Appendix 2); second, it was not adopted as an explanation or used as a motive for government policy, because most economies began to recover of their own accord after 1932.

Recovery within Depression

In most countries of the world, recovery from the Great Depression began in 1933. In the United States, recovery began in early 1933, but the economy did not return to 1929 levels for over a decade. The United States still had an unemployment rate of about 15 percent in 1940, although it was down from the high of 25 percent in 1933.

There is no consensus among economists regarding the motivating force for the US economic expansion that continued through most of the Franklin Roosevelt years (and the 1937 recession that interrupted it). The common view among most economists is that New Deal policies either caused or accelerated the recovery, although these policies were never aggressive enough to bring the economy completely out of recession. It was the rollback of those same reflationary policies that led to the interrupting recession of 1937. One contributing policy that reversed reflation was the Banking Act of 1935, which effectively raised reserve requirements, causing a monetary contraction that helped thwart the recovery.

According to mainstream economist Christine Romer, money supply growth caused by huge international gold inflows was a crucial source of the recovery. The gold inflows were partly due to the devaluation of the dollar. Great Depression expert Ben Bernanke agrees that monetary factors played important roles in the worldwide economic decline and eventual recovery. He also sees a strong role for institutional factors, particularly the rebuilding and restructuring of the financial system, and points out that the Great Depression should be examined in international perspective.

Some economic studies have indicated that just as the downturn was spread worldwide by the rigidities of the gold standard, it was suspending gold convertibility (or devaluing the currency in gold terms) that did the most to make recovery possible. Every major currency left the gold standard during the Great Depression. Great Britain was the first to do so. Japan and the Scandinavian countries also left the gold standard in 1931. Other countries, such as Italy and the United States, remained on the gold standard into 1932 or 1933, and a few countries in the so-called gold bloc, led by France and including Poland, Belgium, and Switzerland, stayed on the standard until 1935–1936.

According to some analyses, the earliness with which a country left the gold standard reliably predicted its economic recovery. For example, Great Britain and Scandinavia, which left the gold standard in 1931, recovered much earlier than did France and Belgium, which remained on gold much longer. The connection between leaving the gold standard as a strong predictor of that country's severity of its depression and the length of time of its recovery has been shown to be consistent for dozens of countries, including those with developing economies. This partly explains why the experience and length of the depression differed from country to county.

By 1936, the US economy had regained the levels of the late 1920s, except for unemployment, which remained high at 11 percent, although this was considerably lower than the 25 percent seen in 1933. In the spring of 1937, industrial production exceeded that of 1929 and remained level until June 1937.

In June 1937, the Roosevelt administration cut spending and increased taxation in an attempt to balance the federal budget. The US economy took a sharp downturn for thirteen months through most of 1938. Industrial production fell almost 30 percent within a few months. Unemployment jumped from 14.3 percent in 1937 to 19.0 percent in 1938, rising from 5 million people to more than 12 million in early 1938. Manufacturing output fell by 37 percent from the 1937 peak and was back to 1934 levels. The 1937 cyclical peak did not end the Depression.

In some empirical investigations,[14] several of these mainstream explanations were put to the test of causality. To pass the test, the hypothesized cause must explain (using 95 percent confidence bands) the depth and duration of the Depression. Neither money nor debt nor gold flow theories passed. Mainstream economics has been at a loss to explain the length and depth of the Great Depression.

More recently, an attempt has been made to argue that the Great Depression was caused by some shock to productivity growth.[15] Productivity rose 5 percent above trend in the 1920s but then fell 14 percent below from 1929 to 1933. Maybe these productivity shocks were more important than any monetary measures or credit moves. The Great Depression was a result of things going wrong in the "real economy," in the productive sectors.

The Marxist Explanation

This brings us to the Marxist explanation. The Marxist view has not been analyzed or tested in any review of the causes of the Great Depression. However, this chapter concludes that just as a Marxist explanation of the nineteenth-century long depression stands, so it is for the Great Depression of the 1930s. Capitalist economies can only recover in a sustained way if average profitability for the productive sectors of the economy rises significantly. That requires sufficient damage to the value of past accumulation of productive capital.

Yet most Marxist economists do not consider the Great Depression a result of this mechanism. Take Duménil and Lévy (D-L).[16] For them, the Great Depression was caused by a combination of factors that mainstream economists have already discerned. A similar approach is adopted by Panitch and Gindin in their prize-winning book.[17] For them, each crisis is unique depending on the particular relationships and alliances forged between workers, business, finance, and the state. There have been four major historical global crises: the long depression in the 1870s, the Great Depression of the 1930s, the Great Recession of 1970s, and what they call the Great Financial Crisis of 2007–9. For them, each has a different cause.[18]

D-L conclude from their analysis of the data that the Great Depression of the 1930s and the Great Recession of 2008 onward cannot have been caused by Marx's law of profitability. Why? In the case of the Great Depression, D-L say that there was no rising organic composition of capital before 1929 (see Figure 3.1). But this is not the case. The "productivity of capital" starts falling (i.e., a rising organic composition) from 1924 onward, and this coincides with a peak in the rate of profit. For five years before the start of the Great Depression, the US rate of profit was falling.

Figure 3.1

US Rate of Profit (Ratio to 1) and Organic Composition of Capital Ratio, 1914–1931

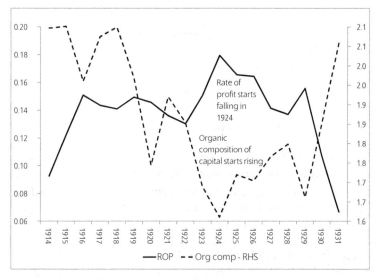

Source: Dumenil and Levy, Author's Calculations

Indeed, the productive sectors of US capital were suffering a profits famine as profits were diverted to the financial sector. Financial sector profits increased 177 percent between 1923 and 1929, while the non-financial sector rose only 14 percent. Profit from capital gains (buying shares low and selling high) increased between 1923 and 1929—five times more than the dividends and interest payments and twenty times faster than wages.[19] Between 1922 and 1929, the volume of shares and debentures released to market for investment in new facilities and equipment remained virtually constant, while new shares and bonds issued for speculative investments was tripled. Profitability had been falling from 1924, and it was all in the productive sectors.

From this also flows the argument that the Great Depression of the 1930s in the US economy lasted so long because profitability did not recover throughout that decade. The evidence is clear: in 1938, the US corporate rate of profit was still less than half the rate of 1929 (see Figure 3.2).

Figure 3.2
US Rate of Profit (%), 1929–1945

Source: US BEA, Author's Calclations

It was the same story for the mass of corporate profits. Even by 1940, profits were still below that of 1929. Indeed, it is clear that profitability only picked up once the war economy was under way, from 1940 onward. So was it necessary for the United States to go to war to establish a sustained recovery in its capitalist economy.

Could Keynesian Policies Have Worked?

But could the New Deal (if Roosevelt had sustained it) and/or Keynesian policies of easy money (low interest rates) and fiscal stimulus (tax cuts and government spending) have done the trick well before the war economy became dominant?

Many economists believe that government spending on the war caused or at least accelerated recovery from the Great Depression, though some believe it did not play a very large role in the recovery. It did help in reducing unemployment. The rearmament policies leading up to World War II helped stimulate the economies of Europe in 1937–39. By 1937, unemployment in Britain had fallen to 1.5 million. But the mobiliation of manpower following the outbreak of war in 1939 ended unemployment completely.

The US entry into the war in 1941 finally eliminated the last effects from the Great Depression and brought the unemployment rate down below 10 percent. Massive war spending doubled the economic growth rate, either masking the effects of the Depression or essentially ending it. Business owners ignored the mounting public debt and heavy new taxes, redoubling their efforts for greater output to take advantage of generous government contracts. It was the mobilization for entry into World War II—or the money creation that financed that mobilization—that eventually got the economy out of depression.[20]

Keynesian economists Brad DeLong and Larry Summers deny this description.[21] They argue that economic recovery was already well under way by 1942 when the United States had already entered the war. DeLong and Summers calculated that more than five-sixths of the decline in output relative to trend that occurred during the Depression had been made up before 1942. They found it "hard to attribute any of the pre-1942 catch-up to the war." So the Marxist and other accounts that war transformed US capitalism and got it out of the Great Depression were wrong.

The DeLong and Summers estimates have been contested by John Vernon.[22] Vernon agreed that the US economy completed its recovery from the Great Depression in 1942, restoring full employment output in that year after twelve years of below full employment performance. However, Keynesian fiscal policies were not the most important factor from 1933 through 1940. World War II fiscal policies were instrumental in the overall restoration of full employment performance. Vernon shows that more than 80 percent of the 1941 increase in real GNP can be attributed to World War II–associated federal fiscal policies: "Thus World War II fiscal policies did much more than simply complete a recovery already largely accomplished: they were, for more than half the recovery, the major determinant in the restoration of full-employment performance."

By 1938, the level of US real GDP was still below the level of 1929. There was no significant rise in US real GDP until 1940, after which GDP really took off to reach twice the 1929 level by 1944. Investment levels did not rise until 1941 and, most interestingly, consumption continued to fall dramatically once the war began.

So there is no evidence that any economic recovery before the war kicked in. Investment rose from 1941 onward to reach, as a share of GDP, far more than double the level that stood in 1940. It was not the result of a pick-up in private sector investment. What happened was a massive rise in government investment and spending (see Figure 3.3). In 1940, private sector investment was still below the level of 1929 and actually fell further during the war. The state sector took over nearly all investment, as resources (value) were diverted to the production of arms and other security measures in a war economy.

Figure 3.3
Ratios of US Private and Government Investment to GDP, 1929–1943

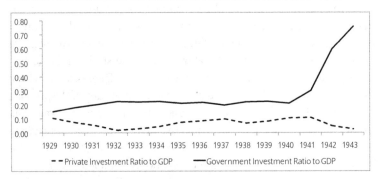

Source: US BEA, Author's Calculations

But is not increased government investment and consumption a form of Keynesian stimulus, just at a higher level? No. The difference is revealed in the continued collapse of consumption. The war economy was paid for by restricting the opportunities for workers to spend their incomes from their wartime jobs. There was forced saving through the purchase of war bonds, rationing, and increased taxation to pay for the war. Government investment meant the direction and planning of production by decree. The war economy did not stimulate the private sector, it *replaced* the free market and capitalist investment for profit. Consumption did not restore economic growth as Keynesians (and those who see the cause of crisis in underconsumption) should expect; instead, it was investment in mainly weapons of destruction.

In many industries, corporate executives resisted converting to military production because they did not want to lose consumer market share to competitors who did not convert. Conversion thus became a goal pursued by public officials and labor leaders. Auto companies only fully converted to war production in 1942 and only began substantially contributing to aircraft production in 1943. The bombing of Pearl Harbor was an enormous spur to conversion. From the beginning of preparedness in 1939 through the peak of war production in 1944, the war economy could not be left to the capitalist sector to deliver. To organize the war economy and ensure that it produced the goods needed for war, the federal government created an array of mobilization agencies, which often purchased goods, closely directed those goods' manufacture, and heavily influenced the operation of private companies and whole industries.

The military services were largely able to curtail production destined for civilians (e.g., automobiles and many nonessential foods) and even for war-related but nonmilitary purposes (e.g., textiles and clothing). The Department of the Treasury introduced the first general income tax in US history, and war bonds were sold to the public. Beginning in 1940, the government extended the income tax to virtually all citizens and collected it by deductions from wages at source. Those subject to income tax rose from 4 million in 1939 to 43 million in 1945!

With such a large pool of taxpayers, the US government took in $45 billion in 1945, an enormous increase over the $8.7 billion collected in 1941, although still far short of the $83 billion spent on the war in 1945. Over that same period, federal tax revenue grew from about 8 percent of GDP to more than 20 percent. All told, taxes provided about $136.8 billion of the war's total cost of $304 billion. To cover the other $167.2 billion, the Treasury expanded its bond program, which served as a valuable source of revenue for the government. By the time war bond sales ended in 1946, 85 million Americans had purchased more than $185 billion worth of the securities, often through automatic deductions from their paychecks.

The Office of Price Administration attempted to curtail inflation by maintaining prices at their March 1942 levels. The National War Labor Board limited wartime wage increases to about 15 percent. Although wages rose about 65 percent over the course of the war, the national living standard barely stayed level or even declined. About 10.5 million Americans either could not have had jobs (the 3.25 million youths who came of age after Pearl Harbor) or would not have sought employment (3.5 million women, for instance). Almost 19 million women (including millions of black women) were working outside the home by 1945. Labor mobility was huge. About 15 million civilians moved. Migration was especially strong along rural–urban axes, especially to war production centers around the country, permanently altering their demographics and economies.[23]

What the story of the Great Depression and World War II shows is that once capitalism is in the depth of a depression, there must be a grinding and deep destruction of all that capitalism had accumulated in value in previous decades before a new era of expansion becomes possible. There is no policy that can avoid that and preserve the capitalist sector.

Keynes summed it up. Having been rebuffed by Roosevelt and the Americans in his prescriptions to deal with the Great Depression, he commented, "It is, it seems, politically impossible for a capitalistic democracy to organize expenditure on the scale necessary to make the grand experiments which would prove my case—except in war conditions."[24]

The war decisively ended the Depression. US industry was revitalized and many sectors were oriented to defense production (for example, aerospace and electronics) or completely dependent on it (atomic energy). The war's rapid scientific and technological changes continued and intensified trends begun during the Great Depression. As the war severely damaged every major economy in the world except for the United States, US capitalism gained economic and political hegemony after 1945.

This leaves us with the legacy of the Great Depression. After the war, Keynesian economics ruled for three decades before giving way to neoclassical and monetarist economics again. Both sides of mainstream economics were convinced that such a terrible depression could not happen again because the lessons of that period had been learned, the global economy was much more integrated, and all central banks are working together to make sure it could not be repeated.[25] We shall see how justified that view proved to be in the next chapter.

Chapter 4
The Profitability Crisis and the Neoliberal Response

World War II established the hegemony of US capital globally. Pax Americana was sealed with the Bretton Woods agreement, which fixed currency rates in the major capitalist economies to the US dollar and established the dollar as the international reserve currency. International agencies like the International Monetary Fund and the World Bank were set up to control and fund international capital flows and deal with financial crises. They were both based in the United States. Finally, the United Nations was founded, and its headquarters were located in the United States.

Globally, profit rates in the major economies were high. There was a plentiful supply of cheap labor, in both the defeated Axis powers and the Allied countries, as the armed forces were demobilized. Huge numbers of displaced unemployed workers were available. In the so-called Third World, there were billions of people in rural areas ready for global exploitation. Technical innovations developed mainly for military purposes could now be invested in to expand labor productivity. Dangerous revolutionary movements appeared briefly after the war as a result of the resistance struggles in Europe and in response to the collapse of Japanese imperialism and the absence of colonial rule in Asia. These were eventually suppressed by a combination of military imposition (Greece, Vietnam) and collaboration with the Allied forces by communist and socialist leaders (Japan, Italy, France).

A Classic Profitability Crisis
The golden age of postwar capitalism began. Investment accelerated, real incomes rose, something like full employment was made possible, and labor pressure led to an expansion of what was called the "welfare state" of pension, social, and health provisions.

But this period was brief. From the mid-1960s, profitability in the major economies began to fall. This happened according to Marx's law of profitability. The organic composition of capital has risen significantly from increased mechanization and investment in new industries. Labor gained bargaining strength from nearly full employment. Wages began to squeeze the share of new value going to profits, so that the increase in the rate of surplus value was not sufficient to compensate for the rise in the organic composition. Moreover, the initial expansion of the global supply of cheap labor had begun to dissipate as Germany, Japan, and other parts of Europe sucked up their "reserve armies."

The evidence is clear that the rate of profit fell from 1965 to 1982 in nearly all the major economies (see Figure 4.1). Indeed, Marxist economists, even those who reject that Marx's law of profitability was relevant to the Great Recession and the current Long Depression, recognize that the period of 1965–82 was a classic profitability crisis.

Figure 4.1
Rate of Profit in Main Capitalist Economis, 1950–2010 (%)

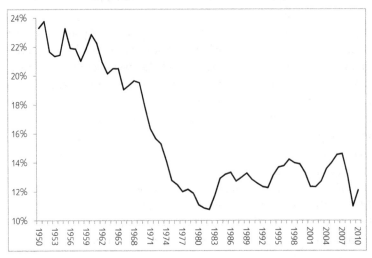

Source: E Maito

The profitability crisis of 1965–82 did not produce a depression. The reasons for that can be explained by the arguments presented in chapter 1. Although profitability of capital was falling, it was not accompanied by a down wave in other cycles of motion of capitalism, namely, in global production prices (where on the contrary energy prices were rising fast) or in a housing bust (the construction cycle was on the upswing). The result was not a depression but stagflation: slower growth alongside rising inflation. This was something inexplicable to neoclassical economics and particularly to Keynesian theory, which reckoned that there was a playoff between unemployment and inflation—namely, you could not have both at once.

What the profitability crisis did produce was the first simultaneous international slump since the 1930s, the recession of 1974–75, and then seven years later, the deepest slump in the industrial sectors of the major economies with the double-dip recession of 1980–82. That culminated in a new trough in the rate of profit.

The Neoliberal Response

These two great slumps created the conditions for a revival in profitability. That is the dialectical nature of Marx's law of profitability. Capital values were destroyed as old plants in old industries were closed, companies went bankrupt, and new companies in new sectors took over. Mass unemployment reduced labor costs and weakened the ability of the trade unions to block reductions in wages and conditions.

Governments came into office and no longer looked to reach compromises with labor over labor costs, market regulation, taxation, and government intervention and services. On the contrary, the Reagan[1] and Thatcher administrations aimed to reverse all the gains of labor during the golden age so that profitability of capital could be raised consistently and the costs of government and labor reduced permanently.[2]

Thus we had the neoliberal "reforms" of anti–trade union legislation, privatization of state companies, cuts in pensions and government services, the lowering of taxes on the corporate sector, and an increase in taxes on spending plus the deregulation of the financial sector.

Profitability did recover as the rate of surplus value or exploitation in the major economies began to outstrip any rise in the organic composition of capital. Indeed, with the development of the high-tech, dot-com revolution in the 1990s, constant capital was cheapened considerably so that the organic composition did not rise at all in many economies (see Figure 4.2).

Figure 4.2

Changes in the US Rate of Profit, Organic Composition of Capital, and Rate of Surplus Value (%), 1950–2011

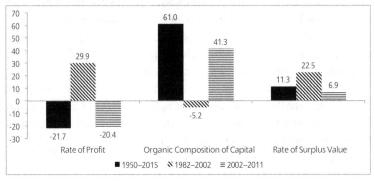

Source: US BEA, Author's Caluclations

Figure 4.3

Global Liquidity as % of Global GDP (Dollar Terms), 1995–2014

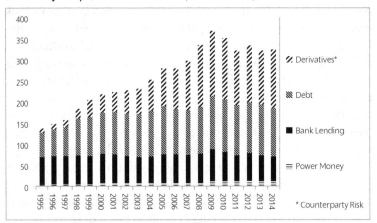

Source: BIS, Author's Calculations

But the rise in profitability at the expense of the conditions and interests of labor was not great. Moreover, it was concentrated in the financial sector, as capital flowed into unproductive sectors like finance and real estate in the search for higher profitability through speculation. There was a sharp growth in fictitious capital (stock and bond prices) and in private sector debt (see Figure 4.3).

As Marx argued: "In practice, however, the rate of profit will fall in the long run."[3] These countervailing influences cannot last forever, and eventually the law of profitability will start to exert its downward pressure on profits. The rate peaked in 1997 with the exhaustion of the gains of new technology in the productive sectors. In the 1990s, it appears that the impact of these countervailing factors faded in the G7 economies.

From 1997 on, profitability began to fall again in the major economies, laying the conditions for the end of the stock market boom. In 2000, the dot-com bonanza in financial markets crashed in spectacular manner, with stock market indexes falling by over 50 percent, even more in the technology-oriented indexes. Shortly after, world capitalism went into a slump.

The recession of 2001 was relatively mild, as the major economies were still being propped up by a significant expansion of credit globally with the deregulation of banking and the attempts of banks to introduce new forms of fictitious capital, such as securitized debt of mortgages and corporate assets and exotic derivatives. Casino capitalism took over, and the major economies went on a credit-fueled binge that accelerated growth from 2002 onward—only to pave the way for the almighty crunch that began in the middle of 2007 (see Figure 4.4).

Figure 4.4

Global Debt to GDP (%): From Credit Bubbles to Credit Crises 1989–2011

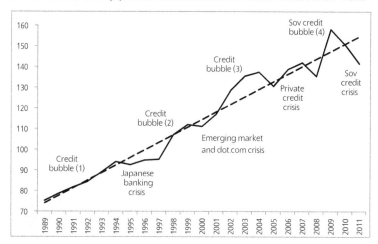

Source: BIS, Author's Calculations

Marx argued that slumps in capitalist production come about when profitability falls to such a level that the cost of new investment in labor and technology rises more than the profits gained, so that the mass of profit begins to fall. Once that starts to happen, the weakest companies begin to have huge losses, lay off labor, and stop investing. This downturn in employment and investment cascades through an economy, generating an overall crisis in production. Then any debt liabilities that had been racked up to invest or speculate in the stock market or real estate cannot be paid, and the profit crisis will trigger a financial crisis. In turn, this financial crisis brings about an even greater fall in investment and production.

This is what happened once profitability began to decline after the late 1990s, only delayed by the credit boom of the early 2000s. Eventually, the Great Recession arrived.

Chapter 5
The Great Recession of the Twenty-First Century

The central problem of depression-prevention has been solved, for all practical purposes.

—Robert Lucas Jr., Nobel Prize winner in economics[1]

The message of this chapter flows from the last. The neoliberal recovery in the major advanced economies did not restore the profitability of capital back to the levels of the golden age of the 1950s and 1960s. Although real gross domestic product (GDP) growth rates were better in the 1980s and 1990s than in the 1970s "profitability crisis" period, they were still below those of the 1960s. Moreover, investment had flowed increasingly into unproductive sectors like finance, insurance, and real estate (FIRE) and less into productive sectors. Speculation in financial assets and property brought higher profits. But that meant that any collapse in housing and stock markets would expose the fictitious nature of this recovery. The dot-com crash of 2001 provided the first indicator of that. After a huge credit-fueled boom from 2002 to 2007, the global financial crash did just that.

How Did It Happen?
The global financial crash started on August 9, 2007, when Bank Paribas National announced that it was closing down one of its funds of US mortgage-backed securities and taking heavy losses.[2] Not long after, other banks across the United States and Europe announced similar losses. The stock market began to plunge from October 2007 (it had been faltering beginning in March). Then there was an avalanche of losses for banks globally. The United States and the rest of the advanced capitalist economies then plunged into the Great Recession that lasted for eighteen months from the beginning of 2008 to the middle of 2009.

This slump in capitalism has been called the Great Recession because it truly was "great." It was the longest and deepest in its contraction of output that the global capitalist economy, as represented by the thirty advanced capitalist nations of the Organization for Economic Co-operation and Development (OECD), has experienced since the Great Depression of 1929–32.

From the peak of the previous boom in real GDP growth from 2007 to the trough of the Great Recession in mid-2009, the OECD economies contracted by 6 percentage points of GDP. If you compare global output in 2009 to where it should have been without a slump, the loss of income was even greater at 8 percentage points. At the trough of the Great Recession, the level of industrial production was 13 percent below its previous peak, and world trade fell 20 percent from its previous peak. World stock markets fell an average of 50 percent from the peak in 2007.

The Great Recession was also the longest since the Great Depression. Since the Great Depression, the US National Bureau of Economic Research (NBER) has tried to date economic recessions with reference to the US economy (see Figure 5.1). There have been eighteen recessions by NBER measures since the Great Depression, now eighty-plus years ago. The average length of these has been ten months, and on average the US economy grows below potential for about nineteen months during those recessions (measured by rising unemployment). The Great Recession lasted about twenty months, making it more than double the average and the longest by far since 1929–32, which lasted forty-three months. Investment crashed and employment followed it down.

Figure 5.1

The Percentage Fall in US Employment from Peak to Trough in Various Recessions

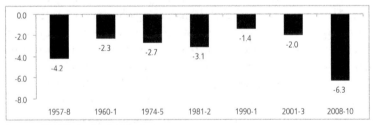

Source: US BIS, Author's Calculations

Investment in real estate took an almighty plunge after the credit-fueled boom up to 2007, but investment in productive assets also tumbled. The mass of profits dropped like a stone, especially for the financial sector, which had appropriated huge shares of profit in the advanced economies from the 1990s up to 2007. In 2007, over 40 percent of US corporate profits went to the financial sector, compared with just 10 percent in 1980. That share dramatically fell.

The financial sector was on its knees and rolling over. Because it has become such an important part of the capitalist system, particularly in the United States, the United Kingdom, and Europe, it now threatened to bring down the productive sector of capitalism through a string of bankruptcies and closures. Governments had to act. Their answer was to bail out the banks, mortgage lenders, and insurance companies (FIRE) with government cash, partly raised by higher taxes on wage earners but mostly by borrowing, that is, selling government bonds to the very banks and insurance companies that were in trouble.

Some banks were allowed to go bust (Lehman Brothers), but most were bailed out. In particular, AIG, the global insurance company which had been insuring all the banks and hedge fund speculators against any losses on their speculations in derivatives of mortgage bonds and other "innovative" forms of fictitious capital, received a massive handout. Why? To meet in full the insurance claims on losses on speculative investments made by the likes of Goldman Sachs and others. So taxpayers ended up fully compensating the big banks for the losses they incurred from their own recklessness and greed.

Government debt rocketed to levels not seen since World War II and not in just a few countries but everywhere (see Figure 5.2). The taxpayer, in particular wage earners, faced a massive bill in terms of increased debt servicing payments to the bondholders (banks, etc.) for the foreseeable future. Annual government budget deficits shot upward to fund the bailouts and because as economies contracted sharply and unemployment spiraled, tax revenues dropped away and spending on welfare benefits mushroomed.

Governments were determined that these deficits be brought down and the new debt reduced in size. As soon as the Great Recession ended, they embarked on what we now call programs of austerity that aim to slash government spending, particularly government investment and social welfare; raise taxes on wage earners in various forms;

and reduce the cost of state pensions by extending the retirement ages, lengthening the time of service, and raising the rate of contributions. Pensions are really deferred wages, as social security contributions are deductions from gross wages and extracted by the state. So the reduction in the value of state pensions was another form of making workers pay for the Great Recession.

Figure 5.2

Top Seven Capitalist Economies' Sovereign Debt to GDP (%), 1950–2012

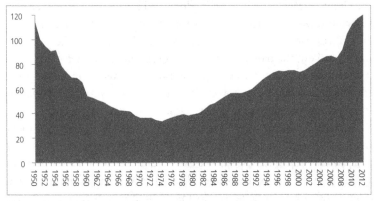

Source: OECD

The Official View: We Did Not See It Coming

Before 2007, no official strategist of economic policy forecast any crisis. US Fed chairman at the time, Alan Greenspan, told us in 2004 that "a national severe price distortion is most unlikely in real estate." In 2006, he said that "the worst may be over for housing," and then the housing bubble burst. As late as March 2008, the newly appointed US Treasury secretary Hank Paulson said the crisis in the overall economy "appears to be contained."[3]

But reality was harsh. As the slump worsened in October 2008, Greenspan told Congress, "I am in a state of shocked disbelief." House Oversight Committee Chair Henry Waxman asked: "In other words, you found that your view of the world, your ideology was not right, it was not working?" Greenspan admitted, "Absolutely, precisely, you know that's precisely the reason I was shocked, because I have been going for forty years or more with very considerable evidence that it was working exceptionally well." He concluded that economics cannot predict a bubble and when it happens there is nothing you can do about it: "You can only break a bubble if you break the underlying basis of the economy."

Greenspan summed up what he had learned in his paper *The Crisis* in March 2010.[4] He told us that what happened was "financial intermediation tried to function with too thin a layer of capital owing to a misreading of the degree of risk embedded in ever-more complex financial products and markets." Something as simple as the lack of capital adequacy in banks was the cause. You would think he might have noticed that as chairman of the Fed.

Moreover, Greenspan reckoned that the bubble that burst in 2008 came about by a conjunction of events that could not be expected. It was the serendipity of the Fall of the Wall, cheap interest rates, and globalization that came together to create excessive risk taking. Could the crisis have been avoided? Because of these serendipitous factors coming together, "I doubt it," he said.

For Greenspan, it was chance, a one-hundred-year event: "The disasters were the results of massive natural forces and they did constitute a perfect storm." This idea was echoed by Paulson: this sort of thing happens "only once or twice" in a hundred years. As economist Daniel Gross commented on the "chance explanation" of the crisis: what's the difference between once or twice? "In this instance, several trillion dollars in losses."[5]

The official leaders of capitalism and the banking community fell back on the argument of Nassim Taleb, a US financial analyst, that the crisis was a "black swan"—something that could not have been expected or even known until it was known, and then with devastating consequences—an unknown unknown.[6] Before Europeans "discovered" Australia, it was thought that all swans were white. But the discovery in the eighteenth century that there were black swans in Australia dispelled that notion. Taleb argues that many events are like that. It is assumed that something just cannot happen: it is ruled out. But Taleb says, even though the chance is small, the very unlikely can happen, and when it does it will have a big impact. The global credit crunch (and the ensuing economic crisis) was another example of the black swan theory.

From a Marxist view, the black swan theory has some attraction. For example, revolution is a rare event in history. So rare that many (mainly apologists of the existing order) would rule it out as impossible. But it can and does happen, as we know. When it does, its impact is profound. In that sense, revolution is a black swan event. But where Marxists would disagree with Taleb is that he argues that chance is what rules history. However, randomness without cause is no way to view the world. This is far too one-sided and undialectical. Sure, chance plays a role in history, but only in the context of necessity.

Another more maverick economist, Nouriel Roubini, correctly argued that financial crises are more like a succession of white swans, or known unknowns, in the sense that the crisis follows a pattern that has happened before.[7] The credit crunch and the current economic slump could have been triggered by some unpredictable event like the collapse of some financial institution or the loss of bets on bond markets by a "rogue trader" in a French bank. The oil price explosion may have been the product of the decision of President George W. Bush to attack Iraq. But those things happened because the laws of motion of capitalism were being played out toward a crisis.

Similarly, the recent spate of natural disasters like tsunamis, earthquakes, and flooding is not an act of God. Climate change is manmade. The current economic crisis was no chance event that no one could have predicted. Greenspan fell back on the old adage of saloon bars, where somebody tells you, "It's human nature. Unless somebody can find a way to change human nature, we will have more crises and none of them will look like this because no two crises have anything in common, except human nature." Greenspan now doubts that stable growth is possible under capitalism.[8]

Ben Bernanke was the Fed chairman who presided over the Great Recession. He is an economist who specialized in the Great Depression. If ever there was an economist who looked at depression economics, to use Keynesian economist Paul Krugman's phrase, it is Bernanke. But as one witty commentator remarked: "Mr. Bernanke, the former head of Princeton University economics department, knows all there is to know about a depression, except what causes them."[9]

Like Greenspan, Bernanke did not see the crunch coming or predict its damage. Thus, in May 2007, he said, "We don't expect significant spillover from the subprime market to the rest of the economy from the financial system."[10] By June, he was saying the losses would be minimal, "between $50–100bn" at most. The losses in the global financial system eventually reached $3–7 trillion, depending on what you include.

Similarly, Sheila Bair, the head of the Federal Deposit Insurance Corporation, a US government agency responsible for regulating and monitoring the banking system, reported in July 2007 that "the banks in this country are well capitalized and my view is that I would be very, very surprised if any institutions of significant size were to get into serious trouble."[11] Then there was a series of banking failures: Bear Stearns, Countrywide Financial, Lehman Brothers, Merrill Lynch, and so on.

Larry Summers was a former Treasury secretary under President Bill Clinton, the president of Harvard University, prominent economist, and (failed) candidate to replace Bernanke as chairman of the Federal Reserve in 2014. Back in 2005, at the Fed's summer school, economist Raghuram Rajan presented a paper arguing that the freeing up of regulations on the financial sector was a recipe for trouble in creating a credit bubble that would burst. Summers was quick to condemn Rajan as being a "Luddite" (a moniker for British hand weavers during the Industrial Revolution who smashed up the new machines that were replacing them).[12] There was no need for restrictions on the new financial innovations, later delightfully called "financial instruments of mass destruction" by Warren Buffett. For Summers, these new instruments brought "substantially more stability" to financial markets.[13]

So the Fed and other official supervisory institutions failed to foresee the greatest economic collapse since the Great Depression. This is not surprising. There is a crude pecuniary connection here. At the *Journal of Monetary Economics*, a respected venue of mainstream economics, more than half of the editorial members are currently on the Fed payroll and the rest have been in the past.[14]

There were 730 economists, statisticians, and others working at the Fed and its regional banks in 1993, according to Greenspan. Over a three-year period ending October 1994, the Fed awarded 305 contracts to 209 professors worth $3 million. The Fed now employs 220 PhD economists. In 2008, the Fed spent $389 million on research into monetary and economic policy, and $433 million was budgeted for 2009. According to the American Economic Association, 487 economists are researching monetary policy and central banking, another 310 on interest rates, and 244 on macroeconomic policy.

The National Association for Business Economics reckons that 611 of its 2,400 members focus on monetary economics and banking. Most of these have worked for or with the Fed. Many editors of prominent academic journals are on the Fed payroll: 84 out of 190 editorial members in seven top economics journals were affiliated with the Fed. "Try to publish an article critical of the Fed with an editor who works for the Fed," complained economist James Galbraith.[15]

Even the late Milton Friedman expressed his concerns about this: "I cannot disagree with you that having something like 500 economists is extremely unhealthy. As you say, it is not conducive to independent objective research. There is censorship of material published."[16] Asked to be a consultant for the Fed: "It's a payoff, like money. I think it's more being one part of a club, being respected, invited to conferences, have a hearing with the chairman, having the prestige is as much as a pay check," said Rob Johnson, Senate Banking Committee economist.[17]

Mainstream Economics: Myriad Causes

That was the response of the officials in government. How did mainstream economists respond? Modern mainstream economics provided myriad causes: it's chance, it's the greed of bankers that got out of hand. Alternatively, there is not enough desire to invest or buy—not enough greed. There is too much credit in the system causing overinvestment or malinvestment. Alternatively, there is not enough credit so investors and buyers are squeezed. Wages are too low to buy more goods and profits are too high, or vice versa, so companies don't invest.

In the modern mainstream, there are two schools of thought, with subdivisions. The neoclassical school is what Marx called "vulgar economics." This school is ideologically committed to a belief in the free market as a starting assumption rather than as a scientifically objective view of economic organization. The neoclassical school can be subdivided into the Walrasian general equilibrium analysis; the monetarists (à la Friedman); and the modern Chicago school of "efficient market" theorists.

Within the mainstream, there is also the Keynesian school, which rejects the microeconomic categories of the neoclassical school as relevant to macroeconomic forces. It is divided again. There are the new Keynesians with their synthesis with neoclassical equilibrium theory, namely, that slumps are really a product of sticky factors of production, particularly wages. For new Keynesians, slumps are also exogenous to the economic model.

There are Keynesians who concentrate on other aspects of Keynes's theory: that slumps are the result of the lack of "effective demand," which in turn is induced by "liquidity preference" in the financial sector or is a product of the irrational movements of "animal spirits" among entrepreneurs and the behavior of consumers (this wing of Keynesianism has now partly migrated into so-called behavioral economics).

Then there are the various schools of heterodox economics, outside the mainstream. There are the post-Keynesians who combine some of the ideas of Marx seen through the lenses of Polish Marxist Michal Kalecki and those of the radical Keynesian Hyman Minsky. There are also the modern monetary theorists, who reckon that crises are the product of reckless banking and excessive private credit. At the other end of spectrum is the Austrian school founded by Ludwig von Mises and Friedrich Hayek who believe that crises are purely the product of excessive credit, caused by the intervention of central banks and government which, if abolished or removed, would cease.

Economic forecasting has not been the strong suit of the mainstream. In March 2001, just as the mild global economic recession of that year began, according to the *Economist*, 95 percent of US economists ruled out such a recession. Economists surveyed by the Philadelphia Reserve Bank in November 2007 forecast that the US economy would grow 2.5 percent in 2008 and employment would rise. The economy fell over 4 percent and unemployment doubled.

Eugene Fama is a Nobel Prize winner and founding exponent of the efficient markets hypothesis, which argues that free markets will ensure that capitalist production will grow smoothly and without struggles if left alone. When asked about the cause of the crisis, Fama responded: "We don't know what causes recessions. I'm not a macroeconomist so I don't feel bad about that! We've never known. Debates go on to this day about what caused the Great Depression. Economics is not very good at explaining swings in economic activity."[18] Asked about the legacy of the financial crisis for mainstream neoclassical economics: "I don't see any. Which way is it going to go? If I could have predicted the crisis, I would have. I don't see it. I'd love to know more what causes business cycles." Can the market economy still be considered "efficient" after this crisis? "Yes. And if it isn't, then it's going to be impossible to tell." Thus the great guru of neoclassical economics sums up his school's contribution to the issue.[19]

Greg Mankiw is a Harvard University economics professor and

author of a main economic textbook used at universities. Looking back at the Great Recession in 2011, he wrote: "After more than a quarter-century as a professional economist, I have a confession to make: There is a lot I don't know about the economy. Indeed, the area of economics where I have devoted most of my energy and attention—the ups and downs of the business cycle—is where I find myself most often confronting important questions without obvious answers."[20]

The Monetarist View: A Financial Panic

In November 2011, top officials and economists at the International Monetary Fund (IMF) and other major international institutions gathered in Washington, DC, for a seminar, "Crises, Yesterday and Today." As the organizers put it: "Several years after the global financial crisis, the world economy is still confronting its painful legacies. Many countries are suffering from lackluster recoveries coupled with high and persistent unemployment. Policymakers are tackling the costs stemming from the crisis, managing the transition from crisis-era policies, and trying to adapt to the associated cross-border spillovers. Against this background, the IMF will take stock of our understanding of past and present crises."[21]

So what did they come up with? Well, the answer was summed up in the keynote speech to the conference from Bernanke. He explained that the global financial collapse of 2008 and the ensuing Great Recession was "best understood as a classic financial panic transposed into the novel institutional context of the 21st century financial system."[22]

What are the common elements of these crises ? Speculative investment in different forms of financial assets gets out of hand every so often, and there is not enough regulation of what financial institutions are doing, so a panic follows. The common factors in capitalist crises thus appear to be that all crises are banking crises and that they are due to excessive speculation and risk-taking by uncontrolled bankers.

Bernanke argued that the Great Recession was similar to the financial panic of 1907. This was triggered by speculative activity in 1907 by "a failed effort by a group of speculators to corner the stock of the United Copper Company." Similarly the 2008 panic "had an identifiable trigger—in this case, the growing realization by market participants that subprime mortgages and certain other credits were seriously deficient in their underwriting and disclosures." In both cases, a fire sale of bank assets and a collapse in the stock market led to a run on bank deposits and liquidity: "In 1907, in the absence of deposit insurance, retail deposits were much more prone to run, whereas in 2008, most withdrawals were of uninsured wholesale funding, in the form of commercial paper, repurchase agreements, and securities lending. Interestingly, a steep decline in interbank lending, a form of wholesale funding, was important in both episodes." In both 1907 and 2008, there was insufficient regulation of financial institutions to ensure that they were not up to their necks in risky dud assets.

In 1907, liquidity injections stopped the rot and "eventually calmed the panic. By then, however, the US financial system had been severely disrupted, and the economy contracted through the middle of 1908." It was the same outcome in 2008. In 1907, extra "liquidity" had to come from the stronger banks like JP Morgan. The experience of 1907 led to the big banks deciding to form the Federal Reserve Bank in response, set up in 1913. The Federal Reserve remains formally owned by the major investment and retail banks and is not owned by the taxpayer, although the Fed is a government-directed agency under the law. From the beginning, the Fed's task has been to meet the interests of Wall Street first and the wider economy second.

Bernanke concluded that depression could be avoided by Fed action. Following his mentor, Friedman, he advocated "printing money" and even "dropping it from helicopters" to the populace to ensure spending is sustained. This monetarist theory led him to concentrate on money supply indicators as a guide to the state of the US economy.

Bernanke was very proud that the Federal Reserve as "lender of last resort" and the provider of liquidity and a monetary injection stopped the 2008 financial collapse from turning into a meltdown. As we have seen in the chapter on the Great Depression, Friedman reckoned that the Fed actually caused the panic of 1929 by injecting too much credit into the economy and then subsequently taking it out too quickly. In 2002, Bernanke famously remarked that Friedman was right and he would not make that mistake with the Fed again.

Bernanke posed the problem for the strategists of capital at the conference: "Our continuing challenge is to make financial crises far less likely and, if they happen, far less costly. The task is complicated by the reality that every financial panic has its own unique features that depend on a particular historical context and the details of the institutional setting." What we need to do is to "strip away the idiosyncratic aspects of individual crises, and hope to reveal the common elements" of these "panics." Then we can "identify and isolate the common factors of crises, thereby allowing us to prevent crises when possible and to respond effectively."

The Mainstream View: The Cat's Stuck Up a Tree

The IMF called another conference in May 2013 to discuss the validity of modern economic theory after the Great Recession.[23] Some five years after the crisis broke, the world's leading macroeconomists gathered together to take first steps and draw early lessons from what happened and how to avoid another disaster in the future.

David Romer concluded that "financial shocks" are not rare but "frequent and hard to predict." Mainstream economics couches all its analysis of crises in terms of shocks to the system, implying that the capitalist process of accumulation and the play of markets is really a stable, steady equilibrium process, but is sometimes subject to shocks from outside (exogenous). This is what is unpredictable, like meteors from the sky (although astronomical theory can now make relatively good predictions on the likelihood of a meteor hitting the Earth).

What's the answer to these unpredictable but frequent shocks? Romer tells us that "the first approach is to reform the financial system so that the shocks that it sends to the real economy are much smaller. I do not know the answers to these questions, but it seems to me that they deserve serious analysis." He saw little progress in understanding crises under capitalism.[24]

Romer's jaundiced view was countered by other eminent economists at the IMF seminar. The then chief economist of the IMF, Olivier Blanchard, claimed that progress was being made: "Rethinking and reforms are both taking place. But we still do not know the final destination, be it for the redefinition of monetary policy, or the contours of financial regulation, or the role of macroprudential tools. We have a general sense of direction, but we are largely navigating by sight." But blindly, it seems, because Blanchard concluded: "There is no agreed vision of what the future financial architecture should look like, and by implication, no agreed vision of what the appropriate financial regulation should be."[25]

George Akerlof is a Nobel Prize winner and a professor at University of California, Berkeley.[26] He is married to Janet Yellen, the successor to Bernanke as the chair of the Federal Reserve. Akerlof is regarded highly as a "behavioral" economist, who with Robert Shiller wrote a book that argued that the crisis was the result of uncertainty among consumers and investors leading to unpredictable movements in "animal spirits."[27]

Akerlof reckoned that "my view is that it's as if a cat has climbed a huge tree. It's up there, and oh my God, we have this cat up there. The cat, of course, is this huge crisis. And everybody at the conference has been commenting about what we should do about this stupid cat and how do we get it down." He was really quite happy with the way things have gone since 2007. He figured that mainstream economics stood the test of the crisis by successfully advising politicians to bail out the banking system and thus avoid a great depression as in the 1930s. It was this policy of "a finger in the dyke" that avoided a tsunami. All the ensuing unemployment, the collapse in investment and GDP, and the sharp reduction in living standards should be balanced against this "success" of saving the banks from themselves.[28]

Akerlof's former joint Nobel Prize winner, Joseph Stiglitz, did not seem quite so sanguine.[29] Stiglitz made the important point that contrary to the economists mentioned above, the capitalist mode of production is not one of perfect stable growth occasionally hit by shocks.[30] He pointed out that after five years or more of crisis, slump, and weak recovery, the crisis was still not resolved.[31] Stiglitz's explanation of the crisis and the subsequent weak recovery was better, but still flawed.[32] The crisis was really due to the mature capitalist economies getting "too mature" or past their sell-by date. But Stiglitz did not see that this long-run "structural problem" had anything to do with a system of capitalist accumulation for a profit, but had more to do with the "switch from manufacturing to a service sector." As this switch has been going on for decades as far back as 1945, can this be the reason for the failure of mature capitalist economies in 2008?

From these comments, it's clear that mainstream economics did not predict the crisis (and even denied it could happen), could not explain how the cat got up the tree, and now has no clear answer about what to do about getting the cat down, short of saying that "it should never happen again."

So how do we get the cat out of the tree? Well, according to Stiglitz, mainstream economics has the tools to solve recurrent crises of capitalism and make the system work "once we revolutionize our flawed models." But it requires some form of government intervention that is more than just monetary policy by the Fed. Unfortunately, there is no sign that mainstream economic models are being revolutionized or that politicians want more government intervention instead of less.

Keynes: A Technical Malfunction

The other main wing of mainstream economics, the Keynesian, also did not predict the banking collapse and the Great Recession. Paul Krugman is the guru of modern Keynesianism and another Nobel Prize winner. He also runs a regular blog for the *New York Times* attacking the policies of austerity and the Republicans. But if you read his books on the crisis (*End the Depression Now!*, for example), you will find lots of ideas about what to do about getting out of the crisis, but very little about how capitalism got there in the first place. If you don't how you got somewhere, it can be difficult to find your way out.

The Keynesian explanation for the crisis is that there was a sudden lack of "effective demand." Households stopped buying so many goods and companies sharply cut back on investment. Suddenly everybody wanted to hold cash rather than buy goods. Even if interest rates for holding cash or borrowing to invest are reduced to zero, people may still hoard cash. There was a liquidity trap. There was a change of what Keynesians call animal spirits: uncertainty about the future suddenly sets in (there is a "lack of confidence," as we hear it put every day by business experts in the media).

It does not really matter why the lack of confidence sets in; the question is what we are going to do about it, says Krugman. He explains: "Keynesian economics rests fundamentally on the proposition that macroeconomics isn't a morality play—that depressions are essentially a technical malfunction."[33] The job of economists is thus simple: "figure out how to repair that technical problem."

For Krugman, capitalist crises can be corrected (if not avoided) if it were not for the pigheaded, ideological insanity on the part of the majority of economists and policy makers who want to see government spending cut, not increased. For him, the crisis is not caused by any fundamental flaw in the capitalist mode of production, but is, borrowing an image Keynes once used, like a magneto problem in a car: "The point is that the problem is not with the economic engine, which is as powerful as ever. Instead, we are talking about what is basically a technical problem, a problem of organization and coordination—a 'colossal muddle' as Keynes described it. Solve this technical problem and the economy will roar back into life." Krugman thinks the capitalist mode of production is fine: all it needs is a new electrical part, not a totally new engine. But the new part is not being supplied because of the colossal muddle on policy that economists and politicians have gotten themselves into.

The Great Recession was because "we are suffering from severe lack of overall demand." It's obvious—just create some more demand. According to Krugman, the lack of demand is due to the hoarding of money. He uses the example of a babysitting co-op. At a certain point, instead of people spending their coupons on babysitting services, they start to save them up, and fewer coupons were then available. Similarly, instead of businesses investing their money or households spending, they start saving (for some unknown subjective, irrational reason), and that creates the lack of demand. Krugman explains: "Collectively, world residents are trying to buy less stuff than they are capable of producing, to spend less than they earn. That's possible for an individual but not for the world around us. And the result is the devastation around us." We can get out of this mess by increasing the supply of money. To do that, governments and central banks must act to break the liquidity trap (money hoarding).[34]

Then it is apparently not as simple as Krugman first tells us. Although he says he wants to discuss what to do to get out of the depression, he cannot escape talking about how we got there in the first place. There is a problem with capitalism beyond simply a sudden lack of demand: the growth of excessive debt in the private sector of the economy "that is arguably at the root of our slump." So there is more to this than meets the magneto. Leaning on Minsky's ideas, Krugman brings in the problem of the financial sector: financial agents take more and more risk to make money, and they borrow more and more to do it. This is inherent in an unregulated financial sector, which becomes vulnerable if things go wrong. So the economy at some point can then have a "Minsky moment," when borrowers can't pay their bills and lenders stop lending. Krugman says that "anything can trigger this." Once the slump has begun and capitalists and households try to reduce their debts, or deleverage, they drive the economy further down by not spending (babysitting co-op again). The economy contracts faster than the debt can be reduced and we enter "debt deflation," as explained by 1930s economist Irving Fisher (see chapter 3 on the Great Depression). Then debtors can't spend and creditors won't lend.

So it was not quite as simple as we first were told. In fact, it is quite complicated. Krugman says there is a paradox (of debt) because although "the root of the crisis" was excessive debt, now we must borrow even more, not deleverage, otherwise we shall remain in a long depression as in the 1930s. His causal factors can be summed up: the deregulation of the US banking system under successive administrations, which led to excessive risk-taking, speculation, and a credit binge along with financial deregulation and instability that turned the "capital development of a country into a by-product of a casino" (to quote Keynes).

Beyond monetary injections, the answer to the current depression is more government spending. What turned things around in the Great Depression was a massive rise in government arms spending before the attacks on Pearl Harbor, according to Krugman.[35] In an appendix in his book, Krugman considers the evidence that government spending on armaments is the way out of depression. He notes that World War II military spending was actually "disappointing" in boosting growth because of "rationing and restrictions on private construction," and the Korean War was also less than effective because of "sharply raised taxes."

Are wars the only way to get big government spending implemented? According to Krugman, "the answer, unfortunately, is yes. Big spending programs rarely happen except in response to war or the threat thereof." It's war Keynesianism or nothing.

Too Much Credit: Minsky, Keen, and the Austrians

Minsky, who was largely ignored until the crisis (but is now fêted in left Keynesian circles), argued that that Keynes had shown capitalism to be inherently unstable and prone to collapse: "instability is an inherent and inescapable flaw of capitalism." This instability was to be found in the financial sector: "The flaw exists because the financial system necessary for capitalist vitality and vigour, which translates entrepreneurial animal spirits into effective demand investment, contains the potential for runaway expansion, powered by an investment boom."[36]

For Minsky, there is no flaw in the capitalist production process— the real economy—but only in the "veil of money" and financial intermediation between production and consumption. As debt accumulates, it brings uncertainty and instability into the process. There are three sorts of borrowers: hedge borrowers, speculative borrowers, and Ponzi borrowers. The first borrows and pays back the principal and interest; the second services the interest only and relies on asset prices to rise to pay the principal; the third group pays the interest only by borrowing more.

In a boom, the first group declines in proportion and the second and third rise as a share, opening up the risk of instability when the pyramid of debt starts to crumble. The actual trigger for this debt crisis could be in the property market as in 2007 or in equities as in 2000. The greater the reliance on leverage and debt to finance investment, the greater the likelihood of collapse. Once house prices stop rising enough to cover debt servicing, there can be a sudden aversion to risk and a desire to deleverage—this is what has now been described as a Minsky moment as in 2007.

Minsky supporters will accept that the Great Recession did not follow his depiction of a financial crisis but argue that his way of looking at an economy would best reveal the cause of the Great Recession, namely, a procyclical burst of credit in a financial sector–dominated economy. Systemic risk in the financial sector eventually collapses into debt deflation.

As Minsky put it: "There is no possibility that we can ever set this right once and for all. Instability, having tested one set of reforms, will after time, emerge in a new guise." So stability will not last forever and crises will always return.

Minsky's view has been extended by Australian economist Steve Keen, who won the Revere Award for Economics for being the first person to predict the credit crunch. His argument is that private credit builds up over and above the "natural" growth of the productive economy, and when it gets so out of line with real production and investment, it becomes a time bomb waiting to go off. For Keen, "capitalism is inherently flawed, being prone to booms, crises and depressions. This instability, in my view, is due to characteristics that the financial system must possess if it is to be consistent with full-blown capitalism."[37]

Keen argues that the key to crises under capitalism is excessive credit or private debt. The modern financial system is trying to expand credit to gain higher returns. This leads to a Minsky type of financial speculation.

Private credit rockets as banks speculate in ever riskier forms of assets (stocks, bonds, property). This creates extra demand in an economy that eventually cannot be satisfied. Increasingly, borrowing is raised just to cover previous borrowing in a Ponzi-like scheme. Eventually, the whole pack of cards collapses in and capitalism falls into a slump.

Keen says the best way to look at Keynesian-style "aggregate demand" in a modern capitalist economy is to add to national income the amount of private debt or borrowing. If you amend "demand" like this, you get a better indicator of when a crisis is coming. US private debt to GDP looks like a "hockey stick" (see Figure 5.3) shooting up from about 1982—a telltale sign of a crisis to come (similar to the graphic for used to warn of the risks of global warming in the climate change debate.

Figure 5.3

US Rpivate Sector Debt to GDP (%), 1952–2009

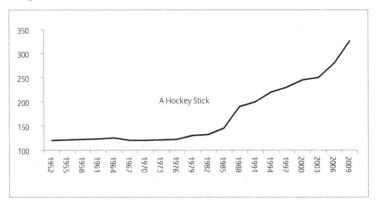

Source: US Federal Reserve

"For Marx, as with Fisher and Minsky before him, the essential element giving rise to Depression is the accumulation of private debt," says Keen. For him, Marx's distinctive contribution is that the cost of borrowing, the market rate of interest, will generally be governed "by the average expectations of the profit of the capitalist class." However, Keen denies any role for actual profitability as a cause of the current crisis. The crisis is the product of insufficient demand when capitalist *expectations* of realizing profits are not met.[38]

The Austrian school of economics is outside the mainstream. The Austrians start from micro-assumptions. This is not the neoclassical view of rational, fully informed human agents, maximizing their utility and profits. On the contrary, human actions are speculative and there is no guarantee of success in investment. According to Carl Menger, the founder of this school of thought, the further out the results of any investment are, the more difficult it is to be sure of success. Thus it is easier to estimate the returns on investment for goods that are for immediate consumption than for those needed for capital goods. Saving rather than consumption is a speculative decision to gain extra returns down the road.

Austrians reckon that the cost of this saving can be measured by the market interest rate, which prices the time involved in delivering future output from savings now. Economic crisis would not happen if it were not for interference in setting that market rate of interest by central banks and governments.

The boom phase in the business cycle takes place because the central bank supplies more money than the public wishes to hold at the current rate of interest, and thus the latter starts to fall. Loanable funds exceed demand and then start to be used in nonproductive areas, as in the case of the 2002–2007 boom in the housing market. These mistakes during the boom are only revealed by the market in the bust.[39]

From an Austrian perspective, the eventual collapse of the house of cards built on inflation (of credit) represents not a failure of capitalism but a largely predictable failure of central banking and other forms of government intervention. The Great Recession was a product of the excessive money creation and artificially low interest rates caused by central banks that on this occasion went into housing. The recession was necessary to correct the mistakes and malinvestment caused by interference with the market pricing of interest rates. The recession is the economy attempting to shed capital and labor from where it is no longer profitable. No amount of government spending and interference will avoid that correction.

Within the Austrian school, there is general agreement that business cycles are primarily caused by periodic credit expansion and contraction of central banks. Business cycles would not be a feature of a "truly free market" economy. As long as capitalists were free to make their own forecasts and investment allocations based on market prices, rather than by bureaucrats, there would be no business cycles. Cycles are due to the manipulation of credit by state institutions. This differs from the neoclassical/monetarist school, which sees recessions as minor interruptions from growth caused by imperfections in market information or markets—not busts caused by artificial credit booms.

As Krugman says about the Austrian school, they reckon that a recession is like a hangover after a heavy night of drinking. In the Austrian view, putting more credit into the economy to solve a recession is like giving more alcohol to a drunken person.

But if the market was left to set the interest rate and allow capitalists to make investment decisions unfettered or misguided by the state, would that end the cycle of boom and slump? The Austrians are perceptive in highlighting that a credit bubble can appear that artificially extends any boom beyond any growth based on real values. That credit boom can be created by government and central banks desperate to sustain growth when profits appear to be waning or consumption and investment weakening.

For the Austrians, the answer to boom and slump is to do away with central banks and state stimulus and let markets decide the rate of interest.[40] But is the rate of interest the driving force of capitalist investment and the price signal that capitalists look for to make investment decisions? As Marx explained, interest is just one part of surplus value, and the latter is key to investment. Value and surplus value are created in the production process, in particular in the exchange of money for labor and through the productivity of labor using capital goods.

Less known to the financial media, but perhaps more discerning in his analysis of crises, is William R. White, formerly at the Bank of International Settlements and now chair of the OECD's Economic Review Committee. For White, mainstream economists have missed the key ingredient that leads to systemic crisis: the build-up of debt. Drawing on the arguments of the Austrians and Minsky, he criticizes the traditional Keynesian view of the economy as a series of flows and wants economists to concentrate on the economic balance sheet and debt stocks in particular.

For White, the theory of rational expectations from the neoclassical school is shown to be flawed when asset prices can move far out of step with underlying values. If the market is so efficient, why is unemployment or the prices of many key commodities like energy unable to adjust? He is no more enamored with Keynesian thought—at least in its mainstream: "They have never been good at forecasting turning points in the business cycle."[41]

For White, the crisis is both financial and real: "The associated concern that weakness in the financial system could feed back into the real economy through tighter credit conditions also feeds the perception that it is only a financial crisis." For him, a credit crisis only becomes a crisis if it feeds back into the real economy—from the credit crunch to the Great Recession.[42] That is surely right: not all financial crises lead to economic contractions or slumps (but all slumps lead to financial crises). White offers no explanation of how this process from the financial to the real might work.

What White and the Austrian school do not explain is why "excess credit" eventually does not work. Apparently, there is a point when credit loses its traction on economic growth and asset prices and then, for no apparent cause, growth collapses. The Austrians ignore the fundamental flaw in the capitalist process identified by Marx in his law of profitability.

For the Austrians and the mainstream economic schools, there is no problem with capitalist production for profit—the problem lies in imperfect information and imperfect markets (neoclassical), the periodic lack of effective demand due to mercantilist hoarding and/or the volatility of animal spirits (Keynesianism), or excessive credit created by the state (Austrian). None of these schools of thought has anything to say about the flawed nature of the social organization of production.

Post-Keynesians: Too Much Inequality

Many leftist and some mainstream economists reckon that restricted incomes for the lower income groups caused the Great Recession because consumption and "effective demand" weakened and because households resorted to taking on more debt to compensate for the lack of growth in the incomes from work.[43]

This view is held by many post-Keynesian economists, as well as some Marxists and even mainstream economists like Stiglitz[44] or the current head of the Indian central bank, Raghuram Rajan.[45] There have been a host of popular books arguing that inequality is the cause of all our problems.[46]

Post-Keynesian economist James Galbraith,[47] son of the famous "New Deal" Keynesian economist J. K. Galbraith, argues that "As Wall

Street rose to dominate the U.S. economy, income and pay inequalities in America came to dance to the tune of the credit cycle." He contends that the rise of the finance sector was the driveshaft that linked inequality to economic instability.

Stiglitz takes the same position: "Growing inequality in most countries of the world has meant that money has gone from those who would spend it to those who are so well off that, try as they might, they can't spend it all." This flood of liquidity then "contributed to the reckless leverage and risk-taking that underlay this crisis."

This Stiglitz hypothesis has been promoted by Anthony Atkinson and Salvatore Morelli, who figure that "in the face of stagnating real incomes, households in the lower part of the distribution borrowed to maintain a rising standard of living," and "this borrowing later proved unsustainable, leading to default and pressure on over-extended financial institutions."[48] Roubini has also raised growing inequality as the key cause of capitalist crisis.[49]

Leftist Democrat Robert Reich also lays the blame for crises at the door of inequality:

> The rich do better with a smaller share of a rapidly-growing economy than they do with a large share of an economy that's barely growing at all. . . . Higher taxes on the wealthy to finance public investments improve future productivity. . . . All of us gain from these investments, including the wealthy. Broadly-shared prosperity isn't just compatible with a healthy economy that benefits everyone—it's essential to it. That isn't crazy left-wing talk. It's common sense. And it is shared by the great majority of people.[50]

Michael Dumhoff and Romain Ranciere from the IMF argue that "long periods of unequal incomes spur borrowing from the rich, increasing the risk of major economic crises."[51] According to these authors, something happens to lead to income stagnation for middle- and low-income workers, while high-income households acquire more capital assets. This increases the savings of wealthy households relative to lower-income households. To keep their living standards from declining, the middle class borrows more. Financial innovations, including new types of securitization, increase the liquidity and lower the cost of loanable funds available to the borrowers.[52]

The evidence for this thesis remains questionable. As Krugman says: "there's no reason to assume that extreme inequality would necessarily lead to economic disaster." Michael Bordo and Christopher Meissner from the Bank of International Settlements analyzed the data and concluded that inequality does not seem to be the reason for a crisis.[53] Credit booms mostly lead to financial crises, but inequality does not necessarily lead to credit booms.[54]

Edward Glaeser also points to research on the US economy that home prices in various parts of the nation did not always increase where there was the most income inequality.[55] That calls into question the claim that income inequality was inflating the housing bubble.[56] Moreover, inequality was higher in two of the six cases where a crisis is identified, which is exactly the same proportion as among the fifteen cases where no crisis is identified. The British think-tank Resolution Foundation published a study by Paolo Lucchino and Salvatore Morelli that looked at all the empirical evidence on this issue. They concluded that "efforts to validate empirically the posited relationship between inequality and crisis have so far been inconclusive."[57]

What has really excited the inequality proponents was a new paper by some IMF economists,[58] which found not only that inequality is bad for economic growth but that redistribution of wealth does little to harm it. Thus it refuted the trickle-down theory on growth and inequality propounded by neoclassical apologists for capitalism that a free market would speed up economic growth and thus everybody would gain. As the rich prospered, their gains would trickle down to the less rich through more jobs, more spending by the rich, and so on.[59] This is not a new conclusion because the two eminent economists on inequality in capitalist economies, Emmanuel Saez and Thomas Piketty, explained: "countries that [have] made large cuts in top tax rates, such as the United Kingdom or the United States, have not grown significantly faster than countries that did not, such as Germany or Denmark . . . we have seen decades of increasing income concentration that have brought about mediocre growth since the 1970s."[60]

It is one thing to recognize that inequality has increased in the past thirty years and could have damaged growth (or at least that reducing inequality won't). It is quite another to claim that this explains the credit crunch and the Great Recession. What is wrong theoretically with this argument is that it assumes, as the Keynesians do, that the fundamental weakness of capitalism lies on the demand side of the economy. Since many people had insufficient income to consume, they borrowed money to maintain their living standards. Radically different conclusions follow if the problem is located on the supply side. From this perspective, the widening of inequality is more a symptom than a cause of economic weakness. The rich became richer with the emergence of the asset bubble, but the underlying economy was far from healthy in the first place.

We did not hear that the slumps of the 1970s and 1980s were caused by rising inequality of income or wealth. Indeed, many mainstream and heterodox economists argued the opposite: that it was caused by wages rising to squeeze profits in overall national income.[61] So it seems that the underlying cause of capitalist crisis can vary. The trouble with this eclectic approach is that it becomes unclear what the cause of capitalist crises is—is it wages squeezing profits as in the 1970s, or is it low wages leading to excessive credit in the 2000s and then a collapse of demand in 2008?

The inequality argument is linked to the Minsky-Keen argument that the great financial crisis was caused by excessive debt, mostly in the private sector. As wages were held down in the United States, households were forced to borrow more to get mortgages or loans to buy cars and maintain their standard of living. They were encouraged to do so by reckless lending from banks even to subprime borrowers. As we know, eventually the sheer weight of this debt could not be supported by rising home prices or the chicken legs of average incomes, and the whole house of cards eventually came tumbling down.

Leading post-Keynesian economist Engelbert Stockhammer from Kingston University argues that the economic imbalances that caused the present crisis should be thought of as the outcome of the interaction of the effects of financial deregulation with the macroeconomic effects of rising inequality.[62] In this sense, rising inequality should be regarded as a root cause of the present crisis. Rising inequality creates a downward pressure on aggregate demand since poorer income groups have high marginal propensities to consume. Higher inequality has led to higher household debt as working-class families have tried to keep up with social consumption norms despite stagnating or falling real wages, while rising inequality has increased the propensity to speculate as richer households tend to hold riskier financial assets than other groups.

For Stockhammer, capitalist economies are either wage-led or profit-led. A wage-led demand regime is one where an increase in the wage share leads to higher aggregate demand, which will occur if the positive consumption effect is larger than the negative investment effect. A profit-led demand regime is one where an increase in the wage share has a negative effect on aggregate demand. The post-Keynesians figure that capitalist economies are wage-led. So when there is a decline in the wage share, as there has been since the 1980s, it reduces aggregate demand in a capitalist economy and thus eventually causes a slump. The banking sector increases the risk of this with its speculative activities.

Stockhammer would say that in the 1970s, capitalist economies were profit-led but now they are wage-led; so each crisis has a different cause.

How did a profit-led capitalist economy become a wage-led one? Perhaps rising inequality is the outcome of the crises of the 1970s and 1980s. It is really the product of the successful attempt to raise profitability during the 1980s and 1990s by raising the rate of surplus value through unemployment, demolishing labor rights, shackling the trade unions, privatizing state assets, freeing up product markets, deregulating industry, reducing corporate tax, and more—in other words, the neoliberal agenda.

French economist Thomas Piketty is one of the leading experts on the rise in inequality of income and wealth in the major economies. His magnum opus, *Capital in the 21st Century*, describes the huge rise in the share of income and wealth held by the top 1 percent. He reckons that the main reason for the huge increase in the incomes and wealth is not higher incomes from wages or work as such, but huge increases in capital income, namely, rising dividends from shares, capital gains from buying and selling shares, rents from property and capital gains from buying and selling property, and interest from loans and bond holdings, and so on. In other words, rising inequality is the result of rising exploitation of labor's creation of value that has been appropriated by the top bankers, corporate chief executives, and the shareholders of capital. This suggests that inequality is a result of an increased rate of surplus value and not the cause.[63] Rising inequality of wealth came about because the share of capital in national income rose, not vice versa.

The inequality theory of crises is not a coherent explanation. It appears to apply to only this current crisis and not previous ones. It appears to apply to just some capitalist economies, like the United States and the United Kingdom, and not to Europe or Japan, where inequality is lower but the crisis is worse.

What's Missing? Profit

What is missing from all these analyses of the causes of crises? It's a role for profit.[64] Modern Keynesian economists usually ignore Keynes's other hint at the cause of capitalist crisis, namely, a falling "marginal efficiency of capital," the closest Keynes comes in his neo-classical model of "diminishing returns" to Marx's analysis of declining profitability in the capital production process. Keynes wrote: "A more typical, and often the predominant, explanation of the crisis is, not primarily a rise in the rate of interest, but a sudden collapse in the marginal efficiency of capital."[65]

But for Keynes, what causes a crisis is when entrepreneurs are overly optimistic about potential profit relative to the going rate of interest. So the problem is not the rate of profit as such, but unpredictable expectation that it will be high enough to justify the going rate of interest. When it is not, then a crisis can ensue. The crisis is a product of wrong judgments, not based on the actual rate of profit relative to the needed reproduction of capital, as Marx would argue. The "marginal efficiency of capital" expresses the return on that factor of production as it tends to equilibrium. So there is nothing wrong with the production process under capitalism. The problem is in the financial sector, where the rate of interest is out of line with profitability.

In his works, Keynes drops this original analysis of profit and moves on to more short-term fluctuations in the financial sector in his analysis of crises. Here the subjective triumphs over the objective, and profits as an objective economic category soon disappears from view, so that modern followers of Keynes concentrate almost entirely on his macro identities for an explanation of the laws of motion of capitalism.

For orthodox Keynesians, a slump is due to the collapse in aggregate or effective demand in the economy (as expressed in a fall of investment and consumption). This fall in investment leads to a decrease in employment and thus to less income. Effective demand is the independent variable, and incomes and employment are the dependent variables. There is no mention of profit or profitability in this schema. Investment creates profits, not vice versa. This is the view of Keynes: "Nothing obviously, can restore employment which does not first restore business profits. Yet nothing, in my judgement, can restore business profits that does not first restore the volume of investment."[66]

But if investment is the independent variable, what causes a fall in investment? It is an ending of animal spirits among entrepreneurs or a lack of confidence. At least Minsky saw a role for profit:[67] "In spite of the greater complexity of financial relations, the key determinant of system behaviour remains the level of profits."[68] But, Minsky went on, investment is dependent on "the subjective nature of expectations about the future course of investment, as well as the subjective determination of bankers and their business clients of the appropriate liability structure for the financing of positions in different types of capital assets." So profits depend on expectations and crises are the result of changed expectations by financial speculators, not profitability of capital.

The Macro Identities: Investment and Profits

Keynes wanted to focus on the macro economy through his key national accounting identities. What are these? National income = National expenditure. National income can then be broken down to Profit + Wages; and then National expenditure can be broken down into Investment + Consumption. So Profit + Wages = Investment + Consumption. If we assume that wages are all spent on consumption and not saved, then Profits = Investment.

But here's the rub. This identity does not tell us the causal direction that can help us develop a theory.

As Krugman says, "accounting identities can only tell you so much. Anyone who claims that the identities tell you everything you know, without an actual model of how things work, is just doing bad economics."[69] In the causal direction of these accounting identities, Marx parts ways with Keynes. Before savings and before investment is the generation of profit (or surplus value) from the activity of labor in the production process. Marxist economics says that it is not the speculative irrationality of investors but the objective movement of profit that decides whether the owners of that profit will invest more or less.

James Montier explains the Keynes-Kalecki interpretation: "This is, of course, an identity—a truism by construction. However it can be interpreted with some causality imposed. After all, profits are a residual: they are a remainder after the factors of production have been paid."[70]

So for Keynes and Kalecki, the causal direction is simply that investment creates profit. But what causes investment? The subjective decisions of individual entrepreneurs. What influences their decisions? Animal spirits, or varying expectations of a return on investment, and so on. We head back to the subjective approach of the neoclassical school, where Keynes remains.

Montier goes on: "Investment drives profits because when a firm or a household decides to invest in some real asset they are effectively buying a good from another firm, creating profits for that entity."[71] So it seems that profits come from buying things (consumption) and not from surplus value created in the labor process, as Marx argued.

This argument is spelled out even more explicitly by the center of Minsky economics, the Jerome Levy Forecasting Center.[72] The authors of a paper state that the profits equation identifies the "sources of profits = investment, non-business saving (households), dividends and profit taxes." How taxes on profits can be a "source" of profit rather than a result is odd. How dividends can be a source of profit rather than a part of profit is also weird. Indeed, take these components out and assume workers don't save and we are back to the source of profit as investment.

The Keynes-Kalecki accounting identity was recently dug up again by another Keynesian, Cullen Roche.[73] According to him, profits depend on investment minus what households and government save. He admits that "it's strange to think of the government as a source of profits because some people don't generally like to think that the government is a large source of private sector profits.[74] "Some people" are right. Government is not the source of profits. Profit does not come from investment or government spending—that's nonsensical. Reality is the opposite. Profits come from the unpaid labor of workers and are distributed to shareholders, government, and foreigners, with what's left being reinvested. Dividends come from profits, not profits from dividends, as Roche wants us to think.

Under the Keynes-Kalecki equation, Profits = Investment − (Non-capitalist) Savings. Savings can be divided into three parts: savings by households, saving by governments, and foreign capitalist savings. If households save more (as they tend to do in a slump) and foreign savings rise (in other words, the national economy's deficit with the rest of the world rises), then investment will be lower and so will profits. However, there is a savior: government savings, or, to be more exact, government "dissaving." If government runs up a big budget deficit, in other words dissaves, it can boost investment and thus profits. Indeed, currently in the United States, using the Kalecki profits equation, it would appear that profits depend on government dissaving or net borrowing. Without it, profits would fall. So the last thing that capitalism should do is cut government spending.

What if we turn the causal direction the other way—the Marxist way? Now investment in an economy depends on profits. If profits are fixed in the equation and cannot be increased, then investment cannot be increased. So capitalist investment (i.e., investment for a profit) will depend on reducing the siphoning off of profits into capitalist consumption and/or on restricting noncapitalist investment, namely, government investment. So capitalism needs more government saving, not more dissaving. Indeed, it is the opposite of the Keynesian policy conclusion. Government borrowing will not boost profits but the opposite—and profits are what matters under capitalism.

So government spending becomes a negative for capitalist investment. Government spending will not boost the capitalist economy because it eats into profitability by depriving the capitalist sector of some of its potential profit. Even Kalecki sort of realized this.[75]

The key point for Marxists here is profit. The huge rise in private debt (measured against GDP) is clearly a very good indicator that a credit bubble is developing. But it alone is not good indicator of when it will burst. Some economists in the Austrian school have tried to gauge when the tipping point might be by measuring the divergence between the growth in credit and GDP growth.[76] But Marxist theory provides a much better guide: it is when the rate of profit starts to fall; then more immediately, when the mass of profits turns down. Then the huge expansion of credit designed to keep profitability up can no longer deliver.

For Keynes, Kalecki, and Krugman, profit and where it comes from is irrelevant to crises. Marx's value theory, based on profit as the unpaid labor of the working class, as Keynes put it (to his student Michael Straight): "was even lower than social credit as an economic concept. It was complicated hocus-pocus."[77] Keynes considered that Das Kapital was "an obsolete economic textbook which I know to be not only scientifically erroneous, but without interest or application to the modern world." Marx's ideas were "characterised . . . by mere logical fallacy" and was a "doctrine so illogical and dull."

Keynes did not need Marx's value theory and law of profitability to explain capitalist crises. They were "technical malfunctions" and were to be found in the financial sector of the economy, the "rentier" part, in the distribution of value or income in an economy and not in any way in the productive sectors of the economy. There was nothing wrong with the capitalist mode of production as such.

Keynes said the crisis comes about through a lack of "effective demand": an unaccountable fall in investment and consumption, causing profits and wages to fall. In contrast, Marx suggests starting with profits. If profits fall, then capitalists would stop investing and lay off workers, wages would drop, and consumption would fall. Then there would be a lack of effective demand, but this would not be due to a drop in animal spirits or a lack of confidence (we often hear that phrase from economists), or even too high interest rates, but because profits are down. The problem lies in the nature of capitalist production, not in the finance sector.

The post-slump austerity policies of most governments are not insane, as Keynesians think. These policies follow from the need to drive down costs, particularly wage costs, but also taxation and interest costs, and the need to weaken the labor movement so that profits can be raised. It is a perfectly rational policy from the point of view of capital, which is why Keynesian policies were never introduced to any degree in the 1930s. Capitalism came out of that Great Depression only when profitability rose and that was when the United States went into a war economy mode, controlling wages and spending and driving up profits for arms manufacturers and others in the war effort. Capitalism needed war, not Keynesian policies.

The Great Recession was just the start of what has turned into a Long Depression, the third that capitalism has experienced in 135 years. You can see where this chapter and the previous ones have taken us. The long depression of 1873–97, the Great Depression of 1929–41, and the Great Recession of 2008–9 have suggested a common reason for these depressions—falling profitability. That is not to deny the important role of credit/debt in the all these crises and depressions. In the next chapter, there is a fuller discussion of the role of debt in the Great Recession and the current Long Depression.

Chapter 6
Debt Matters

Since one unit's liability is another unit's asset, changes in leverage rep-resent no more than a redistribution for one group (debtors) to another (creditors) . . . and should have no significant macroeconomic effects.

—Ben Bernanke[1]

Credit can and will get out of line with capitalist production.[2] Credit is the foundation of fictitious capital, that is, money capital advanced for the titles of ownership of productive and unproductive capital—shares, bonds, derivatives, and so on. The prices of such assets anticipate fu-ture returns on investment in real and financial assets. But the realiza-tion of these returns ultimately depends on the creation of new value and surplus value in the productive capitalist sector. So much of this money capital can easily turn out to be fictitious.

For Marx, the capitalist economy is a monetary economy; it is an economy with credit as a key constituent. Capital exists either in liquid form (i.e., as money) or in fixed form as means and materials of produc-tion. Credit in all its forms increasingly substitutes for money in the general circulation of capital and commodities. This fictitious capital is "a kind of imaginary wealth which is not only an important part of the fortune of individuals and a substantial proportion of bankers."[3] For Marx, financial instruments, both credit and equity, are entitlements to present or future value: "We have previously seen in what manner the credit system creates associated capital. The paper serves as title of ownership, which represents the capital. The stocks of railways, mines, navigation companies, and the like, represent actual capital."[4]

The existence of this fictitious capital imparts flexibility to the economy, but over time it becomes an impediment to the health of the economy.[5] The more fictitious capital distorts the price signals, the more information about the economy disappears. Decisions about production become increasingly unrelated to the underlying economic structure. Pressures build up in the economy, but they are not visible to those who make decisions about production. Fictitious capital retains values that would evaporate if participants in the market were fully aware of the future. They also serve as collateral for a growing network of debt. In effect, the financial system becomes increasingly fragile.

The drive for profit in the capitalist sector is behind the inexorable expansion of credit. A fall in the rate of profit promotes speculation. If the capitalists cannot make enough profit producing commodities, they will try making money betting on the stock exchange or buying various other financial instruments. The capitalists experience the falling rate of profit almost simultaneously, so they start to buy these stocks and assets at the same time, driving prices up. But when stocks and assets prices are rising, everybody wants to buy them—this is the beginning of the bubble on exactly the lines we have seen again and again since the Tulip Crisis of 1637.[6]

This is recognized by even some mainstream economists. As Irving Fisher put it: "Overindebtedness must have had its starters. It may be started by many causes, of which the most common appears to be new opportunities to invest at a big prospective profit, as compared with ordinary profits and interest." But prospective profit eventually gives way to "an expansion of 'the speculative element' and enterprises keep up an appearance of prosperity by accumulating debts, increasing from day to day their capital account."[7]

Fictitious values accumulate during extended boom periods and are subsequently shed in the course of the bust. This shakeout "unsettle[s] all existing relations." As Paul Mattick put it, "speculation may enhance crisis situations by permitting the fictitious overvaluation of capital," which cannot satisfy the profit claims bound up with it.[8] So a debt or credit crisis is really a product of a failure of the capitalist mode of production as a monetary economy.[9]

In the course of a crisis, the elimination of fictitious values serves to increase the rate of profit, at least to the extent that fictitious values and the burden they place on firms are eliminated at a rate that exceeds the fall of prices of tangible assets. The clearing away of these fictitious values removes an important barrier to investment. Consequently, with their elimination, the economy strengthens and the cycle of accumulating capital can begin again. The destruction of fictitious capital is thus closely bound up with the devaluation of tangible capital. And the problem of recovery under the capitalist mode of production is thus intensified when fictitious capital reaches such an unprecedented size that it takes a very long time to eliminate it.

It's Private Sector Debt

The expansion of global liquidity in all its forms (bank loans, securitized debt, and derivatives) has been unprecedented in the past thirty years. The Marxist view is that credit (debt) can help capitalist production take advantage of prospective profit opportunities, but eventually speculation takes over and financial capital becomes fictitious. It becomes fictitious because its price loses connection with value and profitability in capitalist production. This eventually leads to a bursting of the credit bubble, intensifying any economic slump.

Global liquidity expanded at an unprecedented rate from the early 1990s. Liquidity here is defined as bank loans, securitized debt (both public and private), and derivatives. Derivatives are made up of interest-rate hedges, commodities, equities, and foreign exchange (FX). Interest-rate derivatives constitute the bulk, that is, hedging the cost of borrowing. The notional value of derivatives rocketed from the early 1990 to reach over $600 trillion, or ten times global GDP by 2007.

In effect, global liquidity is a measure of what Marx called fictitious capital.[10] On this definition, global liquidity rose from 150 percent of world GDP in 1990 to 350 percent in 2011. The pace of growth accelerated in the late 1990s, and after a pause in the mild recession of 2001, liquidity took off again up to the point of the start of the global credit crunch in mid-2007.

If we exclude derivatives and look at just global credit (bank loans and debt), we can identify four credit bubbles and crunches from the early 1990s (see Figure 6.1). First, there was the credit bubble of late 1980s and early 1990s, mainly visible in Japan, ending in the Japanese banking crisis. The second bubble was the high-tech, dot-com bubble of the late 1990s that ended in the equity crash of 2000 and the recession of 2001. Then there was a very fast credit bubble based on new forms of money (shadow banking and derivatives in the mid-2000s), culminating in the credit crunch of 2007 and subsequent Great Recession of 2008–9.

Before the Great Recession, the rise in credit or debt took place in the private sector, not the public sector. US nonfinancial business and household debt rose to postwar record levels.

Before the crash of 2008, there had been a massive build-up of private sector credit in the United States, reaching over 300 percent of GDP if you include financial sector debt.

Figure 6.1

Change in Global Credit to GDP (%), in Various Periods from 1989 onwards

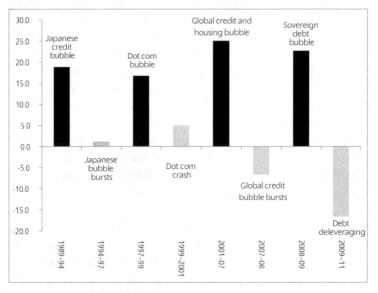

Source: BIS, Author's Calculations

The experience of the United States was repeated more or less in all the major advanced economies. In the United States between 1950 and 1980, the ratio of nonfinancial debt (household, corporate and government) was quite stable at 130 percent of GDP. After 1980, it nearly doubled to more than 250 percent; for advanced economies, the average weighted mean ratio has risen 80 percent. Only about a third of the increase in overall debt has been due to government borrowing. Business and household debt has been consistently higher than government debt. Indeed, in the United States, gross public sector debt now stands at $14.11 trillion but nonfinancial business and household debt stands at just under $25 trillion.

US nonfinancial business debt is higher than it has ever been since World War II and well above its level in 1929 (90 percent of GDP in 2014 compared with 56 percent in 1929). It is only below the 1933 peak because GDP fell 43 percent from 1929, which was a lot faster than the speed at which companies could reduce their 1929 debt. The Great Recession is marked by the sheer size of this debt accrued by companies before the crash. Nonfinancial corporate debt remains the largest component of overall debt in the advanced capitalist economies at 113 percent of GDP compared to 104 percent for government debt and 90 percent for household debt.

The boom in credit went into residential property in the United States and other economies. By mid-2006, the residential property boom in the United States had reached mega proportions. Household debt expanded rapidly during the so-called neoliberal era as a result of falling interest rates that reduced the cost of borrowing and created the ensuing property boom in many advanced capitalist economies in the past fifteen years. The creditors were the banks and other money lenders. The assets (home values) eventually collapsed, placing a severe burden of deleveraging on the financial sector.

The underlying position was worse than the debt figures show because companies shifted much of their debt off the balance sheet. Shadow banking (or nonbank credit institutions) covers money mutual funds, investment funds other than mutual funds, structured financial vehicles, and hedge funds. According to the Basel III Bank of International Settlements (BIS)-IMF Financial Stability Task Force, shadow banking grew rapidly from $27 trillion in 2002 to $60 trillion in 2007 and then declined to $56 trillion in 2008 before recovering to $60 trillion again in 2010. Shadow banking now covers 25–30 percent of the total financial system, or half the size of traditional banking assets globally. The United States has the largest shadow banking sector, with assets of $25 trillion in 2007 ($24 trillion in 2010).[11]

Can we show the relationship between debt and the profitability of capital more directly? One way of showing how the fall in the rate of profit combined with excessive debt to bring US capitalism down is to measure the rate of profit not just conventionally, against tangible corporate assets, but also against fictitious capital.

Marx recognized that fictitious capital will enter into the calculation of profitability for capitalist production. Businesses attempt to follow price setting practices that allow for the recapture of past investments and to repay debt obligations. If they cannot, they face bankruptcy. In that regard, the value of this capital "will continue to be estimated in terms of the former measure of value, which has now become antiquated and illusory."[12]

Throughout the neoliberal period, debt rose, and not just mortgage debt but corporate debt (see Figure 6.2).

We can measure the impact of fictitious capital on profitability if we measure profit against the net worth of companies, and not just their tangible assets. This incorporates financial liabilities (loans from banks, bonds and shares issued). Such a measure for US companies shows that from 1966 to 1982, profitability against net worth falls at a slower pace than profitability measured conventionally against tangible fixed assets. It recovered more quickly in the neoliberal era (1982–97), so profitability against net worth was higher than conventional profitability. In the latest period, 1997–2011, conventional profitability has been broadly flat, but against net worth, profitability has dropped significantly.

Figure 6.2
US Non-Financial Corporate Debt to GDP (%), 1951–2014

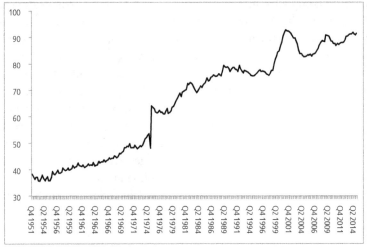

Source: US Federal Reserve

Against net worth, US corporate profitability was nearly cut in half between 1997 and 2000. After 2000, the rate of profit based on net worth remained under the rate against tangible assets for the first time on record, suggesting that the "financial" part of the assets of the capitalist sector became a significant obstacle to the recovery in capital accumulation.

If we decompose the components of US corporate net worth, we find that capitalists increased their borrowing to buy back their shares, and this was exponential after the early 1990s. Companies used the extra debt to buy back their own company shares to boost the share price. UK companies bought back equity at an annual rate of 3 percent of GDP and in the US at 2.3 percent. Up to 1985, US companies issued shares (i.e., they were sellers). Since then they have become by far the most important buyer.

In effect, while corporate profitability relative to net worth has been falling, share prices have been boosted by company share buybacks. Debt is rising to raise stock market prices well out of line with earnings.

Awash with Cash

We now have an apparent conundrum of rising/record profits in the United States and some other major economies, with corporations apparently "awash with cash," but still not investing enough in the "real economy" to achieve a sustained recovery.

Consider the United States. Cash reserves in US companies have reached record levels—just under $2 trillion. The level of corporate fixed investment as a share of corporate cash flow is near to twenty-five-year lows (see Figure 6.3).

Comparing US corporate fixed capital formation to corporate operating surplus, Michael Burke found that

> the increase in profits has not been matched by an increase in nominal investment. In 1971 the investment ratio (GFCF/GoS) was 62 percent. It peaked in 1979 at 69 percent but even by 2000 it was still over 61 percent. It declined steadily to 56 percent in 2008. But in 2012 it had declined to just 46 percent. If US firms' investment ratio were simply to return to its level of 1979 the nominal increase in investment compared to 2012 levels would be over US$1.5 trillion, approaching 10 percent of GDP. This would be enough to resolve the current crisis.[13]

Burke reckons that US companies have used their rising profits to either increase dividends to shareholders or purchase financial assets (stocks): "one estimate of the former shows the dividend payout to shareholders doubling in the 8 years to 2012, an increase of US$320bn per annum." Burke goes onto to point out that cash hoarding is happening in other economies, too.[14] In Canada, both Michal Rozworski[15] and Jim Stanford[16] have noted the same phenomenon.

Figure 6.3
US Fixed Investment as Share of Internal Cash Flow (%), 1991–2013

Source: US Federal Reserve

Burke noted that this hoarding began well before the Great Recession, and this is significant.[17] In the past twenty-five years, firms have been increasingly unwilling to make productive investments, preferring to hold financial assets like bonds, stock, and even cash, which has limited returns in interest. Why is this? Well, it seems that companies have become convinced that the returns on productive investment are too low relative to the risk of making a loss. This is particularly the case for investment in new technology or research and development, which requires considerable upfront funding with no certainty of eventual success.

There was a dramatic increase from 1980 through 2006 in the average cash ratio for US firms. Interestingly, cash hoarding was not taking place among firms that instead paid high dividends to their shareholders. On the contrary,[18] some scholars argue that the "main reasons for the increase in the cash ratio are that inventories have fallen, cash flow risk for firms has increased, capital expenditures have fallen, and R&D expenditures have increased." To compete, companies increasingly must invest in new and untried technology rather than just increase investment in existing equipment. That's riskier.[19] So companies have to build up cash reserves as a fund to cover likely losses on research and development.

In the 1980s, average capital expenditures as a percentage of assets were more than double average R&D expenditures as a percentage of assets (8.9 percent versus 3.2 percent). In contrast, in the 2000s, R&D exceeds capital expenditures (6.7 percent versus 5.4 percent).[20] Rising cash is more a sign of perceived riskier investment than a sign of corporate health.

This story for the United States is also repeated for the UK (see Figure 6.4). Ben Broadbent from the Bank of England noted that UK companies were now setting very high hurdles for profitability before they would invest as they perceived that new investment was too risky.[21] The current net rate of return on UK capital is well below that figure.

Figure 6.4
UK Manufacturing Net Return on Capital (%), 1997–2014

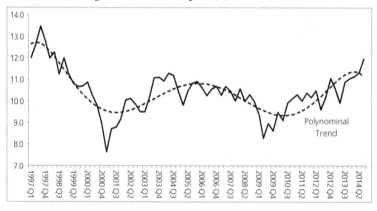

Source: UK Office for National Statistics

But Only by Increasing Debt

Liquid assets (cash and those assets that can be quickly converted into cash) may have risen in total. But US companies were expanding *all* their financial assets (stocks, bonds, insurance, etc.). When we compare the ratio of liquid assets to total financial assets (see Figure 6.5), we see a different story.

US companies reduced their liquidity ratios in the golden age of the 1950s and 1960 to invest more. That stopped in the neoliberal period, but there was still no big rise in cash reserves compared with other financial holdings. The ratio of liquid assets to total financial assets is about the same as it was in the early 1980s. That tells us that corporate profits may have been diverted from real investment into financial assets, but not particularly into cash. Those cash reserves are very concentrated in a few companies and banks. The notion of US corporations being awash with cash does not hold up to scrutiny as a general market characteristic.[22] There has been a rise in the ratio of cash to investment. But that ratio is still below where it was at the beginning of the 1950s (see Figure 6.6).

Figure 6.5
US Corporations Liquid Assets to Total Financial Assets (%), 2951–2014

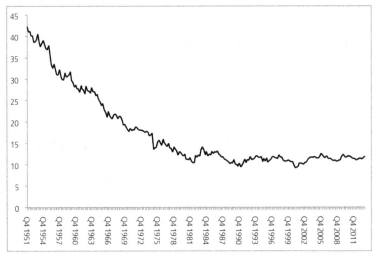

Source: US Federal Reserve

Why does the cash to investment ratio rise after the 1980s? Well, it is not because of a fast rise in cash holdings but because the growth of investment in the real economy slowed in the neoliberal period. The average growth in cash reserves from the 1980s to now has been 7.8 percent a year, which is actually slower than the growth rate of *all* financial assets at 8.6 percent a year. But business investment has increased at only 5.3 percent a year, so the ratio of cash to investment has risen.

If we compare the growth rates of cash reserves and total financial assets since the start of the Great Recession in 2008, we find that corporate cash has risen at a much slower pace at 3.9 percent year-on-year.

That's slightly faster than the rise in total financial assets at 3.3 percent year-on-year. But investment has risen at just 1.5 percent a year. Consequently, the ratio of investment to cash has slumped from an average of two-thirds since the 1980s to just 40 percent in 2014.

So companies are not really awash with cash any more than they were thirty years ago. What has happened is that US corporations have used more and more of their profits to invest in financial assets rather than in productive investment.

Figure 6.6
US Corporations Ratio of Cash Holdings to Investment, 1951–2013

Source: US Federal Reserve

The Specter of Corporate Debt

Corporate debt remains the issue. Sure, interest rates on debt have fallen sharply over the past twenty-five years, so debt servicing costs are down. But corporate debt levels have also risen in the same period, increasing the burden of risk on companies if there is any sign of a downturn in profitability.

Corporate sector debt in the United States has expanded at a rapid pace, with gross issuance reaching a record in 2013. Whereas net debt to assets rose from around 16 percent in 2007 to 22 percent at the depth of the financial crisis, it only fell back to 20 percent by 2011 and was back above 21 percent in 2014. The US corporate sector is much more highly indebted than it has been at this point in previous business cycles. Corporate debt in all the major economies remains high.[23] This increase in debt means that companies must raise profitability or be forced to reduce investment in productive capacity to service rising debt.

The Leap in Sovereign Debt

The global financial crash forced governments to bail out their banking systems, which they did with increased borrowing. In effect, the losses and bankruptcies that threatened the banks were avoided by a sharp rise in public sector debt, which took the losses onto the governments' books.

Although public debt ratios had climbed from the late 1970s until the mid-1990s, they had declined toward their historical peacetime average prior to the global financial crisis of 2008. Private credit maintained a fairly stable relationship with GDP until the 1970s and then surged to unprecedented levels in the decades that followed, right up to the outbreak of the crisis. By the 1970s, private sector debt in the advanced capitalist economies was larger than sovereign debt for the first time since the early 1900s (see Figure 6.7).[24]

In the United States, after the credit binge of 2002–7, private sector debt (households, businesses, and banks) had reached $40.8 trillion in 2008. These sectors have now deleveraged to $38.6 trillion, or down 8 percent, mainly because banks have shrunk and households have defaulted on their mortgages. But this private sector deleveraging has been countered by a huge rise in public sector debt, up over 70 percent from around $8 trillion in 2007 to $13.7 trillion and still rising, if more slowly.

The public sector debt has risen to finance the bailout of the banking system as well as fund widening budget deficits as tax revenues collapsed and unemployment and other benefit payouts rocketed. As a result, the overall debt burden (public and private) in the United States is still rising at a rate that matches nominal GDP growth. So the overall debt to GDP ratio is still not falling.

Indeed, according to a report on global debt by McKinsey, the ratio of debt to GDP has increased in all advanced economies since 2007, mainly in the public sector but also in corporate debt.[25]

In fact, rather than reducing indebtedness, or deleveraging, all major economies today have higher levels of borrowing relative to GDP than they did in 2007. Global debt in these years has grown by $57 trillion, raising the ratio of debt to GDP by 17 percentage points.[26]

Figure 6.7
OECD Private Sector Credit and Public Sector Debt to GDP (%), 1870–
2010

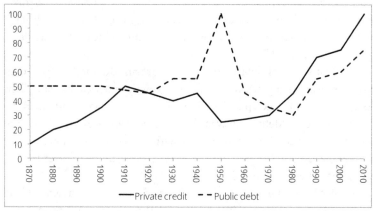

Source: OECD

The Great Recession was triggered by a massive expansion in debt used by households to buy homes in the United States and by companies to support share prices. Wage growth was restricted, and profitability had been falling since the late 1990s. Extra credit was needed to sustain investment in unproductive sectors like property and financial speculation. Eventually, that credit toppled over. But since 2008, total national debt (financial, household, nonfinancial, and government) relative to GDP has not fallen in the major advanced economies.

Debt Matters

The apologists for capitalism want to reduce the public sector debt or at least shift the burden of financing it onto labor and away from capital. Tax struggles are class struggles in disguise. In this sense, the rise in public sector debt becomes part of the overall crisis induced by falling profitability and excessive private sector debt.

Keynesians sometimes argue that debt does not matter and more borrowing is not a problem, at least not for now. Krugman has denied the role of debt in crises because it does not matter in a "closed economy," that is, one where one man's debt is another's asset.[27] It's only a problem if you owe it to foreigners.

The IMF disagrees: "recessions preceded by economy-wide credit booms tend to be deeper and more protracted than other recessions" and "housing busts preceded by larger run-ups in gross household debt are associated with deeper slumps, weaker recoveries and more pronounced household deleveraging."[28] Krugman seems to recognize that there could be "debt-driven slumps," arguing that an "overhang of debt on the part of some agents who are forced into deleveraging is depressing demand."[29]

The historians of debt Carmen Reinhart and Kenneth Rogoff confirm the relationship between debt and growth under capitalism. They looked at twenty-six episodes of public debt overhangs (defined as where the public debt ratio was above 90 percent) and found that on twenty-three occasions, real GDP growth is lowered by an average of 1.2 percentage points a year, and GDP is about 25 percent lower than it would have been at the end of the period of overhang.[30]

Studies by McKinsey and the IMF also found that on average GDP declines by 1.3 percent points for two to three years after a financial crash, and debt to GDP must fall by up to 25 percent to complete deleveraging.[31] There are a host of other studies that reveal pretty much the same thing. The IMF found that when public sector debt levels are above 100 percent of GDP, economies typically experience lower GDP growth than the advanced country average. The IMF also found that where debt levels were between 90 and 100 percent and were decreasing over the fifteen years following the peak, economic growth is faster than for countries even below the 100 percent threshold. So deleveraging is crucial to recovery whatever the level of debt reached.[32]

The correlation between high debt and low growth seems strong, but the causation is not clear. Does a recession cause high debt, and the only way to get debt down is to boost growth (Keynesian)? Or does high debt cause recessions, so the only way to restore growth is to cut debt (Austrian)? The Marxist alternative is that a contraction of profitability leads to a collapse in investment and the economy, which then drives up private debt. If the state has to bail out the capitalist sector (finance), then public debt explodes.[33]

Deleveraging and Depression

What is important is that if the capitalist sector is burdened with heavy debt, it will make it more difficult to launch an economic recovery.[34] The financial sector has deleveraged the most—not surprisingly, as this sector suffered a meltdown in 2008. However, even in this sector, only the United Kingdom and the United States have managed a significant cleansing of debt liabilities relative to GDP. Eurozone banks have taken on more debt since 2008. Japanese financials also took on more debt, at home and abroad, and remain the most leveraged in developed markets.

Households in the countries where the property bust was greatest have deleveraged, mainly through mortgage defaults, downsizing, and refinancing. But households in the Eurozone as a whole have not done so at all, except a small decline since a peak in 2010.

The nonfinancial corporate sector has deleveraged even less than households. Instead, companies have taken advantage of low interest rates and plentiful liquidity to take on more debt to buy back equity to support share prices, pay larger dividends, and hoard cash. In the United States, corporations have expanded their debt relative to GDP by 14 percent. Elsewhere, corporate debt to GDP levels are much the same as they were in 2008, or some 15–20 percent higher than they were at the start of the credit boom in 2003.

The BIS found that of thirty-three advanced and emerging economies, twenty-seven have nonfinancial debt-to-GDP levels above 130 percent. Two of those have ratios above 400 percent, four between 300 and 400 percent. Only six have ratios below 130 percent, and only three are below 100 percent of GDP—Turkey, Mexico, and Indonesia. Of the thirty-three economies, eighteen have rising debt ratios, eleven are flat, and only four have falling debt ratios. Of those four, three are in IMF or Troika bailout programs (Greece, Ireland, and Hungary). Only Norway has reduced its overall nonfinancial debt ratio voluntarily. Only Mexico and Thailand have reduced their overall debt levels in the past fifteen years. Household debt ratios have fallen in some developed markets, including the United Kingdom and the United States, as well as some peripheral European Monetary Union countries. But twenty-seven economies have experienced a rise in private debt-to-GDP ratios since the global financial crisis.

Deleveraging has gone further in the United States.[35] The UK private sector has not been so successful at reducing its debt burden. Strip out the government sector and the United Kingdom has the highest private sector debt ratio (this does not include the banks), although that is mainly due to its very high household debt ratio. Small companies have neither cash reserves nor banks willing to lend to them at sustainable rates. So they are not investing in new equipment at all. There are thousands of heavily indebted small companies that are barely keeping their heads above water despite low interest rates.[36] According to research by the "free market" Adam Smith Institute, 108,000 so-called zombie businesses in the United Kingdom are only able to service the interest on their debt, preventing them from restructuring. In a way, this is holding back a recovery in overall profitability and new investment.[37] In other words, they slow "creative destruction" of capital through the liquidation of the weak for the strong.

As a result, the capitalist sector is not investing in sufficient new productive capacity to engender much higher employment and pre-crisis trend growth. The alternative of public investment is shunned. Public investment in the United States is at its lowest level since 1945. Gross capital investment by the public sector has dropped to just 3.6 percent of US output compared with a postwar average of 5 percent.

Deleveraging excessive debt is part of the task of the current depression. Restoring profitability so that companies will start a period of sustained investment in employment, technology, and plant also depends on reducing the debt burden built up in the period before the crash of 2008. This adds to the duration of the depression.

Some capitalist economies have made more progress in this than others. But there has been no fall in corporate debt in the United States, where many corporations continue to raise cheap debt to support their share prices through buybacks (see Figure 6.8). As a result, corporate leverage (the ratio of net debt to GDP) is higher than at this point of business cycle than in recoveries from previous recessions. That does not bode well for a quick escape from the depression if interest rates on debt start to rise.

As the IMF summed it up: "Increased borrowing has not yet translated into higher investment by nonfinancial corporations whose depressed capital expenditures are taking up a smaller share of internal cash flows than in previous cycles. . . . Firms are more vulnerable to downside risk to growth than in a normal credit cycle."[38] Debt matters, and there is still a way to go in getting it manageable.

Figure 6.8

US Non-Financial Corporations: Net Debt to Assets (%), 2001–2013

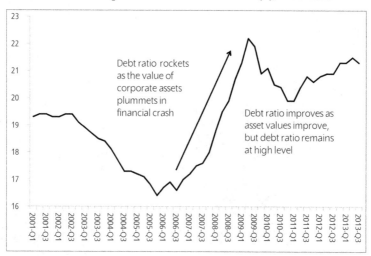

Source: US Federal Reserve

Chapter 7

From Slump to Depression

If in the past, it was depression itself that by cheapening the cost of capital investment made possible a revival in profit rates and renewed prosperity, it is not surprising the debt-fuelled postponement of depression should lead to stagnation.

—Paul Mattick Jr.[1]

The global economy has not yet returned to normal after the end of the Great Recession in mid-2009. Since then, global economic growth, investment, and employment have been below par. The previous chapters on the Great Recession and the role of debt show that there are two main reasons for this.

First, profitability in the major economies is still below the peak reached in 2007 and below the end of the neoliberal recovery peak in 1997. This deters companies from stepping up investment to match previous rates.

Second, the special characteristic of the lead-up to the Great Recession was the unprecedented expansion of global liquidity in all its forms (debt, loans, and derivatives) and, in particular, the rise in private sector debt (household, bank, and nonfinancial corporate debt). When the housing bubble burst in the United States, the size and extent of this debt led to the global financial crash. This exposed the low profitability of capitalist production in the productive sectors as financial profits turned into outright losses. Losses in the private sector were compensated for by increased borrowing in the public sector. But the overhang of debt remains in the corporate sector particularly. Again this deters a pick-up in investment globally.

Global capitalist production and investment will not recover until profitability returns to previous levels and debt is reduced sufficiently to allow new borrowing for investment. It was shown in chapter 1 that profitability stays below previous peaks because the organic composition of capital is so high that even an increased rate of surplus value (through

113

unemployment and wage constraints) is not enough to raise it sufficiently.

Capitalist recessions eventually reduce the costs of production and devalue capital sufficiently to drive up profitability for those enterprises still standing. Unemployment drives down labor costs and bankruptcies, and takeovers reduce capital costs. Businesses gradually start to increase production again, and eventually begin to invest in new capital and rehire those in the reserve army of labor without a job. This boosts demand for investment goods and eventually workers start buying more consumer goods and recovery gets under way.

But this time is different. Such is the overhang of spare capacity in industry and construction and such is the level of debt still owed by businesses, government, and households alike that this recovery is stunted. Every major capitalist economy now finds that it has over 30 percent more capacity than it needs to meet demand. That is a record high. That suggests another slump may be necessary to cleanse the system of zombie companies, unused means of production, and unproductive workers, as well as a write-off of more debt.

The Weak Recovery

The recovery in the global capitalist economy since the trough of the Great Recession in mid-2009 is more like a long depression similar to 1873–97 or 1929–42. In a long depression, as explained earlier, economies grow consistently at well below their previous trend rates, with unemployment stuck at levels well above previous norms, and disinflation (slowing inflation) turning into deflation (falling prices). Above all, it is an economic environment where investment in productive capital is way below previous average levels, with little sign of pick-up.

Historically, excluding the years of the world wars, only 20 percent of all recessions led to output still being lower than before the recession after two years. Just 13 percent persist for more than three years, and only 6 percent for more than five. This time, the United States, Germany, and Canada regained the previous peak level of GDP after some three years.

Since the trough of 2009 in the Great Recession, the major capitalist economies have experienced the weakest recovery of all compared with previous ones from other slumps. Even in the United States, the recovery since mid-2009 has been the weakest following all postwar slumps (see Figure 7.1). Some economies have still not returned to the real output levels achieved before the crisis.

Figure 7.1

Average US Real GDP Growth in Six Years after Trough of Recession (%)

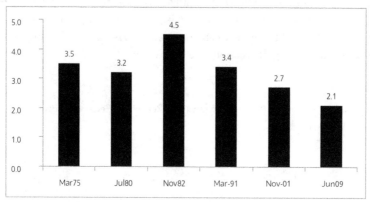

Source: Author's Calculations

There is an even more startling fact: if you measure the loss of real output since 2008 relative to where it should have reached in 2013 if there had been no recession, then Greece and Ireland have lost nearly 40 percent of the potential rise in real output from 2008 to 2013 they should have had. The United Kingdom has lost nearly 20 percent, the United States 12 percent, and even Germany has lost a potential 5 percent (see Figure 7.2).

Figure 7.2

The Loss of National Output Relative to Previous Trend Average Growth (%), 2008–13

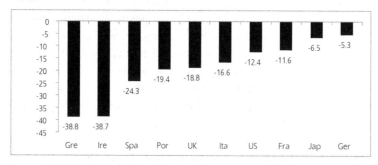

Source: AMECO, Author's Calculations

The Great Recession has led to an overall permanent loss of GDP of about 22 percent from where it would have been if growth had continued on trend—most of that relative loss has been in the slow "recovery" period since 2009. This loss is 50 percent larger than that of the 1980–82 double-dip recession (and it's still rising), confirming that this is really a long depression (see Figure 7.3).

Figure 7.3
Accumulated Loss in Real GDP from Each Recession Relative to Previous Trend Growth (%), 1948–2007

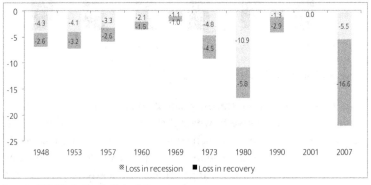

Source: OECD, Author's Calculations

A recent study found that in five previous recessions following major financial collapses, it took about nine years for an economy to return to its growth path. Now the US Congressional Budget Office (CBO) reckons that US real GDP growth will never return to its pre–Great Recession growth path:[2] "The projected decrease in potential GDP is unprecedented, as almost all post-war U.S. recessions, post-war European recessions, slumps associated with European financial crises, and even the Great Depression of the 1930s, were characterized by an eventual return to potential GDP." US real GDP will be permanently 7.2 percent below the prerecession growth path! Such is the waste of jobs, incomes, services, and resources that the Great Recession and recurring capitalist slumps deliver. The CBO calls this a "purely permanent recession." The CBO figures that the US trend growth rate will slow to just 1.7 percent and will not be above 2 percent a year for the foreseeable future.

The International Monetary Fund (IMF) believes that global capitalism will remain in a depression. The IMF says that "a large share of the output loss since the crisis can now be seen as permanent and policies are thus unlikely to return investment fully to its pre-crisis trend."[3] Although potential growth in advanced economies will pick up in the next five years, it will remain well below levels it reached before the financial crisis. Emerging economies will see their potential growth decline over the same period.

In advanced economies, real GDP growth that maximizes potential capacity will "accelerate" to an average of just 1.6 percent over the next five years, compared with 1.3 percent from 2008 to 2014. This growth is weaker than the 2.3 percent pace from 2001 to 2007 and about half the postwar twentieth-century average.

The Global Crawl

This time the recovery is not V-shaped or even L-shaped (as in Japan in the 1990s) but more like a square root sign. Instead of 3–4 percent a year, output in the major economies has been closer to 1–2 percent a year. The slowdown has spread to the so-called emerging economies, too; growth is now closer to 4 percent a year than the previous 7–8 percent.

In its 2015 report, the IMF noted that the global economy continues to crawl along at well below the postwar average trend growth rate, with little sign of improvement. The group argues that the "potential output" of the world economy is growing more slowly than before. In the advanced countries, the decline began in the early 2000s; in emerging economies, after 2009. The concern is that the world economy is now characterized by chronic weak investment, low real and nominal interest rates, credit bubbles, and unmanageable debt. Christine Lagarde, head of the IMF, described the world's current economic performance as "just not good enough."

According to the IMF, although global unemployment is finally back to levels seen before the crisis, employment is growing at just 1.5 percent a year, far slower than the 2.0–2.5 percent growth rate seen before the crisis.[4] Unemployment in advanced economies stood at 7.4 percent in 2014, much higher than the 5.7 percent seen in 2007.

Each year since 2008, the IMF has had to change its forecasts for global real GDP growth. The IMF now expects real GDP growth in the advanced capitalist economies to pick up from 1.8 percent in 2014 to 2.4 percent in 2015. It needs to see that acceleration to achieve its forecast of world growth at 3.5 percent because growth in emerging markets, particularly China and Russia, is slowing or even falling, so growth there will be only 4.3 percent in 2015, down from 5 percent in 2013.

The Organization for Economic Co-operation and Development (OECD) has also reduced its forecast for global economic growth. It warned that weak investment and disappointing productivity growth risk keeping the world economy stuck in a "low-level" equilibrium.[5] The OECD expects the global economy to expand in 2015 by 3.1 percent, a sharp downgrade from its November 2014 forecast of 3.7 percent. "The world economy is muddling through with a B-minus average, but if homework is not done . . . a failing grade is all too possible," said Catherine Mann, chief economist.[6]

The World Bank has also reduced its forecast for global real GDP growth.[7] The bank forecast the world economy will grow 3.0 percent in 2015 and 3.3 percent in 2016, down from its earlier predictions of 3.4 percent and 3.5 percent, respectively. This lower forecast relies on the United States growing faster than the 2.5 percent rate in 2014, or 3.2 percent in 2015. The supposedly stronger US economic growth in 2015 would be unable to compensate for slowing growth and deflation elsewhere—in the Eurozone, Japan, and the major emerging economies of Russia, Brazil, China, South Africa, and Turkey (only India might grow faster this year). The emerging economies cannot help because their economies are running well below their full potential, according to the World Bank.

Also telling is the annual report of the World Trade Organization (WTO).[8] Global trade is poised for at least two more years of disappointing growth, according to the WTO, which believes world trade will grow just 3.3 percent in 2015, below the rate of GDP growth expected by the IMF.

For at least three decades before the 2008 financial crisis, in the era of "globalization," world trade regularly grew at twice the rate of the world GDP. With 2014's growth of 2.8 percent, global trade has now expanded at or below the rate of the broader global economy for three consecutive years. World trade growth continues to fall well behind the trend before the Great Recession (see Figure 7.4).

Roberto Azevêdo, WTO director-general, blamed disappointing trade growth in recent years on the sluggish recovery from the financial crisis. He also warned that economic growth around the world remained "fragile" and vulnerable to geopolitical tensions.[9]

A leading Keynesian, Brad DeLong, has now noticed that the United States "did not experience a rapid V-shaped recovery carrying it back to the previous growth trend of potential output."[10] The trough in the Great Recession of 2008–9 saw the US real GDP level 11 percent lower than the 2005–7 trend. Today, the trend stands 16 percent below that level. Cumulative output losses relative to the 1995–2007 trends now stand at 78 percent of a year's GDP for the United States and 60 percent of a year's GDP for the Eurozone. DeLong goes on:

> A year and a half ago, when some of us were expecting a return to whatever the path of potential output was by 2017, our guess was that the Great Recession would wind up costing the North Atlantic in lost production about 80 percent of one year's output—call it $13 trillion. Today a five-year return to whatever the new normal might be looks optimistic—and even that scenario carries us to $20 trillion. And a pessimistic scenario of five years that have been like 2012-2014 plus then five years of recovery would get us to a total lost-wealth cost of $35 trillion.

DeLong concludes that "at some point we will have to stop calling this thing 'The Great Recession' and start calling it 'The Greater Depression.'"

Figure 7.4

Average Annual Growth in Global Real GDP and World Trade (%), 1992–2013

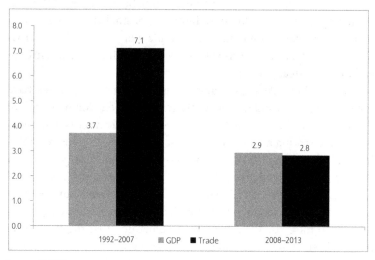

Source: WTO

Why No Recovery?

Ben Bernanke finished his term as chairman of the Federal Reserve in January 2014. He signed off with a speech at the annual meeting of the American Economics Association (AEA).[11] The AEA represents the mainstream economists of North America. Speaking to his colleagues, Bernanke took the opportunity to pronounce the success of his policies in avoiding a financial meltdown when the global crisis erupted in 2008. He emphasized how the Fed had reacted successfully to turn things round.

In this crisis, as he says, he applied monetary policies to avoid certain mistakes. The Fed cut its lending rate to near zero, extended huge financial assistance to the banking system, in particular, the largest investment banks that were "too big to fail," and then applied "unconventional" monetary policies, namely, expanding the quantity of money (quantitative easing) by buying up government, corporate, and mortgage bonds from the banks to stimulate the economy. The Fed's balance sheet has ballooned through these purchases to near $4 trillion, or 25 percent of US GDP.

Bernanke was convinced that this policy was a success in saving the capitalist economy. But was it? First, it did not really avoid a financial meltdown. Sure, the likes of Goldman Sachs, Morgan Stanley, and JP Morgan did not go bust. But Bear Stearns, AIG, and Lehman Brothers did (and Merrill Lynch nearly did). So did many of the leading mortgage lenders. Moreover, hundreds of smaller banks and lenders across the nation went bust. There was a financial meltdown across the world that cost taxpayers something like $3 trillion at least, in cash and loans, to steady the ship.

Second, Bernanke's great antidepression monetary policies have not restored world and US economic growth and employment back to precrisis levels.[12] He claimed that an economic recovery is under way based on restoring a boom in the stock market, keeping interest rates low, and subsidizing the banks. Somehow this financial largesse would stimulate the real and productive parts of the US economy. But has it?

During the crisis, one Keynesian economist, Roger Farmer, reckoned that the Fed should take dramatic action and start buying stocks directly to raise stock market prices (something that the Bank of Japan has been doing in a limited way).[13] Farmer believed that these purchases (by printing money) would boost the stock market and thus restore the wealth of investors, enabling them to start buying more consumer goods and invest and thus raise "effective demand" (to use the Keynesian term). Bernanke did not do that, but the Fed did the next best thing. It injected so much cash into the financial system that it led to massive rise in the stock market. Based on the real (inflation-adjusted) S&P Composite monthly averages of daily closes, the US stock market has more than doubled in real terms since its 2009 low.

This has not led to a restoration of economic growth, employment, and average income, as Farmer claimed and Bernanke hoped. US economic growth remains well below trend; unemployment, especially long-term unemployment, remains well above average; and average household income in real terms is far below precrisis levels (see Figure 7.5).[14]

Figure 7.5

US Real Median Annual Household Income (US Dollars)

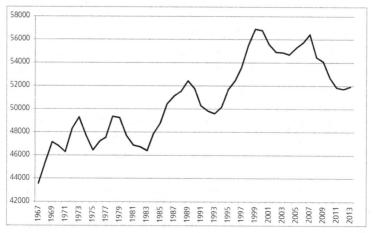

Source: US Federal Reserve

Bernanke's policies may have worked for the big investment banks and stock market and property investors, but it has not worked for Main Street or for the bulk of working people and the unemployed. Main Street corporate America does not appear sufficiently encouraged to start using the huge cash balances they have built up from increased profits engendered by cutting staff and keeping wage increases to the minimum. Profit margins for the large companies are near all-time highs and cash reserves have accumulated, but there is little corresponding investment in the real economy; instead, it is in dividends, stock buybacks, and speculation in financial assets—and, of course, a revival of the property markets. US home prices have shot up from deep lows, to rise at over 13 percent a year (there is a similar phenomenon in the United Kingdom).

Banks: Business as Usual

The global banking sector remains deep in the sludge of scandal, corruption, and mismanagement, with a new revelation nearly every week. It continues to fail in its supposed purpose—to provide liquidity and credit to households and businesses to enable them to pay for working capital and investment to grow.

Take the UK banks: Barclays has been fined $450 million for its part in the so-called Libor scandal, where traders colluded to fix the interest rate for inter-bank lending, which sets the floor for most loan costs across the world. That rigging meant that local authorities, charities, and businesses ended up paying more than they should for loans. HSBC was indicted by the US Congress for laundering Mexican drug gang money and breaches of sanctions on Iran (as was Standard Chartered). Lloyds Bank, along with others, has had to compensate customers for mis-selling them personal injury insurance to the tune of £5.3 billion—money that could have been better used to fund industry and keep loan terms down. In another scandal, HSBC's private banking division, based in Switzerland, has been to found to have engaged in hiding the ill-gotten gains of thousands of rich people in many countries who did not want to pay income tax. HSBC actively arranged ways and tricks to enable these rich people to recycle their cash back to their home countries without tax penalties.

Then there is RBS, a British bank brought to its knees in the financial collapse by a management led by Fred Goodwin, knighted for his services to the banking industry. Goodwin was noted for his bullying of staff and penchant for risk and huge bonuses. He left RBS, but not without taking a fat pension and handshakes from the board, as have all the senior executives of the banks when they have been asked to step down following a scandal. And in May 2015, major banks in the US and the UK were fined $6 billion for rigging foreign exchange markets. No one in these global banks has been charged or convicted in a criminal court for any actions since the scandals and illegal activities were revealed.[15]

On the contrary, the banks have shrugged off all these scandals. JP Morgan continued to run a risky trading outfit engaged in outsized trades in derivatives, the very "financial weapons of mass destruction" (to use the world's greatest investor, Warren Buffett's phrase) that triggered the 2008 crisis. The "London whale," as JP Morgan's derivatives division was called, eventually lost the bank $6 billion! The main trader, Bruno Iksil, told his senior executives that he was worried about the "scary" size of the trades he was involved in. But they ignored him. The US supervisors of JP Morgan, the Office of Comptroller of the Currency, supposedly closely monitoring the banks at that time, also did nothing.

Bob Diamond, the former head of Barclays, eventually sacked over the Libor scandal (but only because the Bank of England governor insisted), made the statement that "for me, the evidence of culture is how people behave when no one is looking."[16] It is clear that the banking culture uses a customers' money, taxpayers' cash and guarantees, and shareholders' investments to make huge profits through risky assets and then pay themselves grotesque bonuses.[17]

Nothing has really changed since these scandals came to light. A secret report recently found that Barclays bank was still engaged in getting "revenue at all costs" and employed "fear and intimidation" on staff to do so. Yet the banks want to continue just as before.[18] It has now been revealed that during the financial collapse when Barclays was threatened with partial nationalization, their board loaned money to investors in Qatar, who then invested in the stock of the bank to the tune £12 billion. In this way, the bank avoided state control by issuing more loans! It is still not clear what commissions were paid to Qatari investors.

Dexia, a Belgian bank eventually forced into nationalization, tried this same trick in 2008, and so did the Iceland bank Kaupthing, which "loaned" money to a Qatari royal, who invested it back into the bank. The Qataris took commissions, and if the shares were worthless, it made no difference to them. It just added to the losses of the bank and to the cost to the taxpayer in any bailout.

Then there is Monte dei Paschi di Siena. This venerable old bank from the heart of Italy was found to be using two sets of accounts to hide the fact that its uncontrolled derivatives division had lost over €700 million in trades. The regulators, this time the Bank of Italy, claim they knew nothing about it until the bank pleaded for money from the taxpayer to save it from bankruptcy. The current head of the European

Central Bank, Mario Draghi, was head of the Bank of Italy at the time.

At the same time, Dutch bank Rabobank has agreed to pay a $1 billion settlement over its role in the Libor rigging. It had rigged Libor and other important benchmark rates for six years. As many as thirty employees of Rabobank, including seven managers, from New York to Utrecht and Tokyo, made more than 500 improperly documented requests to change Libor and Euribor. The bank's chief executive was forced to resign, and he said he did not know what was going on but it was his responsibility.

Similarly, Swiss global bank UBS said it had begun an internal investigation of its foreign exchange business and had "taken and will take appropriate action with respect to certain personnel." It has been forced by the Swiss regulator to increase by half the amount of capital it holds against the risk of litigation. Deutsche Bank said that it had set aside €1.2 billion to deal with litigation. In the United Kingdom, partially publicly owned Lloyds Bank revealed that it had "provisioned" another £750 million for compensation payments for mis-sold payment protection insurance in the third quarter. Its total misconduct bill has now exceeded £8 billion, in effect at the expense of the taxpayer.

What can we say about the UK's Cooperative Bank, supposedly part of the long-standing cooperative movement? In this depression, it was turned into an aggressive speculative financial institution by reckless executives, including a chairman who was a crystal meth user, hired male prostitutes in his spare time, and knew little about banking, let alone the ethical objectives of the co-op movement. The bank has been brought to its knees with debts of $3 billion and still the co-op members are being advised to let bankers run it as a profit-making limited company divorced from its cooperative past.

Nobody has been charged for these immoral and probably illegal activities.[19] Instead, what has happened is that rank-and-file bank workers, most of whom have not been involved these scandals and risk-taking ventures but just do work in back offices or at counters, have been sacked by the thousands to reduce costs. More jobs are going each month.

The number of banking jobs in the United Kingdom peaked at 354,134 in 2007; they are down to under 240,000, according to the Centre for Economics and Business Research. One out of three positions will have been axed since the height of the bubble.[20]

The extent and nature of these continuing banking scandals have forced even supporters of free markets and the City of London, like former Finance minister under Thatcher, Nigel Lawson, to call for the full nationalization of RBS. The bank is already 82 percent owned by taxpayers, but that means nothing because taxpayers have no say in how the bank is run, what bonuses are paid, and what the bank does with deposits, loans, and investments. Lawson now says that far from privatizing it, the bank should be fully nationalized and the government should intervene to "turn it into a vehicle for increasing lending to business." Instead, the British Conservative government has decided to accelerate its sell-off at a loss to taxpayers.

Getting Better?

We are being told by former Fed chief Ben Bernanke and the mainstream economists that things are looking better.[21] But capital accumulation remains at a pretty low ebb, insufficient to restore economic growth and employment back to precrisis levels, let alone that of the 1960s.

This is the main reason for the global crawl: the collapse in the housing bubble in many advanced economies, which was one reason for the drop in private sector investment. But the collapse in business investment was much greater and long lasting.

The IMF found that business investment in the advanced economies was 13 percent lower from 2008 to 2014 than it expected back in spring 2007 before the Great Recession (see Figure 7.6). For the United States, the gap was even bigger at 16 percent—and 18 percent for Japan.

Figure 7.6

Level of Business and Housing Investment Relative in 2014 Compared to 2008 (% Difference)

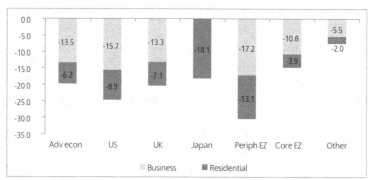

Source: OECD, Author's Calculations

Recently, the Bank for International Settlements (BIS) latched onto the same point—that the Great Recession and the subsequent weak and slow recovery in the major economies was a product of the collapse in business investment, that is, the fault of capitalism.[22] As the BIS put it:

> Business investment is not just a key determinant of long-term growth, but also a highly cyclical component of aggregate demand. It is therefore a major contributor to business cycle fluctuations. This has been in evidence over the past decade. The collapse in investment in 2008 accounted for a large part of the contraction in aggregate demand that led many advanced economies to experience their worst recession in decades. Across advanced economies, private non-residential investment fell by 10-25 percent.

Investment and Profitability

Why is investment lagging? Paul Krugman suggests that investment is lagging because of a general increase in monopoly power: "The most significant answer, I'd suggest, is the growing importance of monopoly rents: profits that don't represent returns on investment but instead reflect the value of market dominance."[23] Although more monopolies might explain higher profits with less investment, there is little evidence that monopoly power has risen in the past few years. After all, capital expenditures are low in competitive industries as well.

Another explanation is a post-Keynesian one: high profits are mirrored in reverse by a fall in real incomes and in labor's share of total national income. Stewart Lansley argues that the sustained squeeze on wages in recent years "sucked out demand," encouraged debt-fueled consumption, and raised economic risk.[24]

On the other hand, Austrian school economist Benjamin Higgins reckons that businesses won't invest because they may be more or less "uncertain about the regime," by which he means they are worried that investors' private property rights in their capital and the income it yields will be attenuated further by government action: regulation, taxation, and other controls.

The IMF believes it is lack of demand. Capitalist companies are not investing enough because there is a lack of demand for their products. This answer prompts the question: why is there a lack of demand? It also fails to recognize that the biggest component in the fluctuation in aggregate demand since 2007 has been investment. After all, investment is part of aggregate demand, as the BIS points out.

There is no need to turn to monopoly power, a squeeze on wages, or the "fear of government" argument for an explanation of the continued depression in business investment. There is the objective reality of low profitability. Cash flow and profits may be up for larger companies, but the rate of profit has not recovered in many capitalist economies, like the United Kingdom and Europe.

Economists at JP Morgan made a study of global corporate profitability. They show a fall from near 9 percent before the Great Recession to under 4 percent in the trough of 2009 before recovering to 8 percent in 2011. But in 2012, it declined again to 7 percent, 13 percent below its peak in February 2008 when the Great Recession began. This decline in global profitability is driven by Europe and a fall in emerging economies.

A UN report also reckoned that the problem was due to a failure in the recovery of returns on corporate investment globally.[25] Profitability on investment in productive sectors of the world in 2011 was some 20 percent below where it was before the global financial crash and the Great Recession for the advanced capitalist economies, and 15 percent down for the world as a whole.

The EU Commission has also commented on corporate profitability and investment in Europe.[26] It noted that nonresidential investment (which excludes households buying houses) as a share of GDP "stands at its lowest level since the mid-1990s." The main reason: "a reduced level of profitability." The report makes the key point that "measures of corporate profits tend to be closely correlated with investment growth" and only companies that don't need to borrow and are cash-rich can invest—and even they are reluctant. The commission found that Europe's profitability "has stayed below pre-crisis levels."

The BIS believes that "the uncertainty about the economic outlook and expected profits play a key role in driving investment, while the effect of financing conditions is apparently small." The bank dismisses the consensus idea that the cause of low growth and poor investment is the lack of cheap financing from banks or the lack of central bank injections of credit.

Instead, the BIS looks for what it calls a "seemingly more plausible explanation for slow growth in capital formation," namely, "a lack of profitable investment opportunities." According to them, companies are finding that the returns from expanding their capital stock "won't exceed the risk-adjusted cost of capital or the returns they may get from more liquid financial assets." So they won't commit the bulk of their profits into tangible productive investment. "Even if they are relatively confident about future demand conditions, firms may be reluctant to invest if they believe that the returns on additional capital will be low."[27]

The profitability of capital has to be high enough to justify riskier high-tech investment and cover a much higher debt burden (even if current servicing costs are low).

If it is the case that the reason for the continuing Long Depression in the major economies (defined as below-trend growth and below-trend investment) is low profitability and excessive debt, then the situation does not look set to improve.

According to JP Morgan, usually an optimist about capitalist economic recovery, US corporate profit margins (i.e. the share going to profit for each unit of production) have been at record highs but now are beginning to fall. "The share of business net value added going to capital, or net operating surplus, has edged down modestly since peaking in 2012. However, the share going to profits, which is essentially net operating surplus less interest payments, has been about unchanged since 2012. Adjusted corporate profits declined at a 5.5 percent annual rate in 4Q14, the latest available data point. However . . . we believe the natural progression of the business cycle will begin gradually squeezing business (and profit) margins."[28]

Sure, in the United States, the total *level* of profits has surpassed the previous precrisis peak, but not the *rate* of profit. In many other advanced capitalist economies, even the mass of profit has not reached the previous peak. We don't have to look for uncertain and unexpected negative shocks or government interference in the market's pricing of labor and capital to explain the stagnation. There just isn't enough profit to get capitalists to invest at previous levels.

The EU Commission believes that Eurozone corporations must deleverage further by an amount equivalent to 12 percent of GDP and that such an adjustment spread over five years would reduce corporate investment by a cumulative 1.6 percent of GDP. Given that nonresidential investment to GDP is at a low of 12 percent at the time of this writing, that's a sizable hit to investment growth.[29]

The Ogre of Deflation

The US Conference Board, which follows productivity growth closely, found that global labor productivity growth, measured as the average change in output (GDP) per person employed, remained stuck at 2.1 percent in 2014, while showing no sign of strengthening to its precrisis average of 2.6 percent (1999–2006).

The Conference Board reckons that the lack of improvement in global productivity growth in 2014 was due to several factors, including a dramatic weakening of productivity growth in the United States and Japan, a longer-term productivity slowdown in China, and an almost total collapse in productivity in Latin America and substantial weakening in Russia.

Labor productivity in the mature capitalist economies grew by only 0.6 percent in 2014, slightly down from 2013, when it was 0.8 percent. Productivity growth in the United States declined from 1.2 percent in 2013 to 0.7 percent in 2014, whereas Japan's fell even more from a feeble 1 percent to negative territory at -0.6 percent. The euro area saw a very small improvement in productivity—from 0.2 percent in 2013 to 0.3 percent in 2014.

For 2015, a further weakening in global productivity growth is projected, down to 2 percent, continuing a longer-term downward trend that started around 2005. Despite a small improvement in the productivity growth performance in mature economies (up to 0.8 percent in 2015 from 0.6 percent in 2014), emerging and developing economies are expected to see a fairly large slowdown in growth from 3.4 percent in 2014 to 2.9 percent in 2015.

Worse, as productivity growth slows, it seems that global inflation is also slowing, with several key economies heading into a deflation of prices—another classic indicator of depression. This is worrying the IMF and its chief Christine Lagarde appealed to central banks to act against this "ogre of deflation."

At the end of 2014, the Eurozone fell into deflation for the first time in more than five years. Japan is nearly back there, and US and UK annual inflation rates are well under central bank targets of 2 percent a year.

We ordinary mortals may think that static or falling prices is good news for our costs of daily living, but for the strategists of capital it means tighter profit margins, weaker investment growth, and an end to "recovery." If people expect prices to fall, they hold back on spending until prices do fall. If there is no inflation, then those corporations with large debts will find no relief from any fall in the real value of debt. They must find more profits to repay debt.

As we have seen in chapter 6, the recovery after the great slump has been hampered and curbed by the deadweight of excessive debt built up in the so-called neoliberal period after the early 1980s and particularly during the credit and property bubble from 2002 on. The level of debt in the world economy has not fallen despite the Great Recession, the banking crash, and bailouts. Deleveraging is not really happening, at least not to any great extent.[30]

The current low-growth world is a reflection of the burden of still-high debt levels on the cost of borrowing relative to potential return on capital and thus on growth. The job of a slump (to devalue assets, both tangible and fictitious) has not yet been achieved. If interest rates should start to rise, that could easily trigger a new slump as the cost of servicing corporate and government debt would rise to unsustainable levels.

A slump will follow to "cleanse" the remaining "excesses" of capital that still hold back a significant rise in profitability. In the meantime, economic growth in the major economies remains well below precrisis trend rates and along with it the underlying ability of capitalist economies to deliver higher productivity. The Long Depression continues.

Chapter 8
America Crawls

*I think it's going to be a while, quite a while before we have another fi-
nancial crisis that will fit the pattern of the 2008 crisis, and others such
as Japan in the late 1980s or the Great Depression. I think those type of
crises are a long time off.*

—*Lawrence Summers*[1]

Among the top capitalist countries, the US economy has made the
best recovery from the Great Recession, but that is hardly anything to
write home about. Growth has not returned to precrisis rates, business
investment levels are similar, and unemployment, although down, is
still worse than it was before the financial crash. Most important, the
profitability of US capital, although recovering from its nadir in 2009,
is still below the level of 2006 and even further below the level of 1997.

The global crisis started in the United States with the collapse
of the housing bubble and the ensuing credit crunch, which spread
across the Atlantic Ocean to Europe. The United States was first into
the slump and first out. Of the major capitalist economies, the United
States was the first to revive to the point of surpassing its previous
level of output.

However, investment remains below peak levels, and the rate of
real GDP growth is still below the trend growth rate of the past thirty
years (see Figure 8.1). US annual real GDP growth in 2014 ended up
about 2.4 percent—pretty much where US economic growth has been
since the end of the Great Recession.

During the Great Recession from the beginning of 2008 to the middle of 2009, the US economy contracted at a 2.9 percent annual rate with
a cumulative decrease of 4.3 percent. During the "recovery" from mid-
2009 to the end of 2014, the US economy grew at only 2.2 percent a year.

The US economic recovery has been weaker than any others in the
postwar period. Moreover, the US real GDP growth rate has been

slowing secularly, with the ten-year average now down to 1.7 percent a year. "The latest [2014] data point (1.43 percent year-on-year) is lower than the onset of all recessions except the one triggered by the Oil Embargo in 1973, with which, at two decimal places, it's tied."[2]

Indeed, this Long Depression has been permanently wasteful of the potential exertion of human ingenuity. Output growth in this recovery has been slower than in either of the past two recoveries, despite the much larger decline in output during the recession. There is no sign of any reduction in the enormous gap that has opened up between actual output and trend. The cumulative loss of output relative to potential approached $6 trillion in 2014, or almost $20,000 for every person in the United States.

Figure 8.1
US Annual Real GDP Growth (%), 1998–2014

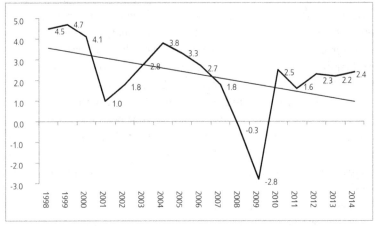

Source: BEA

US average annual real GDP growth (including during the Great Recession) has been just 0.9 percent compared to 2.4 percent in the years before 2007 and way below the average real growth of the 1980s and 1990s (see Figure 8.2).

Even though each year of recovery since 2009 has disappointed the expectations and forecasts of mainstream economics, optimism still reigns among economic forecasters.

For example, according to Deutsche Bank, 2014 would have been the year that US growth tops 3 percent, with 3.8 percent in 2015. The great "vampire squid," Goldman Sachs,[3] reckoned that "the US economy (will) accelerate to an above-trend growth pace in 2014" and its economists outlined the reasons: "The acceleration is likely to be led by faster growth in personal consumption and business capital spending, with continued support from housing."[4] Their hopes were dashed, as US real GDP growth in 2014 came in at just 2.4 percent.

Figure 8.2

US Average Annual Real GDP Growth Over Various Periods (%), 1983–2014

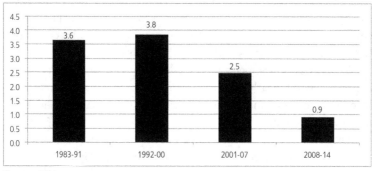

Source: BEA

Much of the increase in real GDP has come from businesses increasing their inventories—meaning they have bought products from suppliers for which there may or may not be demand in the marketplace. Consumer spending growth has averaged less than 2 percent year-on-year since the Great Recession ended, while business spending on equipment and software continues to slow to around a 3 percent rate, hardly enough to replace depreciating and obsolete old equipment.

With 2.2 percent average real GDP growth for the United States in the recovery,[5] the output increase totals an accumulated 10 percent since the summer of 2009. Consumer spending accounted for 65 percent of that growth, a little less than its actual share of GDP at 68 percent. Government spending fell. Residential construction (home building) accounted for 9 percent of the gain in the economy. Net trade deducted from real GDP growth by 0.4 percent. Most significant, inventory-building accounted for a substantial 19 percent of the rise in real GDP. Although it's true that business investment contributed 25 percent of the 10 percent rise in real GDP, that was not enough to get the economy going stronger. This figure includes the dubious new addition by the official statisticians of "intellectual property products" or software.

A Failure to Invest

The failure to invest in new productive capital rather than in financial assets and property is the reason the US economy is experiencing the weakest recovery after a recession since 1947. Overall business investment is still below its 2007 peak, and the rate of growth has been slowing, not accelerating. It fell 16 percent in the 2009 recession, rose 2.5 percent in 2010, accelerated to 7.6 percent in 2011, then slowed a little to 7.3 percent in 2012. But in 2013, it slowed significantly to just 2.7 percent. The level of investment by the top 500 US companies compared to sales or assets remains well below the levels of the 1990s.

Net business investment—after deducting the depreciation of existing stock—is still nearly one-third below the precrisis peak. Net investment in structures is more than half below the previous peak, and down nearly 20 percent in equipment. Even net software investment is still 12 percent down. Net business investment has peaked lower (as a share of GDP) in each successive recovery since the 1980s (see Figure 8.3).

US corporations' capital equipment is getting old, and the average age of structures is the highest it has been since 1964, equipment since 1995, and intellectual property products, like software, since 1983. What is clear is that the US economy will be stuck in its current low-growth trajectory (at best) unless businesses start to invest in new equipment, plant, and technology.

Weak Recovery in Employment

The recovery in US employment has been the weakest ever compared with previous slumps. The number of long-term unemployed workers unable to get back to work has never been higher.

The US unemployment rate has been falling because there are fewer and fewer workers in the labor force. Labor force dropouts are boosting the employed share percentage of a smaller labor force. The stats work like this: if 1,000 people are in the labor force with 70 counted as unemployed and 300 having given up looking for work, the unemployment rate is 7 percent. If the labor force stays at 1,000, but 60 are now counted as unemployed because the number that has given up looking for work has risen to 310, the unemployment rate drops to 6 percent, even though the labor market is actually worse.

Figure 8.3

The Level of US Business Investment in 2014 by Sectors Compared to the Peak at 2008 (%)

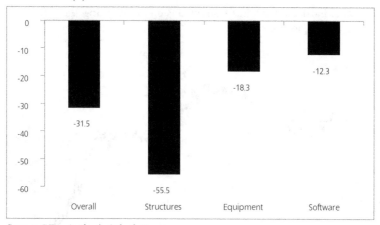

Source: BEA, Author's Calculations

The participation rate—the labor force as a percent of the whole population—dropped to 63 percent by end of 2014 (see Figure 8.4), the lowest rate since 1978 when large numbers of women began entering the workforce for the first time.

The US employed workforce has increasingly become part-time. Back 1968, only 13.5 percent of US employees were part-timers. That number peaked at 20.1 percent in January 2010. The ratio is still above 18 percent.

The annual increase in part-time employment since the early 2000s has been steady, but there was a precipitous decline in full-time jobs from 2002, accelerating in the recession. Since 2002, the number of part-time jobs has risen by 3 million, and full-time jobs have decreased by a similar amount.

In addition, most new jobs are in low-paid sectors like leisure and hospitality, retailing, and fast food. Around 60 percent of the jobs lost during the last recession were mid-wage jobs, whereas 58 percent of the jobs created since then have been low-wage jobs. Approximately one-fourth of all US workers make $10 an hour or less. According to the Working Poor Families Project, "about one-fourth of adults in low-income working families were employed in just eight occupations, as cashiers, cooks, health aids, janitors, maids, retail sales persons, waiters and waitresses, or drivers."[6] The United States actually has a higher percentage of workers doing low-wage work than in any other G7 economy.

Figure 8.4

US Labor Participation Rate (Amount of People of Working Age in Employment) %, 1990–2015

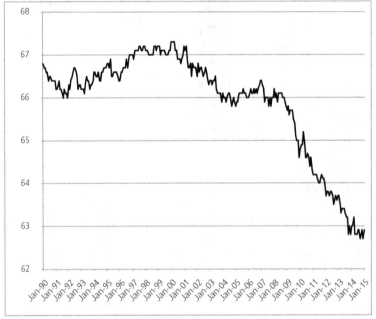

Source: US Bureau of Labor Statistics

Real median household income, that of the household in the middle of the spectrum, is down 8.3 percent from the prerecession 2007 level and off 9.1 percent from the 1999 all-time high. According to one survey, 77 percent of all Americans are now living paycheck to paycheck at least part of the time. The official estimate is that 15 percent of Americans live in poverty. But the highest wage in the bottom half of US earners is about $34,000. The number of Americans who earn between one-half and two times the poverty threshold is 146 million! Put simply, median income has slumped because a very large share of people can no longer find reasonably paid jobs.

The new generation of workers now have trouble finding full-time work and developing the skills needed for the transition to more stable, higher-paying employment. The longer the situation persists, the more difficult making up lost ground and lost time becomes. A recent study by the Brookings Institution found that both short-term and long-term unemployment increased sharply in 2008–9 during the Great Recession.[7] But while short-term unemployment returned to normal levels by 2012, long-term unemployment has remained at historically high levels in the aftermath of the Great Recession. The longer one has been unemployed, the less likely one is to get a call back from an employer, and the job search effort is also likely to decline.

Manufacturing employment has been in relative decline in all the major economies from the 1970s, but the pace of decline accelerated in the so-called neoliberal era, destroying millions of reasonably paid, full-time secure jobs, especially in lower skilled manufacturing sectors. This has enabled the capitalist sector to raise the rate of exploitation to counteract the fall in profitability experienced by most leading capitalist economies between 1965 and the early 1980s. Average income from employment has stagnated, even if average "compensation" (health insurance, pensions, etc.) has risen somewhat. Over the same period, top layers of the employed workforce (chief executives, etc.), as agents of neoliberal policies in the workplace, have seen spectacular rises in income and wealth.

Real Incomes Have Fallen, Inequality Has Risen

US real weekly wages are still falling on average. The top 20 percent has done better, of course. Their average income has risen 6 percent since 2008 in real terms and the top 5 percent of earners had an 8 percent jump. But the bottom 29 percent is still below the prerecession peak. None of this suggests a sharp rise in consumer spending. Indeed, real personal consumption growth per person is still slower than before the Great Recession.

That's not surprising when you find that a study of household incomes over the 2002–12 decade shows that the top 0.01 percent gained 76.2 percent in real terms, but the bottom 90 percent lost 10.7 percent. In 2012, the top 1 percent by income got 19.3 percent of the total. The only year when their share was bigger was 1928 at 19.6 percent!

Despite US households gaining $21 trillion in household wealth since

2009 (from rising property prices), the average family is still poorer than it was in 2007. According to research from economists William Emmons and Bryan North of the Center for Household Financial Stability, the average household's inflation-adjusted net worth is $626,800, 2 percent below its 2007 peak of $645,100. Indeed, almost half of all Americans had no net assets at all in 2009, as their debts exceeded their assets.

These inequalities have worsened in this weak recovery. The Organization for Economic Co-operation and Development (OECD) reckons that "inequality has increased by more over the past three years to the end of 2010 than in the previous twelve," with the United States experiencing one of the widest gaps among OECD countries.[8] According to the Economic Policy Institute, the wealthiest 1 percent of all US households on average have 288 times the amount of wealth that the average middle-class American family does and more than the bottom 90 percent combined.[9] Just twenty rich Americans made as much from their 2012 investments as the entire federal food assistance budget, which is designed to pay for families of four earning no more than $30,000 a year. The six heirs of Wal-Mart founder Sam Walton have a net worth that is roughly equal to the bottom 30 percent of all Americans combined. These facts put a different perspective on the "exciting recovery" that the capitalist media and mainstream economists claimed was on its way for the United States in 2014.

Economists Emmanuel Saez of the University of California, Berkeley, and Gabriel Zucman of the London School of Economics say to forget the top 1 percent.[10] The winners of the race, according to them, have been the 0.1 percent. Since the 1960s, the richest one-thousandth of US households, with a minimum net worth today above $20 million, has more than doubled their share of wealth, from around 10 percent to more than 20 percent. One-thousandth of the country owns one-fifth of the wealth. By comparison, the *entire* top 1 percent of households takes in about 22 percent of US income, counting capital gains (see Figure 8.5).

While the super-rich have risen, the merely affluent have barely budged. The share of wealth belonging to the top 1–5 percent of households has remained about level. The relative gains have been eaten up by the elite—the 0.1 percent and even the 0.01 percent. The top 0.5 percent, with minimum household income of $551,000, have roughly tripled their share of the nation's paycheck since 1978, to about 18 percent. The bottom half of the 1 percent, the work-a-day rich, have upped theirs only to around 4 percent.

An exceptionally tiny circle of Americans is not only commanding a greater and greater share of pay, but—if Saez and Zucman are right— they are successfully consolidating their fortunes far faster than 99.9 percent of the country.

Figure 8.5

Share of US Household Income Going to Top 1% of Households (%), 1913–2008

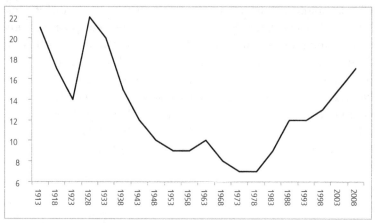

Source: Saez and Zucman

It used to be argued in mainstream economics that inequalities were the result of different skills in the workforce, and the share going to labor was dependent on the race between workers improving their skills and education and the introduction of machines to replace past skills. In most of the nineteenth century, about 25 percent of all agriculture labor threshed grain. That job was automated in the 1860s. The twentieth century was marked by an accelerating mechanization of not only agriculture but also factory work. Harvard University economists Claudia Goldin and Larry Katz have described this as a "race between education and technology."[11]

The evidence now shows that inequalities of income and wealth across US society and the declining share of income going to labor in the capitalist sector are not due to the level of education and skill in the workforce but to deeper factors like the role of capital and profit.[12] We need to start talking about profits and who owns the capital. "I think our eyes have been averted from the capital/labor dimension of inequality, for several reasons. It didn't seem crucial back in the 1990s, and not enough people (me included!) have looked up to notice that things have changed. It has echoes of old-fashioned Marxism—which shouldn't be a reason to ignore facts, but too often is. And it has really uncomfortable implications."[13] Indeed, it does.

To sum up: the US economy has been crawling since the Great Recession ended. Investment remains way below precrisis levels as US corporations hoard cash and raise debt to sustain stock prices. Meanwhile employment for average workers remains poor and precarious and often at lower rates of pay than before the crisis began. Average real incomes are still nearly 10 percent below the peak before the slump. But the richest Americans have lost little and continue to harvest a lion's share of the new value reaped since economic recovery began in 2010. One of the lasting features of the Great Recession and this Long Depression in the United States has been this extraordinary rise in inequality—raising the stakes in the class struggle.

Chapter 9
The Failing Euro Project

The EU decision-making process is hopelessly flawed. . . . The survival of the euro is not, and never was, a matter of pure capitalist economic rationality. No such thing exists. The euro's future will be the outcome of a complex interaction of political and economic factors. [We may have] underestimated the collective stupidity of the EU authorities . . . [so] the euro's survival hangs by a thread.

—*Mick Brooks*[1]

The Crisis of the Euro Is a Crisis of Capitalism

Among the advanced capitalist economies, the region of the Eurozone countries has suffered the most from the Great Recession and the subsequent Long Depression. The message of this chapter is that Europe's stagnant economy is a result of the low rate of profit in the capitalist sector, and this is what is driving austerity in the continent. This exacerbates the inequalities arising from the Eurozone's peculiar combination of advanced and less developed countries in the same currency union. Both neoclassical austerity and Keynesian policies have failed to restore profitability and stimulate economic recovery.

In addition to the general crisis of profitability, there are special features characterizing the euro crisis. Capitalism is a combined but uneven process of development (see Figure 9.1). It is combined in the sense of extending the division of labor and economies of scale and involving the law of value in all sectors, as in globalization. But that expansion is uneven and unequal as the stronger seek to gain market share over the weaker.

The euro project aimed at integrating all European capitalist economies into one unit to compete with the United States and Asia in world capitalism with a single market and a rival currency. But one policy on inflation, one short-term interest rate, and one currency for all members is not enough to overcome the forces of capitalist uneven development, especially when growth for all stops and there is a slump. The professed aim from the beginning of the euro in 1999 was that the weaker economies would converge with the stronger in GDP per capita and fiscal and external imbalances. But the opposite has happened instead, as the International Monetary Fund (IMF) explained.[2] The graph in Figure 9.2 rises up from left to right, instead of being flat. The imbalances have widened and not converged.

Figure 9.1

Eurozone Economy Real GDP (2010 € Terms) Versus Pre-Eurozone Trend Growth, 2000–2016

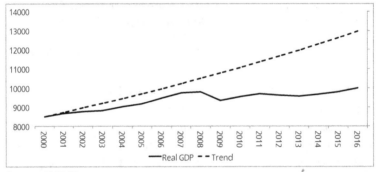

Source: AMECO

Figure 9.2

Eurozone country average current account balances 2000-2007 versus GDP per capita relative to average in 1995 (%)

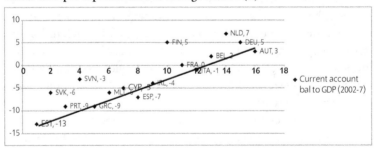

Source: AMECO

The global slump dramatically increased the divergent forces within the euro, threatening to break it apart. The fragmentation of capital flows between the strong and weak Eurozone states exploded. The capitalist sector of the richer economies like Germany stopped lending directly to the weaker capitalist sectors in Greece and Slovenia, and so on. As a result, to maintain a single currency, the official monetary authority, the European Central Bank (ECB), and the national central banks had to provide the loans instead. The Eurosystem's "Target 2" settlement figures (see Figure 9.3) between the national central banks revealed this huge divergence within the Eurozone.

Figure 9.3

Target 2 Eurosystem Credit Balances €—Above the Line Means Net Assets, Below the Line Means Net Liabilities Within the Eurosystem

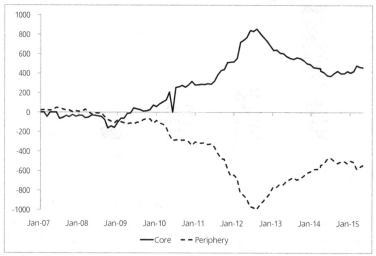

Source: ECB

Those who wish to preserve the euro project, like the EU Commission, the majority of EU politicians, and most capitalist corporations, recognize that the only way to do so is to extend the process toward more integration. That means a banking union so that all the banks in the Eurozone are subject to control by the euro institutions like the ECB and not national government regulators. From January 2016, the ECB and national central banks will provide EU-wide banking supervision under agreed terms for resolution and restructuring.

Better still would be the establishment of a full fiscal union, so that taxes and spending are controlled by Eurozone institutions and deficits in one European Monetary Union (EMU) state are automatically met by transfers from surplus states. That is the nature of a federated state like Canada, the United States, or Australia. These transfers reach 28 percent of US GDP compared with the controlled and conditional transfers under EU budgets and bailouts of less than 10 percent of one state's GDP (see Figure 9.4).

Figure 9.4
Annual Fiscal Transfers as a Share of GDP (%)

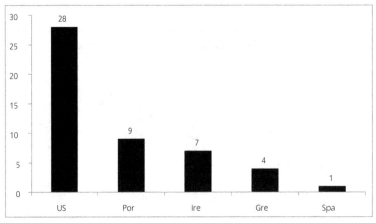

Source: OECD

But the Eurozone does not have such a fiscal union, and there is little prospect of one being created. Instead, after much kicking and screaming, the Germans and the EU agreed to set up some fiscal transfer funds, first through the European Financial Stability Fund and then the European Stability Mechanism. These are not automatic fiscal union transfers; they are contingent on meeting agreed fiscal targets that member states must meet to receive funding. There is growing opposition in Germany and other fiscally prudent states to shelling out cash for what they see as wayward countries who cannot get their public finances in order.

The Policy of Austerity
So instead, the ECB, the EU Commission, and the governments of the

Eurozone proclaimed that so-called austerity, along with neoliberal reforms in labor and product markets, was the only way Europe was to escape from the Great Recession. Control on public spending would force convergence. Supporters of austerity like to cite the example of the Baltic states as showing that these policies could quickly restore profitability and growth.[3] The governments there adopted neoliberal policies forcefully. Estonian unemployment fell back from 20 percent in early 2010 to 10 percent and the economy grew at over 8 percent in 2011. But Estonia's real GDP is still some 9 percent below its peak in 2007, having fallen over 17 percent from peak to trough.

The real aim of austerity was to achieve a sharp fall in real wages and cuts in corporate taxes and thus raise the share of profit. The Estonian labor force has been decimated as thousands left the tiny country to seek work elsewhere in Europe. Estonia also received over €3.4 billion in EU structural funds to finance infrastructure spending and employment. In this way, wage costs have been lowered and profits raised. The other poster child for successful austerity, Ireland, achieved a partially export-led recovery by getting rid of its "excess" workforce in a similar way. Irish emigration is now back at levels not seen since the dark days of the late 1980s.

Austerity should eventually deliver the required reductions in budget deficits and debt. But already there have been years of austerity and very little progress has been achieved in meeting these targets and, more important, in reducing the imbalances within the Eurozone on labor costs or external trade to make the weaker states more competitive.

The adjusted wage share in national income, defined here as compensation per employee as a percentage of GDP at factor cost per person employed (see Figure 9.5), is the cost to the capitalist economy of employing the workforce (wages and benefits) as a percentage of the new value created each year. Every capitalist economy had managed to reduce labor's share of the new value created since 2009. Labor has been paying for this crisis everywhere.

Not surprisingly, the workers of the Baltic states and the distressed Eurozone states of Greece, Ireland, Cyprus, Spain, and Portugal have taken the biggest hit to wage share in GDP. In these countries, real wages have fallen, unemployment has skyrocketed, and hundreds of thousands have left their homelands to look for work elsewhere. That has enabled companies in those countries to sharply increase the rate of exploitation of their reduced workforce, although so far that has not been enough to restore profitability to levels before the Great Recession and thus sustain sufficient new investment to get unemployment down and these economies onto a sustained path of growth—even after five years and in some cases seven.

The major economies of Japan and the United States have also achieved a "moderate" reduction in wage share, which is helping restore profitability. What is worrying for the capitalists of Italy or France is the failure to raise the rate of exploitation much at all. This failure is slowing the pace of return to profitability—no wonder Italy's economy continues to grind down and France is stagnant. As Figure 9.5 shows, Slovenian capitalism needs to do more to reduce wage share there if it is to recover profitability—at least as much as Portugal, Ireland, or Romania.

Figure 9.5

Change in Share of Wages in GDP (Adjusted for Self-Employed) Since 2009 (%)

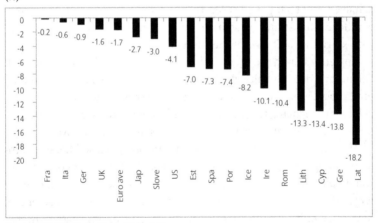

Source: AMECO, Author's Calculations

In these countries, governments are preparing an agenda of labor market reform, spending cuts, and privatizations designed to hit labor's share in the national output. There is more misery to come. Italy's new prime minister, Matteo Renzi, is pledged to such neoliberal measures. France's François Hollande has experienced a conversion to a neoliberal agenda, and Slovenia's "social democrat" coalition is preparing similar measures.

But it is not just the politicians of austerity who have driven or aim to drive down labor's share. Government policy based on the Keynesian alternative of debt restructuring and devaluation of the currency has led to the same result. Iceland's supposedly Keynesian policies have produced a larger fall in labor's share than it has in austerity Spain or Portugal.[4]

Paul Krugman was one leading Keynesian economist (along with some Marxists) who reckoned that austerity could not work and that devaluation and leaving the euro was the only way out. However, he started to backtrack after the ECB said it would do what it takes to ensure sufficient liquidity to give the euro economy breathing space to recover.[5]

Emigration: The Safety Valve

Actually, the breathing space is less the result of the ECB's commitment to provide credit if necessary and has more to do with emigration. One of the striking contributions to the fall in labor's share of new value has been from emigration. It has become an important contribution to reducing costs for the capitalist sector in the larger economies like Spain. Before the crisis, Spain was the largest recipient of immigrants to its workforce: from Latin America, Portugal, and North Africa. That has been completely reversed.

Hundreds of thousands of migrants are heading back home every year, and the country's overall population is falling for the first time since records began. Spain's population jumped from 40 million in 1999 to more than 47 million in 2010, one of the most pronounced demographic shifts experienced by a European country in modern times. The surge was almost entirely the result of migrants from countries such as Ecuador, Bolivia, Romania, and Morocco. The number of foreigners living in Spain increased eightfold in just over a decade, while their share of the population soared from less than 2 percent in 1999 to more than 12 percent in 2009.

Now increasingly they are leaving Spain altogether. In 2008, one year after the start of the crisis, Spain still recorded 310,000 more migrant arrivals than departures. That number fell to just 13,000 the following year before turning negative in 2010. In 2012 there were more than 140,000 more departures than arrivals, and the pace of the exodus is picking up fast. According to the national statistics office, the foreign-born population stands at 6.6 million, down from more than 7 million just two years before.

This net emigration acts a safety valve for Spanish capitalism—unemployment would be even higher without it. It helps the capitalist sector get labor costs down without provoking a social explosion. However, over the longer term, this spells deep trouble for capitalist expansion in Spain. There remains a huge overhang of unfilled real estate from the property boom that triggered the crisis. A falling population means that this form of unproductive capital will continue to weigh down the country's recovery. With a public sector debt to GDP ratio hitting 100 percent, there will be fewer workers to extract value to service that debt.

Unless the productivity of the smaller labor force can be raised, Spain's growth rate will be limited. German capitalism has succeeded to some extent in coping with falling population. Spanish capitalism will be less able. After all, most of the people leaving are the skilled and more productive parts of the workforce. They are going to Germany, France, the United States, even Latin America. Maybe they will return, as many did in the Baltic states or Ireland after past recessions ended. But given the length of this Long Depression, this time could be different.

The recession in the Eurozone, namely, a contraction in real GDP, has made fiscal austerity programs self-defeating. As the denominator for fiscal deficit or debt to GDP has shrunk, the ratios have risen, despite huge cuts in government spending and higher taxes. France, which promised to get below the 3 percent budget deficit to GDP target set by the Eurozone leaders, is forecast to hit 3.4 percent in 2016. And Spain and Portugal will also be above the 3 percent target in 2016, as will of course Greece. Overall, the Eurozone sovereign debt ratio will barely budge over the forecast period, having hit an all-time high of 94.9 percent of GDP in 2014.

More important for labor, the EU Commission sees little improvement in the unemployment rate in the region. It reached an all-time high of 12 percent in 2013 and will still be at 10.5 percent in 2016, nearly 20 percent higher than before the Great Recession. A quarter of the workforce in Spain and Greece will remain without jobs through 2015. Portugal will continue to hover around 17.5 percent.

UK: Booming?

In contrast, maybe austerity has worked in one country that is outside the Eurozone: the United Kingdom, or to be more exact, austerity plus devaluation of the pound, the best of both worlds for mainstream economic policies.

In 2015, we were told that the United Kingdom is booming or in recovery mode. But industrial production is still lower than in 2010 and some 10–15 percent below the level at the beginning of the Great Recession. That puts the "boom" in context.

The British media and the government made much of the news that the UK economy grew faster than the other top seven capitalist economies in 2014. But the UK economy has been one of the slowest to recover of the major economies and it has taken six years to 2014 for national output to return to its precrisis level, although GDP per person remains below that level. What a waste of resources and prosperity.

Indeed, real incomes for hard-working people have only just stopped falling in 2015 after seven years falling average real earnings. For young workers, real incomes have fallen over 12 percent in that period. Workers in the private sector have seen no real raises since 2009, and those in the public sector will see none before 2018 at the earliest.

Average real incomes are still falling. Most British households are not experiencing a boom, even if the top 1 percent in London is having a great time. At best, real GDP growth will be 2.0–2.5 percent from 2014 onward. Is that a boom, even if it is better than other advanced capitalist economies? The low-cost, low-road economy means Britain has the highest proportion of low-skilled jobs in the OECD countries after Spain. Twenty-two percent of UK jobs require no more than primary education, compared with less than 5 percent in countries like Germany and Sweden. Low-skilled jobs obviously mean low pay and carry wider social implications. Working poverty has increased by 20 percent in the past decade, creating a huge benefits bill.[6]

Even if there is economic growth over the next few years, the Resolution Foundation reckons that even by 2019 median working-age real incomes will still be below what they were at the start of the recession.

After a 25 percent depreciation of sterling, Britain's current account deficit has barely improved. British exporters have performed far worse than their counterparts in Ireland, Spain, and Portugal. For example, BAE Systems (a military hardware producer) cut 1,775 jobs at its yards in Scotland and England and ended shipbuilding altogether at Portsmouth. BAE said it had made the cuts because of a "significant" drop in demand.

But this is the producer goods sector of the economy. Surely what matters in the United Kingdom is its powerful services sector: business services, finance, property services, and "creative" industries. Aren't they starting to boom? After all, the services sector has now returned to its precrisis level.

There is little sign of any "balanced growth": it's all in consumer spending and home prices, not in investment or exports; it's all around London and the southeast and not in the other regions.[7] Can rising consumption, based on low interest rates, rising house prices, and central bank and government credit trigger an eventual boom in investment and output? Well, it never has for long in a capitalist economy, which depends on rising profitability and investment—something that is not evident in the United Kingdom. Profitability in the capitalist sector remains low, as does investment, and productivity growth is nonexistent, as employers use temporary and part-time labor at low wages (zero-hours contracts, etc.).

Michael Burke has shown exactly how a slump in investment has been the main reason for the failure of the UK economy to recover.[8] The UK government's policies of austerity have played their role precisely because they have been mainly aimed at reducing government investment. Unless long-term productive investment is restored, modern capitalist economies will not recover, however much extra money is injected or extra government spending takes place.

Despite the proclaimed policy of austerity, the government's budget deficit remains stubbornly high and the public debt to GDP is heading toward 100 percent of GDP. The profitability of UK companies, as measured by their net rate of return, was around 12 percent at the end of 2014. That's up from the trough in 2009, but still lower than in the late 1990s.

Low pay and low skill can become self-perpetuating. If pay is low, employers don't need to invest as much. It costs less to throw cheap workers at a problem than it does to invest in new technology or processes. If the workers are on temporary and zero-hours contracts anyway, why bother to invest in their development? Low investment means that skills stay low and pay stays low.

We see this reflected in the UK productivity figures. If employment increases but the economy doesn't grow, then productivity must fall. Self-employment, which accounts for three-quarters of the growth in employment since the recession, has increased in Britain at a much faster rate than anywhere else in the G7. Incomes, especially those from self-employment, have crashed. While pay rates have recovered in most countries, in the United Kingdom, they are still well below their prerecession level.

With the exception of the United States, productivity took a hit in all the major economies after the financial crash. Most, however, have recovered more quickly than has the United Kingdom.

The United Kingdom was closing the gap in the decade before the recession, only to see it open up again with the financial crisis. The relative gains over the past couple of decades have been completely wiped out. The United Kingdom is now among the hard-working low-productivity countries, not the smart-working high-productivity ones.

The United Kingdom's recovery has been the worst by historical standards and when compared with most of the G7. Growth finally picked up in 2014, but it still feels like watching a slow-moving river after a drought.[9] The UK boom, driven by another housing bubble, is already beginning to wane in summer 2015.

Germany: The Success Story

Germany is the largest and most important capitalist economy in Europe, if not yet the most important European imperialist power (there it vies with the United Kingdom and France). It is the main creditor and funder of the Eurozone member states. On the surface, all looks good for the economic health of Germany, and German capitalism looks set for the status quo for another four years.

Despite the euro debt crisis and the contingent costs to the pockets of the German taxpayers from the bailout payments to the distressed Eurozone states, the German ruling class is still convinced that the euro is worth having over the deutsche mark. That is because German capitalism has gained most from the trade and capital integration of the single currency. The best indicator of that is to look at what has happened to German capital's rate of profit.

Germany's rate of profit fell consistently from the early 1960s to the early 1980s slump (down 30 percent)—much like the rest of the major capitalist economies in that period. Then there was a recovery (some 33 percent up) with a short fall during the recession of the early 1990s and then stagnation during the 1990s as West Germany and East Germany were integrated into a single capitalist economy. The real take-off in German profitability began with the formation of the Eurozone in 1999, generating two-thirds of the rise from the early 1980s to 2007 (see Figure 9.6).

German capitalism benefited hugely from expanding into the Eurozone with goods exports and capital investment until the Great Recession hit in 2008 (see Figure 9.7), while other euro partners lost ground.

Figure 9.6

Germany Net Return on Capital (%), 1960–2014

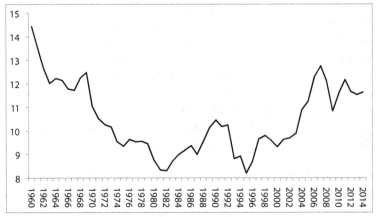

Source: AMECO, Author's Calculations

Figure 9.7

Change in Rate of Profit on Capital Since EMU Was Formed up to 2007 (%)

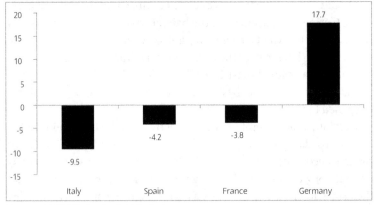

Source: AMECO, Author's Calculations

Once the east was integrated, Germany's manufacturing export base grew just as much as that of the new force in world manufacturing, China. But the fall in profitability during the Great Recession was considerable, and EU forecasts do not suggest a significant recovery in profitability. Indeed, profitability will be below the level of 2005 from now on.

The rise in the rate of profit from the early 1980s to 2007 can be broken down into a rise in the rate of surplus value of 38 percent, much faster than the small rise of 5 percent in the organic composition of capital. This is consistent with Marx's law of profitability in that the rate of profit rises when the increase in the rate of surplus value outstrips the increase in the organic composition of capital. It seems that the ability to extract more surplus value out of the German working class while keeping the cost of constant capital from rising much was the story of German capitalism. In other words, constant capital did not rise due to the cheapening effect of innovations and investment in new technology while the rate of surplus value did, because of the expansion of the workforce using imported labor from Turkey and elsewhere at first and then expansion directly into Europe later.

The real jump in the rate of profit began with the start of the Eurozone. In this period, the organic composition of capital was flat while the rate of surplus value rose 17 percent. German capital was able to exploit cheap labor within the EMU and in Eastern Europe to keep costs down. The export of plant and capital to Spain, Poland, Italy, Greece, Hungary, and so on (without obstacle and in one currency) allowed German industry to dominate Europe and even parts of the rest of the world.

Most important, the fear of the loss of jobs to other parts of Europe enabled German capitalists to impose significant curbs on the ability of labor to raise their wages and conditions. The large rise in the German rate of profit was accompanied by a sharp increase in the rate of surplus value or exploitation, particularly from 2003 onward (see Figure 9.8).

What happened from 2003 to enable German capitalism to exploit its workers so much more? In 2003–2005 the Social Democratic Party–led government implemented a number of wide-ranging labor market reforms, the so-called Hartz reforms. The first three parts of the reform package, Hartz I–III, were mainly concerned with creating new types of employment opportunities (Hartz I), introducing additional wage subsidies (Hartz II), and restructuring the Federal Employment

Agency (Hartz III). The final part, Hartz IV, was implemented in 2005 and resulted in a significant cut in the unemployment benefits for the long-term unemployed. Between 2005 and 2008 the unemployment rate fell from almost 11 percent to 7.5 percent, barely increased during the Great Recession, and then continued its downward trend, reaching 5.5 percent at the end of 2012, although it is still higher than in the golden age of expansion in the 1960s.

Figure 9.8
German Rate of Profit and Rate of Surplus Value (%), 1983–2008

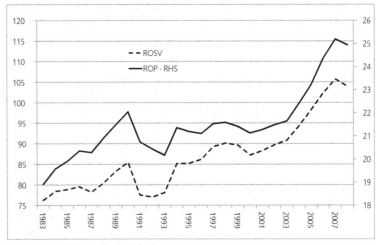

Source: AMECO, Author's Calculations

German Unemployment Rate

A wonderful success—but not for labor. About one quarter of the German workforce now receive a "low-income" wage, using a common definition of one that is less than two-thirds of the median, which is a higher proportion than all seventeen European countries except Lithuania. A recent Institute for Employment Research study found wage inequality in Germany has increased since the 1990s, particularly at the bottom end of the income spectrum. The number of temporary workers in Germany has almost tripled over the past ten years to about 822,000, according to the Federal Employment Agency. This is something we have seen across Europe, the dual labor system in Spain being the prime example.

So the reduced share of unemployed in the German workforce was achieved at the expense of the real incomes of those in work. Fear of low benefits if you became unemployed, along with the threat of moving businesses abroad into the rest of the Eurozone or Eastern Europe, combined to force German workers to accept very low wage increases while capitalists reaped big profit expansion. Real wages fell during the Eurozone era and are below the level of 1999, while German real GDP per capita has risen nearly 30 percent.

No wonder German capitalism has been so competitive in European and world markets. The Hartz reforms may be regarded as a success by German capital and mainstream economists.

Of course, this is not to deny that the German working class is better off than its peers in the rest of the Eurozone. German capitalism may have been a success story over the years since the reunification with East Germany. But its long-term prospects do not look so good from here. It has a declining and aging workforce and fewer areas for exploitation of new labor outside Germany, while competition from the likes of China and Asia will mount. The costs of maintaining the Eurozone will grow. All these are issues for the strategists of German capital.

Spain's Inquisition

German capitalism may have benefited from the euro project, and German capital may have got through the global financial crash with limited damage. But it has been a starkly different story for the rest of Eurozone, in particular, the so-called peripheral member states of Southern and Western Europe.

Spain is the Eurozone's fourth largest economy. The rate of unemployment hit 27 percent in 2013 for the first time since records began, and it stayed there. That's 6 million Spaniards without work in a population of 47 million. Youth unemployment (fifteen to twenty-four years) reached an astronomical 55 percent—only Greek youth are in a worse position for employment.

Even the government admits that the unemployment rate will stay above 25 percent until at least 2016, whereas the IMF reckons it will stay above that level until 2018! For the first time, permanent employment has started to fall as much as temporary employment in this deep economic recession that began in 2008, while long-term unemployment has doubled since 2008.

The unemployment rate would be even higher except that Spaniards are leaving the country to look for work elsewhere in Europe or even Latin America. The rate of net emigration has reached 250,000 a year, draining the economy of some of the most educated and productive young citizens. Average wages are plummeting, down nearly 6 percent in 2012 in nominal terms (i.e., before inflation). Wages fell at a 14 percent annualized rate in the last quarter of 2012. After deducting inflation, real wages are down nearly 9 percent last year as the government hikes value-added tax and other taxes.

While this misery engulfs the 99 percent, the top 1 percent of Spaniards continues to do well. The Spanish stock market has been booming, and government bond prices have recovered. Backed by European Central Bank (ECB) funding to Spain's banks, a new credit bubble is growing. But cash is not getting to where it is needed, to help small and medium business fund the businesses and invest more to restore employment. Spain's small and medium businesses are suffering more than those anywhere else in Europe (except Greece). The banks are not lending to them.

Spain's much-heralded economic boom saw 3.5 percent real growth a year during the 1990s; it stopped being based on productive investment for industry and exports in the 2000s and turned into a housing and real estate credit bubble, just like Ireland's Celtic Tiger boom did. House prices to income peaked at 150 percent, nearly as high as in Ireland. It has fallen back to 120 percent, but Ireland has dropped to 85 percent. Household debt reached 90 percent of GDP. Nonfinancial corporate debt, including that of the developers, reached 200 percent of GDP, the highest in the OECD.

Housing construction doubled from 1995 to 2007, reaching 22 percent of GDP in 2007. Investment in real estate fell from 12.5 percent of GDP in 2006 to 5.3 percent at the end of 2012 and below the historic low of 7 percent in 1997. Oversupply of housing is now around 700,000 units. Sales of new homes have dropped from 400,000 in 2007 to 115,000 in 2012. It will take six years to clear the backlog of unsold homes. House prices are down 31 percent in nominal terms and 38 percent in real terms, but there is still some way to go. (Irish house prices fell 60 percent.) During the property boom, credit grew at 20 percent a year, much faster than nominal GDP at about 7 percent a year. But lending collapsed from 2008. The private sector has deleveraged its debt by 15 percent of GDP since the peak of 2008. Debt is still well above accepted international levels of 160 percent. This is seriously holding back economic recovery. In Spain, capitalists won't invest if they have to meet heavy debt burdens. Spanish corporations are the most indebted among the major economies.

Much of the funding for the property boom came from abroad, mainly other European banks, greedy to get a piece of the property cake. Spanish household savings and corporate profits were not nearly enough to fund the boom and all those consumer purchases it enabled. Costs of production skyrocketed, and the real price of Spanish exports rose 20 percent from 2000 to 2009, increasingly pricing them out of world markets. Spain's external deficit with the rest of Europe and the world mushroomed.

The current account deficit reached 10 percent of GDP in 2007 and net international liabilities (debt and equity) hit 92 percent of GDP, well above the recommended prudent level of 35 percent for a growing emerging economy. Gross external debt is 160 percent of GDP, with nearly half in short-term loans. External debt interest to foreign banks sucks up 2.5 percent of GDP each year. Spanish banks and companies can only borrow from the ECB now. Borrowing from the Eurosystem rose from 6 percent in 2010 to 12 percent of GDP in 2012. The Bank of Spain has net liabilities to the Eurosystem at 30 percent of GDP. This is a huge burden, a burden that cannot be borne because of the hidden Achilles heel of Spanish capitalism: the long-term decline in its profitability (see Figure 9.9).

Figure 9.9

Spain: Rate of Profit on Capital (%), 1950–2010

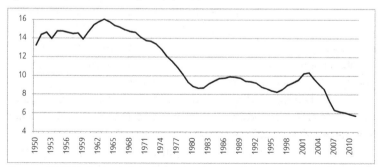

Source: AMECO, Author's Calculations

Spanish capitalism was not a great success under the military rule of General Franco in the post-1945 period. Profitability fell from the great heights of the golden age of postwar capitalism, as it did for all other capitalist economies from 1963 onward, in a classic manner, with the organic composition of capital rising nearly 30 percent while the rate of surplus value fell by about same. After the death of Franco, Spanish capitalism temporarily reversed the decline as foreign investment flooded in to set up new industries, relying on a sharp rise in the rate of exploitation brought about by plentiful surplus labor and a system of temporary employment contracts (while freezing permanent employment), the so-called dual labor policy.

The rate of exploitation rose over 50 percent to 1996, accompanied by the foreign-led investment boom in the 1990s. This drove up the ratio of capital to labor (by 19 percent), as German and other capitalist companies relocated to Spain in search of cheaper labor and higher profits. That eventually put renewed pressure on the rate of profit. From 1996, profitability dropped sharply as wages squeezed profits in the boom of the 2000s.

Spanish capitalists switched to investing in property and riding on the cheap credit boom that disguised weakening profitability in the productive sector. The Spanish economic miracle came to a sorry end in the Great Recession, which in turn led to the property bubble burst, bringing about the banking crash. Indeed, events happened in that order, unlike in the United States and the United Kingdom.

The aim of austerity and high unemployment is to restore Spanish profitability. It's a modern capitalist form of the Spanish Inquisition on the people. Corporate revenues dropped by €3 billion in 2012 (a 0.5 percent drop), but there was a €17 billion (5 percent) cut in wages to employees, so profits rose by €6 billion. Unit labor costs fell by 3.5 percent in 2012 as labor laws were introduced to make it easier to sack permanent staff and end the dual labor system—an ironic reversal of neoliberal policies. The aim, of course, is not to provide rights for temporary workers but to end them for permanent workers.

The IMF believes that economic growth in Spain between 2015 and 2018 will average around 1.5 percent annually. This forecast represents a significant downward revision from earlier optimism.

This terrible depression is also beginning to break up the Spanish state. Regional governments are deeply in debt and are being asked to make huge cuts. Richer regional areas with their own nationalist interests, as in Catalonia and the Basque Country, are making noises about separation from Madrid. The centripetal forces that are raising the odds of a euro break-up are also doing the same to Spain.

Can lower wages and high unemployment eventually make Spanish exports more competitive and thus restore growth through exports? Spanish exports in real terms are up €26.3 billion from 2007 (+10 percent) but its imports are €64.4 billion lower (−20 percent). Lower wages and the cost of labor are helping trade, but this change in net trade has been paltry relative to the complete collapse of investment of €108 billion (−36 percent in real terms). The Spanish depression is a result of the collapse in capitalist investment. To reverse that requires a sharp rise in profitability. Until investment recovers, the depression will not end.

Certainly when unit labor costs are driven down sufficiently, enough weak companies are bankrupted, and exports are cheap enough, then corporate profitability will rise from the ashes of millions of unemployed, much lower living standards, decimated pensions, and destroyed public services that have been burned at the stake of capitalist accumulation. The Spanish Inquisition will eventually have done its job after more years of misery.

Italy: Deep in Stagnation

In some ways, Italy is in the most dire position. Italian capital was in the doldrums even before the Great Recession. Profitability has been falling since 2000, and the rate of profit had fallen back to the level of 1963 (see Figure 9.10).

Since the trough of the Great Recession in mid-2009, Italy's rate of profit has fallen further and is now down nearly 30 percent since 2004, compared with 15 percent for the Eurozone as a whole.

Just as night follows day, with profitability falling, net investment by Italy's capitalists dried up entirely (see Figure 9.11). Since the end of the Great Recession, there has been no recovery in investment. Real investment levels are down 35 percent from the peak in early 2007.

The policies of austerity at first introduced by Silvio Berlusconi in 2010 and then more vigorously by the bankers' man Mario Monti failed, even on their own terms. The public debt to GDP ratio continues to rise and unit labor costs, which have been cut back sharply by austerity in other countries, continue to rise in Italy, despite falling wages, because productivity is falling.

Italian capitalism remains paralyzed, and it is going to take drastic measures to raise profitability and productivity to turn things around on a capitalist basis. Italy's only hope is that economic recovery will return to the rest of the Eurozone to improve growth and employment.

Figure 9.10
Italy Rate of Profit on Capital (%), 1963–2009

The rate of profit was the same in 2007 as in 1963. Since 2000, on joining the Eurozone, Italy's rate of profit has fallen over 20%, double the decline in the UK and the US.

Source: AMECO, Author's Caclulations

Figure 9.11
Italy Net Annual Investment Growth (%), 1964–2009

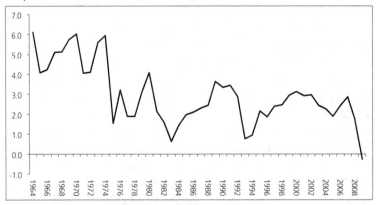

Source: AMECO

Greece: The Ultimate Disaster

And then there is the tragic story of Greece. Greece cannot ever escape the debt deflation trap into which it has descended. Gross public and private debt relative to GDP has risen to record proportions and is still rising. Greek companies have the highest debt to equity ratio of modern economies at 235 percent, more than twice the Eurozone corporate average. These debt ratios are rising partly because the deficit on Greek government budgets has only just been closed, but mainly because nominal GDP growth remains nonexistent while the cost of servicing debt continues to rise.

The public debt ratio is now above 180 percent of GDP. The latest bailout plan forced on Greece by the so-called troika of the EU Commission, the IMF, and the ECB will pile on yet more debt to drive the ratio over 200 percent of GDP, unless debt relief in some form is agreed on. The troika wants the Greek public sector to run a surplus of 3.5 percent of GDP before debt interest payments for the foreseeable future to get its debt ratio down. The reality is that further austerity for another five years is both politically impossible and economically futile.

The election of the anti-austerity left government of Syriza in the January 2015 elections posed a clear challenge to the policies and targets of the troika. It led to a major clash over continuing with austerity policies, with the troika threatening to cut off all credit to the Greek government and its banks, which if implemented, would force Greece out of the Eurozone and the EU. In the event, the Greek government capitulated to the troika's demands and accepted further austerity measures for a new bailout program rather than leave the EU.

At the time, many Keynesian economists and many on the left advocated that Greece break with the euro and the German-led troika bailout packages. Greece should restore the drachma and then devalue it to boost exports and inflate away the real value of debt. In short, Greece should do as Argentina did and default on its public debts.

Two things spring from this alternative policy. First, was the Argentina option of 2002 a success? The experience there was partly exceptional and eventually proved unsuccessful. Second, if the euro crisis is a crisis of capitalism and not just a problem of the euro as a "too strong" currency, then devaluation and debt default on its own would only be a temporary palliative for Greek capitalism—and no more palatable for working people than euro-defined austerity, as it would mean hyperinflation and a collapse of businesses laden with euro debt. The renewal of Argentina's crisis has confirmed that prognosis.[11]

It's true that the crushing of the living standards and wage earnings of Greek households is making Greek industry more "competitive"—total employee compensation has dropped 30 percent since 2010 (see Figure 9.12).

Figure 9.12
Greece Nominal Unit Labor Costs (Indexed 2010=100)

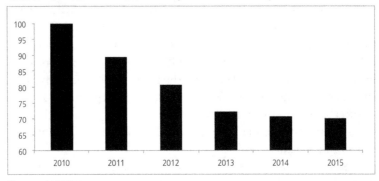

Source: AMECO

Greece is not tiny like Estonia, but it is a relatively small capitalist economy, dependent on trade, mainly of processed minerals, pharmaceuticals, and food, as well as services like tourism.

Austerity in Greece is supposed to be aimed at the public sector. But the reality is that private sector workers have been hit the hardest. Public sector employment shrank by some 56,000 from 2009 to 2011, a 7.8 percent drop. Private sector employment (a much larger share of the labor force) is down 13 percent. Labor costs are down 18.5 percent. This is the real target of austerity.

The Greek rate of profit peaked in 2007, some two years before the crisis really hit the nation. Investment then plummeted 50 percent from 2007 (see Figure 9.13). Austerity has driven the rate of surplus value up by 25 percent since 2009. But Greek capitalism is still encumbered by inefficient capitals, and the organic composition of capital remains elevated. So investment is not yet recovering.

The troika will not allow a haircut on the debt that the Greek government owes to the ECB, the Eurogroup institutions, and the IMF. But it has relaxed the terms of repayment. But just relaxing the repayment burden does not restore Greek capitalism. Unless the Eurozone leaders write off the loans to Greece, and/or the region as a whole makes a dramatic economic recovery in the next few years and this revival trickles down to Greece, Greek capitalism will remain prostrate.

Figure 9.13
Greece Rate of Profit on Capital (%), 1961–2015

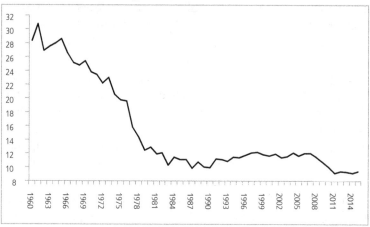

Source: AMECO, Author's Calculations

The Tiny Members Suffer Most

The smaller member states of the Eurozone, like Ireland, Portugal, and Cyprus have suffered badly. Tiny Slovenia, a nation of 2 million people wedged along the Alps between Italy to the west and Austria to the north, is the only Balkan country to be in the Eurozone. Slovenia has been relatively more prosperous than the other Balkan states and avoided the internecine wars that took place between Croatia, Serbia, Bosnia, and Kosovo after the collapse of the communist Yugoslav federation. It entered the European Union and the Eurozone with great hopes of going forward. Then the economic crisis erupted in 2007. Slovenia seemed to avoid the worst for a while. But now it has been hit with tremendous damage. The economy is in a deep recession that began in 2011. The response of all the political parties has been austerity—under the direction of the EU institutions. That has been a disaster, and eventually Slovenians had had enough. In November 2012 there were huge demonstrations demanding an end to austerity. This heightened when it was found that the leaders of the center-right and center-left both appeared have been involved in corruption scandals.

The Slovenian economic crisis is very similar to that of Ireland. The state-owned banks had been engaged in massive loans to Slovenian companies, mainly in construction and real estate, stimulating a huge commercial property boom that came crashing down when the economic slump began. Just as in Ireland, it has been found that the politicians were in collusion with builders and developers to promote a crazy credit boom, taking a slice of the action for their troubles.

For a while this was covered up, but with unpaid loans reaching 20 percent of all lending, the banks are close to a bust. The EU and IMF came up with the usual "Irish solution," which was to shuttle off all the bad debts into a "bad bank," which the taxpayer must "own," while the cleansed banks are given funds to recapitalize, with the aim of selling them off to foreigners or others as soon as possible. The Slovenian government will be left with a public sector debt that will have risen from 23 percent of GDP in 2008 to 70 percent by 2017, a massive burden on taxpaying citizens.

The level of debt built up in the credit boom has destroyed the ability of the banks to provide more credit and companies funds for new investment. Nonresidential capital investment has fallen by nearly 6 percent of GDP since 2007, as the Slovenian capitalist sector went on strike or bust. That drop is second only to Ireland in the Eurozone. The depression is mega-sized for such a small country.

Will the Euro Survive?

There are two ways a capitalist economy can get out of slump. The first is by raising the rate of exploitation of the workforce enough to drive up profits and renew investment. The second is to liquidate weak and unprofitable capital (i.e., companies) or write off old machinery, equipment, and plant from company books (i.e., devalue the stock of capital). Of course, capitalists attempt to do both to restore profits and profitability after a slump.

This is taking a long time in the current crisis since the bottom of the Great Recession in mid-2009. Progress in devaluing and deleveraging the stock of capital and debt built up before is taking time and even being avoided by monetary policy. But progress in raising the rate of exploitation has been considerable.

The Keynesian Solution

The crisis in the Eurozone has been blamed on the rigidity of the single currency area and on the strident austerity policies of the leaders of the Eurozone. But the euro crisis is only partly a result of the policies of austerity being pursued, not just by the EU institutions but also by states outside the Eurozone like the United Kingdom. Alternative Keynesian policies of fiscal stimulus and/or devaluation where applied have done little to end the slump and still made households suffer income losses. Austerity means a loss of jobs and services and thus income. Keynesian policies mean a loss of real income through higher prices, a falling currency, and eventually rising interest rates.

Take Iceland, a tiny country outside the EU and Eurozone. The widely supported Keynesian policy of devaluation of the currency, a policy not available to the member states of the Eurozone, still meant a 50 percent decline in average real incomes in euro terms and nearly 20 percent in krona terms.

Figure 9.14

Greece and Iceland: Net Rate of Return on Capital (Indexed 2010=100), 2005–2015

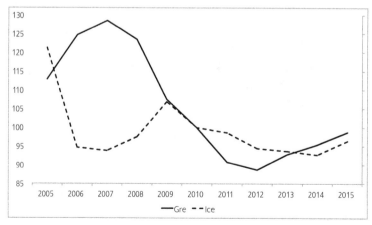

Source: AMECO

Restoring profitability is key for economic recovery under the capitalist mode of production. So which procapitalist policy has done best on this criterion? Let's compare Greece and Iceland. Iceland's rate of profit plummeted from 2005, and eventually the island's real estate bubble burst, and along with it the banks collapsed in 2008–9. Devaluation of the currency started in 2008, but profitability in 2012 remained well under the peak level of 2004, although there has been a slow recovery in profitability from 2008. Greece's profitability stayed up until the global crisis took hold, and then plummeted and only stopped falling in 2014. Profitability in "austerity" Greece and "devaluing" Iceland has fallen by about the same amount since 2005 (see Figure 9.14). You could say that both policies have been equally useless.

The euro crisis is a product of the slump in global capitalism, and the subsequent failure to recover is the same. Profitability in most capitalist economies is still well below the peak of 2007 (the United States is the only exception) and for economies like Italy and Slovenia it is still heading downward.

Figure 9.15

Average Growth in Profitability of Capital Compared to Growth in Real GDP (%), 2009–2012

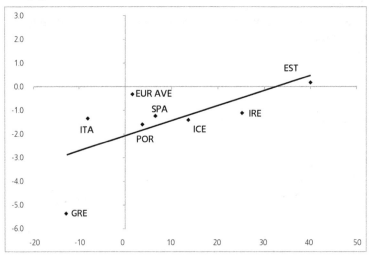

Source: OECD, Author's Calculations

Indeed, if you correlate profitability with growth since the trough of the Great Recession, the trend line is positively sloped (see Figure 9.15). Estonia and Ireland have seen the biggest recovery in profitability (through austerity and cutting wages and living standards for the population, along with massive emigration of the unemployed). As a result, they have had the best GDP recoveries, such as they are. Where the recovery in profitability has been weak or nonexistent, real GDP has contracted the most since 2009.

The correlation between profitability and growth is much better than between government spending and growth (see Figure 9.16), the Keynesian indicator. Countries where government spending to GDP has increased since 2009 (through Keynesian-style stimulus) like Japan and Slovenia have not grown at all, whereas there are many countries that applied austerity and reduced government spending to GDP after 2009 and have achieved some growth. There is no real correlation between growth and austerity (the trend line is almost flat), whatever Keynesian "multipliers" might indicate.[12]

The Failure of the Euro Project

The build-up of debt, not just for banks but also for the nonfinancial capitalist sector, has exerted downward pressure on the ability of Europe's capitalist economies to recover quickly, even after cutting jobs, closing down businesses, and ending investment to reduce the cost of capital. The more the growth in private sector debt before the crisis, the smaller the recovery has been. Balance sheet stress is heavier on the weaker EMU states and the financial centers of the United Kingdom and the United States.

The debt servicing burden of the Eurozone periphery now accounts for almost 10 percent of revenues received by these governments. In the other thirteen Eurozone countries, the same burden averages only 3.5 percent with the difference in the debt service burden between the indebted periphery and the rest of the zone forecast to rise over the next five years. These high levels of debt service, even with lower interest rates, will erode highly indebted countries' ability to make investments and maintain social security nets. For example, Portugal's €7.3 billion interest bill exceeds its education spending and almost matches its health budget.

Figure 9.16

Average Growth in Government Spending to GDP Compared to Real GDP
Growth (%), 2009–2013

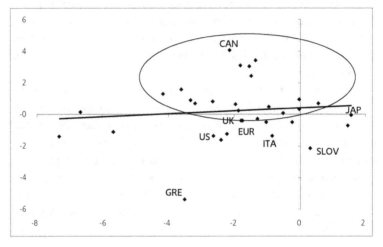

Source: OECD, Author's Calculations

The euro crisis is not really one of sovereign debt or a fiscal crisis.
Its origin lies in the failure of capitalism, the huge banking and private
credit crisis, and the inability of undemocratic pan-European capitalist institutions like the European Commission, the ECB, the Council
of Ministers, and the European Parliament to deal with it.

The ambition of France and Germany to compete with the United
States and Asia on the world stage through the monetary union was
fundamentally flawed. The original dream of a united capitalist Europe, of free markets in production, labor, and finance—ever utopian—
has turned into a mess. Now the single currency union is under threat.
It always was ambitious.

The US investment bank JP Morgan looked at whether the "right
conditions" under capitalism existed for setting up a currency union in
Europe.[13] They measured the difference between countries using data
from the World Economic Forum's Global Competitiveness Report,[14]
which ranks countries using more than 100 variables, from labor markets to government institutions to property rights. JP Morgan found
that there's an incredible amount of variation among the Eurozone's

member nations. The biggest differences come in pay and productivity, the efficiency of the legal systems in settling disputes, antimonopoly policies, government spending, and the quality of scientific research.

Indeed, the Eurozone countries are *more* different from each other than countries in just about any hypothetical currency union you could propose. A currency union for Central America would make more sense. A currency union in East Asia would make more sense. A currency union that involved reconstituting the old Soviet Union or Ottoman Empire would make more sense. In fact, "a currency union of all countries on Earth that happen to reside on the fifth parallel north of the Equator would make more sense."[15]

But the currency union went ahead because of the political ambitions of France and Germany to have a Europe led by them, even after Britain refused to join. Of course, the aim was to bring about a convergence between the weaker and stronger economies. That dismally failed in the boom years of 2002–7. The Great Recession exposed and widened the inequalities.

Can the existing currency union survive? Yes, if economic growth returns big time and/or if German capitalism grasps the nettle and is prepared to pay to help the ailing smaller economies through fiscal transfers. The Germans saying they will do so if the likes of Greece, Portugal, Ireland, and Spain "stick to fiscal targets" is no good. These countries cannot do so. So Germany will have to decide on more transfers without more austerity. Yet the red lines being imposed by the Germans are precisely to avoid recognizing the need to transfer funds to the weaker capitalist economies.

The reason the Germans are balking at this is that a proper fiscal union would not be cheap. It took twenty years, partly via a "solidarity surcharge" on their income taxes, to help integrate and upgrade East Germany. That was roughly two-thirds of West Germany's GDP then. The subsidies helped cover East Germany's budget shortfalls and poured money into its pension and social security systems. At the same time, nearly 2 million East Germans—a full eighth of the population—moved west to seek work. That is the sort of transfer of funds and jobs that will have to take place to support the currency union. Currency unions cannot stay still—Europe's has been around for only fifteen years. Either they break up or they move onto full fiscal union where the revenues of the state are pooled.

Take federal Germany. There is a mechanism of fiscal transfer between the federal states of Germany, the so-called Länderfinanzausgleich. The German constitution states that the objective of this fiscal transfer mechanism is the convergence of financial power across its federal states. The current system consists of vertical payments between the German state (Bund) and the federal states (Länder) as well as horizontal payments from federal state to federal state. The eligibility for transfer payment receipts is determined by an index (Finanzkraftmesszahl), which indicates the relative financial power of the federal states. Bavaria, Baden-Württemberg, and Hesse are currently the only net contributors, and Berlin is the biggest net recipient of these fiscal transfers.

In Germany, fiscal transfers from the south to the northeast have certainly helped these federal states converge in terms of their financial power and standard of living since the German unification in 1990. Nevertheless, after twenty-five years of fiscal transfer payments, the economic situation in these states remains highly unequal. For instance, the German unemployment rate varies significantly across federal states.

Of course, the rich Länder of Bavaria and Hesse are complaining that they are taking too much of the burden in Germany's fiscal union for profligate states like Berlin and Saxony. But that is the point in a nation-state: as Gordon Brown, former UK Labour prime minister, put it during the Scottish independence referendum in September 2014, a nation-state with fiscal union means "from each according to means; to each according to needs"—shades of communism!

Take the example of the United Kingdom. This is a government of four nations and many regions. Taxes are raised by a central state (although there has been some devolution to Scotland, Wales, and Northern Ireland) and raising debt is mostly made by the central state (there are some local government bonds or loans). Wales is a poorer part of the United Kingdom. It runs a trade deficit with the rich southeast of England. Its inhabitants contribute much less in tax revenue than they receive in government handouts. So Wales has twin deficits on its government and capitalist sectors, just as Greece has with the rest of the Eurozone.

Tax revenue per person is 26 percent lower in Wales (at £5,400) and 23 percent lower in Northern Ireland (£5,700) than in the United Kingdom as a whole (£7,300). Wales and Northern Ireland have less income and wealth than the rest of the nations and correspondingly raise less revenue per person from all the main taxes. While the public finance deficit in England was approximately £2,000 per head, it was £6,000 in Wales: a difference of £4,000: a combination of higher public spending of £1,383 and lower tax generation of about £2,400. It's because of higher public spending on tax credits, income support, and housing benefits in Wales with its lower wages, higher unemployment, and greater social needs. Fiscal transfers within a fiscal union ameliorates (but does not eliminate) these disparities.

Tax revenue in Scotland (£7,100 per person in 2012–13) looks much more like that in the United Kingdom as a whole (£7,300). But public spending per person has been higher in Scotland than the rest of the nations and roughly 20 percent greater than in England. So Scottish "budget deficits" are higher than they are in England. Devolution of spending and revenues to Scotland is gradually eroding the UK fiscal union.

Sometimes there are grumbles from the rich south in the United Kingdom that they have to pay for the unemployed Welsh but that argument does not have much traction. After all, the extreme logic of that is to say that the very rich inhabitants of Kensington in the posh part of London should not have their tax revenues redistributed to the poor inhabitants of Wales or the north of England. That would mean Kensington would have to break with the fiscal and currency union that is Britain, put up border controls, and find their own government, armed forces, and central bank. Of course, their riches would soon disappear because they are based on the labor of people all over Britain and even more from abroad. It is a point that many nationalist elements in Germany and Northern Europe forget. If the Eurozone breaks up into its constituent parts, the ongoing (not just immediate) losses to GDP for Northern Europe would be considerable.

The example of the United States also shows the advantages of a federal state over the commonwealth of states that existed to begin with. It took a civil war of bloody proportions to establish a unified state that wiped out the idea of secession. Now the US federal government raises taxes and debt and provides funds to the states (even though they raise their own taxes). A full financial union came later than fiscal union in the United States, when the Federal Reserve Bank was set up by the large private banks after a series of banking collapses. Now dollars are redistributed through the federal reserve system to cover "deficits" on trade and capital between states. As a result, while the average national tax revenue per head is about $8,000, rich states like Delaware, New York, New Jersey, Massachusetts, Minnesota, and Connecticut pay 25–50 percent more per head and poor states like Alabama, Mississippi, West Virginia, Kentucky or Michigan, or "empty" states like Montana pay 25–50 percent less than the average.

If the euro project is to survive, fiscal union along the lines of Germany, the United Kingdom, or the United States is necessary. But it is unachievable in a capitalist European Union, where the national interests of the richer member states are put before a union of "equals." The German view of fiscal union involves a binding agreement between all members to run national budgetary policy so that no intercountry fiscal flows would be necessary! This is impossible to achieve, even if the Eurozone was growing at a reasonable pace, which it is not.

The idea that a central Eurozone budget would gradually grow in size (from its tiny 1 percent of euro GDP) toward a full federal fiscal union is a pipe dream in a Eurozone with big strong states, a huge bureaucracy, an "independent" central bank, and a feeble European Parliament—in other words, no democratic commitment to a federal Europe. Instead, we have a botched, in-between solution, with no democracy, where there are flows of resources from the strong national economies to the weak, but only though euro institutions tied to draconian fiscal targets.

Fiscal union—indeed, a proper democratic federation of Europe, would only be possible through the ending of the capitalist mode of production and its replacement by one based on common ownership and resources transferred from "each according to means and to each according to need."

Neoliberal Disaster

Growth has not been restored by the neoliberal solutions demanded by the euro leaders and the IMF. The OECD keeps claiming that structural reforms will deliver a rise in the level of GDP per capita for the indebted member states (see a recent OECD report for the G20 meeting).[16] What are these wonderful growth-enhancing structural reforms? For Portugal, the IMF/EU decided that they were a reduction of four public holidays a year, three days fewer minimum annual paid holidays, a 50 percent reduction in overtime rates, and the end of collective bargaining agreements. Then there would be more working time management, the removal of restrictions on the power to fire workers, the lowering of severance payments on losing one's job, and the forced arbitration of labor disputes. In other words, workers must work longer and harder for less money and with fewer rights and a higher risk of being sacked. Southern Europe must become a cheap labor center for investment by the north. Those are the reforms.

Then there is deregulation of markets. Utilities are to be opened up to competition. That means companies competing to sell electricity or broadband to customers who must continually change their suppliers to save a few euros. Pharmacies are to have their margins cut, so small pharmacists will earn less, but there is no reduction in the price of drugs from big pharma, the real monopolies. The professions are to be deregulated, so lawyers cannot make such fat fees, but anybody can become a teacher or taxi driver or drive a large truck with minimal or no training. Finally, there is privatization of the remaining state entities sold cheaply to private asset companies to pay down debt and enlarge the profit potential of the capitalist sector. It's more or less the same proposals for Greece, Spain, Italy, and Ireland.

The real aim of these neoliberal solutions from the EU leaders and the OECD is not to restore growth as such but to raise the exploitation of the workforce. This would boost profitability, and so the private sector will then invest to create jobs and more GDP, assuming, of course, that capitalism does not have another slump before then.

Such policies have not worked so far. In the case of the weaker capitalist economies of the Eurozone, they have been disastrous. Can the people of Greece, Portugal, Spain, Italy, Cyprus, Slovenia, and Ireland endure more years of austerity, creating a whole lost generation of unemployed young people, as has already happened in Greece?

The electorate is losing patience and is angry, as the 2014 European Parliament elections showed. The EU leaders and strategists of capital need economic growth to return quickly, or further political explosions are likely. Yet given the current level of profitability, it may take too long before the world economy drops into another slump. Then all bets are off on the survival of the euro.

Chapter 10

Japan Stagnates

It appears as if the slump could go on forever. A dynamic analysis makes it clear that it is a temporary phenomenon—in the model it only lasts one period, although the length of a "period" is unclear (it could be three years, or it could be 20). Even without any policy action, price adjustment or spontaneous structural change will eventually solve the problem. In the long run, Japan will work its way out of the trap, whatever the policy response. But on the other hand, in the long run . . .

—Paul Krugman[1]

Japan's economy has been stagnating for over two decades now. So it is little surprise that its recovery since the end of the Great Recession in mid-2009 has been so weak. The essence of this stagnation lies in the secular decline in the profitability of Japanese capital, driven by a high organic composition of capital and, until recently, an inability of Japanese capital strategists to engineer a sufficient rise in the rate of exploitation of labor to compensate.

Japan has had two elections in fairly quick succession since the end of the Great Recession. Victory was obtained on each occasion by the conservative Liberal Democratic Party (LDP), led by Shinzō Abe. Abe promised he would end stagnation and restore profitability and growth through what have been designated as three arrows of economic policy: monetary stimulus by the Bank of Japan, fiscal stimulus by the government, and most important neoliberal reforms of the labor and product markets to boost profitability.

The great rise of Japanese manufacturing after World War II was driven by a very high rate of profit. That rate fell fast during the late 1960s, and the Japanese "miracle" came to an end in the mid-1970s. After the first worldwide postwar economic crisis of 1974–75, Japan began to struggle. The annual economic growth was 3.8 percent from 1974 to 1990, compared with 9.2 percent from 1956 to 1973.

The Japanese boom was partly driven by the scale of the reserve army (and the mass of low-paid labor in small companies that could be drawn into key sectors of the economy). It was also based on high levels of investment, directed toward key export-oriented sectors, which helped fuel the incredibly high levels of increase in productivity in the 1960s and 1970s. However, after the global recession of 1974–75, Japanese capitalism had exhausted its reserve army of cheap labor, and a rising organic composition of capital kept profitability low.

While domestic consumption remained restricted and the global market expanded outside Japan, this could allow the leading Japanese firms to appropriate surplus value on a global scale by undercutting laggards in Europe and North America. But the Japanese miracle petered out due to a combination of rising wages and a rising organic composition of capital in the domestic sector (see Figure 10.1), the saturation of foreign markets in consumer goods, renewed competition from the United States from the 1980s, on the one hand, and the Asian Tiger economies, on the other. The final straw was the rise in the value of the yen imposed by the Plaza Accord after 1985. These factors led to the subsequent asset price bubble in Japan from the late 1980s.

Figure 10.1

Japan Rate of Proft on Capital (%) and Organic Composition of Capital

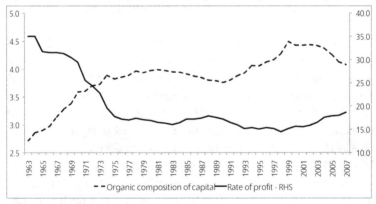

Source: Penn World Tables and Author's Caclulations

Japanese capitalism tried to boost profitability by looking for higher profits in unproductive sectors like real estate and finance in a forerunner of the great credit boom that the United States and Europe entered after 2002. Japan's credit bubble burst in 1989 in a disastrous way similar to the global financial crash of 2007–8. The country entered a recession that also coincided with a worldwide slump in 1990–91. But while the other major capitalist economies made a relative recovery after that slump, Japanese profitability declined further during the 1990s.

The main reason was an unwillingness on the part of the ruling elite in the banks, big corporations, and government to entertain a deleveraging of the overextended financial sector. Just as the US and European governments did in 2009, they got the taxpayers and the state to bail out the banks and the big institutions. As a result, Japan was left with enormous public sector debt that weighed down on the productive sectors of the economy, sucking up new value and savings (as a proportion of national output, public debt is more than double that of Europe and the United States). Japanese capitalism became zombie capitalism.

In 2001, Japan's political elite tried to reform under a neoliberal Prime Minister Junichirō Koizumi who opted for the restructuring of the banks, privatization of state agencies, and higher taxes. This produced a short revival in profitability, at the expense of average living standards, reduced pensions, and worse work benefits. The electorate hoped that the new Democratic Party, an amalgam of former socialists, social democrats, and liberals, would be a driving force to clean up Japanese politics, end corruption, and restore growth. But the triple whammy of the earthquake/tsunami in March 2011, the ensuing nuclear plant meltdown disaster, and the global economic crisis knocked Japanese capitalism over again. By 2010, the nation's nominal GDP was lower than that of 1994.

Since 2013, the LDP has been back in the saddle, pledging to spend more on government projects, not raise taxes, boost exports by devaluing the yen, restore the nuclear facilities, raise military spending, and act "tougher" with China—the same tired policies of the past thirty years.

There are three tools of procapitalist macroeconomic policy: fiscal, monetary, and currency. There is confusion among mainstream economic advisers on which of these policy tools is best to use to get capitalism out of its depression. Monetarists like Ben Bernanke are wedded to cutting interest rates and "printing" piles of money. Keynesians want go further: they want to reverse neoliberal fiscal austerity measures and let the government spending multiplier work its magic. Some less vocal thinkers advocate the benefits of devaluing the currency to boost exports. The newly elected Japanese government went for all three solutions at once.

The government's answer has been to add yet more fiscal stimulus to the economy, pump in yet more liquidity, and drive down the value of the yen against the currencies of its major trading rivals. That's particularly important for Japanese capitalism, which relies on exports and investment for any marginal improvement in growth. As a result, the yen depreciated by as much as 20 percent against the US dollar from its peak.

This was necessary, in the minds of the Japanese, because the yen had been left behind in a "race to the bottom" for the major currencies since the Great Recession began. At one point, the yen had appreciated in real terms (taking into account relative inflation rates) against the currencies of its trading rivals by 30–40 percent since the Great Recession started. Over the same period, the British pound sterling had dropped 25 percent and the euro by 10–15 percent. Even the currencies of faster-growing emerging capitalist economies had not moved up.

Did these Japanese measures work? Keynesian guru Paul Krugman was doubtful.[2] For him, Japan's problem is a monetary one, namely, that the country is in a classic Keynesian liquidity trap where near-zero interest rates do not restore investment or spending because debt deflation is in operation. What's needed is a huge fiscal stimulus.[3] So the answer is more fiscal spending and monetization to increase inflation deliberately. Indeed, that's what the US government should be doing as well.[4]

Interestingly, another Keynesian who would usually agree with Krugman seems to reject this explanation of Japan's stagnation and the Krugman/Adair solution. Martin Wolf, a *Financial Times* columnist, pointed out that Japan has had plenty of "fiscal stimulus" over the years and it has done little to get the economy back on track.[5] Monetary stimulus and yen devaluation to cause inflation won't work either because the problem is not deflation, as Krugman argues.[6] The problem, according to Wolf, is that Japanese industry is profitable but unwilling to invest: "So what is that underlying cause? 'Excess private savings' is the answer or, more precisely, a huge structural excess of corporate gross retained earnings over investment."[7]

There is some truth in Wolf's view. Over the past two decades, Japanese industry has not been investing nearly as much of its rising cash flow back into the real economy. So the economy has struggled.

Japan's capitalist sector, just as in other major capitalist economies, is not stepping up to the plate and investing in plant, equipment, and employment to restore economic growth. But the explanation for this also lies in the profitability of the Japanese corporate sector. From 2002, Japan's rate of profit rose 60 percent (Figure 10.2, solid black line, left scale) while investment stayed pretty flat (dotted black line, right scale). In the Great Recession, profitability plunged and along with it, investment. Profitability has now recovered, but it remains below the 2007 peak, so investment remains very much in the doldrums.

Figure 10.2

Japan Net Return on Capital and Gross Investment (Indexed 2010=100), 1999–2015

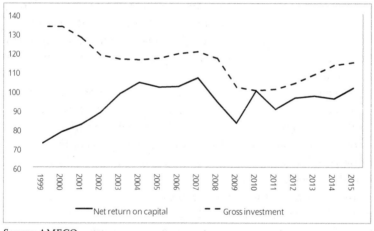

Source: AMECO

Wolf calls for these "excess savings" (i.e., profits) to be taken away from the corporate "oligopolies" and used for the greater good.[8] How is this to be done? He proposes to raise corporate taxes, not cut them, and shift profits into dividends for shareholders to spend and raise wages. But these proposals would be anathema to the capitalist sector and will fall on deaf ears. They would not work because profitability would fall again.

Instead, the Japanese government continues to look to devalue its currency and inject inflation into the economy as a way of restoring growth. This is very much in the tradition of the "beggar-thy-neighbor" policies of the 1930s, as it is of any Keynesian alternative. The aim is to steal back world market share by making Japanese exports cheaper.

Historically, devaluation does not work for long because it leads to other governments adopting the same policy in a race to the bottom. There is little evidence that a weaker currency will help create better growth. Look at the record since the Great Recession. The biggest depreciation in currency value since 2007 has been with the pound and the euro, but average real GDP growth has been tiny while the US dollar has appreciated, and yet the US economy has recorded a much better growth rate in the period.

Keynesian Noah Smith asked what caused Japan's growth speed-up from 2000 to 2007. There is a good reason he wants to know: the economic performance of Japan is a mystery to him and does not seem to fit any Keynesian explanations. You see, as Smith points out, during that period, Japan remained in a Keynesian liquidity trap with interest rates near zero, while prices were deflating. According to Keynesian theory, the nation should have been in another decade of depression. But it wasn't, really.

Instead, Japan picked up its growth rate in the 2000s compared to the lost decade of the 1990s. Indeed, it partially reversed the decline in GDP per capita relative to the United States that it experienced in the 1990s. Smith went through the possible explanations of this relative recovery which took place during the Koizumi era, again hardly fitting in with Keynesian policies.

The improvement was only relative. Real GDP growth averaged 4.6 percent between 1981 and 1990, the so-called bubble years. The bubble was followed by a crash in the 1990s and average growth dropped to just 0.7 percent a year between 1993 and 1999 (excluding the slump years of 1991 and 1992). Then after the slump years of 1998 and 1999, annual average growth improved to 1.5 percent between 2000 and 2007. This was double the rate of the 1990s, although still way below the bubble years. In the last seven years of the Long Depression, Japan's economy has risen by just 0.2 percent a year.

Smith notes that Japan continued to be in a Keynesian-style liquidity trap and in deflation throughout the 2000s. Also, the relative recovery cannot be explained by Keynesian-style fiscal stimulus, because government spending fell in absolute terms and as a percentage of GDP, and budget deficits as a share of GDP also narrowed. In the 1990s, in contrast, there was considerable extra government spending and rising budget deficits, but these Keynesian prescriptions failed to revive the Japanese economy. Then in the 2000s, there was fiscal austerity under Koizumi and yet economic growth was faster! Of course, part of this paradox is that poor growth in the 1990s meant the ratio of government spending and deficits to GDP rose, but in absolute terms, government spending and deficits rose—to little effect, it seems.

The contribution from net exports did not seem to contribute much either in the 2000s. But Smith notes that bank lending, which had collapsed in the 1990s when banks were deleveraging their debts from the bubble years, rose in the 2000s. But Smith is at a loss to explain this.[9]

If growth and investment picked up in the 2000s, then the main reason must be a recovery in profitability. That's exactly what the data show. Japan's rate of profit was held up during the 1980s by a massive credit and property boom, but that could not last. After the credit bubble burst in 1989, the average rate of profit in the Japanese economy fell nearly 20 percent during the 1990s. But from 1998 to 2007, it rose nearly 30 percent.

The organic composition of capital (the value of plant, equipment, and raw materials relative to the cost of labor employed) fell for the first time since World War II, while the rate of exploitation of the labor force rose nearly 25 percent. In other words, Japanese companies devalued old assets, reduced the labor force, and boosted profits per unit of labor. This was the classic way out for capitalist production—at the expense of labor (see Figure 10.3).

Japanese capital also devalued and deleveraged much of the debt that it had built up during the bubble decade of the 1980s, when non-financial corporate debt rose nearly 25 percent as a share of GDP and household debt (financial and property) jumped by 37 percent. During the 1990s, the corporate sector deleveraged by 15 percent, laying the basis for profitability to recover. Japanese corporations had much higher debt levels (relative to GDP) compared with German, British, and US corporations. But they began deleveraging that debt during the 1990s, with the bulk of that done by 2002. The opposite was happening in the other countries.

Average real GDP growth came back (relatively) because Japanese capital had written off old capital (tangible and fictitious) enough, and banks were in better shape to lend again—at the expense of a lost decade of income and jobs for its population in the 1990s, culminating in the dire deflationary slump of 1998. The global slump of 2008–9 hit Japan hard, because much of its profitability and growth depend on world markets. This is the mystery explained.

Figure 10.3
Japan Change in Components of Rate of Profit (%), 1988–2007

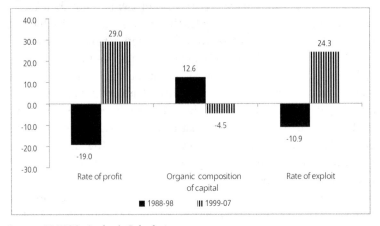

Source: AMECO, Author's Calculations

Japan's economic growth has been pretty much nonexistent since the trough of the Great Recession, and the current right-wing government is now throwing the kitchen sink of Keynesian policies at the problem.

Not only does Japanese capital still have large debts and lower profitability, it also has a declining and aging population. The ability to generate more value and surplus value from the workforce is limited by a contraction in labor supply. That means capital must exploit the workforce even more intensively or invest more in costly new technology to try and raise relative surplus value to boost profitability.

Japan is also suffering from the lack of expansion of its workforce. In the short term, that makes GDP per capita growth in Japan look better than GDP growth, so US GDP per capita growth in recent years is little better than it is in Japan (see Figure 10.4). Longer term, this is bad news for Japan, as its debt burden will mount and its ratio of working population to dependents will decline. This is a growth and debt time bomb.

The move to crisis may be slow because Japan has huge reserves of foreign exchange and foreign assets built up over decades, so it has lots of funds to fall back on. The nation's net international investment position (foreign assets to liabilities) is 56 percent in the positive, whereas the United States is 19 percent in the negative. Also, its debt is mostly owned by its own citizens (only 7 percent by foreigners), while US government debt is 40 percent owned by foreigners. However, the US dollar is still the world's reserve currency, giving the United States considerable leeway in funding its deficits and debt. Japan's banks and government are intertwined. In the 1990s, the banks were bailed out by government; currently the banks are bailing out the government. Next time, they both go down together.

Figure 10.4
Average Annual Per Capita Real GDP Growth, 1989–2014

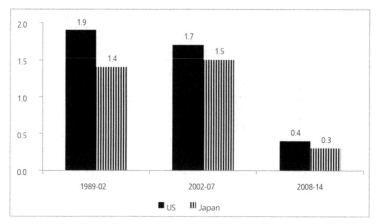

Source: OECD

Keynesian policies in the 1990s did not work for Japan, and they won't work in this decade either. The 2010s will be another lost decade. Fiscal austerity has not worked; indeed, it has made the situation worse. But neither has fiscal stimulus where it has been applied, as in Japan. Keynesians say it has not been applied enough and needs to be combined with a depreciation of the currency and even a boost to inflation with monetary injections. In other words, try all three tools of capitalist economic policy at once. That is what Japan has tried. But the depression continues.

Chapter 11
The Rest Cannot Escape

Emerging markets will not save the world if the West slides back into recession. In an interconnected global economy, decoupling is a beguiling myth.

—DK Matai, August 23, 2011[1]

The Long Depression has engulfed every corner of the world, including the emerging markets. They emerged as new centers of capital accumulation during the neoliberal boom and as part of the further globalization of capital. For that reason, these emerging economies are not immune to the dynamics of the world system and its current Long Depression.

One of the factors that enabled the world economy to expand since the 1970s was the globalization of trade and investment. Trade expanded and so did capital flows. As profitability fell in the advanced capitalist economies, companies moved to plants overseas and used the cheap, plentiful supply of labor in Asia and Latin America. China, India, and some smaller Asian economies in particular were huge new sources for the expansion of value and surplus value (see Figure 11.1).[2]

There was a divergence between the G7 rate of profit and the world rate of profit after the early 1990s. This indicates that non-G7 economies have played an increasing role in sustaining the rate of profit. Profitability has peaked in the major emerging economies, and world capitalism is now in a down phase for profitability. But the history of the past thirty years suggests that emerging economies will retain their differential premium for some time.

China and other emerging economies have not yet reached the point where the working population is no longer rising and the expansion of absolute surplus value is restricted—the so-called Lewis turning point.[3] But China is not far away. In the meantime, the nation is pushing ahead with a sweeping plan to move 250 million rural

185

residents into newly constructed towns and cities over the next several years—a massive expansion of labor power into production. The broad trend began decades ago. In the early 1980s, about 80 percent of Chinese lived in the countryside, but only 47 percent do today, plus an additional 17 percent that works in cities but are classified as rural.

Figure 11.1
Investment to GDP Ratios in Advanced and Emerging Capitalist Economis (%), 1980–2012

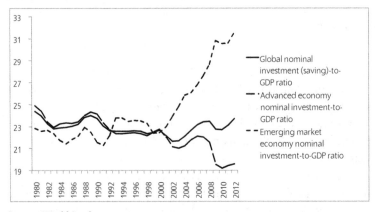

Source: World Bank

The wider global story is revealed by the rise in the industrial workforce in emerging economies and the fall in advanced economies.[4] China's population is expected to go into decline, whereas India's is expected to grow strongly for another fifty years. Indonesia's populations are projected to grow steadily. Nigeria's population is expected to explode eightfold this century.

From BRICS to Fragile Five

Even if there is still latent potential in emerging economies for capital to expand, the effects of the global depression are seriously affecting emerging economies. These economies experienced a boost to growth (and inflation) from the transfer of cheap credit from the advanced economies to their markets since the Great Recession ended in mid-2009.

The expansion there is now being revealed as fictitious, too, as growth slows in the large emerging economies and as central banks start to reduce injections of credit into the financial sector globally.

The World Bank has recently published an estimate of the impact of quantitative easing.[5] It found that 60 percent of the increase in private capital flows from advanced capitalist economies to emerging ones in the recent recovery was due to central bank credit injections, not improved corporate earnings. The World Bank data also show that the flow of foreign direct investment globally relative to investment domestically has not recovered (see Figure 11.2)—and we know that investment domestically in most major economies remains in a slump.

Figure 11.2

Global Foreign Direct Investment as a Share of Gross Fixed Capital Formation (%), 1990–2012

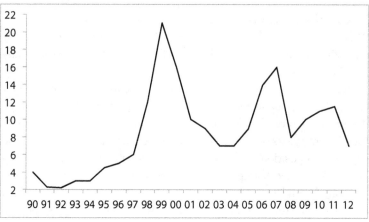

Source: World Bank

Stock markets may have been booming, but tangible investment in the productive sectors of capitalism has not. The United Nations Commission on Trade and Development (UNCTAD) revealed that the problem is due to a failure in the recovery of returns on corporate investment globally.[6] Profitability on investment in productive sectors of the world in 2011 was some 20 percent below where it was before the global financial crash (2007) and the Great Recession for the advanced capitalist economies—and 15 percent down for the world. It will still be below precrisis levels in most of the world.

As a result, the BRICS (Brazil, Russia, India, China, and South Africa, named by former Goldman Sachs chief economics Jim O'Neill) were supposed to be the saviors of global capitalist growth but have now turned into the "fragile five" (India, Brazil, Indonesia, Turkey, and South Africa). This is a heterogeneous group, as many of these struggling emerging economies depend on selling not so much manufacturing goods or services but agricultural or metals commodities. This is particularly the case for Argentina, Brazil, South Africa, and Chile.

As credit has been reeled back globally, investment in infrastructure is dropping. The demand for raw materials in construction—copper, iron ore, steel, coal, and so on—is also waning relatively. The result is a loss of demand for the exports of Australia, Chile, Brazil, and others. The Great Recession and the subsequent weak recovery have led to a significant fall in trade and investment flows to the emerging economies. Their growth rates have also begun to fall away. The crisis is worldwide.

Brazil: The Carnival Is Over

We can look at the Brazilian economy from a Marxist viewpoint by analyzing the movement in the rate of profit for the whole economy (see Figure 11.3).

Between 1963 and 2008, the rate of profit declined secularly by about 19 percent. But this secular fall was really the product of the very large decline in the rate of profit from 1963 to the early 1980s and 1990s. Over these twenty years or so, the rate of profit fell over 30 percent while the organic composition rose 23 percent and the rate of exploitation fell 17 percent—a classic example of Marx's law of profitability at work.

From the mid-1990s, Brazil's ruling elite adopted neoliberal policies designed to restore the rate of profit. Between 1993 and 2004, the rate of profit rose 35 percent. The organic composition of capital rose 20 percent as foreign investment flooded into industry (autos, chemicals, and petroleum), but the rate of exploitation rose even more, up 55 percent, as more Brazilians entered the industrial and agro processing labor force with intensive capitalist production methods, while wages were held down.

Brazil became a major agricultural producer and exporter to the world market. Leading exports include soybeans and soy products, beef, poultry, sugar, ethanol, coffee, orange juice, and tobacco. Brazil's agrifood sector now accounts for about 28 percent of the country's GDP. It is now the world's third largest agricultural exporter (in value terms), after the United States and the European Union. Rapid export growth was accompanied by changes in the composition of agricultural exports away from tropical products to processed products—up the value-added scale. Processed products now account for about three-fifths of agricultural exports.

Figure 11.3
Brazil Rate of Profit on Capital (%), 1953–2010

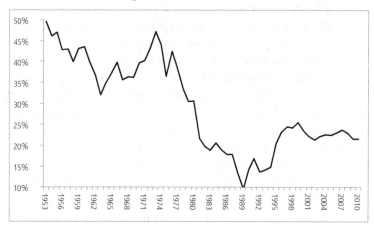

Source: E Maito

Like some other emerging economies, Brazil benefited from some favorable external factors that supported the neoliberal policies at home. Food commodities prices rose. In a way, it was like the discovery of North Sea oil that helped Britain's Thatcher government in the 1980s. The income windfall to Latin America from persistently high commodities prices over the past decade has been unprecedented. It averaged 15 percent of domestic income on an annual basis and close to 90 percent on a cumulative basis.[7] A combination of rising commodities prices driven by Chinese demand, productivity gains as the rate of exploitation rose, and the expansion of employment from the rural areas boosted profitability and growth for a decade. After the 2002 crisis, GDP growth averaged above 4 percent a year until 2010. This led to significant improvements in living standards and life in general.

But the inequalities of capitalist development remained embedded in the system. Inequality of income and wealth in Brazil remains at extreme levels, exceeded only by post-apartheid South Africa—and, when measured by a Gini coefficient per capita, Mexico.

Despite the boom of the last decade, average household net-adjusted disposable income in Brazil is still way lower than the OECD average of $23,047 a year—and that's the *average*. Over 16 million people are still living in what is deemed extreme poverty, with monthly incomes of below 70 reais (about US$33). Some 80 percent of men are in paid work, compared with 56 percent of women, and 12 percent of employees work very long hours, higher than the OECD average of 9 percent, with 15 percent of men working very long hours compared with 9 percent of women. Around 7.9 percent of people reported falling victim to assault over the previous twelve months, nearly twice the OECD average of 4.0 percent. Brazil's homicide rate is 21.0 per 100,000 people, almost ten times the OECD average of 2.2, and one of the highest in the world. Violence is concentrated among young people and over the past fifteen years, violence—including armed violence—has become a major social problem in the country. Brazil's regional disparities remain very high: average GDP varies from just 46 percent of the national average in the northeast region to 34 percent above the average in the southeast.

Under the government of former president Luiz Inácio Lula da Silva and during the commodities boom, there were some important gains for the working class: a social protection system, increasing credit at low interest rates for workers, and universal health care and education. The Bolsa Família, or family allowance program, is the most visible face of these policies. Between 2004 and 2011, the number of families benefiting from income transfers more than doubled, from 6.5 million to 13.3 million, representing nearly one-quarter of the population. In the more isolated regions, payments under this program have become the principal engine of the local economy. Another pillar of government policy, adopted through negotiations with the unions, was to raise the minimum wage and associated pension. Wages went up by 211 percent in nominal terms between 2002 and 2012, for a real inflation-discounted increase of 66 percent. The unemployment rate plunged from 12.3 percent to 6.7 percent and the labor force expanded at a 1.6 percent yearly rate.

However, during this boom, Marx's law of profitability was still at work. From 2004, the rate of profit began to fall (down 8 percent in 2008 and more since), as wages shot up and the rate of exploitation dropped 25 percent. Only the continued boom in commodities prices kept growth going.

When the global slump came in 2008–9, the emerging capitalist economies could not avoid the consequences. In the case of Brazil, it seemed that rising commodities prices plus a deliberate policy by the government to increase state-financed investment had enabled the nation to avoid the worst of the slump compared with others.

But prices for Brazil's key agricultural exports began to falter from 2011 onward. Global commodity prices have fallen back sharply and profitability began to fall further. The export profitability is some 20 percent below its best years before 2004.

Brazil's GDP growth has consequently slowed since 2011. There has been a sharp fall in manufacturing investment and exports since 2013. Although public investment increased by 0.4 percent points to 5.4 percent of GDP, it has not been enough to compensate for the fall in the ratio of private investment to GDP from 14.3 percent to 12.7 percent. Industry has not returned to its precrisis production level.

The government has tried to get private sector investment going through tax cuts and incentives for the corporate sector, but at the cost of running up a deficit on its budget. Interest costs on the public debt have been mounting, forcing the government to cut subsidies to transport, housing, and education on which the majority rely. The last straw was spending huge amounts on football and the Olympic Games (partly to boost capitalist sector profits) at the expense of basic public services.

Subsequent unrest has prompted the government to make concessions, but it has no intention of reversing its neoliberal policies. Finance Minister Guido Mantega made that clear when he said that he will "raise taxes or cut public spending to compensate for any future subsidies it offers to support struggling sectors." Profitability in the capitalist sector will not recover without further hits to living standards, and economic growth will remain low as long as the world economic recovery remains weak and China slows down. The carnival is over.

South Africa: Mandela's Legacy

The death of Nelson Mandela in 2013 was a reminder of the great victory that the black masses of South Africa achieved over the vicious, cruel, and regressive apartheid system first encouraged by British imperialism and then adopted by a reactionary and racist white South African ruling class to preserve the privileges of a tiny minority.

Mandela spent twenty-seven years as a political prisoner, and the people he represented fought a long, hard battle to overthrow a grotesque regime, backed by the major imperialist powers, including the United States, for decades.

But the end of apartheid in the 1990s was also attributable to a change of attitude by the white ruling class in South Africa and the ruling classes of the major capitalist states. There was a hard-headed decision to no longer consider Mandela a terrorist and recognize that a black president was inevitable and even necessary.

At the time, South Africa's capitalist economy was on its knees. That was not just because of global boycotting of its exports but because the productivity of the black labor in the mines and factories had dropped away. The quality of investment in industry and availability of investment from abroad had fallen sharply. This was expressed in the profitability of capital reaching a postwar low in the global recession of the early 1980s (see Figure 11.4). Unlike other capitalist economies, apartheid South Africa could find no way of turning that around through the further exploitation of the black labor force.

Figure 11.4
South Africa Rate of Profit on Capital (%), 1963–2008

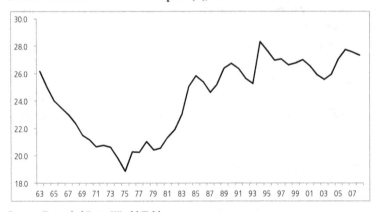

Source: Extended Penn World Tables

The ruling class had to change strategy. The white leadership under F. W. de Klerk reversed decades of previous policy, opted to release Mandela, and go for black majority government that could restore labor discipline and revive profitability. For his deserts, de Klerk shared the Nobel Peace Prize with Mandela, who was elected president at the age of seventy-six! Profitability did rise dramatically under the first Mandela administration as foreign investment poured in and the rate of exploitation of the workforce rocketed (see Figure 11.5).

Figure 11.5
South Africa Rate of Exploitation or Surplus Value (Ratio to Wages)

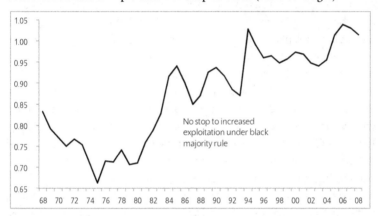

Source: Extended Penn World Tables

The rise in profitability tapered off in the early 2000s as the organic composition of capital rose sharply. South African industry is now in difficulty; unemployment and crime remain at global highs, and economic growth is foundering.

South Africa under Mandela and later Thabo Mbeki saw some improvement in the truly awful living situation of the black majority, in sanitation, housing, electricity, education, health, and so on, ending the cruel and arbitrary control of movement and the inequality of the apartheid regime. But South Africa still has the highest inequality of income and wealth in the world and inequality has never been higher as black capitalists have joined white ones in the economy. Despite its professed socialist ideology, the African National Congress (ANC) never went toward replacing the capitalist mode of production with common ownership, not even of the mines or resource industries.[8]

The tiny, wealthy white minority have remained pretty much unaffected by the ending of apartheid.[9] Now the rich whites are joined by rich blacks who dominate businesses and exert overwhelming influence over the black leadership of the ruling ANC. The party expresses the sharp divisions between the majority of working-class blacks and the small black ruling class that has developed. These fissures erupt every so often, as yet without a decisive break. Mandela's legacy was the end of apartheid; the struggle for equality and a better life continues.

Turkey: Can't See the Trees for the Woods

An explosion of protests in Turkey began in 2013 when people tried to stop the pulling down of trees in Taksim Gezi Park as part of a government plan to replace the park with yet another shopping center that would include yet another mosque and the demolition of the secular Atatürk Cultural Center and its replacement with an Ottoman-style military barracks. This was no accident of history, because the loss of green spaces to development has been increasingly objected to by wide varieties of Turks—working class and middle class. According to the OECD, 33 percent of Turks feel they lack access to green spaces, much more than the 12 percent average of OECD European countries, and the highest level of dissatisfaction in the region.

Turkish capitalism has been on the move in the past decade and, as far as the ruling Justice and Development (AK) Party and domestic and foreign capital are concerned, nothing must stand in its way (including trees). Turkey wants to move up the ladder of the rich club of the OECD and is still vying to join the EU by the end of decade. At the same time, the government is autocratically trying to impose an Islamic-style state superstructure onto this capitalist expansion, with strict rules on alcohol, religious observance, dress, and the subjugation of women, Iran-style.

Up to the protests, the AK Party had been riding high, winning election after election, enabling it to cut the former Atatürk secular military down to size and disperse the secular opposition of corrupt middle-class parties. The AK was backed in this by the huge urban poor of the cities, where it had carefully built a base over a decade or longer. Of course, on obtaining unchallenged power, it had become the tool of big business and foreign capital (despite the occasional rift over policy). The government increasingly saw itself as a regional power able and willing to intervene in the various clashes of the region: Iran, Palestine, and Syria.

On the surface, it would appear that Turkish capital is moving on and up without much problem. It is true that economic growth has accelerated in recent years while foreign investment has flooded in to exploit a labor force coming into the urban areas from the impoverished countryside—a classic emerging capitalist development. This apparent economic success was founded on the shaky legs of a weak capitalism and was also weighed down by corruption, religious backwardness, and scant regard for human rights and laws. Inequality of income is measured by a Gini coefficient of around 40, according to the IMF, making it higher than the United States, the most unequal of the advanced capitalist economies and the highest in emerging Europe, apart from Russia.

It's no surprise that Turkey was ranked 154th in Reporters Without Borders' Press Freedom Index in 2014.[10] Not only is the country "currently the world's biggest prison for journalists," media bosses fire journalists because of pressure from the government. Only 48 percent of the working-age population aged fifteen to sixty-four has a paid job, a figure much lower than the OECD employment average of 66 percent and the lowest rate in the OECD. People in Turkey work 1,877 hours a year, more than the OECD average of 1,776 hours. In Turkey, however, 46 percent of employees work very long hours, by far the highest rate in the OECD, where the average is 9 percent.

Around 67 percent of people say they are satisfied with their current housing situation, much less than the OECD average of 87 percent and the lowest level among OECD countries. In Turkey, the average home contains 0.9 room per person, less than the OECD average of 1.6 rooms per person. In terms of basic facilities, 87.3 percent of people in Turkey live in dwellings with private access to an indoor flushing toilet, less than the OECD average of 97.8 percent and the lowest rate across OECD countries.

The best-performing school systems manage to provide high-quality education to all students. In Turkey, the average difference in results between the 20 percent with the highest socioeconomic background and the 20 percent with the lowest socioeconomic background is 106 points, higher than the OECD average of 99 points. This suggests the school system in Turkey mainly provides higher quality education for the better-off.

Total health spending accounts for 6.1 percent of GDP in Turkey, more than three points below the average of 9.5 percent across OECD countries. At $913 in 2008, Turkey's level of health spending per person is the lowest in the OECD, where the average is of $3,268. In Turkey, only 61 percent of people say they are satisfied with water quality. This figure is the lowest in the OECD, where the average satisfaction level is 84 percent, and suggests Turkey still faces difficulties in providing good-quality water to its inhabitants.

The Great Recession hit Turkish capitalism just as hard as it did elsewhere. The answer of the government (against IMF advice) was to let loose a credit boom to fuel domestic demand. This pushed the inflation rate to double digits and widened the current accounts deficit to 10 percent of GDP (the second largest in the world in dollar terms) in 2011, exposing Turkey to the risks of capital flow reversal at a time of continued global uncertainty. External financing needs are around 25 percent of GDP, so Turkish banks rely on short-term foreign borrowing. The nation has jumped from an agricultural to a services economy within two decades, and the recession weakened the manufacturing base. Conglomerates like Eczacıbaşı and Zorlu have built huge shopping malls in the past few years rather than investing in their core businesses.

Between 2003 and 2011, real GDP growth averaged 5.3 percent a year, but the unemployment rate remained in double digits, thus creating a reserve army of labor to exploit. The deficit on trade and income with other countries was over 5 percent of GDP on average. These were the good years for Turkish capitalism. Economic growth is expected to slow to less than 4 percent a year for the rest of the 2010s, at best, while the external deficit will widen to 7.5 percent of GDP. The boom of the last decade was partly based on real estate, credit, and services and construction and less on manufacturing, exports, and investment.

This is because the profitability of Turkish capital has declined as the expansion of the labor force began to slow. The decline was visible during the 1990s (see Figure 11.6). It was no accident that the AK Party won a landslide victory with the backing of big business in the 2002 elections, just one year after its foundation. Under the AK Party, profitability made a dramatic recovery (based partly on unproductive investment). The Great Recession brought another reversal, and this time the recovery in profitability has faltered. Although profitability recovered to the previous peak by early 2010, since then it has taken a tumble and is still below the peak before the Great Recession.

Figure 11.6

Turkey Rate of Profit on Capital (%), 1950–2010

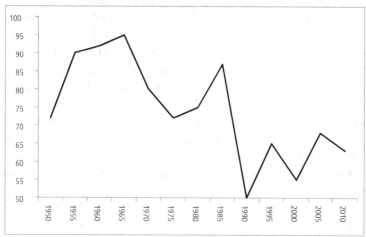

Source: Extended Penn World Tables

Since 2013, the economy has slowed, driven by weakening domestic demand. The national savings rate has fallen dramatically over the past fifteen years, from 25 percent of GDP in the late 1990s to less than 15 percent now. This decline has been larger than in any G20 country over this period and stands in stark contrast to the experience in other emerging economies. Turkey is forced into making its labor force competitive to attract more FDI flows into the tradables sector. At around 2.0 percent of GDP, foreign direct investment inflows are still below the G20 average, with most flows tilted toward unproductive sectors, such as banking and real estate.

Turkey remains prone to boom-bust cycles driven by foreign capital flows. The health of global imperialism is still the overriding factor in Turkey's own growth.

India's Modinomics

In April–May 2014, India conducted the biggest democratic election in human history, if we mean "democracy" to mean a vote for a parliament. Around 814 million Indians were eligible to vote. The Bharatiya Janata Party (BJP), led by Narendra Modi, won. The BJP has ruled before, from 1998 to 2004, but proved to be an unreliable party for Indian capital, riddled as it is with former members of what is basically a Hindu religious fascist party, the Rashtriya Swayamsevak Sangh (RSS), an organization modeled on Mussolini's Black Brigades.

Modi is a longtime member of the RSS who has moved seamlessly into the BJP. He claims, of course, that he has moved on and will now be doing the bidding of capital as a whole and will no longer push his former Hindu communalism. But Modi had been chief minister in Gujarat state since 2001, where pogroms of Muslims have taken place without a blink from the government. But that does not matter to India's capitalist class, as long as it does not get out of hand. For them, Modi is leading a "business-friendly" government as he proved in Gujarat, where multinational companies were welcomed with cheap land deals, reduced taxes, and deregulated environmental laws. This is what he likes to call Modinomics.

The problems for Indian capitalism are mounting. After achieving spectacular growth averaging above 9 percent over the past decade, India has started to slow in the last few years.

The slump in infrastructure and corporate investment has been the single biggest contributor to India's recent growth slowdown. India's investment growth, averaging above 12 percent during the last decade, fell toward zero in the last two years (see Figure 11.7).

Mainstream Indian economists blame high interest rates and "too rigid" labor rights. The IMF in turn blames "heightened uncertainty regarding the future course of broader economic policies and deteriorating business confidence."[11] The IMF wants the Indian government to raise energy prices to make the state-owned companies profitable and stop labor unions from preserving wages and employment so the young unemployed can get work (at lower wages, of course).

Two-thirds of Indian workers are employed in small businesses with fewer than ten workers, where labor rights are ignored—indeed, most are paid on a casual basis and in cash rupees, the so-called informal sector that avoids taxes and regulations. India has the largest informal sector among the main emerging economies.

But small businesses are not very productive. Indeed, India has the lowest productivity levels in Asia. Productivity would rise if generally underemployed peasants could move to the cities and get manufacturing jobs. This is how China transformed its workforce, of course to be exploited more by capital but also to raise productivity and wages.

China did this through state planning of labor migration and building up infrastructure. India's rate of urbanization is way behind that of China. So Indian and foreign capital are still not fully exploiting the huge reserves of mainly youthful labor for profit.

Figure 11.7

India Investment Growth (%), 1997–2013

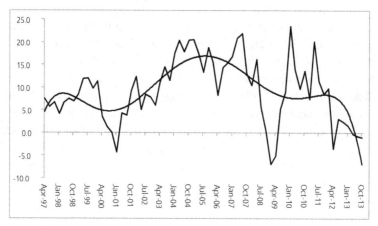

Source: Extended Penn World Tables

As a result, employment growth is pathetically slow. An estimated 10–12 million young Indian people are entering the workforce each year, but many cannot find jobs because they lack the right skills or there are no jobs. The Congress Party says it will find jobs for low-caste rural people by introducing "affirmative action" in companies. This would do little except enrage large and small capitalists alike. At the same time, it goes along with the IMF for "a more flexible labor policy."

There is the issue of basic resources for India's 1.2 billion people. Mechanically pumped groundwater now provides 85 percent of drinking water and is the main water source for all uses. North India's groundwater is declining at one of the fastest rates in the world, and many areas may have already passed "peak water" (that is, being sustainably managed). The World Bank predicted that a majority of India's underground water resources will reach a critical state within twenty years.

The big demand from Indian capital is to cut back the size of the state. Bureaucratic and inefficient as it is, the nation's central and state government, as well as state enterprises set up in the early days of independence, have provided some solidity to the economy. But the multinationals and large Indian capitalists want this to go. Central and state government run up significant annual budget deficits because they subsidize food and fuel for millions of poorer Indians. Those deficits are funded by borrowing, and the cost of that borrowing has steadily eaten into the available revenue from taxes, leaving little for education, health, or transport.

Government tax revenues are low because Indian companies pay little tax and rich individuals pay even less. Inequality of income in India is not as high as in China, Brazil, or South Africa, but it is probably higher than the official Gini index because of huge hidden income among the rich, and it has been rising. According to the OECD, income inequality has doubled in India since the early 1990s.[12] The richest 10 percent of Indians earn more than twelve times as much as the poorest 10 percent, compared with roughly six times in 1990.

The answer for Indian capital, endorsed by Modi, is privatization, cuts in food and fuel subsidies, and a new sales tax, a tax that is the most regressive way to get revenue because it hits the poor the most. The aim here, as it always is with neoliberal economic policy, is to raise the labor exploitation rate so that profitability of capital is boosted and thus provide an incentive to invest, something Indian capital is refusing to do right now.

Figure 11.8
India Rate of Profit on Capital (%), 1980–2008

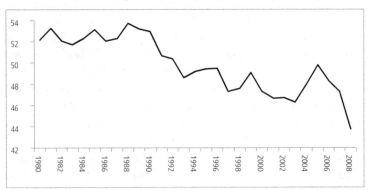

Source: Extended Penn World Tables

Indian companies are increasingly heavily in debt: corporate debt to GDP is one of the highest in Asia. The cost of servicing that debt has risen sharply as the Reserve Bank of India has been hiking interest rates to try to control the highest inflation in Asia.

Indian capital's profitability had been falling steadily (if from a high "emerging market" level) even before the global economic slump started (see Figure 11.8). It has fallen further and is some 20 percent below the levels of the 1980s. The double-digit growth boom years of the early 2000s, when all the talk was about India's software outsourcing industry and new auto companies, seem unlikely to return without drastic reductions in the share of value going to labor. Modinomics will not "solve" Indian capitalism's failure to deliver sufficient growth and better profitability.

The Transitional Economies of Eastern Europe

It has been about 25 years since the so-called transition economies of Europe broke from the Soviet bloc. By "transition," I mean those economies within the Soviet bloc that were transformed from mainly state-owned centrally planned economies into fully fledged capitalist economies with privately owned companies.

It would be wrong to describe Europe's transitional economies in one breath, as the 180 million people who live in these countries face different issues and problems. The richest and fastest growing have been the so-called Visegrád Group of Poland, the Czech Republic, Hungary, and Slovakia. They are close to the advanced capitalist economies of Western Europe, both geographically and economically. Western Europe, particularly Germany, provides them with rich markets for exporting to and the potential for inward foreign investment as German and other companies relocate and outsource their business to take advantage of cheap and skilled labor, weak regulation, low taxes, and little environmental controls.

Hourly compensation for workers in the Visegrád and the Baltic states was under 10 percent of West German wages when the Soviet bloc fell. Even in 2011, it is still no more than 25 percent of average compensation in Germany.[13]

Then there is a swath of small countries in southeastern Europe and the Balkans, some ten countries in total, with not more than 50 million people. These small economies, particularly once the Yugoslav federation fell apart, face an uphill struggle to become richer because they depend so much on foreign investment, which exploits rather than enriches labor. They increasingly have become satellites of Germany, who pushed for the break-up of Yugoslavia the most.

Then there are the tiny Baltic states sandwiched between Scandinavia, Poland, Germany, and Russia and historically at the mercy of these larger powers. But it does not take much funding or investment to sustain such small populations. So Sweden plays a big role in their banking systems, and the Baltics have found it easier to integrate with Europe to the west without provoking Russian ire.

Finally and bottom of the list are the border states to Russia (Ukraine, Belarus, and Moldova). These are populous but poor, still very beholden to the whims and investment of Russia, and contain sizeable Russian minorities.

So after twenty-five years of capitalism in the transition economies, have the majority of these 180 million people gained? If we measure prosperity by per capita GDP, capitalism has not been a great success. Back in 1990, per capita GDP in Central, Eastern, and southeastern Europe was about 35 percent that of Germany. In 2011, it was 38 percent. That is after a huge collapse when the Soviet bloc fell, down to 25 percent of German per capita GDP in 1993. Things improved after that terrible slump and at an accelerating pace in the 2000s. But then came the global financial collapse and the Great Recession of capitalism and the credit and property bubbles in many transitional economies burst and they went backward.[14]

Of course, convergence toward the so-called heaven of Western Europe has not even happened among all states. The Visegráds have done by far the best, driven by their advantages exporting into the Eurozone. The share of exports to GDP in the central European economies is about 80 percent. Europe is the world's trade center, accounting for almost half of global trade in goods and services. For just the goods trade, the ratio for Central and Eastern Europe rose from 44 percent of GDP in 2002 to more than 70 percent today. In Southern Europe it is less than 20 percent. Western Europe is the region's largest export market. Many of the countries in the region have become part of a supply chain that provides inputs to final producers in Western Europe. German automakers, for instance, have set up production facilities in Central Europe and shifted part of their production to that region.

As central as trade is to the relationship, financial links—mainly through banks—are more important still. The region's banking systems are tightly integrated with Western European banks in terms of ownership and financing. Foreign-owned banks (here meaning those in which a foreign entity has a stake of more than 25 percent and is the largest shareholder) account for about 35 percent of the market in Belarus, Russia, Slovenia, and Turkey, whereas in Bosnia and Herzegovina, Croatia, the Czech Republic, Estonia, Romania, and the Slovak Republic foreign banks have up to 80 percent of the market. By contrast, foreign banks on average account for less than 20 percent of the market in the euro area. Cross-border funding by foreign banks is important in many economies in the region. It exceeded 30 percent of GDP in Bulgaria, Croatia, Estonia, Hungary, Latvia, Lithuania, Montenegro, and Slovenia at the end of 2011.

These tight financial linkages portended a big impact on Central, Eastern, and southeastern Europe from shocks originating in Western Europe. That is what happened during 2008–9. Before the Lehman Brothers failure, Western European parent banks financed the rapid expansion of domestic credit, which fueled an asset price and domestic demand boom. But when the global crisis hit western Europe, those flows suddenly stopped, plunging the region into a deep recession, which began to abate only after a revival of exports to western Europe in 2010. The need to refinance large external debt keeps borrowing requirements high. Large stocks of foreign currency loans constrain exchange rate and monetary policy. Russia and Ukraine remain susceptible to declines in commodity prices. Fiscal deficits are still substantial in a number of countries, despite consolidation efforts to reduce deficits and debt. Banking systems are saddled with a large stock of nonperforming loans—a problem that did not exist prior to 2008.

Labor productivity growth was much higher in the transitional economies than in advanced Western Europe in the period up to the Great Recession—in other words, the rise in the rate of exploitation was greater. But even the Visegrád states still have a long way to go to reach Eurozone productivity levels. They are just half that of countries such as Germany and Sweden. The rest of the transitional economies have made little progress in closing the productivity gap (with the United States as benchmark). The gap between the Visegrád and the others is widening.

Within the "successful" Visegrád economies, there is also considerable divergence. Hungary has been a disaster in its ability to compete through higher productivity. Back in 1990, productivity levels were some 50 percent higher than Poland's. Now Poland's productivity is higher, while the Czech Republic and Slovakia are in a different league. Yet Hungary was the model that mainstream capitalist economists put up as the one to follow, with its "liberalization" of capital flows and markets. Now it is struggling with a huge foreign debt burden.

Again, the Visegrád economies have been able to attract direct foreign investment in new plants and operations that create more jobs. The others have had to try to borrow to make investments themselves. Debt in foreign currencies has risen more. Most of the transitional economies are increasingly just colonies of German and US imperialism. But even the Visegrád economies are beholden to foreign capital in a big way.

The southeastern transitional economies are too small to develop as capitalist success stories on their own. In most of Europe, enterprises with fewer than ten workers account for around one fifth of value added, but in the south-east it is almost one third. Such micro-enterprises have neither the skills nor the resources to "go abroad." So they must be swallowed up by the EU but without any possibility of becoming prosperous and equal with the leading Eurozone states or even the Visegrád. They will remain at the bottom of the heap.

The Baltics, although also tiny, have a better chance of convergence because they are close to the capital of Scandinavia and Germany and are not so "troublesome." But they will also struggle, as the impact of the Great Recession has shown. Indeed, depression is the rule of this decade for the southeast, the Balkans, and the Baltics. The border states (Ukraine, Belarus) are populous and have resources, but they are tied to the gangster capitalism of Russia.

There is another development that is usually neglected by mainstream economics when discussing the progress (or otherwise) of the transitional economies. That's the increased inequality of income and wealth that has been generated over the past twenty-five years since the fall of the Berlin Wall.

Emerging Europe was the most egalitarian area of all emerging economies in 1990 at a Gini coefficient of 29.4 compared with 49.7 in Latin America, 34.7 in Asia, 34.5 in the Middle East, and 47.2 in sub-Saharan Africa. However, the transition to capitalism and the privatization of state assets saw the biggest jump in the coefficient of all the emerging market areas. For this region, it was up 3.6 points, compared with 2.6 in Asia, 2.2 in the Middle East, and a fall of 1.1 points in Latin America and 3.2 in Africa. Within the region, the most equal societies in 1990 were the Baltic states, southeastern Europe, and the Balkans—the poorest transitional economies. But by 2010, Bulgaria had become the most unequal society in Eastern Europe outside Russia, followed by the Baltics. The transition to capitalism has meant a huge rise in inequality. Any gains in national income in the past twenty-five years have not been shared fairly.

None of the formerly communist economies have escaped the impact of a global capitalist crisis, because they are either too small or too integrated into world trade and capital markets. The prosperous years, supported largely by easy credit from Western Europe, came crashing to an end with the global banking collapse, triggering a sharp contraction in domestic demand in most Central and Eastern European economies. A massive slump in global trade exacerbated the crisis, battering exports. As a result, the countries in the region suffered an unprecedented economic contraction in 2008 and 2009. By the time the region started to recover in 2010, GDP had declined by as much as 25 percent in some countries, although a few, such as Albania and Poland, escaped relatively unscathed.

All three Baltic states had a rollercoaster ride through the global economic crisis. The precrisis boom was fueled by strong capital inflows from EU funds and through Scandinavian banks. In the global slump, they chose the path of strict austerity, not just to control government spending but also to put downward pressure on prices and wages with the aim of restoring competitiveness. Wage deflation was also supposed to facilitate a shift of labor and other resources from nontradable sectors like construction to tradable ones like manufacturing, farming, and forest products, allowing an export-led recovery.

Internal devaluation brought down manufacturing wages and reduced unit labor costs, which reflect changes in wages and productivity. But real GDP is still not back to precrisis peaks. Real GDP per capita is higher than before the crisis, but only partly because of substantial emigration. Unemployment remains high. Bulgaria has lost no fewer than 582,000 people over the past decade. In a country of 7.3 million inhabitants, this is a big deal. Furthermore, it has lost 1.5 million people from its population since 1985, a record in depopulation not just for the EU but by global standards. The country, which had a population of almost 9 million in 1985, now has almost the same number of inhabitants as in 1945 after World War II. The decline continues.

Poland was hit less hard by the Great Recession. It was the only EU member to dodge recession in 2009. Their economy is still eking out growth of about 2 percent, far better than in the troubled fringes of the Eurozone. Although unemployment was at 14.2 percent in 2013, a six-year high, it is much lower in large cities—the kinds of places that are drawing growing numbers of investors building back-office and outsourcing centers, as well as language schools and other businesses.

Despite the recent improvements in financial markets, growth in the region has slowed sharply this year—a spillover from the recession in the euro area. Moreover, tight trade and financial linkages keep the region at risk from renewed deterioration in the euro area.

If the euro area crisis were to intensify, Central, Eastern, and southeastern Europe would be severely affected through both trade and financial channels. Exports would suffer if euro-area growth declined rapidly: financial markets strains would intensify, parent bank funding would likely be scaled back, and capital inflows would drop—further affecting domestic demand.

Now that these economies are broadly wedded to capitalism, and many are still small nations, they are at the mercy of the booms and slumps of global capitalism, particularly profitability. Profitability is the life blood of capitalist accumulation. Without rising or high profits, capitalists will not invest, people will not be employed, and economies will not grow.

The capitalist mode of production accelerates absorption of plentiful labor supplies. Like other emerging economies, Eastern European capitalism has developed through the expansion of absolute surplus value. However, that growth is beginning to dissipate. The growth of the workforce in Eastern Europe has been the smallest of the emerging capitalist regions since 1997 (see Figure 11.9).[15]

Indeed, in some transitional economies, the workforce is shrinking fast. So these economies will need to raise profitability by raising relative surplus value, that is, the rate of exploitation through better technology and lower unit costs of production. That will be increasingly difficult.

Figure 11.9
Annual Growth in Workforce by Region (%), 1997–2007

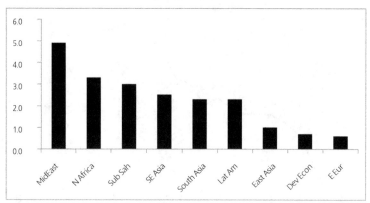

Source: UN

If we look more closely at the profitability of the transitional economies, we find that profitability grew quite fast after the transition—at least if Poland, the largest and most important of the Eastern European economies, is a guide. Poland's profitability rose from 35 percent in 1990 to 45 percent by the end of the decade (see Figure 11.10). It continued to rise up to a peak of 50 percent in 2004.[16] Since then it has stagnated, and that peak has not been surpassed. That suggests Polish investment and GDP growth will be lower from now on.

What was the impact on profitability during the Great Recession? Only Lithuania has a higher profit rate now than before the slump. Romania, Bulgaria, Slovenia, and Latvia have profit rates that are still more than 30 percent below their peaks before the crisis. The smallest decreases during the crisis were in Poland and Slovakia, and the largest was in Latvia. The biggest recovery has been in the Baltics, although only Lithuania is back to previous levels. There has been no recovery in Poland, the Czech Republic, and southeastern Europe (see Figure 11.11).[17]

Figure 11.10
Poland Rate of Profit on Capital (%), 1991–2013

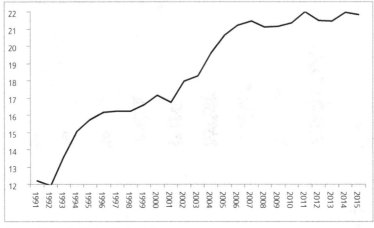

Source: Extended Penn World Tables

Figure 11.11
Change in the Rate of Profit in Transitional Economies from their Peaks in 2008 to the trough in 2009 and then to 2013 (%)

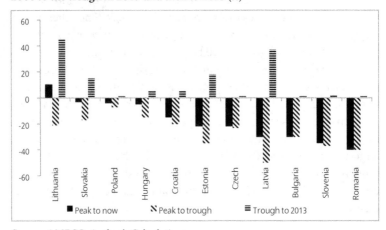

Source: AMECO, Author's Calculations

All this suggests that the transitional economies remain very vulnerable to any new economic recession in world capitalism, particularly in Western Europe.

The next question for these capitalist states is whether further integration into the European Union or the Eurozone is the best way forward. Up to now, all the leaders and business elites could think of little else but driving toward accession to the EU and even further into the single currency. That idea has cooled. So far, the Visegrád and Baltic states have joined the EU, along with southeast Europe and a few Balkan states. The small states of Estonia, Slovakia, and Slovenia have gone a step further and joined the euro area.

But joining or not joining has not been decisive in the health of these economies. Slovenia is now in a deep crisis, but Slovakia is not. Estonia suffered a sharp recession, but so did Lithuania and Latvia, as well as Hungary. The issue is not whether to be inside or outside, but the impact of the world capitalist crisis on each state.

The forces for convergence were strong in Europe during the good years, but now opposing forces are more powerful. That has made it difficult for the Visegrád to integrate further and impossible for the south. As for the border states, they are still divided between moving toward Europe to escape the grip of the Russian bear or facing its embrace.

If the euro debt crisis and the depression continues, political fragmentation of the bourgeois consensus will increase and the euro will come under the threat of breaking up if Germany decides to ditch the project. This will lead to even more divergence within the transitional economies. The likes of the Czech Republic, Slovakia, and probably Poland will become even closer satellites of German imperialism in a new alliance of Northern Europe. The Baltic states will tag along behind. Hungary, southeastern Europe, and the Balkans will descend into further depression and poverty. The border states are in the middle of a tug-of-war between the interests of Russian capital and that of German-led Europe. The experience of the turmoil and potential break-up of Ukraine shows that.

China: The Exception?

There is one great exception to the story of the emerging economies and their ability to escape from the impact of the Long Depression in the advanced economies: China.

Leading up to the National People's Congress in 2013, the procapitalist wing was loudly demanding a change of direction by the government. This was highlighted by a World Bank report on China's future,[18] published in conjunction with the Development Research Center of China's State Council. The report argued that there would be an economic crisis in China unless state-run firms were scaled back. The country needed to implement "deep reforms," selling off state-owned enterprises or making them operate more like commercial firms. According to the World Bank, China's growth would decelerate rapidly once people reached a certain income level, a phenomenon these economists call the "middle-income trap." The report said the answer was to set up "asset management firms" to sell off state industries, overhaul local government finances, and promote "competition and entrepreneurship."

The first of its six strategic measures is the privatization of the state. There is no mention of the democratization of the state, ending one-party rule, ending the suppression of individual rights and freedoms, allowing trade union rights, and so on. The World Bank authors want capitalism, but they don't care about democracy. The report admits that the capitalist mode of production still does not dominate in China—indeed, that is the problem according to the World Bank and its domestic supporters. The report recognizes that China's incredible economic success over the past three decades was based on an economy where growth was achieved through bureaucratic state planning and government control of investment. China has raised 620 million people out of internationally defined poverty. Its rate of economic growth may have been matched by emerging capitalist economies for a while back in the nineteenth century when they were taking off. But no country has ever grown so fast and been so large (with 22 percent of the world's population)—only India, with 16 percent of the world's people, is close. As John Ross has pointed out,[19] in 2010, eighty-seven countries had a higher per capita GDP than China, but eighty-three were lower. Back in the early 1980s, three-quarters of the world's people were better off than the average Chinese. Now only 31 percent are. This is an achievement without precedent.

Even if China slows down over the medium run, as the World Bank predicts, it will still add over $21 trillion to its GDP before the end of the 2010s and reach the size of the US economy by then. Even though China's consumption as a share of GDP is very low by capitalist standards (anywhere between 35 and 45 percent of GDP, depending how you measure it, compared with 65–75 percent in mature capitalist economies), it will add another $10 trillion in annual consumption by 2020, equivalent to the size of US annual consumption. These figures come from the World Bank report.

This has been achieved without the capitalist mode of production being dominant. China's "socialism with Chinese characteristics" is a weird beast. Of course, it is not socialism by any Marxist definition or by any benchmark of democratic workers control. There has been a significant expansion of privately owned companies, both foreign and domestic over the past thirty years, with the establishment of a stock market and other financial institutions. But the vast majority of employment and investment is undertaken by publicly owned companies or institutions that are under the direction and control of the Communist Party. The biggest part of China's world-beating industry is not foreign-owned multinationals, but state-owned enterprises.[20]

The major banks are state-owned, and their lending and deposit policies are directed by the government (much to the chagrin of China's central bank and other procapitalist elements). There is no free flow of foreign capital into and out of the country. Capital controls are imposed and enforced, and the currency's value is manipulated to set economic targets (much to the annoyance of the US Congress).

At the same time, the single-party state machine infiltrates all levels of industry and activity in China. According to a report by Joseph Fan and others[21], there are party organizations within every corporation that employs more than three Communist Party members. Each party organization elects a secretary, who is the lynchpin of the alternative management system of each enterprise. This extends party control beyond the state-owned enterprises, partly privatized corporations, and village or local government–owned enterprises into the private sector or "new economic organizations" as these are called. In 1999, only 3 percent of these had party cells. In 2013, the figure was nearly 13 percent.[22]

The reality is that almost all Chinese companies employing more than 100 people have an internal party cell–based control system. This is no relic of the Maoist era. It is the current structure set up specifically to maintain control of the economy.[23] This does not look like the normal relationship of state-owned companies or agencies in mature capitalist economies, where the recently nationalized banks in the United Kingdom or the briefly publicly owned General Motors in the United States are controlled at arm's length. The taxpayers fund these, but they operate purely on the profit motive. In contrast, Chinese banks have targets for lending and investment set by the government which they must meet, whatever the impact on profits.

The law of value does operate in China, mainly through foreign trade and capital inflows, as well as through domestic markets for goods, services, and funds. Insofar as it does, profitability becomes relevant to investment and growth. There have been various attempts to estimate the rate of profit in China.[24]

There were three cycles of profitability. Between 1978 and 1990, there was an upswing as capitalist production expanded through the Deng Xiaoping reforms and the opening of foreign trade. But from 1990 to the end of that decade, there was a decline, as overinvestment picked up steam and other economies, particularly in the emerging world, went through a series of crises (Mexico in 1994, Asia in 1997–98, Latin America in 1998–2001). The falling rate of profit was accompanied by slowing in the GDP growth. From about 1999 onward, there has been a rise in profitability, which also saw a significant rise in the rate of economic growth (as the world expanded at a credit-fueled pace). A more recent study by the Fung Global Institute suggests that profitability peaked in 2004.[25]

After 2007, the slump in world capitalism drove Chinese profitability down. Rising wages were not matched by increased sales abroad, so the rate of surplus value slumped (see dotted black line in Figure 11.12) while investment in fixed capital remained high. So profitability fell. Inevitably, this had a deleterious effect on GDP growth, as profits lead investment and investment leads growth, particularly in China.

China's Gini coefficient, an index of income inequality has risen from 0.30 in 1978 when the Communist Party began to open the economy to market forces to 0.46 recently, according to Sun Liping. Indeed, China's Gini coefficient has risen more than any other Asian economy in the past two decades. The rise in inequality is partly the result of the urbanization of the economy as rural peasants move to the cities. Urban wages in the sweatshops and factories are increasingly leaving peasant incomes behind (not that those urban wages are anything to write home about when workers assembling Apple iPads are paid under

$2 an hour). But it is also partly the result of the elite controlling the levers of power while allowing some Chinese billionaires to flourish.

Figure 11.12

China Rate of Profit (%) and the Rate of Surplus Value (Ratio to Wages), 1978–2010

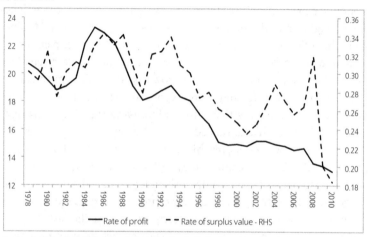

Source: China National Statistics, Author's Calculations

By the end of the 2010s, China's GDP will be higher than that of the United States, although average living standards, even in the urban and coastal belts, will be only one-third of that of Americans. As living standards rise and the population ages (by 2025, the workforce will stop increasing and the number of retirees will rise sharply), the Chinese people will want to obtain the material benefits of a modern economy. That does not mean just cars, high-tech gadgets, and fashion as mainstream economics emphasizes. It also means decent pensions, proper transport and infrastructure, health services, and education—so-called public goods.

If the capitalist path is adopted and the law of value becomes dominant, it will expose the Chinese people to chronic economic instability (booms and slumps), insecurity of employment and income, and greater inequalities. On the other hand, if the surplus created by the Chinese people remains under the control of an elite backed by an army and police, ruling without dissent, then the needs and aspirations of a more affluent and educated population will not be met.

Mainstream economics is confused about which way the Chinese economy is going. Some media and economists reckon Chinese growth is slowing fast from its double-digit pace and indeed is heading toward a crisis or slump brought on by overinvestment, a reversal of a credit-fueled property bubble and a spiraling of hidden bad debts in the banking system. On the other hand, some economists believe that economic growth may be slowing, but the Chinese authorities will be able to engineer a soft landing through the easing of credit and financing of the write-off of debt from cash reserves built up over past years.

Behind this debate on the immediate future also lies a discussion on whether China can continue to grow fast through investment in industry, infrastructure, and more exports or will need to switch to a consumer-led economy that imports more and supplies goods to a rising middle class, like advanced capitalist economies supposedly do. Mainstream economics figures this cannot be done without developing a more "market-based" economy (i.e., capitalism), because the complexity of a consumer society can only work under capitalism and not under "heavy-handed" central planning of government and state industries.

Chinese economic growth has clearly slowed. At the last People's Congress, the leaders targeted real growth at just 7.5 percent a year, something not seen since the depth of the Great Recession in 2008. By global standards, that's a growth rate to envy: the United States can barely manage 2 percent; Europe and Japan are flat at best, and even fast-growing India will not achieve that rate of growth in the near future.

But the Chinese economy needs to grow by at least 8 percent a year in real terms if it is to generate enough jobs to absorb the influx of workers from rural areas into the cities without unemployment rising. So there would appear to be a problem ahead.

The main argument presented for expecting that China is heading for a sharp slowdown, or even what is called a hard landing, is that its fast growth in recent years was based on excessive credit injections by its banks, creating a property bubble that is now bursting. Much of the property bubble was engendered by local authorities borrowing huge hidden amounts from the banks and financing their spending by selling off land to private developers, often over the heads of the local villagers.

That property bubble has burst. Property prices have fallen in most Chinese cities. Huge debts have been run up by local authorities and developers and were hidden in special-purpose vehicles off the balance sheets of the banks. The level of what is called the total social funding of the economy by the banks has reached 180 percent of GDP. This shadow banking is similar to the off-balance sheet mess that US and European banks got into that led to the financial collapse of 2008. The risk is that China is heading the same way. But is it?

China has borrowed to fund investment, rather than consumption; companies are the main borrowers. Corporate indebtedness has risen significantly. This rising corporate debt is outstripping any growth in profits.

The country is not dependent on foreign lenders. In addition, the renminbi is not freely convertible into foreign currency. China not only is a net creditor but also has exchange controls. Domestic creditors cannot take their money out of China. If they pull out of one part of the financial system, they will have to put it back into other domestic assets. The People's Bank can deal with any run. Moreover, according to the IMF, even China's "augmented public debt"—which includes spending by local governments that is not always captured in official data—was only 45 percent of GDP. The Chinese government could certainly bear any conceivable losses if it wanted to—particularly since, unlike Japan in 1990, the country has a relatively undeveloped economy that still possesses good long-term catch-up potential.

The argument of mainstream economics is that a move to full consumer-led capitalism is necessary to enable China to escape from the so-called middle income trap. Emerging economies can grow fast with big capital investment and exports using cheap labor and new technology—the Chinese model. But less than a fifth of the 180 countries in the world have made it to being advanced economies. Of the 101 countries that were "middle-income" in 1960, only 13 managed to break from the pack to become advanced economies by 2008.

Mainstream economics asserts that then there must be a switch to boosting domestic consumption that a state-led economy cannot do. So the cry is: liberalize with free trade and capital—that's the only way to move on.[26]

Leftist economist John Ross takes a different view.[27] Raising consumption indeed should be an economic policy aim. Unfortunately, Ross argues, this has become confused with a different idea of sharply increasing the percentage of consumption in China's GDP. These two goals are actually contradictory as GDP growth is largely driven by investment, and this underpins sustainable consumption. But sharply increasing consumption's percentage in GDP cuts investment levels, thereby inadvertently leading to lower GDP and consequently lower consumption growth. This illustrates why the phrase "consumer-led growth" is confusing.

The Chinese Communist Party's Third Plenum[28] discussed what to do over the next five to ten years.[29] There was no change in the general philosophy of "socialism with Chinese characteristics," and thus the maintenance of the dominance of the state sector. There was no move toward any more democracy or control of even local legal systems and decisions by the people. On the contrary, the leadership is setting up even more repressive state security services to monitor and control the population and curb any dissidence.

There is nothing in the aims and policy proposals agreed on by the Chinese political elite that changes the nature of the Chinese economic, social, and political model. The majority in the leadership will continue with an economic model that is dominated by state corporations directed at all levels by the communist cadres. Markets will not rule, and the law of value will not dominate prices, labor incomes, or domestic trade.

Can the elite continue with this "halfway house" without provoking either a crisis or slump that will force them to follow the "capitalist road" as the World Bank and the procapitalist elements want? Will the elite face an eruption from below as the fast-growing working-class urban population starts to flex its muscles for a say in running the country?

As Ross has pointed out, China's industrial growth remains truly staggering.[30] The nation will continue to grow at least 6–7 percent in annual real GDP terms for at least another decade. The working population is still growing, although it will soon peak; there are still hundreds of millions of rural workers and peasants to be incorporated into the industrial machine. China is increasingly sucking up as much of the world's raw materials as it needs to sustain its expansion. The great Chinese economic miracle is not exhausted quite yet.

Chapter 12
Cycles within Cycles

All of you know that, from reasons I have not now to explain, capitalistic production moves through certain periodical cycles.

—Karl Marx to Friedrich Engels, 1865[1]

We consider long cycles in the capitalistic economy only as probable.

—N. Kondratiev[2]

The general economic crisis that was unleashed across the world in 2008 is a Great Depression. It was triggered by a financial crisis in the US, but that was not its cause. This crisis is an absolutely normal phase of a long-standing recurrent pattern of capitalist accumulation in which long booms eventually give way to long downturns.

—Anwar Shaikh[3]

This chapter looks ahead. It takes the discussion of the nature and causes of the Long Depression to a more theoretical and probably contentious level. It aims to generalize on the historical examination of capitalism's three great depressions into a broader theory of cycles and crises in capitalism.

In many ways, this chapter is really a series of propositions that are not fully confirmed by evidence. The first proposition is that crises are endemic to capitalism and continue to occur, the explanation for which lies in Marx's law of profitability, discussed in a previous chapter. This chapter goes on to argue that these crises occur in regular periods that can be measured and possibly predicted.

In particular, there is a cycle of profitability in each of the major capitalist economies, although its length varies. If we develop a world rate of profit measure, we can develop a cycle of profitability globally. The cycle seems to be completed over a thirty-two- to thirty-six-year period, from trough to trough.

In addition, it is proposed that this cycle of profitability is linked with other cycles operating within capitalism. The first cycle we can identify is the very short one based on the flow of working capital in capitalist companies, that is, raw materials and inventories built up and run down as production takes place. This inventory cycle, first identified by Joseph Kitchin, usually completes every four years.

The second is the most well known, the business cycle of boom and slump that seems to complete every eight to ten years, sometimes called the Juglar cycle. This cycle is based on the overall motion of a capitalist economy in investment, employment, and output, and not just profitability.

The third is the construction cycle of major plant, infrastructure, and housing. This seems to span a period about double that of the business cycle, about eighteen years. It's usually referred to as the Kuznets cycle after the economist Simon Kuznets.

Finally, there is the most controversial and disputed of all, a cycle that lasts about fifty to seventy years, which is driven by the movement of world trade in the prices of production and commodities and seems to depend on global demographic and resource factors. This is commonly called the Kondratiev cycle after the proponent of its existence, Nikolai Kondratiev.

The main proposition of this chapter is that a depression, as opposed to a recession or slump (Juglar style), comes along at a point when all the cycles are in a certain conjunction, that is, they are all in a downward phase: the Kondratiev cycle is in its downward twenty-five- to thirty-five-year phase, the profit cycle is in its sixteen- to eighteen-year downward phase, and so on.

This conjunction does not happen very often. Indeed, given the duration of the long Kondratiev cycle, it can only happen once every fifty to seventy years. If this is right, then it explains why the start of the nineteenth-century depression in 1873 was only repeated fifty-six years later with the start of the Great Depression in 1929 and with the start of the current Long Depression in 2008, some seventy-nine years after that.

Specifically it explains why the collapse of the property market in 2005 in the United States led to the Great Recession. The previous property slump in the United States took place in the early 1990s in commercial property (the savings and loan scandal), coinciding with the slump of 1991. But there was no Great Recession as the profit cycle was in an up phase. But the next slump in property was timed for 2009–10, exactly at the point of eventual trough in the Great Recession.

Cycles

What is a cycle? It has been described as a "harmonic wave."[4] It comes from some sort of restorative force. With a restorative force, being up high is what makes you more likely to come back down, and being low is what makes you more likely to go back up. Imagine a ball on a spring; when the spring is really stretched, all the force is pulling the ball in the direction opposite to the stretch. This causes cycles.

In mainstream economic models, business cycles are not cycles under this definition. They are modeled as shocks to an equilibrium trend. After a temporary shock, the system reverts to the mean (i.e., to the "trend"). This is very different from harmonic motion. In the mainstream economics model, boom need not be followed by bust.[5]

The idea that all deviations from trend growth or equilibrium are simply random shocks or temporary does not hold water. There are plenty of detailed case studies from baseball, elections, climate change, the financial crash, poker, and weather forecasting of significant changes from the norm that are not temporary or insignificant.[6]

Any support for the concept of harmonic cycles in capitalism usually gets dismissed for two main reasons. The first is that statistics or data showing cycles are spurious and really just an expression of random shocks; by extension, there are so few turning points in the longer cycles that no statistical significance can be applied. The second is that there is no theoretical model that can explain apparent economic cycles and, without that, the search for cycles is pointless.

But everything depends on the quality of the "priors" or assumptions, from which statistical techniques can provide degrees of probability for outcomes. The best economic theory and explanation comes from looking at the aggregate, the average, and the outliers. In short, defining and identifying cycles is not impossible and if found can deliver significant explanatory power.

What Marx Said on Cycles

Marx thought there were cycles in capitalism: "Once the cycle begins, it is regularly repeated. Effects, in their turn, become causes, and the varying accidents of the whole process, which always reproduces its own conditions, take on the form of periodicity."[7]

Marx spent some considerable time and research in trying to identify cycles in the capitalist economy.[8] He particularly looked for periodicity in cycles. Right up to the end of his research on the capitalist economy, Marx continued to look for cyclical movements. He wrote to Engels in May 1873 about "a problem which I have been wrestling with in private for a long tim[e]." He had been examining "tables which give prices, discount rate, etc. etc. . . . I have tried several times—for the analysis of crises—to calculate these ups and downs as irregular curves, and thought (I still think that it is possible with enough tangible material) that I could determine the main laws of crises mathematically."[9]

Marx saw the immobility of fixed capital as a part of the explanation of the periodicity of the cycle. He thought that duration of the accumulation cycle (boom and slump) was about five to seven years, a view he revised to ten years when the expected crisis did not strike in 1852.

So Marx developed the idea that the cycle was connected with the replacement of fixed capital. On this basis, he argued, "there can be no doubt at all that the cycle through which industry has been passing in *plus ou moins* ten-year periods since the large-scale development of fixed capital, is linked with the total reproduction phase of capital determined in this way. We shall find other determining factors too, but this is one of them."[10]

Engels told Marx that it was normal to set aside 7.5 percent for depreciation, which implied a replacement cycle of thirteen years, although he noted twenty- and thirty-year-old machines still working.[11] Marx concluded that "The figure of 13 years corresponds closely enough to the theory, since it establishes a unit for one epoch of industrial reproduction which plus ou moins coincides with the period in which major crises recur; needless to say their course is also determined by factors of a quite different kind, depending on their period of reproduction. For me the important thing is to discover, in the immediate material postulates of big industry, one factor that determines cycles."[12]

The key point for Marx was that "the cycle of related turnovers, extending over a number of years, within which the capital is confined by its fixed component, is one of the material foundations for the periodic cycle [crisis] . . . But a crisis is always the starting point of a large volume of new investment. It is also, therefore, if we consider the society as a whole, more or less a new material basis for the next turnover cycle."[13] So Marx connected his theory of crisis to cycles in the turnover of fixed capital.

Marx considered that "So far the period of these cycles has been ten or twelve years, but there is no reason to consider this a constant figure." Indeed, he thought that the cycle of replacement capital would shorten. Later Engels began to argue that "the acute form of the periodic process, with its former ten-year cycle, appears to have given way to a more chronic, long drawn out, alternation between a relatively short and slight business improvement and a relatively long, indecisive depression—taking place in the various industrial countries at different times."[14] So the cycle could be longer than ten to thirteen years.

The Profit Cycle

Marx and Engels were trying to identify what we now call the business or Juglar cycle. This cycle is driven by the growth and decline of investment in fixed capital: plant, machinery, and new technology.

Modern scholars have also identified a profit cycle, namely upward and downward movement in the trajectory of the overall profitability of capital in any one country or the world economy. Anwar Shaikh found such a profit cycle with seventeen-year up and down waves.[15] Minqi Li and colleagues found that since the mid-nineteenth century there have been four long waves in the movement of the profit rate and rate of accumulation in the major economies.[16] The second half of the late nineteenth-century profit rate long wave, from peak to trough, lasted for twenty-three years or longer from the early 1870s to the late 1890s. The early twentieth-century profit rate long wave lasted for forty-two years from 1897 to 1939, and the mid-twentieth-century profit rate long wave (including the World War II period) lasted for forty-four years. Therefore, each of the previous profit rate long waves lasted for about forty to forty-five years from 1939 to 1983. The current profit rate long wave started in 1983 and peaked in 1997 and presumably to trough by the end of the 2010s.

Basu and Manolakis took this further in their analysis of the postwar US economy.[17] Their analysis is much more sophisticated statistically than any done before. They point out that "most empirical studies have simply examined time series plots and fit a trend to these data. However, existence or nonexistence of a downward trend is not a valid test of Marx's hypothesis unless the counter-tendencies are appropriately controlled for." They found that "scholars have speculated that long waves of aggregate economic activity might be related to long waves of the general rate of profit. A plot of the general rate of profit for the U.S. economy since 1869 indeed displays long waves."

For Basu and Manolakis, there are four waves or phases, beginning with a contraction during the period 1869–94. This contraction coincides with the depression of the 1890s. In the next phase, which coincides with the period from 1894 until the onset of the Great Depression, there is no strong trend but minor period cycles. In the third phase, there is a substantial contraction coincident with the Great Depression and a substantial expansion coincident with World War II. In the final phase, the rate of profit contracts till about the early 1980s and is followed by an expansion. "Thus, the series displays considerable persistence and it is plausible to suppose that there is a stochastic trend in these data."[18] In other words, there are cycles.

Why does this profit cycle exist? It is really a product of Marx's law of profitability as countertendencies play out against the tendency to fall.[19] The evidence suggests, at least for the United States, that there is an upward cycle in profitability driven by countertendencies overpowering the underlying tendency to fall, but after about sixteen to eighteen years that gives way to a fall in profitability as Marx's law takes over again.

Britain in the Second Half of Nineteenth Century

Can we discern this cycle of profitability in various capitalist economies? Consider two case studies. The first is the British economy when it was the hegemonic capitalist economy during Marx's time from 1850 to 1914; second is the US economy in the post–World War II period.

I dealt with the first in the chapter on the depression of the late nineteenth century. Now let us consider that period from the point of view of cycles. As we have seen, Marx found it difficult to test any of his hypotheses against empirical evidence available for Britain in his time. We now have better data. We can plot the rate of profit in Marxist terms.

First, the rate of profit for the UK economy between 1855 and 1914 moved in a cycle of about thirty-plus years from trough to trough, or in two phases of about fifteen years each. The up phase of 1885–71 was followed by a down phase of 1871–84, a period noted for frequent and deep recessions—indeed, the 1880s were considered a Great Depression like the 1930s. After 1884 we get another (volatile) up phase in the rate of profit until 1899. Finally, there was a fall back in profitability from 1900 up to the start of World War I in 1914.

The data show that the main reason for the cycle of profitability under British capitalism between 1855 and 1914 was the movement in the organic composition of capital. There is a significant inverse relationship between the organic composition and the rate of profit.

The US Postwar Cycles

In the second case for the US economy from 1946 to 2007, we find a similar profit cycle with up waves and down waves, each of about fifteen to seventeen years. In the first wave, which has been called the golden age, profitability was very high throughout. After falling back in the 1950s, it rose to reach a peak in 1965. From then, the organic composition of capital rose and the rate of profit fell to reach a low in the economic recession of 1982. The rate fell sharply in the first great postwar economic recession of 1974–75. But the seeds had been planted for these falls by the steady decline in the rate of profitability from 1966. By 1982 after two big economic recessions, such was the reduction in the organic composition of capital, the rate of profit steadily rose, apart from the merest of pauses in the recession of 1990–92, up to a new peak in 1997. After 1997, the rate of profit declined. We are in the down wave of the profit cycle similar to the period 1965–82. These two studies provide a powerful correlation between the cycle of profitability and Marx's law of profitability.

The postwar profit cycle appears to have been replicated in the other major capitalist economies (see Figure 12.1). In a set of fourteen countries, Maito finds that the golden age of postwar capitalism from 1950 to the mid-1960s, when the rate of profit was high, gave way to a period of falling profitability to 1982. Then there was a recovery in the neoliberal period to the late 1990s. Now the major economies are in a down wave of profitability, culminating in the Great Recession and depression.

Again, the data suggest that this cycle of profitability is driven by Marx's law of the tendency of the rate of profit to fall and the countertendencies. In the G7 economies, the rate of profit fell secularly between 1950 and 2011 because in that period, the organic composition of capital rose much more than did the rate of surplus value (see Figure 12.2). But in the neoliberal period, when profitability rose, organic composition actually fell slightly while the rate of surplus value rose significantly. In the period of the current Long Depression, the rate of profit has fallen over 20 percent because the organic composition has outstripped the rise in the rate of surplus value.

Figure 12.1

A World Rate of Profit (Simple Mean Average) of 14 Countries (%), 1950–2009

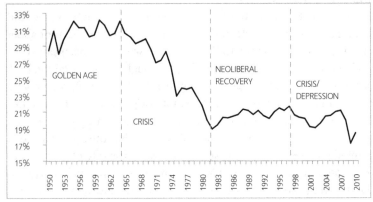

Source: E Maito

Figure 12.2

Changes in the Profitability, Organic Composition of Capital, and Rate of Exploitation in Top Seven Capitalist Economies, 1950–2014

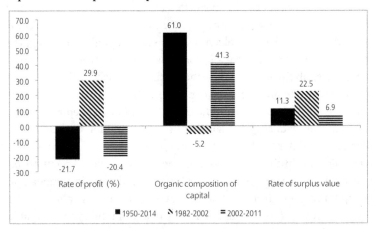

Source: Penn World Tables, Author's Calculations

If Marx's law of profitability is cyclical in this way, it can significantly help in the debate about whether it is relevant to the Great Recession or whether that was just a financial crisis. If the cyclical approach is correct, then we are still in a down phase for profitability that began in 1997 and won't trough until the end of the 2010s (or earlier). Another recession would be needed before capital is sufficiently devalued (and, in the case of labor, weakened) to create the environment for rising profitability.

If we extend the data back to 1929 for the US and the G7 economies, we notice a significant rise in profitability from 1938 to 1944. This period covers World War II. War adds a new dimension to "creative destruction." Physical destruction of the stock of capital accompanies value destruction. This produces a dramatic fall in the cost of capital. War is an exogenous event that can sharply interfere in these endogenous profit cycles.[20]

What would have happened to profitability without World War II? The US rate of profit was turning downward in 1938. Without war, it may have dropped to a cyclical low by, say, 1946, before entering an upward phase up to 1964. If that is accurate, then the 1946–64 period is really an upward phase.

How close were Marx and Engels to being right on their estimate of the replacement cycle? The US Bureau of Economic Analysis provides data on the age structure of replacement for private nonresidential fixed assets. From 1963 the US rate of profit peaked and began to fall. It seems that the age structure fell from about 17 years to 14.5 years at the turning point in US profitability that began after the slump of 1980–82. From 1982, the organic composition of capital fell and investment growth slowed. The age structure rose back toward seventeen years. It is clear that if the replacement of fixed assets is the model for explaining any cycles in capitalist accumulation, the cycle can be expected to be around fifteen to seventeen years.

Profit Cycles and the Stock and Credit Markets

This length in the profit cycle is supported by the stock market cycle in all the leading financial centers. The US stock market cycle appears pretty much the same in length (a bull cycle of eighteen years followed by a bear cycle of a similar length) as the US profit cycle. The stock market seems to peak in value a couple of years after the rate of profit does. This is really what one would expect, because the stock market is closely connected to the profitability of companies, much more than bank loans or bonds. When the rate of profit enters its down wave, the stock market soon follows, if with a short lag.

That close relationship can be established by measuring the market capitalization of companies in an economy against the accumulated assets. Tobin's Q takes the "market capitalization" of the companies in the stock market (in this case the top 500 companies in the S&P 500 index) and divides that by the replacement value of tangible assets accumulated by those companies (these figures are provided again by the US Bureau of Economic Analysis and by the S&P's data on company accounts). The replacement value is the price that companies would have to pay to replace all the physical assets that they own (plant, equipment, etc.).

Tobin's Q measures the value that speculators on the stock exchange can get over or below the actual real value of the company's assets. As we can see from Figure 12.3, for the period 1948–2013, Tobin's Q starts at about 0.33. The value of stock market shares was approximately only one-third of the real value of the assets owned by the companies—very cheap. It rose to nearly 1.00 in 1968. That was the peak of Tobin's Q then. Afterward it fell back to just 0.30 in 1981. That was the trough. From 1982, it rose to reach 1.70 in 1999. So the stock market value was 70 percent over the real value of the company's assets. From 1999, it fell back to 0.60 in 2009, but then rallied somewhat to near 1.00 in 2014.

There was a secular bull market from 1948 to 1968, followed by a bear market until 1981 and then another bull market until 1999. The US stock market cycle appears pretty much the same as the US profit cycle, although slightly different in its turning points.

New research has started to identify a credit cycle, at least in the major capitalist economies, with a duration of sixteen to eighteen years. Claudio Borio finds what he calls a "financial cycle" using a composite of property prices (house prices to income) and changes in credit (credit to GDP).[21] Borio is struck by the fact that the duration is longer than the business cycle. His financial cycle matches the length of the profit cycle. But it appears to run inversely with the profit cycle, at least in the United States—namely, when profitability is in its downward phase, the financial cycle is in its upward phase. This suggests that capitalists look for unproductive investments like property to replace investment in production when profitability in productive assets falls. This is very relevant to understanding the relation between the productive and financial sectors of capitalism culminating in the Great Recession of 2008–9.

Figure 12.3

Tobin's Q: The Market Capital Value as a Ratio of the Net Stock of Capital in US Corporations

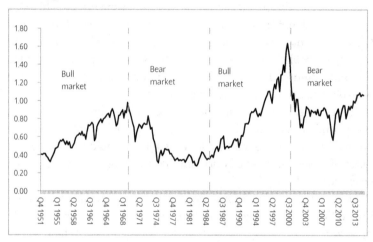

Source: Federal Reserve

Kondratiev Cycles

Let's talk about even longer cycles in capitalist production. Just as the capitalist profit cycle appears to be spread over approximately thirty-two to thirty-six years from trough to trough, and so does the stock market and credit market cycles, there also appears to be a cycle in prices that is about double that size, or around sixty-four to seventy-two years. This cycle was first identified properly by Nicolai Kondratiev, a Russian economist, in the 1920s. He argued that there appeared to be a period when prices and interest rates moved up for about twenty-seven years or so, and then a period when the opposite occurred.

Kondratiev "long cycles" have been critiqued at three levels. First, it is argued that there is no firm statistical evidence that such cycles of fifty years or longer really exist. There are few data points, and the economic series analyzed by Kondratiev have been considered unconvincing.

Second, Kondratiev's argument that cycles should be considered endogenous to the capitalist mode of production has been rejected. The alternative consensus is that changes in the relative pace of economic growth or in prices of production are caused by external factors like wars, revolutions, disease, weather, or more specifically new stages of capitalist economic organization (imperialism, financialization, etc.).

Third, there is no convincing theory or model to explain these long cycles, if they do exist. Kondratiev defended his theory from all these criticisms. He admitted that the available data were inadequate to "assert beyond doubt the cyclical character of these cycles. Nevertheless, the available data were sufficient to declare this cyclical character to be very probable." In particular, the time series for prices of production and commodities bore the greatest support for cycles "and cannot be explained by external random causes."[22]

He reckoned the long duration of the cycles was based on the gestation period of large capital projects that could not be completed in the normal business cycle, and these investments would take place in a series of waves. He rejected criticism that any long cycles were caused by exogenous factors.[23]

Later scholars have provided empirical support for endogenous Kondratiev cycles.[24] Theoretical and empirical backing has been developed for Kondratiev's suggestion that long cycles are the result of clusters of innovation or long duration capital projects. Ernest Mandel attempted to link long cycles to movements in profitability, although he claimed, rather oddly, that the down phase in such cycles was endogenous to capitalist production but the up phase was exogenous.[25]

Interest rates are a very good proxy for the Kondratiev prices cycle. The level of the US short-term interest rate (the Fed Funds rate, as set by the Federal Reserve Bank), rose from 1946 to a peak in 1981 and then fell back after that.

Can we bring together the claimed Kondratiev cycle with the cycles of profitability discerned earlier for the United Kingdom in the nineteenth century and the United States in the twentieth century? Figure 12.4 shows K-cycles on the left side, with the phases of the profit cycle. The first K-cycle begins in about 1785, rises to a prices peak around 1818, and then goes to a trough in the early 1840s. The second cycle peaked in the mid-1860s and then troughed in the mid-1880s or early 1890s. The third K-cycle peaked in 1920 and troughed in 1946. The fourth K-cycle peaked in 1980 and will trough around 2018.

The Cycle of Innovation

The graph also depicts the so-called innovation cycle that Joseph Schumpeter identified.[26] In this cycle, a scientific discovery is made. Eventually, this leads to the development or growth of a new technology in capitalist production. Later this technology takes off and is applied across sectors or in newly expanding sectors. Then it reaches a period of maturity, where its added value consolidates. Eventually it enters a period of saturation when it has run out of expansion profitably. Finally the technology goes into decline and disappears.

Figure 12.4
Cycles in Capitalism

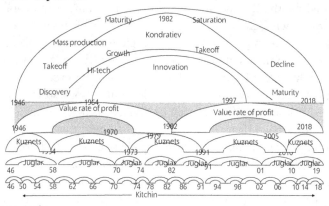

Source: Author

There are six stages, each of which fits into the change in the phases of the profit cycle. There are two examples. There is the mass production technology of cars, the so-called Fordist industrial model. In 1946, this was in its take-off phase of huge expansion. But by the mid-1960s, it entered a period of maturity where output and sales rose steadily. In the neoliberal period after the early 1980s, auto production found a "saturated" market (at least in the advanced economies) and fell back as one of the leading sectors, at least relatively. In the current profit cycle down phase after 1997, auto production has been in significant decline in the United States, Europe, and even Japan, and has shifted to Asia and Latin America.

The other example is high technology (computers, Internet communications, etc.). The major scientific discoveries here were made in the postwar period of the 1950s and early 1960s. In the period from the mid-1960s to the early 1980s, these discoveries were turned into applicable new technology (PCs, digital media, etc.). Through the 1980s and 1990s, high tech took off in a big way, culminating in the dot-com boom that busted in 2000. Now high tech and its applications have become the leading technology sector. It is in its mature stage. In this schema, these technologies will enter saturation, perhaps even globally, in the 2020s and 2030s and decline as important profit creators for capitalism by mid-century. The innovation cycle fits into the K-cycle.

The K-cycle has been lengthening in duration from Kondratiev's time, from about fifty-five years to sixty-four years in the third cycle and seventy-two years in the fourth cycle. Various reasons have been proposed for the lengthening of the cycle, including demographics and government debt financing. The K-cycle now follows much more closely the cycle in profitability as the capitalist mode of production has become dominant globally, particularly since the postwar period.

The right side of Figure 12.4 shows how the profit cycle integrates with the K-cycle into what have been called four seasons: spring (rising profitability); summer (falling profitability) alongside the rising phase of the K-cycle; and then autumn (rising profitability) and winter (falling profitability), alongside the declining phase of K-cycle. In the winter phase, the model would expect to reveal a period of depression (falling prices or slowing inflation alongside high or rising unemployment and poor economic growth). Previous winter periods have been the 1840s, the 1880–90s (the first long depression), and the 1930s (the Great Depression)—and we are now in another one (the Long Depression).

More Cycles of Motion

There are three more cycles of motion that operate under modern capitalism: the cycle in real estate prices and construction, the cycle of economic boom and slump (the so-called business cycle), and the inventory cycle.

There appears to be a cycle of about eighteen years based on the movement of real estate prices. The US economist Simon Kuznets discovered the existence of this cycle back in the 1930s. We can measure the cycle in the United States by looking at house prices (see Figure 12.5). The first peak after 1945 was in 1951. The prices fell back to a trough in 1958, then rose to a new peak in 1969 before slumping back to another trough in 1971. The next peak was in 1979–80 and the next trough was in 1991. Assuming an eighteen-year cycle, then the next trough in US house prices should have been around 2009–10.[27] It was.

The real estate cycle is not aligned with the Marxist profit cycle, the stock market cycle, or the Kondratiev prices/money cycle. These latter cycles are products of the laws of motion of capitalist accumulation. They operate in the productive sector of the economy. In contrast, the real estate cycle operates mostly in the unproductive sector of the capitalist economy. Housing is a big user of consumer income. So the cycle in house prices reflects the spending behavior of capitalists and workers, not the profitability of capital. For these reasons, the real estate cycle has different timings in its turns than does the profit cycle. The US profit cycle reached a trough in 1982 before rising for fifteen or sixteen years to peak in 1997. The stock market cycle also troughed in 1982 and then ran up to a peak in 2000, eighteen years later. In contrast, the US real estate cycle troughed some nine years later in 1991 and only reached its peak in 2005 before troughing in 2010.

Figure 12.5

US House Prices YOY Change (%)

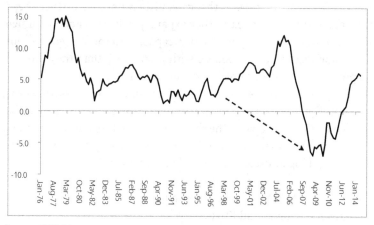

Source: US BEA

Clément Juglar was the first mainstream economist to notice a business cycle of about ten years. This cycle of economic growth and recession now seems to be about nine to ten years. That is the average time between troughs of each recession in the recent period. Capitalist economists define a recession as two consecutive quarters of a fall in GDP or annual output, after taking inflation into account. On that basis, there have been seven recessions over the past sixty years, with varying degrees of severity and length. Over two profit cycles since 1946, there have been seven Juglar cycles with one still to come to complete the current profit cycle—implying that there are four business cycles in every full profit cycle.

The Juglar cycle has different turning points from the Marxist profit cycle. The cycle is of the whole economy, the productive and unproductive sectors, including the government sector. Thus the movements in the profit cycle and the productive sectors of capitalism feed through with a lag to the rest of the economy. If profitability declines and the mass of profits start to fall, this will feed through to falling investment and then employment and incomes. The recession (falling output and rising unemployment) will come months, quarters, and even years later.

Finally, there is an even shorter business cycle of about four to five years. Kitchin discovered this in the 1930s. This cycle seems to be the product of even more short-term decisions by capitalists on how much stock to keep to sell. It seems that capitalists cannot see further ahead than about two to four years. They expand production and maximize the utilization of existing production capacity. In the struggle to compete, capitalist producers end up with more stock than they can sell. So production is slowed until stocks are run down.

As Figure 12.4 shows, these cycles can be integrated. In other words, the long Kondratiev cycle of sixty-four to seventy-two years can be divided all the way down to the short Kitchin cycle of four to five years. Thus, there are two profit cycles in the Kondratiev cycle, four Kuznets cycles, eight Juglar cycles, and eighteen Kitchin cycles.

The profit cycle is key. The up wave in the profit cycle from 1946 to 1965 coincided with the up wave in the Kondratiev cycle. Thus the troughs in the Juglar and Kuznets cycles in the mid-1950s did not produce a very deep recession or downturn in economic growth and employment. Because the Kitchin cycle troughed also in 1958, the "pause" was longer than in 1954. But high and rising profitability in an environment of a Kondratiev up wave was generally good news for capitalism.

From 1965 to 1982, the rate of profit fell. The Kondratiev cycle was still in an up wave of prices, though. What we got was successively worse economic slumps (1970, 1974, and 1980–82) alongside rising prices—in other words "stagflation." In 1974, the Kuznets, Juglar, and Kitchin cycles troughed together. In an environment of falling profitability, world capitalism suffered its first postwar simultaneous economic slump. The 1980–82 recession was deep and long-lasting because profitability reached lows and the Kondratiev prices cycle peaked. But the real estate Kuznets cycle was also at a peak, so output and employment fell while prices stayed up—the ultimate stagflation crisis.

The next up wave of profitability (1982–97) coincided with the down wave in the Kondratiev prices cycle, which we are still in. Thus rising profitability was accompanied by falling inflation, from 15 percent in 1982 to just 2–3 percent by the late 1990s. Rising and high profitability (by 1997) also meant that the Juglar cycle troughs of 1991 and 2001 were not nearly as deep or severe as in 1974 and 1980–82. The Kuznets cycle troughed again in 1991, making the 1991 economic recession much more severe than the 2001 recession when the housing market in the United States and elsewhere was booming.

The Winter of Discontent

We are now in another profit downwave that should not reach a bottom until around 2018. So output and employment slumps should be at least as severe and long-lasting as they were in 1974–75 and 1980–82. This is because the profit down wave now coincides with the down wave in the Kondratriev prices cycle that started in 1982 and won't reach its trough until 2018 or so.

The three depressions—the one in the late nineteenth century, the Great Depression of the 1930s, and the current Long Depression—coincided with the winter phase of a Kondratiev cycle. They also coincided with different stages of capitalism. The depression of the late nineteenth century was an impulse for the development of imperialism, the expansion of finance capital into the "colonies," and the battle among imperialist powers to divide up the world, which eventually led to World War I.

The Great Depression led to a new imperialist battle, one that was not resolved by World War I. The hegemonic imperialist power, Great Britain, had been irretrievably weakened by the 1914–18 war, but the rising hegemonic power, the United States, was not ready or willing to assume the mantle of imperialist dominance. The rival imperialist powers, German and Japan, tried to gain a bigger cut of the spoils. That led to World War II and the eventual inception of Pax Americana after 1945.

The autumn phase of the current Kondratiev cycle from 1982 to 2000 saw the collapse of the Soviet Union. The current Long Depression threatens the hegemony of US imperialism, already in relative decline to new ambitious powers like China, Brazil, India, and Russia. Renewed rivalry threatens to unleash major conflicts in the next decade or so.

Eventually, the winter phase of the current K-cycle will give way to a Kondratiev spring and the start of the fifth K-cycle in modern capitalism. Capitalism will enter a new up phase on the back of the destruction of capital values from the series of slumps in the winter phase (2001 recession, the Great Recession of 2008–9, and probably a final slump in 2016–17?). From the mid-2030s, we would enter another Kondratiev summer, when profitability would fall, capitalism would be in crisis again, and class struggle would intensify. This would last until the 2050s. This is really what we call the long view!

This tentative scenario assumes no exogenous forces cutting across the inherent cyclical motion of capitalism. Those exogenous forces include a new world war (or revolutions in major economies), but also damaging changes in the planet itself. In the final chapter, we examine some of those exogenous forces and the longer-term future of capitalism after the Long Depression.

Chapter 13

Past Its Use-By Date?

In principle, in developed capitalism, any great crisis can become the final crisis. But if it does not, it remains a presupposition for further accumulation. But permanent crisis is just as conceivable in the Marxian system as surmountable crises . . . under present day conditions of world capital, a state of persistent economic and political crisis can arise, just as it is possible that the crisis will give capital a chance of beginning a new expansion.

—Paul Mattick[1]

Those who subscribe to the conventional view fail to see that untold millions of competing and collaborating global workers are ultimately likely to be flattened by the major force that will truly shape the century. Globalisation is certainly significant but it is really a mere offshoot of the primary force driving us toward change and the force continues to be technology.

—Martin Ford[2]

The world economy is in a Long Depression. That has been the main message of this book. However, world capitalism will not stay in this depressed state. Eventually, probably after another slump that will destroy more capital values (the value of means of production, fictitious capital, and employment), profitability for those that survive will rise sufficiently to start an upwave in investment and growth. This assumes, of course, that the class struggle does not lead to the forces of labor triumphing over capital in any major economy.

So the Long Depression is not some final crisis. There are yet more human beings in the world to be exploited, and there are always new technological innovations that can provide a new Kondratiev cycle for expansion of value and surplus value.

In the twenty-first century, capitalism is creating new contradictions for itself that threaten its survival as a dominant mode of production and social organization—and, for that matter, the very existence of a healthy planet.

Growing Inequality

The first contradiction in capitalism is the growing inequality of income and wealth. The gulf between rich and poor can only exacerbate the class struggle. This is the inequality of wealth and income between nations, as well as within.

The United Nations has analyzed this closely in a recent study.[3] It revealed that the top 1 percent of wealth holders in the world had 48 percent of the wealth and the top 10 percent had 86 percent. Remember this is wealth across the whole world, not just inequality of wealth within a country. Indeed, most of the top 10 percent of wealth holders live in the top seven (G7) advanced capitalist economies.

Globally, 393 million people have net worth (wealth after all debt is accounted for) of over $100,000. Over $100,000 in net wealth may not seem that much if you own a home in any G7 country without a mortgage. But many millions of people in the United Kingdom or the United States are in this group and so are in the top 10 percent of global wealth holders. This shows just how little two-thirds of adults in the world have—under $100,000 of net wealth each—and billions have nothing at all.

This is not annual income but wealth—in other words, 3.2 billion adults own virtually nothing at all. At the other end of the spectrum, just 32 million people own $98 trillion in wealth or 41 percent of all household wealth or more than $1 million each. Just 98,700 people with ultra-high net worth have more than $50 million each, and of these 33,900 are worth over $100 million each. Half of these super-rich live in the United States.

All this comes in the global wealth report authored by Anthony Shorrocks and Jim Davies.[4] The authors find that global wealth has reached an all-time high of $241 trillion, with the United States accounting for most of the rise. Average wealth hit a new peak of $51,600 per adult, but the distribution of that wealth is wildly unequal. The study finds that there is little or no social mobility globally between rich and poor over generations—87 percent of people stay rich or poor, hardly moving up or down the wealth pyramid.

Global wealth is projected to rise by nearly 40 percent over the next several years, reaching $334 trillion by 2018. Emerging markets will be responsible for 29 percent of the growth, although they account for just 21 percent of current wealth, and China will account for nearly 50 percent of the increase in emerging economies' wealth. Wealth will primarily be driven by growth in the middle segment, but the number of millionaires will also grow markedly.

Branco Milanović, formerly of the World Bank, recently updated his definitive study of the inequality of incomes (not wealth) globally.[5] In 2005, Milanović had carefully documented in his book *Worlds Apart* that the global inequality of income (and wealth), was "20:80" (i.e., that 80 percent of world's population of 6.6 billion could be classed as poor) and the situation was getting worse, not better, even if you take into account the booming so-called BRICS (Brazil, Russia, India, China, and South Africa).

The usual measure of income inequality is the Gini coefficient. This measure takes its name from the Italian statistician and economist Corrado Gini. The Gini coefficient ranges from 0—when everybody has the same income—to 1 (or 100, expressed as a percentage or an index), when one person gets the entire income (of a city, province, nation, world—whatever the relevant population over which we calculate the inequality). Milanović uses national household surveys from dozens of countries over time as raw data to work out his Gini indexes for each country and the world. Later he revised his data and it's a 92:9 world now—even more unequal in income than he measured before.[6]

Milanović notes that global inequality between nations is much greater than inequality within any individual country. The global Gini is around 0.7, substantially greater than inequality within Brazil, the highest for a country. It is almost twice as great as inequality in the United States. Milanović finds that the 60 million or so people who constitute the world's top 1 percent of income "earners" have seen their incomes rise by 60 percent since 1988. About half of these are the richest 12 percent of Americans. The rest of the top 1 percent is made up by the top 3–6 percent of Britons, Japanese, French, and German, and the top 1 percent of several other countries, including Russia, Brazil, and South Africa. These people include the world capitalist class—the owners and controllers of the capitalist system and the strategists and policy makers of imperialism.

But Milanović finds that those who have gained income even more in the past twenty years are the ones in the global middle. These people are not capitalists. These are mainly people in India and China, formerly peasants or rural workers who migrated to the cities to work in the sweat shops and factories of globalization. Their real incomes have jumped from a very low base, even if their conditions and rights have not.

The biggest losers are the very poorest (mainly African rural farmers) who have gained nothing in twenty years. The other losers appear to be some of the better off globally, but they are in fact mainly working-class people in the former communist countries of Eastern Europe whose living standards were slashed with the return of capitalism in the 1990s and the broad working class in the advanced capitalist economies whose real wages have stagnated in the past twenty years.

Milanović shows that since the Industrial Revolution that accompanied the rise to dominance of the capitalist mode of production, inequality in world income has risen.[7] However, he is struck by a decline in his measure of global inequality since 2002, which "may be historically important." He explains this by the catching-up of poor and large countries (China and India), overcoming upward pressures in inequality within countries.

Does this mean that global inequality will decline from now on? Don't bet on it for long, if growth in China and India should slow. Using a Theil coefficient of global inequality in two baseline years (1870 and 2000), Milanović shows that overall global inequality today is greater than it was in 1870.

However, Milanović makes some controversial assertions. Global inequality can be decomposed into two parts. The first part is due to differences in incomes within nations, which means that part of total inequality is due to income differences between rich and poor Americans, rich and poor Chinese, rich and poor Egyptians, and so on, for all countries. If one adds up all of these within-national inequalities, one gets the aggregate contribution to global inequality. Milanović calls this the traditional Marxist class component of global inequality because it accounts for (the sum) of income inequalities between different income classes within countries. The second component, which he calls the "location" component, refers to the differences between mean incomes of all the countries. Around 1870, "class" explained more than two-thirds of global inequality. Now more than two-thirds of total inequality is due to location. Over the period since 1870, more than 50 percent of income for an individual has depended on the average income of the country where a person lives or was born.

Milanović concludes from this that the Marxist class analysis has been proven wrong. But inequality of income (and wealth) within the imperialist countries has risen in the past thirty years and is now as

high, if not higher, than in 1870. That's a fairly Marxist class component of inequality. All class societies have generated extremes of inequality in wealth and income. That is the point of a rich elite (whether
feudal landlords, Asiatic warlords, religious castes, slave owners, etc.)
usurping control of the surplus produced by labor. But past class societies considered that normal and God-given. Capitalism, on the other
hand, talks about free markets, equal exchange, and equality of opportunity. But the reality is no different from previous class societies.

Falling Productivity Growth

The main thesis of this book has been that the world capitalist economy (led by the major economies) is in a Long Depression similar to
those experienced by the leading capitalist economies in the late nineteenth century and then again in the mid-twentieth century.

Global productivity growth is slowing. The US Conference Board,
which follows productivity growth closely, found that global labor productivity growth, measured as the average change in output (GDP) per
person employed, remained stuck at 2.1 percent in 2014, while showing no
sign of strengthening to its precrisis average of 2.6 percent (1999–2006).

This slowdown is another signal that the world economy is struggling with a depression. Increasingly world capitalism is failing to provide dynamic growth (see Figure 13.1).

Figure 13.1

OECD Labor Productivity Per Hour Worked (% YOY)

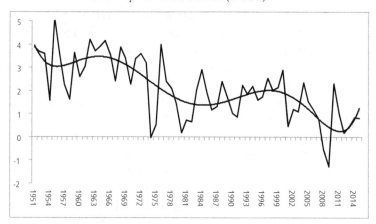

Source: OECD

Globalization and the high-tech revolution reversed the productivity growth decline in the 1990s, but in this century productivity growth in the advanced economies has headed toward stagnation. Only productivity growth in the emerging economies has enabled world productivity growth to stay near 2 percent a year. Since the Great Recession, productivity growth has dropped to under 1 percent a year.

Real GDP growth can be considered as comprising two components: productivity growth and employment growth. The first shows the change in new value per worker employed, and second shows the number of extra workers employed. The mainstream neoclassical economics view is that these components are independent and exogenous to the economy. Technological advances and population growth are independent variables to the processes of the capitalist mode of production.

The Marxist view is the opposite: that they are endogenous. In Marxist economics, employment growth does not depend on population growth as such but on the demand for labor by the capitalist sector of the economy. Capitalist investment is the determining variable, and employment is the dependent one. Capital accumulation can be positive for employment as investment grows, but it can also be negative as machines and technology (robots) replace labor. Similarly, productivity growth is really the flip side of the growth in investment. Capital accumulation aims to raise profitability by the introduction of new techniques that raise productivity and relative surplus value. No new technique is introduced unless the individual capitalist reckons it will deliver more value than otherwise.

The flaw in the capitalist productivity process is that the drive for more productivity to undercut rival capitalists leads to a tendency of the rate of profit to fall that over time exerts itself over the rise in the rate of surplus value and other counteracting factors to that tendency. This leads to a crisis of profitability that can only be resolved by a slump and the devaluation of the existing capital employed to start the process of accumulation and growth again.

What the productivity growth figures show is that the ability of capitalism (or at least the advanced capitalist economies) to generate better productivity is waning. Thus capitalists have squeezed the share of new value going to labor and raised the profit share to compensate. Above all, they have cut back on the rate of capital accumulation in the "real economy," increasingly trying to find extra profit in financial and property speculation. Look at the growth in the accumulated stock of capital in the advanced capitalist economies in Figure 13.2.

Figure 13.2
Annual Growth in Net Stock of Capital in Advanced Capitalist Economies, 1961–2015

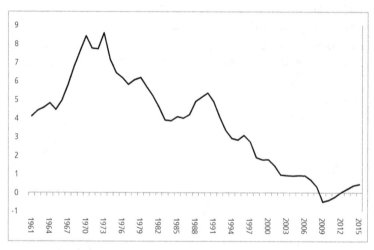

Source: OECD

We have productivity growth of under 2 percent a year in the world—that's about 3 percent in emerging economies and under 1 percent for the advanced economies, which currently represent 52 percent of world GDP (the forecast is for that share to slip to 48 percent by 2025).

The story for productivity is repeated for employment growth in the advanced economies. Employment growth is far less than 1 percent a year in the twenty-first century.

If you add (to productivity growth) an employment growth rate globally of 1 percent a year, then global growth is going to be little more than 3 percent a year for the next decade (and a maximum of just 2 percent a year for the advanced economies), unless this depression rate of growth and employment is simply a cyclical downturn that will swing up as the world economy recovers. The evidence in the data suggests that it is not and the dynamism of world capitalism is waning.

Neoclassical economics likes to use a more sophisticated measure of productivity called total factor productivity. This measure, not just the productivity of labor employed but also the productivity achieved from innovations. Actually it is just a residual from the gap between real GDP growth and the productivity of labor and "capital" inputs. So it is really a rather bogus figure. But taking it at face value, the Conference Board finds that total factor productivity dropped below zero for the global economy in 2013 indicating "stalling efficiency in the optimal allocation and use of resources."

Worse, as productivity growth slows, it seems that global inflation is also slowing (see Figure 13.3) with several key economies heading into a deflation of prices—another classic indicator of depression.

Figure 13.3
Global Annual Inflation Rate (%)

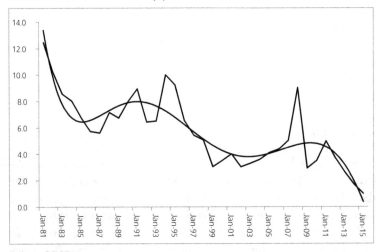

Source: OECD

Permanent Stagnation?

Slowing productivity and creeping deflation—these are serious indicators of this depressionary era. The designation of "depression" has not had a lot of support among economists of any theoretical slant until now. But the idea of "permanent depression" has surfaced from the "great and good" in mainstream economics. At an IMF conference on the causes of the crisis,[8] Larry Summers pronounced that the efforts of central banks to revive the economy with low or zero interest rates or with the "printing of money" through quantitative easing (QE)-type purchases of government and private sector financial paper, was not working to return economies to "normal growth."[9]

Apparently even "unconventional" monetary policies are not doing the trick for the economy, except to drive up stock market prices in a new (noninflationary) bubble. Summers's view has been echoed by a litany of Keynesian epigones like Paul Krugman, Gavyn Davies, and Martin Wolf. For them, it seems that capitalism is not working "automatically" to return to "equilibrium growth" and deflationary pressures are becoming dominant.[10] It appears that the major capitalist economies cannot grow at rates that would achieve full employment any longer even with negative real interest rates.

But this view of depression is not the same as what is argued here. First, for the Keynesians, the depression is a product of money hoarding by capitalists, leading to a permanent lack of "effective demand." What the likes of Krugman do not explain is why this hoarding suddenly happened and why it won't end, even with negative real rates. Should we not look elsewhere from the financial sector and central bank policy toward what is going on in the real economy? Under capitalism, that means examining what has happened to the profitability of capital.

Krugman talks about "secular stagnation" under capitalism since the 1980s, echoing the arguments of neo-Keynesian economist Alvin Hansen in the immediate postwar period who extrapolated Keynes's theory to mean the gradual slowdown in growth. Krugman reckons this secular stagnation may be caused by "slowing population growth," keeping effective demand low, or by "persistent trade deficits," which emerged in the 1980s and "since then have fluctuated but never gone away."[11] The first explanation looks outside of the motions of capitalist accumulation to some exogenous law of nature, and the second refers to imbalances and uneven development between capitalist economies, rather than capitalism as a world economy. Both causes deny any fault in the fundamental workings of modern capitalism, and neither sounds convincing.

Martin Wolf also takes up the theme of "stagnation."[12] For him, the cause of this new depression is a "global savings glut" or a "dearth of investment" caused by "excessive hoarding" of savings by capitalists unwilling to invest: "The world economy has been generating more savings than businesses wish to use, even at very low interest rates.

This is true not just in the US, but also in most significant high-income economies." So the problem of the Long Depression is a surplus of profits (savings), not low profitability.

This is a hoary old argument that originated from Ben Bernanke, former chief of the Fed, back in the early 2000s, when he argued that the cause of the "persistent trade deficits" in the United States and the United Kingdom were caused by "too much saving" in the "surplus" Asian and OPEC countries. Thus the credit binge and the subsequent credit crunch was really the fault of Japan or China not spending enough on US goods! Now it is everybody's fault for not spending enough. Again, the question is why are people not spending enough?

That's not difficult to answer when it comes to average households, decimated by reduced incomes and unemployment, but why don't capitalist companies in the United States or the United Kingdom or Europe invest more? Wolf thinks it may be due to "excessive debt" being built up during the credit binge before the Great Recession. So the crisis was caused by "excessive spending" and now the depression is caused by "excessive saving."[13] Capitalism swings from one to the other.

Wolf also thinks the failure to invest may be due to a change in the culture of capitalist firms, which no longer want to invest in productive capital but prefer to play the stock market or buy financial assets. That is what the great capitalist system has come to—a "rentier" economy. Once again, the idea of the profitability of capital in what is, after all, a profit economy by definition, where people invest to make a profit, is totally absent from the explanations by Krugman or Wolf.

Noah Smith, a Keynesian blogger, recently considered how to get out of the depression:[14] for him, the explanation of the depression was high debt still being deleveraged, "low expectations" (of profit?) and "low confidence" (in what?).[15] Again, there is no mention of what is happening to profitability or why capital is idle. Could it be that it is not sufficiently profitable? The only way to revive profitability is through slumps that destroy the value of accumulated unproductive capital, so that profits (relative to the remaining value of capital) will then rise and allow the process of accumulation to resume. As in the Great Depression of the 1930s, capitalism cannot get out of this long slump without a massive destruction of dead capital. World War II eventually managed to do that. In the 1880s and 1890s, it took a series of major slumps before sustained growth resumed. That is similar to now.

Profitability: The Health Indicator

Does this mean that capitalism still has room to expand for many decades, or has it passed its use-by date as a mode of production that can take human society further forward? We can consider the answer to this question by looking at the profitability of global capital. The rate of profit is the best indicator of the health of a capitalist economy. It provides significant predictive value on future investment and the likelihood of recession or slump. The level and direction of a world rate of profit can be an important guide to the future development of the world capitalist economy.

Marx's model of capitalism starts from capital in general. It was at that level of abstraction that Marx developed his model of the laws of motion of capitalism and, in particular, what he considered the most important law of motion in the capitalist process of production: the tendency of the rate of profit to fall.

However, in the real world, there are many capitals—not just one world capitalist economy, but many national capitalist states. There are barriers to the establishment of a world economy and a world rate of profit from labor, trade, and capital restrictions designed to preserve and protect national and regional markets from the flow of global capital. Can we realistically talk about a world rate of profit? What would it tell us if we could?

As early as 1848, Marx forecast that capitalism would become the dominant mode of production and would rule the world. He expected that all the countries and their labor forces would be brought under the control of capitalism and market forces. That would mean two things: the urbanization and industrialization of the peasant and other noncapitalist sectors of economies as they were incorporated into the capitalist sector, and the conflict and tension between global capitalism and national state interests.

The biggest move toward the globalization of capital began in the late nineteenth century with the expansion of capital flows from the leading capitalist states into their colonial territories. This new era of modern imperialism, Marx explained, was part of the need for capitalism in the leading capitalist states to maintain a rate of profit that was falling or under pressure. Foreign trade and investment was an important counteracting factor to the law of falling profitability. It could cheapen the value of constant capital through cheap raw materials, and it could raise the rate of surplus value through the exploitation of a newly emerging labor force for capitalism in the colonial territories. That surplus value could be transferred to the imperialist economies and thus raise the rate of profit there.

This process of globalization begun in the late nineteenth century was arrested by two world wars, the product of imperialist rivalry that resulted from the drive to sustain the rate of profit in the major capitalist economies. However, from about the 1980s onward, with the rate of profit in the major economies at new lows, the leading capitalist states again looked to counteract Marx's law through renewed capital flows into countries that had massive potential reserves of labor that would be submissive and accept "super-exploitation" wages. World trade barriers were lowered, restrictions on cross-border capital flows were reduced, and multinational corporations began to move capital within their corporate accounts.

In the twenty-first century, for the first time in the history of capitalism, we can begin to recognize a world rate of profit that is meaningful. Can we measure this world rate of profit? There have been a few studies that attempt to integrate national rates of profit into a world rate of profit. Minqi Li and colleagues developed a world rate of profit for a long period going back to 1870. For the nineteenth century, the study integrates just the UK, US, and Japanese rates of profit. For the period after 1963, the authors bring in Germany, France, and Italy to make the G6. Among other things, they found that the world rate of profit fell from 1970 to 1983 and then rose from 1984 to 2005, although the data also show a peak in the world rate of profit in 1997. The authors suggest that this could signal that the world rate of profit is now in a down phase.[16]

Goldman Sachs analysts Kevin Daly and Ben Broadbent developed a global rate of profit based on data from the ten largest capitalist economies. Using national sources, their study used a net yield of capital measure, which excludes capital gains. On this measure, they found that the global rate of profit also rose from 1982, but was only a little higher at the peak of the boom in the last decade compared to the trough in 1982. Interestingly, they also show that US profitability followed the same trajectory: the rate of profit peaked in 1997 and has not been surpassed since. Daly and Broadbent also concluded that a rising rate of profit in the so-called emerging economies was the key driver of the global rate of profit.[17]

More recently, Esteban Maito constructed a world rate of profit based on fourteen countries.[18] He finds pretty much a secular decline since the mid-nineteenth century, but also a relative stabilization or recovery from the mid-1980s. Excluding China, Maito's world rate of profit peaked in 1997, though still at a lower level than in the 1960s, and has fallen since.

We can also measure a world rate of profit that includes all the G7 economies plus the BRICS. There was a fall in the world rate of profit from the starting point of the data in 1963, and the world rate has not recovered to the 1963 level in the past fifty years (see Figure 13.4). The rate of profit reached a low in 1975, and then rose to a peak in the mid-1990s. Since then, the world rate of profit has been static or slightly falling and has not returned to its peak of the 1990s. The data seem to confirm that world capitalism is now in a down phase for profitability. The trends are similar to Maito's.

Figure 13.4

A World Rate of Profit (Indexed 1963=100)

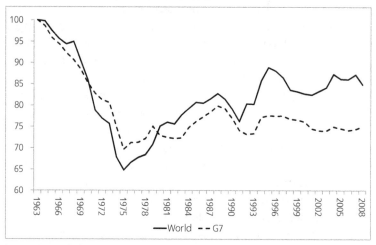

Source: Extended Penn World Tables, Author's Calculations

The other outcome is the divergence between the G7 rate of profit and the world rate of profit after the early 1990s. This indicates that non-G7 economies have played an increasing role in sustaining the rate of profit, especially as the emerging economies have increased their share of world output during this period. The G7 capitalist economies appear to have been suffering a profitability crisis since the late 1980s, certainly since the mid-1990s.

What are the implications of these outcomes? The world rate of profit indicates what most analysts have concluded looking at national rates, particularly that of the United States. The rate of profit rose during what is called the neoliberal period. Marx's law of the tendency of the rate of profit to fall includes a series of countervailing factors that can dominate over the law as such and create conditions for a rise in profitability for some time. Marx said that the most likely conditions for such a rise in the rate of profit were when "a rise in the rate of surplus value was coupled with a significant reduction in the value of the elements of constant capital and fixed capital in particular."[19]

These were precisely the conditions of accumulation from 1982 onward. The two deep economic slumps of 1974–75 and 1980–82 had sufficiently reduced the value of constant capital. At the same time, the slumps had driven up unemployment and weakened the ability of the labor movement to protect wages (the cost of variable capital). The productivity of labor rose as new techniques (and high-tech ones at that) were introduced to many sectors of the economy, while wages were not allowed to rise as much. The wage share in the US economy plunged. The rate of surplus value rose. At the same time, constant capital fell in value relative to variable capital.

As Marx argued: "In practice, however, the rate of profit will fall in the long run."[20] These countervailing influences cannot last forever, and eventually the law of profitability will exert its downward pressure on profits. The rate peaked in 1997 with the exhaustion of the gains of new technology in the productive sectors. In the 1990s, it appears that the impact of these countervailing factors faded in the G7 economies. But this was not the case for the world as a whole.

Globalization was the major force that enabled the counteracting factors to dominate in the 1990s. The connection between globalization and the rate of profit can take two forms. The first is that national capitalist economies can gain a higher rate of profit from investment abroad, to compensate for a fall in the domestic rate of profit. More important, globalization meant a huge growth in international trade and capital flows. This was particularly the case from the 1990s, explaining the divergence between the G7 and world rate of profit.

Capitalism became truly global in the late twentieth century, in a period that was similar but more powerful than in the globalization period of the late nineteenth century. That's because the huge increase in capitalist investment into emerging capitalist economies brought into the capitalist mode of production a huge supply of peasant and noncapitalist labor, and much of it at a cost below the value of labor power in those regions—that is, super-exploitation.

The emerging economies have much faster growth in population than the mature capitalist economies. Since the mid-1970s, the emerging economies have had a larger industrial workforce than the advanced capitalist economies. The gap continues to widen. Value and surplus value in the world capitalist economy are increasingly created from outside the mature capitalist economies. At the same time, this global workforce is super-exploited. The global reserve army of unemployed, underemployed, or inactive is some 80 percent larger than those at work.

This would suggest that as long as there is a significant source of labor supply to be used and exploited under the now dominant capitalist mode of production, capitalism has not reached its absolute limits. China's industrial workforce is still growing, although it is likely to peak by the end of the 2010s. India's workforce has much further to go. There are still areas of the world that are yet to be fully exploited.

Capitalists are permanently engaged in the search for value, or more specifically, surplus value. They can get that globally by drawing more of the population into capitalist production. The big issue is how much longer capitalism can continue to appropriate value from human labor power when the workforce globally can no longer expand sufficiently.[21]

More important, more people means more potential value to be appropriated by capital. But getting more value and surplus value through extending the size of the workforce is increasingly difficult or even impossible in many advanced capitalist economies.

Instead, in these economies, capitalists must try to raise surplus value though the increased intensity of work and through more mechanization and technology that saves labor, that is, increasing relative surplus value. But that, as Marx explained, brings into operation the law of the tendency of the rate of profit to fall and the ultimate barrier to further accumulation and growth in value.

Indeed the crisis in the south of the Eurozone is creating permanent damage to these economies. It is not just that their GDPs are shrinking; there is also an exodus of the workforce. The number of Greek and Spanish residents moving to other EU countries has doubled since 2007, reaching 39,000 and 72,000, respectively, in 2011, according to new figures on immigration published by the OECD. In contrast, Germany saw a 73 percent increase in Greek immigrants between 2011 and 2012, almost 50 percent for Spanish and Portuguese, and 35 percent for Italians.

George Magnus recently pointed out that the "support ratio" (i.e., the amount of people of working age to the total population) in the United States and Europe in the early 2000s was similar to that of Japan ten years earlier.[22] From about 2016, the decline in China's support ratio starts to speed up, so that by 2050, it will have fewer workers per older citizen than the United States has. It also includes India, by way of comparison, as the representative of the bulk of emerging markets and developing countries. India's support ratio is predicted to go lower, but even by 2050, it will still be the same as that in Western countries in the 1990s. From the 1960s onward—a little earlier in Japan—the total support ratio rose everywhere and more or less continuously, until about 1990 in Japan, and 2005–10 in the United States and Europe. Japan's support ratio is now approaching 1.5 workers per older citizen and is predicted to carry on falling to parity in the middle of the century. The United States and Europe are predicted to follow Japan, though support ratios are not expected to fall as far.

There are still huge reserves of labor as yet untapped, particularly in Africa. The latest UN projections for the world's economies show that Africa is expected to dominate population growth over the next ninety years as populations in many of the world's developed economies and China shrink.[23] Africa's population is expected to more than quadruple over just ninety years, while Asia will continue to grow but peak about fifty years from now and then start declining. Europe will continue to shrink. South America's population will rise until about 2050, at which point it will begin a gradual decline. North America will continue to grow at a slow, sustainable rate, surpassing South America's overall population around 2070.

China's population is soon expected to go into decline, whereas India's is expected to grow strongly for another fifty years. Indonesia's populations is projected to grow steadily. Nigeria's population is expected to explode eightfold this century.

Can capitalism get a further kick forward from exploiting the hundreds of millions coming into the labor forces of Asia, South America, and the Middle East? This would be a classic way of compensating for the falling rate of profit in the mature capitalist economies. John Smith has showed the massive increase in the global industrial workforce, now well over 600 million people.[24] Most important, while the industrial workforce in the mature capitalist economies has shrunk to under 150 million; in the so-called emerging economies, the industrial workforce now stands at 500 million, having surpassed the industrial workforce in the imperialist countries by the early 1980s. In addition, there is a large reserve army of labor composed of unemployed, underemployed, or inactive adults of another 2.3 billion people that could also be exploited for new value.

Capitalism in a Terminal Stage?

Despite further room for exploitation of labor globally and in the still-growing emerging economies, maybe capitalism has really passed it use-by date. Is the future of capitalism just one of recurrent and even regular crises of booms and slumps in capitalist accumulation? Or is it more than that, namely, one of eventual breakdown, where capitalism cannot continue indefinitely (even if it has regular crises) but must reach its limits as a system of social organization, then break down and be replaced by a new system?

The Marxist theory of crisis and its laws could be described schematically in Figure 13.5, as showing that capitalism proceeds in cycles of boom and slump.

Such a path of economic development is hugely wasteful of human life and time, as it involves not just the loss of potential output or use values to society but also loss of employment and livelihood of hundreds of millions of working people and their families at recurrent intervals. It breeds social inequality and instability and frequent wars. Unless the working class seizes political power and replaces the capitalist system with another, the figure suggests that capitalism will find a way out. There is no permanent crisis in the sense of total endogenous breakdown.

The alternative of "breakdown theory" of capitalist crisis would look more like what is shown in Figure 13.6.

Figure 13.5
Recurrent Crisis Theory

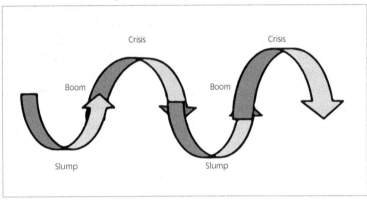

Source: Author

Figure 13.6
Breakdown Theory

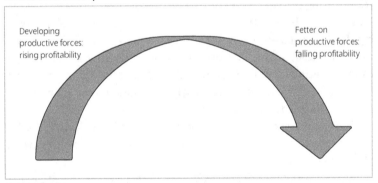

Source: Author

In this model, the capitalist economy rises as it is still a progressive system in developing the productive forces, but eventually the contradictions of capitalist accumulation become so great that capitalism becomes a fetter on human progress. It no longer reduces labor time or increases use values sufficiently. Capitalism then heads for breakdown and the final confrontation with the working class. It's socialism or barbarism.

Thomas Piketty seems to suggest the latter with his book.[25] Piketty's view of the golden age is that it was a very special and unrepeatable phenomenon in the history of capitalism. Due to the process of convergence, Europe's capitalist economies and Japan grew faster than they would have if they were at the technological frontier. Increasing population growth rates also drove the sum of population growth and the growth of per capita income ever higher. On the other hand, institutional factors, including high taxation and the threat of communism (which Piketty does not mention) kept the net return on capital low and, uniquely in the history of capitalism, allowed growth of total income to exceed it. All positive developments during the golden age flowed from the reversal of that inequality.

In Piketty's interpretation, this extraordinary parabolic curve, while being "ignited" by the Industrial Revolution as well as by the French and American revolutions, was held "alive" in the twentieth century by the convergence economics, demographic growth, and paradoxically cataclysmic developments during the two world wars. This is now coming to an end, or after China converges to the rich countries' income levels, will indeed come to a final stop. From a convex curve we are likely to go back to a rather flat line, implying barely rising or even stagnant per capita incomes (see Figure 13.7).

Figure 13.7

Annual Growth Rate of World Per Capita Output From Antiquity Until 2100 (%)

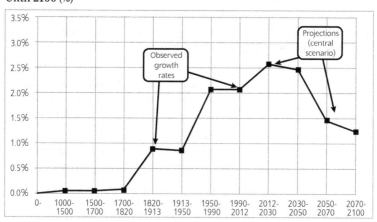

Source: Piketty

Robert Kurz argues something like that, as well.[26] Kurz highlights some key indicators in modern capitalism that tell you it is in its terminal stage. First, there is the growth of unproductive labor. Most labor is increasingly employed in sectors that do not provide surplus value for accumulation, but in circulating existing capital or preserving the capitalist state. This is a very telling indicator of the decline in the "progressive" nature of capitalism on the productive forces.

Kurz is not convinced that the huge supplies of value-creating labor in the emerging economies can be exploited to compensate for the growing unproductive nature of mature capitalist economies.

Another key indicator of the terminal stage of capitalism for Kurz is the huge growth of state credit or debt, which has become a "new normal" condition for capital to accumulate. Fictitious capital in the form of state credit and the abolition of a physical base to money with the ending of the gold standard are big signs. Money is no longer a reliable store of value because value is increasingly difficult to extract from labor. Indeed, financialization and the pyramid of private credit that eventually collapsed in 2007 suggest the decaying nature of this formerly progressive mode of social production.

Sure, says Kurz, the globalization of the capitalist mode of production into noncapitalist areas and the development of the world market is an important way capitalism can stave off breakdown or collapse. It is a powerful counteracting factor, yet another indication that capitalism is in its mature phase historically. He doubts that China or Asia can provide a new lease on life for capitalism with the exploitation of technology and labor there.

But Kurz was writing in 1995, and can we say now that China/India/Asia is not providing new capitalist accumulation? Has "the basis of capitalist reproduction" truly reached its absolute limit, as Kurz argued? Kurz recognized that capitalism could revive itself after crises and slumps through the devaluation of capital, but he doubted that after even the most destructive process that capitalism could still rise from the ashes of a long depression like the mythological Phoenix for two reasons. First, it can no longer properly exploit the technical advances to deliver new levels of profitability and second, the productive sector in industry is now too weak and small to do so. So capitalism is "a walking corpse" that cannot start again from the beginning on a purified terrain. Society is faced with proceeding to socialism or back to precapitalist barbarism, because it cannot continue in its current form.

The idea that capitalism can no longer exploit technology success-fully is the theme adopted by David Graeber.[27] He argues that capi-talism has failed to deliver on the hopes and promises of technologi-cal advances in the past fifty years: what happened to robot factories, moon bases, personal jet packs, and robots in the home? Leisure time has not increased for the average working household—on the con-trary. "Blue skies" research that does not require or lead to immediate practical applications is disappearing as universities fight to provide business with any small improvement in profit-making rather than in-novations that could transform society. Bureaucracy rules: "no popu-lation in history has spent nearly so much time engaged in paperwork." Modern capitalism cannot afford to solve the climate crisis and other environmental nightmares or find a cure for cancer.

Why has it failed? Because capitalism is a mode of production for profit; profitability is in secular and terminal decline, in Graeber's view. He says there are three claims that capitalism makes to justify itself as a progressive mode of social organization: it fosters scientific and technological growth, it increases overall prosperity, and it cre-ates a more secure and democratic world. But it increasingly fails to deliver on all three: Backing up this view is Mariana Mazzucato, who has shown that the real story of high-tech innovation over the past thirty years has not been one of risk-taking entrepreneurs out of Sili-con Valley but government-funded projects.[28]

Robert J. Gordon argues that the United States is in just such a ter-minal stage.[29] Indeed, he states provocatively that the rapid technolog-ical progress under the capitalist mode of production in the past 250 years is over. The ability of capitalist accumulation to foster economic growth is faltering, and real GDP per capita, at least in the US econ-omy, will be slower that in any extended period since the Civil War, when US capitalism first leaped onto the world stage. Gordon argues six headwinds will slow future innovation: an aging population in the mature economies, rising inequality, an increasing lack of competitive advantage for the mature capitalist economies, poorer education be-cause public investment in education is being destroyed, increasing en-vironmental regulations, and excessive debt. He concludes that US real economic growth could fall to just an average 0.2 percent a year for the foreseeable future compared 2–3 percent of the past. Whether those headwinds justify such slower economic growth is open to question.

Gordon suggests that capitalism drove the productive forces (and thus economic growth) upward from about 1750 to 1950. Now we are in the downward spiral of capitalism that no longer takes the productive forces forward. He illustrates UK and US economic growth rates over the period. Capitalism, at least in the mature economies, has had its day.

However, Gordon's arguments have been attacked. Krugman and Chicago neoclassical economist John Cochrane agreed that their "gut feeling" was that Gordon is too pessimistic about the future of technology.[30]

Gordon admitted that he was talking about the United States and no other economies where the "headwinds" may be weaker and agreed that "there is plenty of room for 'catch-up growth' in the emerging markets of the world."[31] He was looking at potential growth, not actual real GDP. But he claims that he does not need to predict poor innovation from here still to conclude that US economic growth is set to slow to a trickle over the next few decades.[32]

Gordon predicts the real living standards of all but the top 1 percent in the income distribution will barely grow at all in the decades ahead and that this experience of the vast bulk of the population has been no better than that since 1973. Over the whole of that period, median real household income has actually risen by only 0.1 percent a year. What cannot be denied is the productivity growth in the United States and other major capitalist economies has been slowing since the 1970s—neoliberalism has failed to innovate. US output per hour of work since 1972 has risen by only about 1.3 percent a year, apart from the brief dot-com boom in the late 1990s. Real output growth per worker has slowed from a mediocre 2.4 percent a year (as Gordon recorded) in the past 20 years to just 1 percent a year since 2009.

Many critics of Gordon's view argue that this slowdown is temporary and is caused by the effects of the Great Recession and the cyclically weak recovery. Once capitalists start to invest more, productivity growth will recover to the previous trend. The only problem with that argument is that there is still little sign of any significant return to the previous trend in business investment growth.

In 2013, real spending on business investment in the United States rose 3.8 percent, little more than half the rate achieved prior to the Great Recession (see Figure 13.8). What is especially noticeable is that spending on high-tech innovative equipment, the previously dynamic high growth sector with an average of 10–20 percent annual growth, is very weak, now growing at a pace slower than overall real GDP.

High-tech spending on both equipment and software has fallen as a share from 4.7 percent of US GDP in 2000 to 3.5 percent in 2013. This area is key to boosting productivity. What is the reason for this slowdown in investment in new technology? It appears to be that the cost of new equipment and software is just too high relative to the realized and expected return on those investments—in other words, the rate of profit is not high enough.

Kenneth Rogoff pitched in on Gordon's predictions.[33] He agreed that there were obstacles to continuing the "previous success" of capitalism. Yet he remained optimistic that capitalism can overcome these challenges,[34] as he reckoned that technological progress has trumped obstacles to economic growth in the past.[35]

Robots, AI, and Labor Power

Is technology and innovation really going to fail to deliver better growth over the next few decades? Contrary to Graeber, the rise of robots and artificial intelligence is predicted by some to start very soon and have an exponential effect in what has been called the "second machine age"[36] or "the march of the robots."

Figure 13.8

Annual Growth in US Real Business Spending on Hi-Tech Equipment % yoy

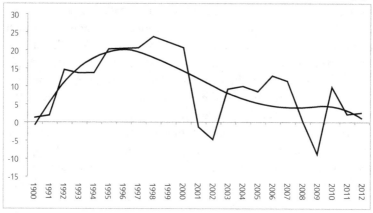

Source: BEA

One of the basic Marxist theoretical arguments is that the competitive pressure to make more profit forces capitalist producers to find new technologies that can save on the overall costs of production. It may be possible for newly expanding capitalist economies to use huge supplies of cheap labor to create surplus value rather than using new technology (or ideally a combination of both, as in China and East Asia). But in more mature (and aging) economies, the supply of cheap labor has run out and capitalists in the West can only compete in world markets by either exporting their capital into the emerging economies (imperialism or globalization) or finding new technologies that raise labor productivity exponentially.

Globalization was the story of the period from the late 1970s to early 2000s as the "solution" to falling profitability in the major capitalist economies. But a new downturn in profitability in the late 1990s and the recessions of 2001 and 2008–9 has put that solution in jeopardy. Indeed, it is being argued that it is no longer cheaper to build factories and expand business in emerging economies because wages there are rising fast. According to the International Labour Organization in its World of Work report, inflation-adjusted average wages in China more than tripled over the decade from 2000 to 2010.[37] In Asia as a whole, they have doubled. In Eastern Europe and Central Asia, average wages almost tripled. Yet in the developed world, wages are just barely higher than they were in 2000.

This has led some to argue that after its sixty-year decline, manufacturing may start to return to the advanced capitalist economies. Then profitability will rise again in the major capitalist economies through a new manufacturing revolution. Much is being made of the likes of Apple opening up factories in the United States rather than Asia. Apple says it will invest $100 million in producing some of its Mac computers in the United States, beyond the assembly work it already does in the United States.[38] Over the past few years, companies across various industries, including electronics, automotive, and medical devices, have announced that they are "reshoring" jobs after decades of shipping them abroad. Lenovo, the computer giant based in China, said it would begin making its ThinkPad-branded computers, including notebooks, desktops, and some tablets, in the United States.[39]

This is really just so much wishful thinking in the US media. General Electric has hired American workers to build water heaters, refrigerators, dishwashers, and high-efficiency top-load washing machines, but continues to add more jobs overseas as well. Apple's iPad and iPhone products, which amount to nearly 70 percent of its sales, will continue to be made in low-cost centers of manufacturing like China, mostly on contract with outside companies like Foxconn. American manufacturing has been growing in the past few years, but the sector still has 2 million fewer jobs than when the recession began in December 2007. Worldwide manufacturing is growing much faster, even for many of the American-owned companies that are expanding at home. Wage levels may have risen in emerging economies and stagnated in the advanced economies, but the gap is still huge. As of 2010 (the latest year for which data are available), hourly compensation costs for manufacturing in the United States were about four times those in Taiwan and twenty times those in the Philippines.

Although some manufacturing may return to the United States, it will not bring jobs with it. A new study by McKinsey finds that manufacturing now makes up 20 percent of global economic output and 37 percent of global productivity growth since 1995.[40] But because investment in manufacturing is "capital-biased," it does not create jobs and is designed to avoid raising wages. Indeed, according to McKinsey, manufacturing employment fell 24 percent in the advanced economies between 1995 and 2005.

In the advanced economies, higher profits can only come from raising the productivity of labor or by a reduction in raw material (energy) costs, rather than lowering or holding wages down through the use of more cheap labor. The shale oil and gas revolution in North America and parts of Europe may help reduce energy costs over the next decade (maybe). But getting overall costs down depends on the new technologies.

That brings up the issue of robots, something that is being raised as the imminent way out for advanced capitalist economies to compete in world manufacturing markets. If manufacturers increasingly use robots, they can do away with expensive labor and all will be well for capitalism.

In some high-profile industries, technology is displacing workers of almost all kinds. For example, one of the reasons some high-technology manufacturing has lately been moving back to the United States is that the most valuable piece of a computer, the motherboard, is basically made by robots, so cheap Asian labor is no longer a reason to produce them abroad. Robots mean that labor costs don't matter so much and capitalists can then locate in advanced countries with large markets and better infrastructure. Even the low wages earned by factory workers in China have not insulated them from being undercut by new machinery. In 2011, Terry Gou, the founder of Foxconn, announced a plan to purchase a million robots to replace much of his workforce.[41] The robots will take over routine jobs like spraying paint, welding, and basic assembly.

Now mainstream economics has noticed that this is not good news for labor and have suggested that a capital bias in technology could explain the falling labor share and growing inequalities. Computer engineer and Silicon Valley software entrepreneur Martin Ford puts it this way: "Over time, as technology advances, industries become more capital intensive and less labor intensive. And technology can create new industries and these are nearly always capital intensive."[42] The struggle between capital and labor is thus intensified.[43]

So much depends on the development of the class struggle between labor and capital over the appropriation of the value created by the productivity of labor. Clearly labor has been losing that battle, particularly in recent decades, under the pressure of anti–trade union laws, ending of employment protection and tenure, the reduction of benefits, a growing reserve army of unemployed and underemployed, and the globalization of manufacturing.

According to the ILO report, in sixteen developed economies, labor took a 75 percent share of national income in the mid-1970s, but this dropped to 65 percent in the years before the economic crisis. It rose in 2008 and 2009—but only because national income itself shrank in those years—before resuming its downward course. Even in China, where wages have tripled over the past decade, workers' share of the national income has gone down.

Overall compensation for workers as a share of national income in the advanced economies did not fall in the 1980s and 1990s because nonwage benefits like health insurance, pensions, and state benefits compensated. These extra costs to capital have been ruthlessly crushed in the past decade.

Capital bias is not new in economic theory. Marx explained in detail that this is one of the key features in capitalist accumulation—something continually ignored by mainstream economics, until now it seems. Marx put it differently. Investment under capitalism takes place for profit only, not to raise output or productivity as such. If profit cannot be sufficiently raised through more labor hours (i.e., more workers and longer hours) or by intensifying efforts (speed and efficiency—time and motion), then the productivity of labor can only be increased by better technology. So in Marxist terms, the organic composition of capital (the amount of machinery and plant relative to the number of workers) will rise secularly. Workers can fight to keep as much of the new value that they have created as part of their compensation, but capitalism will only invest for growth if that wage share does not rise so much that it causes profitability to decline. So capitalist accumulation implies a falling share to labor over time or what Marx would call a rising rate of exploitation (or surplus value).

Will capitalism be saved by robots, while workers live the happy life of leisure that John Maynard Keynes believed would be achieved by capitalism? Well, clearly, past technology did not do that. Predictions of the 1970s—that workers would have to worry more about what to do with their leisure time than if they could work enough to make ends meet—have not materialized.

Keynes predicted that with technology the capitalist world would achieve superabundance and a three-hour day—the socialist dream, but under capitalism.[44] The average working week in the United States in 1930—if you had a job—was about fifty hours. It is still above forty hours (including overtime) for full-time permanent employment. Indeed, in 1980, the average hours worked in a year was about 1,800 for the advanced economies. Currently, it is about 1,800 hours—no change there.

Would robots do the trick? Existing robots allow tasks to be carried out repeatedly (and indefinitely) to a predictable standard. Autonomous, intelligent robots will allow this approach to be applied to a wider variety of tasks, from warehouses to care homes. Examples on the horizon include flexible assembly robots that can be taught to use new tools or assemble new prototype products, logistics robots that can safely choose the best routes through a busy warehouse, and cleaning robots that can learn which areas get dirty and when. For businesses, this means that more tasks can be automated (and thus predictably and accurately performed). By using learning software, robots could be retrained to work on new problems as required.

One study shows, however, that as many as 47 percent of positions currently filled by humans could be done by a computerized workforce "over some unspecified number of years, perhaps a decade or two."[45] Most likely to be replaced are telemarketers, title examiners, mathematical technicians, watch repairers, and insurance underwriters—the research suggests a 99 percent chance that these roles will be performed by robots in the future. Just like ATMs have reduced bank teller positions and self-driving cars might replace taxi drivers, this frees up a lot of labor.

As the use of robots accelerates, this technology is contributing to a reduction in the number of manufacturing jobs. The mainstream economics view on balance is that this can mean better standards of living alongside lower hours of toil for humans. After all, hasn't the technical progress under capitalism done just that in the past century?

Well no. In the 1930s, Keynes thought that the world was moving toward a decrease in social differences, but globalization in the second half of the twentieth century has created social inequalities without precedent. As work becomes increasingly social and production processes interpenetrate and overlap between countries and continents, power and wealth have increased for the rich elite and exploitation and oppression have increased for the rest. In virtually all countries, surveys show that in recent decades workers have increased job insecurity and feelings of oppression in the workplace.

Will it be different with robots? Marxist economics would say no, for two key reasons. First, Marxist economic theory starts from the undeniable fact that only when human beings do any work or perform labor is anything or any service produced, apart from that provided by natural resources (and even then that has to be found and used). So crucially, only labor can create value under capitalism, and value is specific to capitalism. Living labor can create things and provide services (what Marx called use values). But value is the substance of the capitalist mode of producing things. Capital (the owners) controls the means of production created by labor and will only put them to use to appropriate value created by labor. Capital does not create value itself.

Now if the whole world of technology, consumer products, and services could reproduce itself without living labor going to work and could do so through robots, then things and services would be produced, but the creation of value (in particular, profit or surplus value) would not.

As Ford puts it: "the more machines begin to run themselves, the value that the average worker adds begins to decline."[46] So accumulation under capitalism would cease well before robots took over fully, because profitability would disappear under the weight of capital bias.

The most important law of motion under capitalism, as Marx called it, would be in operation, namely, the tendency for the rate of profit to fall. As capital-biased technology increases, the organic composition of capital would also rise and thus labor would eventually create insufficient value to sustain profitability (i.e., surplus value relative to all costs of capital). We would never get to a robotic society; we would never get to a workless leisure society—not under capitalism. Crises and social explosions would intervene well before that.

The falling share of value going to labor already exposes this contradiction. Capital accumulates through increased centralization and concentration of the means of production in the hands of a few. This ensures that the value created by labor is appropriated by capital and that the share going to the 99 percent is minimized. This is not monopoly as an imperfection of perfect competition, it is the monopoly of ownership of the means of production by a few. This is the straightforward functioning of capitalism, warts and all.

It's not monopoly power or rising rents going to the robber barons of the monopolies that forces down labor's share, it's just capitalism. Labor's share in the capitalist sector in the United States and other major capitalist economies is down because of increased technology and capital bias from globalization and cheap labor abroad, from the destruction of trade unions, from the creation of a larger reserve army of labor (unemployed and underemployed), and from ending work benefits and secured tenure contracts. Companies that are not monopolies in their markets probably did more of this than monopolies. Indeed, this is exactly what Marx meant by the "immiseration of the working class." This contradiction cannot be resolved under capitalism.[47]

Climate Change and Capitalism

Before we can even imagine a capitalist world of robots and no living labor, capitalism is faced with a new barrier to its expansion and even survival—one of its own making. This is irreparable damage to the planet from rapacious capitalist production and the increase in the atmospheric warming of the planet from greenhouse gases.

Minqi Li argues the global warming crisis and the peak of energy production will make it impossible for capitalism to avoid collapse or breakdown. Like Gordon and echoing the views of Immanuel Wallerstein, Li predicts that world economic growth will grind to halt by the 2040s as a result. Capitalism cannot survive beyond that and there must be a new system of human social organization or total chaos.[48] Socialism or ecological disaster is Li's forecast. Richard Smith makes a devastating case for a similar outcome.[49]

Are they right? The International Panel for Climate Change (IPCC) brings together hundreds of scientists in the field of climate change to cooperate in drawing up a comprehensive analysis of the state of the Earth's climate and forecasts about its future. The latest IPCC report raised its estimate of the probability that human activities, led by the burning of fossil fuels, are the main cause of climate change since the mid-twentieth century to "extremely likely," or at least 95 percent, from "very likely" (90 percent) in its previous report in 2007 and "likely" (66 percent) in 2001.[50]

The IPCC said that short periods are influenced by natural variability and do not generally reflect long-term climate trends. Those who deny climate change is man-made or is not getting worse cannot rely on the slowing of the rise in average atmospheric temperatures in the past fifteen years. The IPCC went on to say that temperatures were likely to rise by 0.3–4.8°C (0.5 to 8.6°F) by the late twenty-first century. Sea levels are likely to rise by 26–82 cm (10–32 inches) by the late twenty-first century, after a 19 cm rise in the nineteenth century. In the worst case, seas could be 98 cm higher in 2100.

The IPCC estimates that a doubling of carbon dioxide concentrations in the atmosphere would lead to a warming of 1.5–4.5°C (2.7–8.1°F), lowering the bottom of the range from 2.0°C (3.6°F) estimated in a 2007 report. The new range, however, is the same as in other IPCC reports before 2007. It said the Earth was set for more heat waves, floods, droughts, and rising sea levels from melting ice sheets that could swamp coasts and low-lying islands as greenhouse gases build up in the atmosphere.

The IPCC admitted that it was still unclear about the causes for the slowdown in climate change in the past fifteen years, but insisted that the long-term trends were beyond doubt and that a decade and a half was far too short a period in which to draw any firm conclusions.

The temperature rise has slowed from 0.12°C per decade since 1951 to 0.05°C per decade in the past fifteen years—a point seized on by climate skeptics to discredit climate science.[51] Explaining a recent slower pace of warming, the report said the past fifteen-year period was skewed by the fact that 1998 was an extremely warm year with an El Niño event—a warming of the ocean surface—in the Pacific. It said warming had slowed because of random variations in the climate and the impact of factors such as volcanic eruptions when ash dims sunshine, and a cyclical decline in the sun's output.

But the deniers of climate change remain unconvinced. Judith Curry of the Georgia Institute of Technology responded by saying, "Well, IPCC has thrown down the gauntlet—if the pause continues beyond 15 years (well it already has), they are toast."[52] Rajendra Pachauri, chair of the IPCC, retorted that the reduction in warming would have to last far longer—"three or four decades"—to be a sign of a new trend.[53] The IPCC report predicted that the reduction in warming would not last, saying temperatures in 2016–2035 were likely to be 0.3–0.7°C (0.5–1.3°F) warmer than in 1986–2005.[54]

The skeptics or deniers are a tiny percentage of scientists in the field of climate change. An analysis of abstracts of 11,944 peer-reviewed scientific papers, published between 1991 and 2011 and written by 29,083 authors, concludes that 98.4 percent of authors who took a position endorsed man-made (anthropogenic) global warming, 1.2 percent rejected it, and 0.4 percent were uncertain.[55] More recent studies made after the laborious IPCC compilations[56] confirm that the Earth is warming up at a rate that can only be explained by human activity. Indeed, the concentration of carbon dioxide in the atmosphere was reported to have passed 400 parts per million for the first time in 4.5 million years.

The evidence of climate change and its man-made nature is increasingly overwhelming. The potentially disastrous effects from higher temperatures, rising sea levels, and extreme weather formations will be hugely damaging especially to the poorest and most vulnerable people on the planet. But industrialization and human activity need not produce these effects if human beings organized their activities in a planned way with due regard for the protection of natural resources and the wider impact on the environment and public health. That seems impossible under capitalism.

The environmental and ecological impact of the capitalist mode of production was highlighted by Marx and Engels way back in the early part of industrialization in Europe. As Engels put it, capitalism is production for profit and not human need, and so takes no account of the impact on wider society of accumulation for profit.[57] This drive for profit leads to ecological catastrophe.[58]

Marx summed up the impact of capitalist production on nature: "All progress in capitalistic agriculture is a progress in the art, not only of robbing the laborer, but of robbing the soil; all progress in increasing the fertility of the soil for a given time, is a progress toward ruining the lasting sources of that fertility . . . Capitalist production, therefore, develops technology, and the combining together of various processes into a social whole, only by sapping the original sources of all wealth—the soil and the laborer."[59]

There is modern evidence that climate change is the result of capitalist accumulation. Jose Tapia Granados and Oscar Carpintero have shown that there is a procyclical correlation between the rate of increase of atmospheric CO_2 and the rate of growth of the global economy, providing strong evidence that the world economy is linked with the build-up of the greenhouse effect and, therefore, with the process of global warming.[60]

Tapia Granados uses multivariate analysis of the influence of the world economy, volcanic activity, and El Niño Southern Oscillation activity on CO_2 levels to show that the annual increase in atmospheric CO_2 is significantly linked to the growth of the global economy. Years of above-trend GDP growth are years of greater rise in CO_2 concentrations, and similarly, years of below-trend growth are years of smaller rise in CO_2 concentrations. So global emissions of CO_2 have increased at rates strongly correlated with the absolute growth of the global economy.

This might well provide part of the explanation of the slowdown in global warming from 1998, because world economic growth slowed since then. A major drop in the growth of estimated emissions occurred in 2009 as a consequence of the Great Recession. When capitalist production stops, so does global warming. Of course, that does not end the story.[61]

Most of the rise in emissions comes from emerging economies where economic growth has been fastest. China was responsible for 24 percent of the global total emissions in 2009, against 17 percent for the United States and 8 percent for the Eurozone. But each Chinese person emits only a third as much as an American and less than four-fifths of a resident of the Eurozone. China is a relatively wasteful emerging economy, in terms of its emissions per unit of output. But it still emits less per person than the high-income countries because its people remain relatively poor. As emerging countries develop, emissions per person will tend to rise toward levels in high-income countries, raising the global average. This is why global emissions per person rose by 16 percent between 2000 and 2009, which was a period of fast growth in emerging economies.

European Climate Commissioner Connie Hedegaard said: "If your doctor was 95 percent sure you had a serious disease, you would immediately start looking for a cure."[62] But what are the solutions? The skeptics say nothing should be done to weaken the drive to get more energy "for the poor"—but they really mean not restricting the profits of the fossil fuel companies. So the leaders of this capitalist world will not adopt energy policies that keep emissions below the "safe" level of 450 parts per million. There is an urgent search for new sources of energy supply that are cleaner and cheaper. But capitalism has failed to deliver. Investment in renewables and other low-carbon sources has just not been enough, and the technical advantages of such sources are disappointing. Offshore wind is a technology that is not profitable. Nuclear energy, as shown by the stations being built in Finland and France, is getting more rather than less expensive.

What about changing behavior? The chair of the IPCC reckoned that the only way to reduce large-scale fossil fuel use is to "price" carbon emissions.[63] But is the neoclassical economics solution of pricing going to work to change the behavior of energy and manufacturing companies? What governments will "interfere" with the market for energy to do so? The EU carbon emissions permits scheme, designed to drive up carbon pricing, has failed miserably.

An alternative solution from some mainstream economists is carbon taxation. Taxing bad things like cigarettes may have some effect, but high taxes on tobacco also hit the incomes of the poorest. What is really needed is proper planning of available resources globally, plus a drive, through public investment, to develop new technologies that could work (like carbon capture, transport not based on fossil fuels, goods produced locally with low carbon footprints, etc.) and, of course, a shift out of fossil fuels into renewables. Also, it is not just a problem of carbon and other gas emissions, but of cleaning up the environment, which is already damaged. All these tasks require public control and ownership of the energy and transport industries and public investment in the environment for the public good.

The world is already experiencing extreme weather. In the United States, California's drought in 2014 was the worst in 100 years while the East Coast faced a massive snowstorm with freezing temperatures. On the other side of the world, Australia has dealt with intense summer heat and droughts, causing major bush fires. There has been severe winter flooding in the United Kingdom and Europe, and so on.

Now this may just be random—outliers in the normal distribution of weather conditions—or maybe the globe is reaching a peak in a cycle of weather, or it could be the ever-growing impact of climate change as the world heats up. In fact, it could be all three, because the first two possible causes can be considered as immediate or cyclical and the last (climate change) as structural or "ultimate." The facts speak. Since 1997, the world has experienced the thirteen warmest years ever recorded out of fifteen, according to the United Nations. June 2012 marked the 328th consecutive month with a global temperature above the twentieth century average. In 2013, extreme weather events included several all-time temperature records. Snow cover in Europe and North America was above average, while the Arctic ice was 4.5 percent below the 1981–2010 average.

Northern Hemisphere weather extremes have been linked to Arctic sea ice melting. In January alone, 11,233 weather-related deaths were reported in India. Bangladesh faced the lowest temperature since the country's independence in 1971. In Europe, summer 2014's weather was bizarre. Finland and most of the northern countries got the highest temperatures in Europe during May and June, while Western and Middle Europe faced much cooler weather and even their wettest May and June ever.

Every year there is a major disaster in the emerging economies, with thousands dying and hundreds of thousands losing their homes and livelihoods. But the media only remembers the events that hit the rich economies. The most infamous was Hurricane Katrina, the bursting of the levees, and the flooding of homes in New Orleans. Not only did the federal and local governments fail to act quickly and efficiently, we know that warnings of such a calamity had been voiced years before. Instead of spending more to upgrade the levees, federal and state governments actually cut back on such infrastructure funding. After all, such spending was of no value to the rich, living up on their hilltop homes.

Even the classical economist of capitalism and the so-called guru of free markets Adam Smith recognized the need for public spending in infrastructure because the private sector could not do it.[64] The American Society of Civil Engineers (ASCE) has continually complained that America's infrastructure is rotting away. It found that one in five US bridges were "structurally deficient." Although the number of miles traveled by cars and trucks has doubled in the past twenty-five years, highway lane miles rose only 45 percent. Demand for electricity has increased by 25 percent, but the construction of new transmission facilities has fallen by 30 percent. This deterioration has cost 870,000 jobs that could have been secured with new projects, while the costs of moving goods has risen significantly. The ASCE reckoned that there was $100 billion of potential work available. Instead, the US Congress plans to cut such spending by 35 percent to the end of this decade.

The evidence is overwhelming that unless the capitalist system is replaced in the next fifty years, the planet will be suffering from such damage to its natural development that economic growth will slow, natural disasters will become common, and the cost of restoration and prevention will become too much for a profit-making mode of production to handle.[65]

Crisis or Breakdown?

This chapter has argued that the world capitalist economy is in a Long Depression that began with the Great Recession of 2008–9 and probably won't end until 2018 or so—and then only after another major slump or recession. It has also argued that capitalism is not in some permanent stagnation brought on by causes of Keynesian origin, like permanently stuck interest rates and lack of effective demand, or on the other side of the coin, by excessive saving and not enough spending.

The Long Depression can come to an end when profitability in the major economies has been sufficiently restored by a further devaluation of capital values through another slump. Assuming that capitalism in any major economy is not replaced by a planned economy owned in common and controlled by the majority, or that there is not a new and devastating world war in the next decade, capitalism will eventually recover.

That does not mean capitalism will march on forever in a series of booms and slumps. There is a limit to the exploitation of absolute surplus value through new areas of surplus labor coming under the control of capital globally. Increasingly, surplus value will only be expanded relatively through new technology. That new technology will include a robot revolution. Artificial intelligence will be exploited by capital to replace labor in many jobs that seem untouchable right now.

But the robotic revolution will exacerbate the contradiction under capitalism between developing the productivity of labor and appropriating more value in profit for capital. The first will exert increased limits on the latter.

Moreover, before we get to that contradiction, capital in its rapacious drive for more value has so seriously damaged the planet that we face an environmental and ecological crisis over the next generation that will increase already growing inequalities and pose major struggles over land, water, and resources.

What is the right schema for capitalism over the next thirty years? Regular crises or one big breakdown—neither is the full story. The schema for capitalism looks more like Figure 13.9. There will be recurring crises or cycles that spin around the secular downtrend for capitalist development.

Capitalism will not just collapse of its own accord. Crises and even a breakdown are endogenous because of the main contradiction within the capitalist mode of production, of accumulation for profit and not need. But also it is possible for capitalism to recover and soldier on "endogenously" when sufficient old capital is destroyed in value (and sometimes physically) to allow a new period of rising profitability.

Capitalism can only be replaced by a new system of social organization through conscious action of human beings, in particular by the majority of people (the working class globally). Without such conscious action, capitalism can stumble on or society may eventually fall back into barbarism. By "barbarism," I mean a decisive drop back in the productivity of labor and living conditions to precapitalist times. The Roman republic rose tooth and claw over 500 years based on a war machine financed by the work of free peasant farming and land-owning estates. Then a predominantly slaveholding Roman empire slid down over 400 years before the European world collapsed into barbarism. The technology of the Romans (derived from the innovations of the Greeks before them) was mostly forgotten and became unused. That could happen again and much more quickly in a world where things move so much more rapidly.

Figure 13.9

Combined Secular Trend and Cyclical Motion of Capitalism

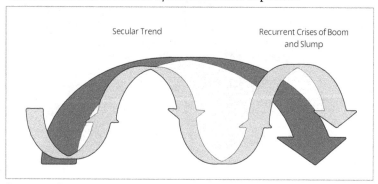

Source: Author

Appendix 1
Measuring the Rate of Profit

The cause of a crisis like the Great Recession must lie with the key laws of motion of capitalism. The most important law of motion of capitalism, Marx argued, was the law of the tendency of the rate of profit to fall. So it must be relevant to a Marxist explanation.[1]

Marx was clear on what his definition of the rate of profit (ROP) was—the general or overall rate of profit in an economy was the surplus value generated by the labor force divided by the cost of employing that labor force and the cost of physical or tangible assets and raw materials that are employed in production. His famous formula followed: $P = s/c + v$, where P is the rate of profit, s is surplus value, c is constant capital (means of production), and v is the cost of the labor power.

Marx is clear that the ROP applies to the whole economy. It is a general rate of profit derived from the total surplus value produced in an economy as a ratio to the total costs of capitalist production. All that surplus is produced by the labor power of workers employed in the "productive" capitalist sectors of production. Some of that value is also transferred to unproductive sectors in the form of wages and profits and to noncapitalist sectors in the form of wages and taxes.

So the rate of profit is the total surplus value divided by total value of labor in all sectors and the cost of fixed and circulating assets in the capitalist sector. That means fixed and circulating capital in the noncapitalist sector is not counted in the denominator for calculating the ROP. But their wages are.

Profit as a category applies to the capitalist sector of the economy. Wages as a category applies to the noncapitalist sector, too. The value measured in the noncapitalist sector has been transferred from the capitalist sector through taxation, sales of noncapitalist production to the capitalist sector, and the raising of debt.

There are many ways of measuring a rate of profit à la Marx.[2] Take

273

constant capital. This is fixed assets of capitalist production plus raw materials used in the production process (circulating capital). In measuring the rate of profit, we must therefore exclude the residential assets (homes) of households and the assets of government and other nonprofit activities.

A capitalist economy can be divided between a productive and unproductive sector. The productive sector (goods producing, transport, and communications) creates all the value and surplus value. The unproductive sector (commercial trading, real estate, financial services) appropriates some of that value.

Then you could just look at the business sector of the capitalist economy for all parts of Marx's ROP formula and exclude the wages of public sector workers. You could narrow it further and exclude the wages of unproductive workers within the productive sector (supervisors, marketing staff, etc.). You can measure constant capital in current costs or in historic costs.[3] You can measure profit before or after tax.

In my view, the simplest is the best. Most measures of the rate of profit in this book follow a simple formula. S = net national product (that's GDP less depreciation) less v (employee compensation); c = net fixed assets (either on a historic or current cost basis); and v = employee compensation, that is, wages plus benefits. The measure of value is usually for the whole economy and not just for the corporate sector (which would exclude employee costs or the product appropriated by government from the private sector through taxation). It also includes the value and profits appropriated by the financial sector, even though it is not productive in the Marxist sense. The measure of constant capital is for the capitalist sector only and so excludes household investment in homes and government investment.

Do These Different Measures Matter? Yes and No

In one way, it does not seem to matter how you measure the Marxist rate of profit. All measures show that for the US economy—the largest capitalist economy with 25 percent of annual world GDP and twice as large as the next largest capitalist economy—there has been a secular trend downward in the rate of profit for any period in which we have data. This is correlated with a trend upward in the organic composition of capital, suggesting that Marx's most important law of motion of capitalism, the tendency of the rate of profit to fall as the organic composition capital rises, is confirmed by the evidence.

Duménil and Lévy find that "the profit rate in 2000 is still only half of its value in 1948. Finally, we show that the decline of the productivity of capital was the main factor of the fall of the profit rate, though the decline of the share of profits also contributed to this evolution."[4]

But it may matter when it comes to applying Marx's law to the causes of capitalist crisis. Most of those who have provided measures of the rate of profit à la Marx, have found that the ROP peaked in 1997 after the rise from the trough of 1982 and was not surpassed even in the boom of 2002–7.

Simon Mohun spells out his thesis "that US capitalism is characterised by long secular periods of falling profitability and long secular periods of rising profitability and crises are associated with major turning points."[5] His turning points seem to be a 1946 trough in profitability, a 1965 peak, a 1982 trough, and a 1997 peak—similar to mine.

Li Minqi, Fenq Xiao, and Andong Zu looked at the movement of the profit rate and related variables in the United Kingdom, the United States, Japan, and the Eurozone.[6] According to them, since the mid-nineteenth century there have been four long waves in the movement of the average profit rate and rate of accumulation. They find a peak at 1997 in the ROP for the United States.

David M. Kotz uses an after-tax ROP measure of the nonfinancial corporate business sector as a percentage of net worth.[7] Kotz finds that the US ROP rose rapidly to 1997. Then it peaked and fell sharply thereafter.

Anwar Shaikh, using another measure of ROP as profits of enterprise that excludes rent, interest, and taxes, finds that that the US ROP peaked in 1997.[8]

George Economakis, Alexis Anastasiadis, and Maria Markaki measure the Marxist ROP by the net product less employee compensation divided by net fixed capital of US nonfinancial corporations,[9] which is very close to my broader measure. They find that the ROP rose from 10.6 percent in 1946 to a peak of 19 percent in 1966, falling back to 9.6 percent in 1983 and then rising to a peak of 18.2 percent in 1997 before dropping back again remaining under the peak of 1997 thereafter. They also find that adding the financial sector into the equation makes no difference to the turning points or trend of the ROP.

Erdogan Bakir and Al Campbell find that US after-tax profit rate peaked in 1997 at about 7.5 percent before falling back, and the next peak in 2006 was still below that of 1997.[10]

All these studies not only confirm the secular decline in the US ROP since 1946 but also agree that there was a cyclical movement in the ROP, with turning points of a peak in 1965–66, a trough at 1982 and then a peak in 1997, not surpassed since.

Andrew Kliman has several measures of US ROP. He includes the financial sector in his measures.[11] But his favored one of "property income" measured against the historic cost of net fixed assets has shown no cyclical turning points but a "persistent" fall in the ROP. He argues that the rise in ROP since 1982 as shown by others is because they measure the ROP against current costs and not historic costs, as Marx would. But my measure uses historic costs and still shows a rise in ROP after 1982.

Appendix 2
The Failure of Keynesianism

There are two great merits of Keynes's contribution to understanding an economy. The first was a return to analyzing an economy in its aggregate, not at the level of an individual consumer's or firm's behavior or preferences. This meant that the fluctuations in a capitalist economy could be considered in their whole and not just ignored or dismissed. In other words, macroeconomics replaced microeconomics.

The second contribution was to assert that capitalist free markets do not clear and so supply does not equal demand, at least at a macro level. So the capitalist mode of production can be in equilibrium at less than full employment for some time. Keynes saw this discovery as a refutation of the old economic rule, called Say's law, that supply always equals demand, namely, that where there is seller there must be a buyer. This law is still held to in one form or another by neoclassical and Austrian economics schools. Keynes was attempting to break with the old adage of Thomas Carlyle: "Teach any parrot the words supply and demand and you've got an economist."

For Keynes, Say's law was an example of the fallacy of composition, the false assumption that what is true for a part will also be true for the whole. In macroeconomics, the other-things-being-equal assumption of demand matching supply does not hold. The paradox of thrift is the traditional Keynesian example of the fallacy of composition. The paradox states that if everyone tries to save more money during times of slump, then aggregate demand will fall and will in turn lower total savings in the population because of the decrease in consumption. The paradox is that total savings may fall even when individuals attempt to save more and that increase in savings may be harmful to an economy.

These great insights have been whittled away over the past three decades for two reasons. First, it became clear to mainstream economists that Keynesian economics did not work in explaining modern

capitalism. Keynes's theory would suggest that if there is high unemployment, aggregate demand would be low and there would be
oversupply, so inflation would be low or nonexistent. Thus, boosting
demand by tax cuts and/or government spending could restore aggregate demand and reduce unemployment without generating inflation
in prices of commodities. Once full employment was reached, however, further stimulus could start to drive up inflation. So there was a
trade-off between inflation and employment. This led to the famous
Phillips curve that attempted to confirm this trade-off empirically.
Unfortunately, the experience of the 1970s demolished this theory,
when the major economies had high unemployment and high inflation or stagflation.

Neoclassical economics and monetarism regained the stage, with
likes of Friedrich Hayek and Milton Friedman, who claimed that interference of the state or central bankers caused inflation and unemployment at the same time. The adoption of these theories was not an
accident because the strategists of capital needed theoretical support
for the counterrevolution they launched against the welfare state and
labor to reverse the squeeze on profits and profitability of capital in
the latter part of the 1970s.

Now Marxist economics could have told both sides that they were
looking in the wrong place for an explanation of stagflation. If they
had looked at the causes of falling profitability in the capitalist mode
of production, that would have explained why fiscal stimulus and easy
money was not restoring full employment but merely stoking up inflation. Stagflation was the outcome of capitalist crisis plus Keynesian
policy prescriptions, unlike the 1930s, which was capitalist crisis without Keynesian stimulus.

The power of aggregate was now rejected.[1] As Keynesian aggregate
econometrics explained nothing, mainstream economics returned to
microeconomic theory. Although Keynes had brought mainstream
economic theory to the macro and the aggregate, he had never broken
with neoclassical marginal utility and general equilibrium theory at
the level of the micro. He rejected any objective labor theory of value
as a foundation for an explanation of economic processes. He held to
the neoclassical "belief" that starts with individual consumer preferences and moves onto market-clearing anomalies before establishing
an equilibrium of supply and demand. So any anomalies were external

shocks to the market system, not endogenous to the process of capitalist production and consumption.

So Keynes's more radical insights were now reduced to the infamous Investment-Savings and Liquidity Preference–Money Supply (IS-LM) curve that argued an unemployment equilibrium would not occur under capitalism unless there was "stickiness" in wages or other "shocks" to the market system. In other words, market capitalism would not have slumps if labor did not resist wage cuts and government did not interfere. This reduced Keynes to a Friedman-style monetarism where central banks "enrich thy neighbor"[2] by controlling the money supply.

During the Great Moderation, when fluctuations in economic growth and prices supposedly fell away during the 1990s, mainstream Keynesian economics concentrated on explaining business cycles or fluctuations in an economy using modern techniques of modeling from what it called microfoundations. Econometric analysis like the Phillips curve were ditched because such correlations between employment and inflation had been proven wrong. The job now was not to look at macro or aggregate data but to work out some model that started with some premises of agent (consumer) behavior or preferences and then incorporated some possible shocks to the general equilibrium of the market and then considered the number and probability of possible outcomes.

Thus were born the dynamic stochastic general equilibrium (DSGE) models. They had *equilibrium* because they started from the premise that supply would equal demand ideally; they were *dynamic* because the models incorporated changing behavior by individuals or firms (agents); and they were *stochastic* as shocks to the system (trade union wage push, government spending action) were considered as random with a range of outcomes, unless confirmed otherwise.

This is now what most Keynesian economists spend their time doing. Forget empirical evidence, forget macro data, find a "micro" foundation (model) that might help offer a guide to what might happen. Keynesians accepted the critique of the neoclassical school, as presented by the Nobel Prize winner Robert Lucas ("the problem of depressions has been solved"), that just looking at economic statistics provides no theoretical base and thus was open to the distortion of spurious correlation. You needed to have firm microtheory. As Lars Syll points out, those neoclassical micro-foundations bear no relation to the real world.[3]

This is the hole that Keynesian economics has descended into. And it *is* a hole because DSGE models have been proven worthless in explaining anything. These models failed to predict or explain the Great Recession and are unable to explain the subsequent weak recovery or Long Depression. It is not hard to see why. There is a total absence of investment or profit as shocks in these models. Everything starts with consumer preferences; the consumer is king as in the neoclassical world and Keynesian aggregate demand is reduced to just consumption.[4]

The DSGE models' capitulation to the concept of general equilibrium stands in contrast to Keynesian "lack of effective demand" at a macro level. As Edward Glaeser puts it: "There is no market mechanism that leads, even in principle, to a general equilibrium. Nor is there any basis for assuming that, if a general equilibrium does exist, it is unique, and that if it is unique, it is necessarily stable."[5]

After the experience of the Great Recession, even some leading Keynesians started to disown DSGE modeling, just as Keynesians had disowned econometrics after the 1970s. The failure of DSGE models has led some Keynesians to return to the macro and empirical analysis from the premise that markets do not "clear" at the aggregate.[6] Larry Summers is one.[7] Summers now preaches what he did not practice when an adviser to the Clinton administration. He opposed regulatory and prudential controls for financial markets and joined Fed Chairman Alan Greenspan and his political sponsor, former Treasury Secretary Robert Rubin, in smearing Commodity Futures Trading Commission chair Brooksley Born, so as to make the world safe for OTC derivatives.[8]

The reality is that Keynesian economics fell into the neoclassical DSGE trap because it accepted the neoclassical theory of value, denied any role for profit even in its aggregate analysis, and relied in essence on the implausible belief that capitalist markets will clear and some form of equilibrium will be the norm, whether it is the great moderation of the neoliberal period or an inherent smoothness in the capitalist production process. Keynesian economics failed to explain stagflation in the 1970s and the Great Recession in 2008. That makes its prescriptions of monetary easing and fiscal stimulus doubtful as a way out of the Long Depression.

Bibliography

Akerlof, George. 2013. "The Cat in the Tree and Further Observations." *IMF Direct*, May 1.

Angrist, Joshua, and Jorn-Steffen Pischke. 2010. "The Credibility Revolution in Empirical Economics: How Better Research Design Is Taking the Con Out of Econometrics." *Journal of Economic Perspectives* 24: 3–30.

Aziz, J. 2013. "On Depressions, the Structure of Production and Fiscal Policy," *Noahpinion*, October 25. http://noahpinionblog.blogspot.co.uk/2013/10/on-depressions-structure-of-production.html.

Bakir, E., and A. Cambell. 2010. "Neoliberalism, the Rate of Profit and the Rate of Accumulation." *Science and Society*, July.

Bank of England. *Financial Stability Report*. 2014. (London: Bank of England).

Bastiat, F. 2013. *The Law: Selected Essays on Political Economy*. Irvington-on-Hudson, NY: Foundation for Economic Education.

Basu, Deepankar, and Panayiotis T. Manolakis. 2013. "Is There a Tendency for the Rate of Profit to Fall? Econometric Evidence for the US Economy, 1948–2007." *Review of Radical Political Economics* 45 (1): 76–95.

Bates, T., K. Kahle, and R. Stulz. 2009. "Why Do US Firms Hold so Much More Cash Than They Used To?" *Journal of Finance* 64: 1985–2021.

Bayes, Thomas, and Richard Price. 1764. "An Essay towards Solving a Problem in the Doctrine of Chance. By the Late Rev. Mr. Bayes, Communicated by Mr. Price, in a Letter to John Canton, A. M. F. R. S." *Philosophical Transactions of the Royal Society of London* 53: 370–418. doi: 10.1098/rstl.1763.0053.

Beales, H. L., and R. S. Lambert. 1934. *Memoirs of the Unemployed*. London: Victor Gollancz.

Bernanke, Ben S. 2004. *Essays on the Great Depression*. Princeton, NJ: Princeton University Press.

———. 2007. "The Subprime Mortgage Market" (speech). Federal Reserve Bank of Chicago's 43rd Annual Conference on Bank Structure and Competition, Chicago, Illinois, May 17.

———. 2013. "Monetary Policy and the Global Economy" (speech). Department of Economics and STICERD Public Discussion in Association with the Bank of England, London School of Economics, London, March 25, http://www.federalreserve.gov/newsevents/speech/bernanke20130325a.htm.

———. 2014. "The Federal Reserve Looking Back, Looking Forward" (speech). Annual Meeting of the American Economic Association, Philadelphia, PA, January 3.

Blanchard, Olivier, Ben Bernanke, Stanley Fischer, Kenneth Rogoff, and Lawrence H. Summers. 2013. "Economic Forum: Policy Responses to Crises" (panel). IMF Economic Forum video, 1:32:55. November 8. http://www.imf.org/external/mmedia/view.aspx?vid=2821294542001.

Blanchard, Olivier, C. Rhee, and L. Summers. 1993. "The Stock Market, Profit, and Investment." *Quarterly Journal of Economics* 108: 115–36.

Bleaney, M. 1976. *Underconsumption Theories: A History and Critical Analysis.* London: Lawrence and Wishart.

Bonner, B. 2010. "Economic Instability as a Result of Extreme Imbecility." *Daily Reckoning*, February 12. http://dailyreckoning.com/economic-instability-a-result-of-extreme-imbecility/.

Bordo, Michael, and Christopher Meissner. 2012. "Does Inequality Lead to a Financial Crisis?" NBER Working Paper 17896.

Borio, C. 2012. "The Financial Cycle and Macroeconomics: What Have We Learnt?" BIS Working Paper 395.

Borio, C., and P. White. 2002. "Asset Prices, Financial and Monetary Stability: Exploring the Nexus." BIS Working Paper 114.

Bourne, Ryan. 2012. "Estonia: A Case Study." Report, Center for Policy Studies.

British Academy. 2009. "The Global Financial Crisis—Why Didn't Anybody Notice." *British Academy Review* 14: 8–10.

Broadbent, Ben. 2012. "Costly Capital and the Risk of Rare Disasters" (speech). Bank of England, London, May 28.

Brooks, Mick. 2012. "The Crisis of Capitalism and the Euro." *KarlMarx.net*, May 27. http://www.karlmarx.net/topics/europe/thecrisisofcapitalismandtheeuro.

———. 2013. *Capitalist Crisis: Theory and Practice.* London: Expedia.

Brynjolfsson, E., and Andrew McAfee. 2011. *Race against the Machine: How the Digital Revolution Is Accelerating Innovation.* Lexington, MA: Digital Frontier Press.

Buckley, George. 2013. "UK Economy Grew in 2012—Reaction." *Telegraph*, February 27. http://www.telegraph.co.uk/finance/economics/9896971/UK-economy-grew-in-2012-reaction.html.

Burke, Michael. 2013. "The Cash Hoard of Western Companies." *Socialist Economic Bulletin*, October 21.

Carchedi, Guglielmo. 2010. "Zombie Capitalism and the Origin of Crises." *International Socialism* 125.

———. 2011. *Behind the Crisis.* Leiden: Brill.

Carchedi, Guglielmo, and Michael Roberts. 2013. "The Long Roots of the Present Crisis: Keynesians, Austerians, and Marx's Law." *World Review of Political Economy* 4: 86–115.

Carchedi, Guglielmo, and Michael Roberts. 2014. "Old and New Misconceptions of Marx's Law." *Critique: Journal of Socialist Theory* 41: 571–94.

Cassidy, J. 2010. "Interview with Eugene Fama." *New Yorker*, January 13. http://www.newyorker.com/news/john-cassidy/interview-with-eugene-fama.

———. 2010. "Is Larry Summers the New Henry Kissinger?" *New Yorker*, May 18. http://www.newyorker.com/rational-irrationality/is-larry-summers-the-new-henry-kissinger.

Cecchetti, Stephen G., M. S. Mohanty, and Fabrizio Zampolli. 2011. "The Real Effects of Debt." Paper presented at Achieving Maximum Long-Run Growth symposium, Federal Reserve Bank, Kansas City, KS, August 25–27.

Chan, Edwin, and Nicola Leskie. 2012. "Apple to Return MAC Production to US in 2013," Reuters, December 7, 2012, http://uk.reuters.com/article/2012/12/07/us-apple-manufacturing-idUSBRE8B50R120121207

Chernow, R. 1998. *Titan*. New York: Vintage Books.

China Copyright and Media. 2013. "CCP Central Committee Resolution Concerning Some Major Issues in Comprehensively Deepening Reform." *China Copyright and Media*, November 12. https://chinacopyrightand-media.wordpress.com/2013/11/15/ccp-central-committee-resolution-concerning-some-major-issues-in-comprehensively-deepening-reform/.

China.org. 2013. "Third Plenum." http://wiki.china.org.cn/wiki/index.php/Third_Plenum.

Cochrane, J. 2012. "Two Views of Debt and Stagnation." *Grumpy Economist*, September 20. http://johnhcochrane.blogspot.com/2012/09/two-views-of-debt-and-stagnation.html.

Coibion, Olivier, Yuriy Gorodnichenko, and Dmitri Koustas. 2013. "Amer-isclerosis? The Puzzling Rise of US Unemployment Persistence." *Brookings Papers on Economic Activity* 47 (2): 193–260. http://www.brookings.edu/~/media/Projects/BPEA/Fall%202013/2013b%20coibion%20unemployment%20persistence.pdf.

Cowan, T. 2011. "The Deflation of 1873–1896." *Marginal Revolution*, August 28. http://marginalrevolution.com/marginalrevolution/2011/08/the-deflation-of-1873-1896.html.

Crafts, Nicholas F. R. 1983. "British Economic Growth 1700–1831." *Economic History Review* 36 (2): 177–99.

Davies, J., and T. Shorrocks. 2014. *Credit Suisse Global Wealth Report.* Credit Suisse.

Dobbs, Richard, Susan Lund, Jonathan Woetzel, and Mina Mutafchieva.

2015. "Debt and (Not Much) Deleveraging." McKinsey Global Institute, February. http://www.mckinsey.com/insights/economic_studies/debt_and_not_much_deleveraging.

Duménil, Gérard, and Dominique Lévy. 1994. *The US Economy since the Civil War: Sources and Construction of the Series.* Paris: EconomiX PSE.

———. 2012. "The Crisis of the Early 21st Century: Marxian Perspectives." http://www.jourdan.ens.fr/levy/dle2012f.pdf.

Economakis, George, Alexis Anastasiadis, and Maria Markaki. 2010. "An Empirical Investigation on the US Economic Performance from 1929 to 2008." *Critique: Journal of Socialist Theory* 38 (3): 465–87.

Eggertsson, Gauti, and Neil Melhotra. 2014. "A Model of Secular Stagnation." NBER Working Paper 20574.

Engels, Friedrich. 1877. *Socialism.* Part 3 of *Anti-Dühring.* Leipzig: Vorwärts.

———. 1976. *The Dialectics of Nature.* Moscow: Progress Publishers.

European Commission. 2014. *European Economic Forecast: Winter 2014.* Brussels: European Commission. http://ec.europa.eu/economy_finance/publications/european_economy/2014/pdf/ee2_en.pdf.

Fackler, James S., and Randall E. Parker. (1994) 2011. "Accounting for the Great Depression: A Historical Decomposition." In *The Seminal Works of the Great Depression,* vol. 2, edited by Randall E. Parker. Cheltenham, UK: Edward Elgar.

Fan, Joseph, Randall Morck, and Bernard Yeung. 2011. "Capitalizing China." NBER Working Paper 17687. Cambridge, MA: National Bureau of Economic Research. http://www.nber.org/papers/w17687.

Farmer, R. 2010. *Expectations, Employment and Prices.* Oxford: Oxford University Press.

Feinstein, C. H., and John C. Odling-Smee. 1982. *British Economic Growth, 1856–1973.* Stanford, CA: Stanford University Press.

Fels, R. 1959. *American Business Cycles, 1865–1897.* Chapel Hill: University of North Carolina Press.

Fisher, I. 1933. "The Debt Deflation History of Great Depressions." *Econometrica* 1 (4): 337–57.

Ford, Martin. 2009. *The Lights in the Tunnel: Automation, Accelerating Technology and the Economy of the Future.* Acculant.

Freeman, A. 2009. "What Makes the US Rate of Profit Fall?" Working Paper, University of Greenwich.

Friedman, Milton, and Anna Schwartz. 1971. *A Monetary History of the United States 1867–1960.* Princeton, NJ: Princeton University Press.

FSB (Financial Stability Board). 2011. *Defining and Measuring the Shadow Banking System.* Basel, Switzerland: Financial Stability Board.

Galbraith, J. 2012. *Inequality and Instability.* Oxford: Oxford University Press.

Garrison, Roger W. 1999. "*The Great Depression Revisited* (Review)." *Independent Reviews*, March 22.

Gaulard, Mylene. 2010. "Baisse du taux de profit et croissance chinoise." http://gesd.free.fr/m6gaulard.pdf.

Giffen, R. 1886. *Essays in Finance*, 2 vols. London: George Bell and Sons.

Glaeser, Edward. 2010. "Does Economic Inequality Cause Crises?" Rappaport Institute, December 14. http://www.hks. harvard.edu/centers/rappaport/events-and-news/op-eds/ does-economic-inequality-cause-crises.

Glasner, David, and Thomas Cooley. 1997. "Crisis of 1873." In *Business Cycles and Depressions: An Encyclopedia*, edited by David Glasner, 132–33. New York: Garland.

Goldstein, J. 1985. "Kondratieff Waves as War Cycles." *International Studies Quarterly* 29: 411–44.

Gordon, R. J. 2009. "Is Modern Macro or 1978 Macro More Relevant?" Paper presented at International Colloquium on the History of Economic Thought, São Paulo, September 12. http://economics.weinberg.northwestern.edu/robert-gordon/GRU_Combined_090909.pdf.

———. 2012. "Is US Economic Growth Over? Faltering Innovation Confronts Six Headwinds." NBER Working Paper 18315. Cambridge, MA: National Bureau of Economic Research.

———. 2014. "The Demise of US Economic Growth: Restatement, Rebuttal and Reflections." NBER Working Paper 19895. Cambridge, MA: National Bureau of Economic Research.

Graeber, David. 2012. "Of Flying Cars and the Rate of Profit." *Baffler* 19, http://www.thebaffler.com/salvos/ of-flying-cars-and-the-declining-rate-of-profit.

Granados, José Tapia. 2012. "Statistical Evidence of Falling Profits as a Cause of Recessions: Short Note." *Review of Radical Political Economics* 44: 484–93.

———. 2013. "Does Investment Call the Tune? Empirical Evidence and Endogenous Theories of the Business Cycle." *Research in Political Economy* 28: 229–40.

Granados, José Tapia, and Óscar Carpintero. 2013. "Dynamics and Economic Aspects of Climate Change." In *Combating Climate Change: An Agricultural Perspective*, edited by Manajit S. Kang and Surinder S. Banga, 29–58. Boca Raton, FL: CRC Press.

Greenspan, Alan. n.d. "Testimony to Congress." http://www. ft.com/cms/s/0/aee9e3a2-a11f-11dd-82fd-000077b07658. html?siteedition=uk#axzz3SVATArZd.

——. 2010. "The Crisis." *Brookings Papers on Economic Activity*, Spring: 201–61. http://www.brookings.edu/~/media/projects/bpea/spring-2010/2010a_bpea_greenspan.pdf.

Grim, R. 2009. "How the Federal Reserve Bought the Economics Profession." *Huffington Post*, October 23.

Grossman, H., 1992. *The Law of Accumulation and Capitalist Breakdown*. London: Pluto Press.

Haldane, Andrew, Simon Brennan, and Vasileios Madouros. 2010. "What Is the Contribution of the Financial Sector? Miracle or Mirage?" In *The Future of Finance: The LSE Report*, edited by Adair Turner, 87–120. London: London School of Economics.

Harman, Chris. 2007. "The Rate of Profit and the World Today." *International Socialism* 115. http://isj.org.uk/the-rate-of-profit-and-the-world-today/.

Heath, Allister. 2013. "Imagine if the Price of Food Had Gone Up as Fast as Homes." *City AM*, June 14. http://www.cityam.com/article/imagine-if-price-food-had-gone-fast-homes.

Hoover, Herbert. 1952. *The Great Depression*. Vol. 3 of *The Memoirs of Herbert Hoover*. Herbert Hoover Presidential Library and Museum.

Howard, M. C., and J. E. King. 2014. *History of Marxian Economics*, vol. 1, *1883–1929*. Princeton, NJ: Princeton University Press.

ILO (International Labour Organization). 2011. *Income Inequality: The Cause of the Great Recession?* Geneva: International Labour Organization.

IMF (International Monetary Fund). 2012. "Dealing with Household Debt." In *World Economic Outlook: Growth Resuming, Dangers Remain*, 89–124. Washington, DC: International Monetary Fund.

——. 2013. *World Economic Outlook: Hopes, Realities, Risks*. Washington, DC: International Monetary Fund.

——. 2014. *Global Financial Stability Report April 2014: Navigating Monetary Policy Challenges and Managing Risks*. Washington, DC: International Monetary Fund.

IPCC (Intergovernmental Panel on Climate Change). 2013. *Fifth Assessment Report*, October. Intergovernmental Panel on Climate Change.

Izquierdo, Sergio Cámara. 2010. "Short and Long-Term Dynamics of the US Profit Rate (1946–2009)." Paper presented at the First International Conference in Political Economy, University of Crete, Greece, September 10–12.

Jordà, Òscar, Moritz Schularick, and Alan M. Taylor. 2013. "Sovereigns versus Banks: Crises, Causes and Consequences." CEPR Working Paper. Washington, DC: Center for Economic Policy and Research.

Kalecki, M. 1943. "Political Aspects of Full Employment." *Political Quarterly* 14 (4): 322–30.

Kalogerakos, Themistoklis. 2013. "Technology, Distribution, and Long-Run Profit Rate Dynamics in the US Manufacturing Sector, 1948–2011: Evidence from a Vector Error Correction Model (VECM)." MA thesis, Lund University.

Keen, Steve. 2001. "The Minsky Thesis: Keynesian or Marxian?" In *Financial Keynesianism and Market Instability: The Economic Legacy of Hyman Minsky*, vol. 1, edited by R. Bellofiore and P. Ferri, 106–20. Cheltenham, UK: Edward Elgar.

Kennedy, Paul. 1989. *The Rise and Fall of the Great Powers*. London: Fontana Press.

Keynes, John Maynard. 1971. *A Treatise on Money*. London: Palgrave MacMillan.

———. 1931. *Essays in Persuasion*. New York: Harcourt Brace.

———. 1978. *Collected Writings*, vol. 13. Cambridge: Cambridge University Press.

Kliman, Andrew. 2007. *Reclaiming Marx's Capital*. New York: Lexington Books.

———. 2010. *The Persistent Fall in Profitability Underlying the Crisis: New Temporal Evidence*. Marxist Humanist Initiative.

———. 2011. *The Failure of Capitalist Production*. London: Pluto Press.

Kondratiev, Nikolai. (1925) 1984. *The Long Wave Cycle*. New York: E. P. Dutton.

Kotz, David M. 2008. "Contradictions of Economic Growth in the Neoliberal Era: Accumulation and Crisis in Contemporary US Economy." *Review of Radical Political Economics* 40 (2): 174–88.

Krugman, Paul. 1998. "Japan's Trap." http://web.mit.edu/krugman/www/japtrap.html.

———. 2011. "Debt Is Mostly Money We Owe to Ourselves." *New York Times*, December 28. http://krugman.blogs.nytimes.com/2011/12/28/debt-is-mostly-money-we-owe-to-ourselves/?_r=0.

———. 2012. "Technology and Wages." *New York Times*, December 10. http://krugman.blogs.nytimes.com/2012/12/10/technology-and-wages-the-analytics-wonkish/.

———. 2012. "Human versus Physical Capital." *New York Times*, December 11. http://krugman.blogs.nytimes.com/2012/12/11/human-versus-physical-capital/.

———. 2013. *End This Depression Now!* New York: Norton.

———. 2013. "The Japan Story." *New York Times*, February 5. http://krugman.blogs.nytimes.com/2013/02/05/the-japan-story/.

———. 2013. "Secular Stagnation, Coalmines, Bubbles and Larry Summers." *New York Times*, November 16. http://krugman.blogs.nytimes.com/2013/11/16/secular-stagnation-coalmines-bubbles-and-larry-summers.

———. 2014. "The State of the Euro." *New York Times*, January 1. http://krugman.blogs.nytimes.com/2014/01/01/the-state-of-the-euro-in-one-graph/.

Kuhn, R. 2007. *Henryk Grossman and the Recovery of Marxism.* Chicago: University of Illinois Press.

Kumhof, Michael, and Romain Rancière. 2010. "Leveraging Inequality." *Finance and Development* 47 (4): 28–31.

Kurz, Robert. (1995) 2012. "The Apotheosis of Money: The Structural Limits of Capital Valorization, Casino Capitalism and the Global Financial Crisis." *Libcom.org*, January 26. http://libcom.org/library/apotheosis-money-structural-limits-capital-valorization-casino-capitalism-global-financi.

Landes, D. 1969. *The Unbound Prometheus.* Cambridge: University of Cambridge Press.

Lansley, Stewart. 2013. "Wage Led Growth Is an Economic Imperative." *New Left Project*, September 2. http://www.newleftproject.org/index.php/site/article_comments/wage_led_growth_is_an_economic_imperative.

Levy, David, Martin Farnham, and Samira Ryan. 2008. "Where Profits Come From: Answering the Critical Question That Few Ever Ask." Mount Kisco, NY: Report, Jerome Levy Forecasting Center.

Lewis, A. C. 1967. *The Deceleration of British Growth 1871–1913.* Development Research Project, Woodrow Wilson School, Princeton University.

Li, Minqi. 2009. *The Rise of China and the Demise of the World Economy.* New York: Monthly Review Press.

Li, Minqi, Feng Xiao, and Andong Zhu. 2007. "Long Waves, Institutional Changes, and Historical Trends." *Journal of World Systems Research* 13: 33–54. http://gesd.free.fr/lietal.pdf.

Lucchino, Paolo, and Salvatore Morelli. 2012. "Inequality, Debt and Growth." Report, Resolution Foundation.

Magnus, George. 2013. *Demographics: From Dividend to Drag, American Women, and Abenomics.* London: UBS Investment Research.

Maito, Esteban Ezequiel. 2014. "The Historical Transience of Capital: The Downward Trend in the Rate of Profit since XIX Century." Working Paper, University of Buenos Aires, Argentina. http://gesd.free.fr/maito14.pdf.

Mandel, E. 1995. *Long Waves in Capitalist Development.* New York: Random House.

Manyika, James, Jeff Sinclair, Richard Dobbs, Gernot Strube, Louis Rassey, Jan Mischke, Jaana Remes, et al. 2012. *Manufacturing the Future:*

The Next Era of Global Growth and Innovation. Report, McKinsey Global Institute. http://www.mckinsey.com/insights/manufacturing/the_future_of_manufacturing.

Marquetti, Adalmir. 2012. "Extended Penn World Tables." Duncan Foley homepage, March 25. https://sites.google.com/a/newschool.edu/duncan-foley-homepage/home/EPWT.

Marx, Karl. 1858. *Grundrisse Notebook VII.* London: Allen Lane, October 1973.

———. 1865. *Value Price and Profit.* London: Wildside Press, 2008.

———. 1867. *Capital,* vol. 1. London: Penguin, 2004.

———. 1868. "Marx to Kugelman in Hanover." Letter, July 11. https://www.marxists.org/archive/marx/works/1868/letters/68_07_11-abs.htm.

———. 1873. *Letters to Engels.* London: New Park Publications, 1983.

———. 1885. *Capital,* vol. 2. London: Penguin, 1992.

———. 1895. *Capital,* vol. 3. London: Penguin, 1992.

———. 1990. *Collected Works.* London: Lawrence and Wishart.

———. 2009. *Das Kapital.* The Skeptical Reader Series. Washington, DC: Regnery Publishing.

Mason, R. S. 1989. *Robert Giffen and the Giffen Paradox.* Lanham, MD: Rowman and Littlefield.

Mattick, Paul. 1974. *Economic Crisis and Crisis Theory.* London: Merlin Press.

———. 2011. *Business as Usual.* London: Reaktion Books.

Mazzucato, Mariana. 2013. *The Entrepreneurial State: Debunking Private versus Public Sector Myths.* London: Anthem Press.

McGregor, James. 2012. *No Ancient Wisdom, No Followers: The Challenges of Chinese Authoritarian Capitalism.* Westport CT: Prospecta Press.

Milanović, B. 2012. "Global Inequality by the Numbers." World Bank Policy Research Working Paper. Washington, DC: World Bank.

Minsky, Hyman P. 1992. "The Financial Instability Hypothesis." Levy Economics Institute Working Paper 74. Annandale, NY: Bard College.

Mitchell, W. 1913. *Business Cycles.* Berkeley: University of California Press.

Mohun, S. 2010. "The Present Crisis in Historical Perspective." Paper presented at Historical Materialism Conference, November. London.

Montier, J. 2012. "What Goes Up Must Come Down." GMO White Paper. London.

Murphy, R. P. 2011. "My Reply to Krugman on Austrian Business-Cycle Theory." *Mises Institute,* January 24. https://mises.org/library/my-reply-krugman-austrian-business-cycle-theory.

Musson, A. E. 1959. "The Great Depression in Britain 1873–96: A

Reappraisal." *Journal of Economic History* 19: 199–228.

NBER (National Bureau of Economic Research). 2012. "US Business Cycle Expansions and Contractions." April 23. Cambridge, MA. http://www.nber.org/cycles/cyclesmain.html.

OECD (Organisation for Economic Co-operation and Development). 2011. *Special Focus: Inequality in Emerging Economies.* Paris: OECD.

———. 2013. *OECD Skills Outlook.* Paris: OECD.

Ostry, Jonathan D., Andrew Berg, and Charalambos G. Tsangarides. 2014. "Redistribution, Debt and Growth." IMF Staff Discussion Note 14/02, February.

Panitch, Leo, and Sam Gindin. 2014. *The Making of Global Capitalism: The Political Economy of the American Empire.* New York: Verso Books.

Papell, David H., and Ruxandra Prodan. 2011. "The Statistical Behavior of GDP after Financial Crises and Severe Recessions." University of Houston Research Paper. http://papers.ssrn.com/sol3/papers.cfm?abstract_id=1933988.

Parker, Randall E. 2002. *Reflections on the Great Depression.* Northampton, MA: Edward Elgar.

Phelps-Brown, E. H., and P. E. Hart. 1952. "The Share of Wages in National Income." *Economic Journal* 62 (246): 253–77.

Pigou, A. 1927. *Industrial Fluctuations.* London: Macmillan.

Piketty, T. 2014. *Capital in the 21st Century.* Cambridge, MA: Harvard Belknap Press.

Popper, Karl. (1934) 2002. *The Logic of Scientific Discovery.* New York: Routledge.

Rajan, R. 2010. *Faultlines.* Princeton, NJ: Princeton University Press.

Reich, Robert B. 2011. *Aftershock.* New York: Vintage.

Reinhart, Carmen M., and Kenneth S. Rogoff. 2009. *This Time Is Different: Eight Centuries of Financial Folly.* Princeton, NJ: Princeton University Press.

Roberts, Brandon, Deborah Povich, and Mark Mather. 2012–13. "Low-Income Working Families: The Growing Economic Gap." Policy Brief, Working Poor Families Project. http://www.workingpoorfamilies.org/wp-content/uploads/2013/01/Winter-2012_2013-WPFP-Data-Brief.pdf.

Roberts, Michael. 2009. *The Great Recession.* London: Lulu.

———. 2011. "The Crisis of Neoliberalism and Gerard Dumenil." Michael Roberts blog, March 3. https://thenextrecession.wordpress.com/2011/03/03/the-crisis-of-neoliberalism-and-gerard-dumenil/.

———. 2011. "Measuring the Rate of Profit, Profit Cycles and the Next Recession." Paper prepared for the Association of Heterodox Economics,

November. https://thenextrecession.files.wordpress.com/2011/11/
the-profit-cycle-and-economic-recession.pdf.

———. 2011. "Review of *The Failure of Capitalist Production*." Michael
Roberts blog, December 8. http://thenextrecession.wordpress.
com/2011/12/08/andrew-kliman-and-the-failure-of-capitalist-production/.

———. 2012. "Eurozone Debt, Monetary Union and Argentina." Michael
Roberts blog, May 10. http://thenextrecession.wordpress.com/2012/05/10/
eurozone-debtmonetary-union-and-argentina/

———. 2012. "China's Transition: New Leaders, Old Policies." Michael
Roberts blog, November 16. http://thenextrecession.wordpress.
com/2012/11/16/chinas-transition-new-leaders-old-policies/.

———. 2013. "Revising the two RRs." Michael Roberts blog, April 17. http://
thenextrecession.wordpress.com/2013/04/17/revising-the-two-rrs/.

———. 2013. "The Cat Is Stuck Up a Tree." Michael Roberts blog, May 10.
https://thenextrecession.wordpress.com/2013/05/10/the-cat-is-stuck-up-
a-tree-how-did-it-get-there-and-how-do-you-get-it-down/.

———. 2014. "Argentina, Paul Krugman and the Great Recession." Michael Roberts blog, February 3. http://thenextrecession.wordpress.
com/2014/02/03/argentina-paul-krugman-and-the-great-recession/.

Roberts, Michael, and Mick Brooks. 2011. *It's Time to Take Over the Banks.*
Fire Brigades Union pamphlet, November.

Roche, Cullen. 2013. "Budget Deficits Contribute to Corporate Profits, but Don't Matter, Right?" *Pragmatic
Capitalism*, October 16. http://www.pragcap.com/
budget-deficits-contribute-to-corporate-profits-but-dont-matter-right/.

Rogoff, K. 2014. "Malthus, Marx and Modern Growth." *Project Syndicate*,
March 4. http://www.project-syndicate.org/commentary/kenneth-ro-
goff-identifies-several-obstacles-to-keeping-living-standards-on-an-up-
ward-trajectory.

Romer, Christina D. 1999. "Changes in Business Cycles: Evidence and Explanations." *Journal of Economic Perspectives* 13: 23–44.

Ross, John. 2013. "China Has Overtaken the US." *Key Trends in Globalisation*, September 9. http://ablog.typepad.com/keytrendsinglobalisa-
tion/2013/09/china-has-overtaken-the-us.html.

———. 2013. "Investment will Boost China's Economy." *Key Trends in Globalisation*, November 15. http://ablog.typepad.com/keytrendsinglobalisa-
tion/2012/10/investment-will-boost-chinas-economy.html.

Rothbard, M. 1969. *Economic Depressions: Causes and Cures.* Lansing, MI:
Ludwig von Mises Institute.

Roubini, Nouriel. 2011. "Full Analysis: The Instability of Inequality." *Econo-
Monitor*, October 17. http://www.economonitor.com/nouriel/2011/10/17/

full-analysis-the-instability-of-inequality/.

Roxburgh, Charles, Susan Lund, Toos Daruvala, James Manyika, Richard Dobbs, Ramon Forn, and Karen Croxson. 2012. "Debt and Deleveraging: Uneven Progress on the Path to Growth." Report, McKinsey Global Institute, January.

Rozworski, Michal. 2013. "Canada's Profitability Puzzle." *Political Eh-conomy*, December 3. http://politicalehconomy.wordpress.com/2013/12/03/canadas-profitability-puzzle/.

Saez, Emmanuel, and Gabriel Zucman. 2014. "Wealth Inequality in the US since 1913: Evidence from Capitalized Income Tax Data." NBER Working Paper 20625. Cambridge, MA: National Bureau of Economic Research.

Schumpeter, Joseph. 1939. *Business Cycles: A Theoretical, Historical and Statistical Analysis of the Capitalist Process.* New York: McGraw-Hill.

Selgin George A. 1997. *Less Than Zero: The Case for Falling Price Levels in a Growing Economy.* London: Institute of Economic Affairs.

Shafik, Nemat. 2012. "Convergence, Crisis and Capacity Building in Emerging Europe." *IMF Direct*, July 27. http://blog-imfdirect.imf.org/2012/07/27/convergence-crisis-and-capacity-building-in-emerging-europe/.

Shaikh, Anwar. 1992. "The Falling Rate of Profit as the Cause of Long Waves." In *New Findings in Long Wave Research*, edited by A. Kleinknecht, Ernest Mandel, and Immanuel Wallerstein, 174–95. London: Macmillan. http://gesd.free.fr/shaikh92w.pdf.

———. 2011. "First Great Depression of the 21st Century." *Socialist Register* 47.

Shilling, G. 2010. *The Age of Deleveraging.* New York: Wiley.

Short, D. 2014. *Advisor Perspectives.* http://www.advisorperspectives.com/dshort/.

Silver, N. 2012. *The Signal and the Noise: Why Most Predictions Fail—but Some Don't.* New York: Penguin Press.

Skidelsky, R. 1995. *John Maynard Keynes: The Economist as Savior, 1920–1937.* New York: Penguin.

Smith, Adam. (1776) 2004. *The Wealth of Nations.* New York: Barnes and Noble.

Smith, John. 2010. "Imperialism and the Globalisation of Production." PhD thesis, University of Sheffield.

Smith, John. 2011. "Imperialism and the Law of Value." *Global Discourse* 2. https://globaldiscourse.files.wordpress.com/2011/05/john-smith.pdf.

Smith, Noah. 2013. "The Koizumi Years: A Macroeconomic Puzzle." *Noahpinion*, February 9. http://noahpinionblog.blogspot.co.uk/2013/02/the-koizumi-years-macroeconomic-puzzle.html.

———. 2013. "Is the Business Cycle a Cycle?" *Noahpinion*, February 15. http://noahpinionblog.blogspot.co.uk/2013/02/is-business-cycle-cycle.html.

Smith, Richard. 2014. "Beyond Growth or Beyond Capitalism." *Truthout*, January 15. http://www.truth-out.org/news/
item/21215-beyond-growth-or-beyond-capitalism.

Societe Generale. 2013. "On Our Minds Today: UK SMEs Still in the Doldrums." *Societe Generale*, October 30.

*Solow, Robert. 2008. "The State of Macroeconomics." Journal of Economic
Perspectives 22 (1): 243–49.*

Stamp, Josiah. 1931. *Criticism and Other Addresses*. London: E. Benn.

Stanford, J. 2013. "Good Time to Rethink Corporate Tax Cuts." *Progressive Economics*, November 14. http://www.progressive-economics.
ca/2013/11/14/good-time-to-rethink-corporate-tax-cuts/.

Stiglitz, Joseph E. 2012. *The Price of Inequality: How Today's Divided Society
Endangers Our Future*. New York: Norton.

———. 2013. "The Lessons of the North Atlantic Crisis for Economic Theory
and Policy." *IMF Direct*, May 3. http://blog-imfdirect.imf.org/2013/05/03/
the-lessons-of-the-north-atlantic-crisis-for-economic-theory-and-policy/.

Stockhammer, Engelbert. 2013. "Rising Inequality as a Cause of the Present
Crisis." *Cambridge Journal of Economics* 39. doi: 10.1093/cje/bet052.

Summers, Lawrence H., Axel Weber, Mervyn King, Ben Bernanke, and
Olivier Blanchard. 2013. "'I Do Not Believe the Long Run Can Be Ceded
to the Avatars of Austerity' Weblogging." *Brad DeLong's Grasping Reality*,
March 25. http://delong.typepad.com/sdj/2013/03/mervyn-king-ben-ber-
nanke-olivier-blanchard-lawrence-summers-axel-weber.html.

Syll, Lars P. 2012. "The State of Microfoundations and Macroeconomics—
Robert Solow Says It All." Lars P. Syll blog, March 16. https://larspsyll.
wordpress.com/2012/03/16/the-state-of-microfoundations-and-macro-
economics-robert-solow-says-it-all/

Szamosszegi, Andrew, and Cole Kyle. 2011. "An Analysis of State-Owned
Enterprises and State Capitalism in China." US-China Economic and
Security Review Commission. http://origin.www.uscc.gov/sites/default/
files/Research/10_26_11_CapitalTradeSOEStudy.pdf.

Taibi, Matt. 2009. "The Great American Bubble Machine." *Rolling Stone*
1082, July 9.

———. 2010. *Griftopia*. New York: Spiegel and Grau.

Taleb, Nassim Nicholas. 2007. *The Black Swan: The Impact of the Highly
Improbable*. New York: Penguin.

Tapia, José A. 2015. "Money and Say's Law: On the Macroeconomic Models
of Kalecki, Keen, and Marx." *Real-World Economics Review* 70: 110–20.
http://www.paecon.net/PAEReview/issue70/Tapia70.pdf.

Tapia, José A., and Rolando Astarita. 2011. *La Gran Recesión y el capitalismo
del siglo XXI*. Madrid: Catarata.

Thompson, Earl A., and Jonathan Treussard. 2002. "The Tulipmania: Fact or Artifact?" UCLA Working Paper.

Tinbergen, J. 1939. *Statistical Testing of Business-Cycle Theories*, vol. 2. Geneva: League of Nations.

Tylecote, A. 1993. *The Long Wave in the World Economy.* London: Routledge.

UNCTAD (United Nations Conference on Trade and Development). 2013. *World Investment Report 2013—Global Value Chains: Investment and Trade for Development.* New York: United Nations.

US Bureau of Labor Statistics. 2011. "International Comparison of Hourly Compensation Costs." Washington, DC.

Vernon, J. R. 1994. "World War II Fiscal Policies and the End of the Great Depression." *Journal of Economic History* 54 (4): 850–68.

Vistesen, Claus. March 25. "The Big Disconnect between Leverage and Spreads." *Seeking Alpha*, March 25. http://seekingalpha.com/article/2107013-the-big-disconnect-between-leverage-and-spreads.

Wells, David Ames. 1890. *Recent Economic Changes and Their Effect on Production and Distribution of Wealth and Well-Being of Society.* New York: Appleton.

Werner, Alejandro. 2013. "After a Golden Decade Can Latin America Keep Its Luster?" *EconoMonitor*, May 7. http://www.economonitor.com/blog/2013/05/after-a-golden-decade-can-latin-america-keep-its-luster/.

White, William. 2009. "Modern Macroeconomics Is on the Wrong Track." *Finance & Development* 46 (4): 15–18.

Winters, B. 2013. "Banker Bashing." *City AM*, February 6.

Wolf, Martin. 2012. "Lunch with the FT." *Financial Times*.

———. 2013. "Japan Can Put People before Profits." *Financial Times*, February 5.

———. 2013. "Why the Future Looks Sluggish." *Financial Times*, November 20.

World Bank and the Development Research Center of the State Council, P. R. China. 2013. *China 2030: Building a Modern, Harmonious, and Creative Society.* Washington, DC: World Bank. doi:10.1596/978-0-8213-9545-5.

Wren-Lewis, Simon. 2012. "Microfoundations—Is There an Alternative?" *Mainly Macro*, March 13. http://mainlymacro.blogspot.co.uk/2012/03/microfoundations-is-there-alternative.html.

Zhang Yu and Zhao Feng. 2006. "Rate of Profit in China." http://www.seruc.com/bgl/paper%202006/Zhao-Zhang.pdf.

NOTES

Introduction

1. Paul Krugman, "The Third Depression," *New York Times*, June 27, 2010, http://www.nytimes.com/2010/06/28/opinion/28krugman.html.

2. "The global recession is a huge development, and it is reasonable to ask to what extent it could have been foreseen. What's more, we can't say 'never again' if we don't fully understand what occurred." "The academy tried to argue that some people had seen the crisis coming. But they admitted that most had not and, in particular, officials in government, the heads of the banks and most economists and all in the mainstream. And these are the people that matter. So in summary, Your Majesty, the failure to foresee the timing, extent and severity of the crisis and to head it off, while it had many causes, was principally a failure of the collective imagination of many bright people, both in this country and internationally, to understand the risks to the system as a whole." British Academy, "The Global Financial Crisis—Why Didn't Anybody Notice?," *British Academy Review* (July 2009).

3. Ryan Grim, "How the Federal Reserve Bought the Economics Profession," *Huffington Post*, October 23, 2009.

4. But as Marx once said: "The vulgar economist has not the faintest idea that the actual everyday exchange relations cannot be directly identical with the magnitudes of value. The essence of bourgeois society consists precisely in this, that a priori there is no conscious social regulation of production. The rational and naturally necessary asserts itself only as a blindly working average. And then the vulgar economist thinks he has made a great discovery when, as against the revelation of the inner interconnection, he proudly claims that in appearance things look different. In fact, he boasts that he holds fast to appearance, and takes it for the ultimate. Why, then, have any science at all?" Letter to Kugelman in Hanover, July 11, 1868, Marxists Internet Archive (marxists.org), https://www.marxists.org/archive/marx/works/1868/letters/68_07_11-abs.htm.

5. If you read Nicholas Taleb's book *The Black Swan*, you would think that the recession was random. Taleb Nassim, T*he Black Swan: The Impact of the Highly Improbable* (New York: Penguin, 2007) and Michael Roberts, *The Great Recession* (London: Lulu, 2009), chapter 31.

6. Nate Silver, *The Signal and the Noise: Why Most Predictions Fail—But*

Some Don't (New York: Penguin, 2012), 302.

7.   Like "'the probability of Obama winning the electoral college is 83% and the probability of him winning the popular vote is 50.1%.' This is different from much statistical method in colleges and universities today that rely on idealized modelling assumptions that rarely hold true. Often such models reduce complex questions to overly simple 'hypothesis tests' using arbitrary 'significance levels' to 'accept or reject' a single parameter value. In contrast, the practical statistician needs a sound understanding of how baseball, poker, elections or other uncertain processes work, what measures are reliable and which not, what scales of aggregation are useful, and then to utilize the statistical tool kit as well as possible. You need extensive data sets, preferably collected over long periods of time, from which one can then use statistical techniques to incrementally change probabilities up or down relative to prior data." Silver, *The Signal and the Noise*, 23, and see http://fivethirtyeight.blogs. nytimes.com/2012/11/03/nov-2-for-romney-to-win-state-polls-must-be-statistically-biased/.

8.   Thomas Bayes and Richard Price, "An Essay towards Solving a Problem in the Doctrine of Chance. By the late Rev. Mr. Bayes, communicated by Mr. Price, in a letter to John Canton, A. M. F. R. S.," *Philosophical Transactions of the Royal Society of London* 53 (1763), 295.

9.   Karl Popper, *The Logic of Scientific Discovery* (1934; New York: Routledge, 2002), 19.

10.   Alan Greenspan, testimony to Congress, October 23, 2008; available at Financial Times website and at http://www.theguardian.com/business/2008/oct/24/economics-creditcrunch-federal-reserve-greenspan.

11.   Christina Romer, key economic adviser to President Barack Obama, argues that "economists cannot predict recessions and economic discontinuities because they are inherently unpredictable." It is impossible to see the shocks coming. . . . But is that really so? "Predictions involve modelling. The difference is that for many people the models are poorly specified, based on little information and cannot be tested. Those who rail against models and the 'folly of forecasting,' while still making predictions, are still doing modelling but doing it very poorly." Christina Romer, "Changes in Business Cycles: Evidence and Explanations," *Journal of Economic Perspectives* 13, no. 2 (1999), 23–44.

12.   "Many macroeconomists abandoned traditional empirical work entirely, focusing instead on computational experiments. Researchers choose a question, build a theoretical model economy, calibrate the model so it mimics the real economy along some key statistical dimensions and then run a computational experiment by changing model parameters to address the original question. The last two decades have seen countless studies in this mould, often in a dynamic stochastic general equilibrium framework. Whatever might be said in defence of this framework as a tool for clarifying the implications of economic models, it produces no

direct evidence on the magnitude or existence of causal affects. An effort to put reasonable numbers on theoretical relations is harmless and
may even be helpful. But it's still theory." Joshua Angrist and Jorn-Steffen Pischke, "The Credibility Revolution in Empirical Economics: How
Better Research Design Is Taking the Con out of Econometrics," *Journal
of Economic Perspectives* 24 (2010), 3–30.

13. Roberts, *The Great Recession* (London: Lulu Publications, 2009), 72.

14. Ernest Mandel, *Long Waves in Capitalist Development* (New York:
Random House, 1995).

15. Some scholars doubt that Marx even had a theory of crises and that we
can talk about a Marxist theory of crisis. See Michael Heinrich, "Crisis
Theory, the Law of the Tendency of the Rate of Profit to Fall, and Marx's
Studies in the 1870s," *Monthly Review* 64, no. 11 (April 2012), http://
monthlyreview.org/2013/04/01/crisis-theory-the-law-of-the-tendency-
of-the-profit-rate-to-fall-and-marxs-studies-in-the-1870s/.

Chapter 1

1. M. Brooks, Capitalist Crisis—Theory and Practice (London: Expedia,
2013).

2. Anwar Shaikh, "First Great Depression of 21st Century," Socialist Register 47 (2011).

3. National Bureau of Economic Research, "US Business Cycle Expansions
and Contractions," April 23, 2012; http://www.nber.org/cycles/cycles-
main.html.

4. In Appendix 1, I explain how I have measured the rate of profit in a
capitalist economy, with all its technical pitfalls.

5. Karl Marx, *Marx Engels Collected Works*, vol. 33 (London: Lawrence
and Wishart, 1990), 104; Karl Marx, *The Grundrisse* (London: Penguin,
1973), 748.

6. Karl Marx, *Collected Works* (London: Lawrence and Wishart, 1990),
563.

7. "Since the mass of the employed living labour is continually on the
decline relative to the productively consumed means of production,
it follows that the portion of living labour, unpaid and congealed in
surplus-value, must also be continually on the decrease compared to
the amount of value represented by the invested total capital. Since the
ratio of the mass of surplus-value to the value of the invested total capital forms the rate of profit, this rate must constantly fall." Marx, *Capital*,
vol. 3 (1895).

8. "In light of the fact that 'the principal laws governing crises' are, as all
social laws, tendential and contradictory, 'to determine mathematically'
the laws is an impossible task. First, mathematics is a branch of formal
logic. As seen above, premises in formal logic cannot be contradictory.
However, to account for the laws of movement in society one has to
start from contradictory premises and this is why the laws of movement

are tendential. Second, even if all the 'factors involved' were known, it would be practically impossible to consider all of them. This is why econometric models, even large ones involving thousands of relations, have such a dismal record as tools of prediction. But if it is impossible to determine the laws of crises purely in terms of mathematics, it is certainly possible to analyse the cyclical movement of economic indicators (the ups and downs) by using 'higher mathematics'. This was Marx's intuition." G. Carchedi, *Behind the Crisis* (Leiden: Brill, 2011).

9.   C. Harman, "The Rate of Profit and the World Today," *International Socialism* 115 (2007); available at http://isj.org.uk/the-rate-of-profit-and-the-world-today/.

10. This holds per unit of capital invested. Total employment depends also on capital accumulation.

11. For a fuller analysis of Marx's law and a defense of the critical arguments against it, see G. Carchedi and M. Roberts, "Old and New Misconceptions of Marx's Law," *Critique: Journal of Socialist Theory* 41 (2014), 571–94.

12. H. Grossman, *The Law of Accumulation and Capitalist Breakdown*, (London: Pluto Press, 1992), 72.

13. "The periodical depreciation of existing capital—one of the means immanent in capitalist production to check the fall of the rate of profit and hasten accumulation of capital—value through formation of new capital—disturbs the given conditions, within which the process of circulation and reproduction of capital takes place, and is therefore accompanied by sudden stoppages and crises in the production process." Marx, *Capital*, vol. 3, chapter 15.

14. J. Tinbergen, *Statistical Testing of Business-Cycle Theories*, vol. 2 (Geneva: League of Nations, 1939).

15. W. Mitchell, *Business Cycles* (Berkeley: University of California Press, 1913).

16. O. Blanchard, C. Rhee, and L. Summers, "The Stock Market, Profit and Investment," *Quarterly Journal of Economics* 108 (1993), 115–36.

17. Marx, Capital, vol. 3, (1990), 615.

18. Paul Sweezy, *Theory of Capitalist Development* (New York: Monthly Review Press, 1970), 177. For a fuller explanation of underconsumption theory and its faults, see Michael Bleaney, *Underconsumption Theories: A History and Critical Analysis* (London: Lawrence and Wishart, 1976) and Andrew Kliman, *The Failure of Capitalist Production* (London: Pluto Press, 2011), chapter 9, 165–67.

19. "It is sheer tautology to say that crises are caused by the scarcity of effective consumption, or of effective consumers." Marx, *Capital*, vol. 2 (London: Lawrence and Wishart, 1971), chapter 20.

20. "The so-called plethora of capital always applies essentially to a plethora of the capital for which the fall in the rate of profit is not compensated through the mass of profit—this is always true of newly developing

fresh offshoots of capital—or to a plethora which places capitals incapable of action on their own at the disposal of the managers of large enterprises in the form of credit. This plethora of capital arises from the same causes as those which call forth relative over-population, and is, therefore, a phenomenon supplementing the latter, although they stand at opposite poles—unemployed capital at one pole, and unemployed worker population at the other. Over-production of capital, not of individual commodities—although over-production of capital always includes over-production of commodities—is therefore simply over-accumulation of capital." Marx, *Capital*, vol. 3.

21. For an excellent account of the positions of the Marxist leaders at the turn of century despite its dismissal of the theory itself, see M. C. Howard and J. E. King, *History of Marxian Economics*, vol. 1, 1883–1929 (Princeton, NJ: Princeton University Press, 1989).

22. Rick Kuhn, *Henryk Grossman and the Recovery of Marxism* (Chicago: University of Illinois Press, 2007).

23. Costas Lapavitsas: "the tendency of the rate of profit to fall is the cause of capitalist crises is really a fairly new idea, one that has arisen only post-war and mainly comes from Anglo-Saxon sources . . . Sure, it might have fitted the facts in the 1970s, but not after. Classical Continental European Marxists of the prewar era never proposed profitability as the cause of crisis." M. Roberts, "The Crisis of Neoliberalism and Gerard Dumenil," thenextrecession.wordpress.com (March 3, 2011).

24. See reply to Heinrich in Carchedi and Roberts, "Old and New Misconceptions of Marx's Law."

25. Yanis Varoufakis criticizes Marx's theory of crises as failing to explain depressions as opposed to slumps. "Marx told the story of redemptive recessions occurring due to the twin nature of labour and giving rise to periods of growth that are pregnant with the next downturn which, in turn, begets the next recovery, and so on. However, there was nothing redemptive about the Great Depression. The 1930s slump was just that: a slump that behaved very much like a static equilibrium—a state of the economy that seemed perfectly capable of perpetuating itself, with the anticipated recovery stubbornly refusing to appear over the horizon even after the rate of profit recovered in response to the collapse of wages and interest rates." See http://yanisvaroufakis.eu/2013/12/10/confessions-of-an-erratic-marxist-in-the-midst-of-a-repugnant-european-crisis/#_edn2. It could be retorted that Keynesian theory does not explain the reason for slumps.

26. Andrew Kliman, *Reclaiming Marx's Capital* (New York: Lexington Books, 2007).

27. Kliman, *Reclaiming Marx's Capital*.

28. See my review of Kliman, The Failure of Capitalist Production, Michael Roberts blog, December 8, 2011, http://thenextrecession.wordpress.com/2011/12/08/andrew-kliman-and-the-failure-of-capitalist-production/.

29. Esteban Maito, "The Historical Transience of Capital: The Downward Trend in the Rate of Profit Since the 19th Century," Working Paper, University of Buenos Aires, Argentina, 2014, http://gesd.free.fr/maito14. pdf.

30. All empirical research on the US rate of profit agrees with this statement. See M. Roberts, *The Great Recession* (London: Lulu, 2009) and "Measuring the Rate of Profit, Profit Cycles and the Next Recession," paper at AHE (2011); Carchedi, *Behind the Crisis*; and Kliman, *Failure of Capitalist Production*, among others. D. Basu and P. T. Manolakis. "Is There a Tendency for the Rate of Profit to Fall? Econometric Evidence for the U.S. Economy, 1948–2007," *Review of Radical Political Economy* 45 (2013) applied econometric analysis to the US economy between 1948 and 2007 and found that there was a secular tendency for the rate of profit to fall with a measurable decline of about 0.3 percent a year "after controlling for counter-tendencies." Roberts finds an average decline of 0.4 percent a year through 2009 using the latest data.

31. Guglielmo Carchedi and Michael Roberts, "The Long Roots of the Present Crisis: Keynesians, Austerians, and Marx's Law," *World Review of Political Economy* 4 (2013), 86–115.

32. Carchedi and Roberts, "The Long Roots of the Present Crisis."

33. But falling employee compensation when net social security benefits are excluded, see Kliman, *The Failure of Capitalist Production*.

34. Both Alan Freeman ("What Makes the US Rate of Profit Fall?," Working Paper, University of Greenwich, 2009) and Kliman, *The Failure of Capitalist Production*, have found similar correlations. Izquierdo finds that "the drop in the productivity the capital from the 1946–1973 period to the 1974–1983 period explains 78% of the fall in the rate of profit, while the minor decrease in the profit share explains only 22%. Therefore, the declining profitability manifested during the Keynesian period is explained by the technological component of the rate of profit, confirming the expectations of the Marxian law of the tendency of the rate of profit to fall. The scant recovery of the general rate of profit during the neoliberal period is also explained mostly by the productivity of capital, which accounts for 84% of the relative increase in profitability, while the profit share remains nearly constant; it grows only 1% in relative terms—and explains only 16% of the recovery." Sergio Camara Izquierdo, "Short and Long Term Dynamics of the US Rate of Profit 1946–2009," First International Conference in Political Economy, University of Crete (2010).

35. Themis Kalogerakos, "Technology, Distribution, and Long-Run Profit Rate Dynamics in the US Manufacturing Sector, 1948–2011: Evidence from a Vector Error Correction Model (VECM)," master's thesis, Lund University (2013).

36. Roberts, *The Great Recession* (2009).

37. Broad measure = profits before tax and interest, narrow = after tax, or retained funds and so on, for the whole corporate sector or just the

nonfinancial sector, historic or current cost.

38. Carchedi and I reach the same results in Carchedi and Roberts, "Old and New Misconceptions of Marx's Law."

39. As Kalogerakos puts it: "in the last period, that includes the Great Recession and the years leading up to it, the CAGRs (compound annual growth rates) of all profit measures are negative in both sectors. The average profit rates are slightly higher than in the preceding period, but still lower than in any other phase of the long wave and lower than the average rates for the whole period under scrutiny (except for the after-tax profit rate for the whole corporate sector). In addition to that, the trend of the TSVR (total surplus value rate) in both sectors is slightly descending and that of the other measures is leveling off. What is more, it is obvious from the peak-to peak and trough-to-trough CAGRs, that the long-term profitability in the corporate and non-financial corporate sectors, aside from the partial revival of profit rates during the 1980–1997 period, is one of declining or at best stagnating nature. This denotes that prior to the crisis, the accumulation process in the US economy was certainly problematic, and profit rates in the 'real' economy may have led to the boom of the financial sector." Kalogerakos, *Financialisation, the Great Recession and the Rate of Profit.*

40. Carchedi comments: "if crises are recurrent and if they have all different causes, these different causes can explain the different crises, but not their recurrence. If they are recurrent, they must have a common cause that manifests itself recurrently as different causes of different crises. There is no way around the 'monocausality' of crises." See Guglielmo Carchedi, "Zombie Capitalism and the Origin of Crises," *International Socialism* 125 (2010).

41. More recently, Jose Tapia Granados, using regression analysis, finds that over 251 quarters of US economic activity from 1947, profits started declining long before investment did and that pretax profits can explain 44 percent of all movement in investment, while there is no evidence that investment can explain any movement in profits. Jose Tapia Granados, "Does Investment Call the Tune? Empirical Evidence and Endogenous Theories of the Business Cycle," *Research in Political Economy* 28 (2013), 229–40, and "Statistical Evidence of Falling Profits as a Cause of Recessions: Short Note," *Review of Radical Political Economics* 44 (2012), 484–93.

42. Granados, "Does Investment Call the Tune?"

43. Izquierdo, "Short and Long Term Dynamics of the US Rate of Profit."

44. "The monetary crisis defined as a particular phase of every general industrial and commercial crisis, must clearly be distinguished from the special sort of crisis, also called a monetary crisis, which may appear independently of the rest and only affects industry and commerce by its backwash. The pivot of these crises is to be found in money capital and their immediate sphere of impact is therefore banking, the stock exchange

and finance." Karl Marx, *Capital*, vol. 1 (1867; London: Penguin, 2004).

45.	The basic point is that financial crises are caused by the shrinking productive base of the economy. A point is thus reached at which there has to be a sudden and massive deflation in the financial and speculative sectors. Even though it looks as though the crisis has been generated in these sectors, the ultimate cause resides in the productive sphere and the attendant falling rate of profit in this sphere." Carchedi, *Behind the Crisis*.

Chapter 2

1.	Murray Rothbard, *Economic Depressions: Causes and Cures* (Lansing, MI: Ludwig von Mises Institute, 1969).

2.	Arthur C. Lewis, T*he Deceleration of British Growth 1871–1913*, Development Research Project, Woodrow Wilson School, Princeton University, 1967.

3.	David Glasner and Thomas Cooley, "Crisis of 1873," in *Business Cycles and Depressions: An Encyclopedia*, ed. David Glasner (New York: Garland, 1997). Although the 1857 slump has a strong claim to being the first international recession.

4.	Ron Chernow, *Titan* (New York: Vintage Books, 1998).

5.	As cited in Glasner and Cooley, "Crisis of 1873."

6.	Milton Friedman and Anna Schwartz, *A Monetary History of the United States, 1867–1960* (Princeton, NJ: Princeton University Press, 1971).

7.	Robert Giffin, *Essays on Finance*, 2 vols. (London: George Bell and Sons, 1884); R. S. Mason, *Robert Giffen and the Giffen Paradox* (Lanham, MD: Rowman and Littlefield, 1989).

8.	David Landes, *The Unbound Prometheus* (Cambridge: Cambridge University Press, 1969).

9.	Landes, *Unbound Prometheus*.

10.	Josiah Stamp, *Criticism and Other Addresses* (London: E. Benn, 1931).

11.	"Unfortunately, most historians and economists are conditioned to believe that steadily and sharply falling prices must result in depression: hence their amazement at the obvious prosperity and economic growth during this era. For they have overlooked the fact that in the natural course of events, when government and the banking system do not increase the money supply very rapidly, free market capitalism will result in an increase of production and economic growth so great as to swamp the increase of money supply. Prices will fall, and the consequences will be not depression or stagnation, but prosperity (since costs are falling, too) economic growth, and the spread of the increased living standard to all the consumers." Rothbard, *Economic Depressions*.

12.	"Prices certainly fell, but almost every other index of economic activity—output of coal and pig iron, tonnage of ships built, consumption of raw wool and cotton, import and export figures, shipping entries and clearances, railway freight clearances, joint-stock company formations, trading profits, consumption per head of wheat, meat, tea, beer, and tobacco—all of these showed an upward trend." A. E. Musson, "The Great Depression in Britain 1873–96: A Reappraisal," *Journal of Economic History* 19 (1959), 199–228.

13. "A large part at least of the deflation commencing in the 1870s was a reflection of unprecedented advances in factor productivity. Real unit production costs for most final goods dropped steadily throughout the 19th century, and especially from 1873 to 1896. At no previous time had there been an equivalent 'harvest of technological advances' that was so general in their application and so radical in their implications." George Selgin, *Less than Zero: The Case for a Falling Price Level in a Growing Economy* (London: Institute of Economic Affairs, 1997).

14. David A. Wells, *Recent Economic Changes and Their Effect on Production and Distribution of Wealth and Well-being of Society* (New York: Appleton, 1890).

15. Tyler Cowan, "The Deflation of 1873–1896," marginal revolution, August 18, 2011, http://marginalrevolution.com/marginalrevolution/2011/08/the-deflation-of-1873-1896.html.

16. Rendigs Fels, *American Business Cycles, 1865–1897* (Chapel Hill: University of North Carolina Press, 1959).

17. Andrew Tylecote, *The Long Wave in the World Economy* (London: Routledge, 1993).

18. Paul Kennedy, *The Rise and Fall of the Great Powers* (Waukegan, IL: Fontana Press, 1989).

19. Carmen M. Reinhart and Kenneth S. Rogoff, *This Time Is Different: Eight Centuries of Financial Folly* (Princeton, NJ: Princeton University Press, 2009).

20. H. L. Beales and R. S. Lambert, *Memoirs of the Unemployed* (London: Victor Gollancz, 1934).

21. Musson, *The Great Depression in Britain*, 227.

22. Arthur Pigou, *Industrial Fluctuations* (London: Macmillan, 1927), 27.

23. Lewis, *Deceleration of British Growth*, 11–12.

24. C. Feinstein, "British Economic Growth 1700–1831," *Economic History Review* (1983), 374.

25. Lewis, *Deceleration of British Growth*, 17.

26. E. H. Phelps-Brown and P. E. Hart, "The Share of Wages in National Income," *Economic Journal* 62, no. 246 (1952), 253–77; Lewis, *Deceleration of British Growth*, 26.

27. "In the low level of profits in the last quarter of the century we have an explanation which is powerful enough to explain the retardation of industrial growth in the 1880s and 1890s . . . we have here also, in low domestic profits, the solution to the great mystery of British foreign investment, namely why Britain poured so much capital overseas . . . home industry was so unprofitable in the 1880s through the squeeze on profits between wages and prices." Lewis, *Deceleration of British Growth*, 28.

28. Lewis, *Deceleration of British Growth*, 28.
29. Lewis, *Deceleration of British Growth*, 95, table on composite industrial production index to highlight key recessions and booms.
30. "Recessions which occur against a background of prices falling are bound to last longer than those which occur against a background of rising prices . . . the longer the recession lasts, the more prices fall and so the more difficult it is to climb up again." Lewis, *Deceleration of British Growth*, 43.
31. See my explanation for this length of cycle in my book and the reference to the Kuznets cycle, Michael Roberts, *The Great Recession* (London: Lulu, 2009).
32. Lewis, *Deceleration of British Growth*, 45.
33. As Lewis says: "the fundamental objection is that the supply of bank money in this period in not closely related to changes in the supply of gold . . . bank money, the supply of credit seems to have responded to changes in demand, rather than to have initiated the change." But "We are dealing with cumulative forces. If depression leads to bank failures, the decline in the money supply aggravates the depression and if prosperity leads to credit creation, the expansion in money supply may outrun the expansion of trade and reinforce inflation. But neither can one find anything in the monetary history of 1873–1913 which can explain why prices should fall drastically for 20 years and then reverse their movement of the next 20 . . . If the price movement was not due to monetary factors, it must have been due to real factors and the dynamic factor in demand was the rapid growth of industrial production." Lewis, *Deceleration of British Growth*, 67.
34. Lewis, *Deceleration of British Growth*, 77.
35. This chapter will not explain this law but only look at the data that confirm it operated in the Long Depression. The reader must refer to Chapter 6 for a full explanation.
36. For source of data, see Roberts, *The Great Recession*.
37. Gerard Duménil and Dominique Lévy, *The U.S. Economy since the Civil War: Sources and Construction of the Series* (Paris: Economix PSE, 1994).
38. Lewis, *Deceleration of British Growth*, 78.

Chapter 3

1. Randall E. Parker, *Reflections on the Great Depression* (Northampton, MA: Edward Elgar, 2002).
2. Ben Bernanke, *Essays on the Great Depression* (Princeton, NJ: Princeton University Press, 2004).
3. Arthur C. Lewis, *The Deceleration of British Growth*.
4. "The Great Depression was (and in many ways remains) a great puzzle as there were millions of the world's citizens who wanted to consume more housing, food and clothing; and producers by the hundreds

of thousands who wanted to manufacture more housing, food and clothing and yet the two sides could not get together. Why? What was preventing these economically improving, mutually beneficial changes taking place? What was it that prevented people from working and producing more? At this moment, the answer remains largely unknown." Parker, *Reflections on the Great Depression.*

5. John D. Rockefeller, July 8, 1932, in Jeffery Hirsh, *Super Boom* (Hoboken, NJ: John Wiley, 2011), 87.

6. Roger W. Garrison, "The Great Depression Revisited, Review," *Independent Reviews*, March 22, 1999, http://www.highbeam.com/doc/1G1-54504268.html.

7. Andrew Mellon from Herbert Hoover, *The Great Depression*, vol. 3 of The Memoirs of Herbert Hoover, Herbert Hoover Presidential Library and Museum, 1952, www.hoover.nara.gov.

8. Milton Friedman and Anna Schwartz, *A Monetary History of the United States 1867–1960* (Princeton, NJ: Princeton University Press, 1971).

9. "Monetary developments [in the early 1930s] were the major explanation for the depth and the length of the contraction. As I've said over and over again, I'm not saying that that caused the initial recession. . . . And I don't doubt for a moment that the collapse of the stock market in 1929 played a role in the initial recession." There is no boom and slump mechanism in capitalism. "I don't believe there is such a thing as a business cycle [i.e., a boom-bust cycle]. I believe there are economic fluctuations [i.e., occasional lapses from full employment followed by recoveries]." Parker, *Reflections on the Great Depression.*

10. The monetarists considered the Fisher perspective "overblown." Friedman's colleague Anna Schwartz comments: "I'm not impressed with Fisher's contribution as an intellectual contribution. I think he was just explaining his own life [laughter]. I mean here's this guy who's a million dollars in debt to his sister-in-law because he had played the stock market. . . . I don't blame him for expecting that the stock market would just continue in the direction in which it had been moving because he didn't really know what the Federal Reserve was going to do. But then when he got stuck with this enormous debt that he couldn't repay his sister-in-law, I think this seemed to him the explanation of why the Depression had happened." Parker, *Reflections on the Great Depression.*

11. Lee Ohanian, a neoclassical economist who has studied the Great Depression, appeared surprised in an interview by these empirical aspects of the banking crisis during the Great Depression. Ohanian said that "according to the standard financial theory, one would expect that in states in which they were most serious crises and bank runs, depression would have been more intense. However when we try to verify this hypothesis, we were not able to find any correlation between changes in income level of states and the severity of the banking crisis." Parker, *Reflections on the Great Depression.*

12. John Maynard Keynes, *Collected Writings*, vol. 13 (Cambridge: Cambridge University Press, 1978).

13. Keynes, *Collected Writings*, vol. 13.

14. James S. Fackler and Randall E. Parker, "Accounting for the Great Depression: A Historical Decomposition," in *The Seminal Works of the Great Depression*, ed. Randall E. Parker (Cheltenham: Edward Elgar, 2011).

15. These economists use the total factor productivity as their measure, a neoclassical category with dubious validity. But at least the authors look to the supply side for their causes. They go on to blame New Deal employment programs for lowering productivity. Thus the depression was prolonged because of supply-side factors, not a lack of demand as in the Keynesian view. Ohanian in Parker, *Reflections on the Great Depression*.

16. "Nothing similar happened before the Great Depression and the current crisis; instead a sequence of phases of explosion of financial mechanisms—notably the dramatic rise of stock-market indices, unsustainable levels of indebtedness, and the involvement in speculative financial investment—and financial crashes was observed." Gérard Duménil and Dominique Lévy, "The Crisis of the Early 21st Century: Marxian Perspectives," 2012, http://www.jourdan.ens.fr/levy/dle2012f.pdf.

17. Leo Panitch and Sam Gindin, *The Making of Global Capitalism: The Political Economy of the American Empire* (New York: Verso Books, 2014).

18. Panitch and Gindin, *The Making of Global Capitalism*.

19. J. A. Tapia and R. Astarita, *La Gran Recesión y el capitalismo del siglo XXI* (Madrid: Catarata, 2011).

20. Yanis Varoufakis criticizes Marx's theory of crises as failing to explain depressions as opposed to slumps. "Marx told the story of redemptive recessions occurring due to the twin nature of labour and giving rise to periods of growth that are pregnant with the next downturn which, in turn, begets the next recovery, and so on. However, there was nothing redemptive about the Great Depression. The 1930s slump was just that: a slump that behaved very much like a static equilibrium—a state of the economy that seemed perfectly capable of perpetuating itself, with the anticipated recovery stubbornly refusing to appear over the horizon even after the rate of profit recovered in response to the collapse of wages and interest rates." Yanis Varoufakis, "Confessions of an Erratic Marxist in the Midst of a Repugnant European Crisis," December 10, 2013, http://yanisvaroufakis.eu/2013/12/10/confessions-of-an-erratic-marxist-in-the-midst-of-a-repugnant-european-crisis/#_edn2. It could be retorted that Keynesian theory does not explain the reason for slumps.

21. J. Bradford DeLong and Lawrence Summers, "Does Macroeconomic Policy Affect Output?," Brookings Papers on Economic Activity, 1988, 2.

22. J. R. Vernon, "World War II Fiscal Policies and the End of the Great Depression," *Journal of Economic History* 54 (1994), 850–68.

23. Carchedi has summed it up: "Why did the war bring about such a jump in profitability in the 1940–5 period? The denominator of the rate not only did not rise, but dropped because the physical depreciation of the means of production was greater than new investments. At the same time, unemployment practically disappeared. Decreasing unemployment made higher wages possible. But higher wages did not dent profitability. In fact, the conversion of civilian into military industries reduced the supply of civilian goods. Higher wages and the limited production of consumer goods meant that labour's purchasing power had to be greatly compressed in order to avoid inflation. This was achieved by instituting the first general income tax, discouraging consumer spending (consumer credit was prohibited) and stimulating consumer saving, principally through investment in war bonds. Consequently, labour was forced to postpone the expenditure of a sizeable portion of wages. At the same time labour's rate of exploitation increased. In essence, the war effort was a labour-financed massive production of means of destruction." G. Carchedi, *Behind the Crisis* (Leiden: Brill, 2011).

24. J. M. Keynes, *Essays in Persuasion* (New York: Harcourt Brace, 1931).

25. Ben Bernanke, "The Federal Reserve: Looking Back, Looking Forward," speech, Federal Reserve, January 3, 2014.

Chapter 4

1. I will not accept the excuse that the Federal Government has grown so big and powerful that it is beyond the control of any President, any administration or Congress. We are going to put an end to the notion that the American taxpayer exists to fund the Federal Government. .....I will stimulate our economy, increase productivity and put America back to work. The time is now to limit Federal spending," Ronald Reagan, Acceptance speech for the Republican nomination for President, July 17, Transcipt, Public Broadcasting Network, 1980, http://www.pbs.org/wgbh/american-experience/features/primary-resources/reagan-nomination/

2. James Callaghan UK Prime Minister, "We used to think you could spend your way out of recession and increase employment by boosting government spending," 1976 Labour Party Conference, *Daily Telegraph*, "The message from the 1970s on state spending," August 18, 2012.

3. Karl Marx, *Capital* vol. , chapter 13. (Londong: Penguin, 1993).

Chapter 5

1. Robert Lucas papers, 2003 in "Robert E. Lucas Papers, 1960–2004 and undated." Rubenstein library, Duke University.

2. The first rumblings of the crisis could be dated even earlier, to February 2007, when some subprime mortgage securities started to lose value. M. Roberts, *The Great Recession* (London: Lulu, 2009).

3. Alan Greenspan, testimony to Congress, October 23, 2008, http://www.ft.com/cms/s/0/aee9e3a2-a11f-11dd-82fd-000077b07658.html?siteedi-

tion=uk#axzz3SVATArZd.

4.   Greenspan, testimony.

5.   Daniel Gross, *Dumb Money* (New York: Free Press, 2009), 15.

6.   Nassim Nicholas Taleb, T*he Black Swan: The Impact of the Highly Improbable* (New York: Penguin, 2007).

7.   "Crises are neither freak events that modern economics has made them seem nor the rare black swans that others have made them out to be. Rather, they are commonplace and relatively easy to foresee and to comprehend. Call them white swans." Most crises begin with a bubble in which the price of particular asset rises far above its underlying fundamental value. Crises are not black swans but white swans: the elements of boom and bust are remarkably predictable. N. Roubini, "Full Analysis: The Instability of Inequality," *EconoMonitor*, October 17, 2011, http://www.economonitor.com/nouriel/2011/10/17/full-analysis-the-instability-of-inequality/.

8.   "I strongly doubt that stability is achievable in capitalist economies, given the always turbulent competitive markets continuously being drawn toward but never quite achieving equilibrium." He went on, "unless there is a societal choice to abandon dynamic markets and leverage for some form of central planning, I fear that preventing bubbles will in the end turn out to be infeasible. Assuaging the aftermath is all we can hope for." Greenspan, testimony.

9.   Bill Bonner, "Economic Instability as a Result of Extreme Imbecility," *Daily Reckoning*, February 12, 2010, http://dailyreckoning.com/economic-instability-a-result-of-extreme-imbecility/.

10. Ben Bernanke, speech at Federal Reserve Bank of Chicago's 43rd Annual Conference on Bank Structure and Competition, Chicago, May 17, 2007.

11. Federal Deposit Insurance Corporation, Annual report, July 2007, https://www.fdic.gov/about/strategic/report/2007annualreport/chairman.html.

12. Raghuram Rajan, "Has Financial Development Made the World Riskier?," Kansas Federal Reserve symposium, Jackson Hole, August 2005, https://www.kansascityfed.org/PUBLICAT/SYMPOS/2005/PDF/Rajan2005.pdf and Yves Smith, Econned (New York: Palgrave Macmillan, 2010), 10.

13. Lawrence Summers, remarks to the Coalition of Service Industries and Congressional Economic Leadership Council, Washington, DC, August 12, 1997, https://www.treasury.gov/press-center/press-releases/Pages/rr1879.aspx. And Lawrence Summers, testimony before the Joint Senate Committees on Agriculture, Nutrition, and Forestry and Banking, Housing and Urban Affairs, June 21, 2000. Also see Charlie Ferguson, "Larry Summers and the Subversion of Economics," *Chronicle Review*, October 2, 2010, http://chronicle.com/article/Larry-Summersthe/124790/.

14. Alan Greenspan, "The Crisis," Brookings Papers on Economic Activity,

Spring (2010), 201–61, http://www.brookings.edu/~/media/projects/bpea/spring-2010/2010a_bpea_greenspan.pdf.

15. Ryan Grim, "How the Federal Reserve Bought the Economics Profession," *Huffington Post*, October 23, 2009.

16. Robert Auerbach, *Deception and Abuse at the Fed* (Houston: University of Texas Press, 2008), 142.

17. Grim, "How the Federal Reserve Bought the Economics Profession."

18. John Cassidy, "Interview with Eugene Fama," *New Yorker*, January 13, 2010, http://www.newyorker.com/news/john-cassidy/interview-with-eugene-fama.

19. Grim, "How the Federal Reserve Bought the Economics Profession."

20. Grim, "How the Federal Reserve Bought the Economics Profession."

21. Grim, "How the Federal Reserve Bought the Economics Profession."

22. Ben Bernanke, "Monetary Policy and the Global Economy," speech, Department of Economics and STICERD Public Discussion in Association with the Bankof England, London School of Economics, London, March 25, 2013, http://www.federalreserve.gov/newsevents/speech/bernanke20130325a.htm.

23. *Crises: Yesterday and Today*, International Monetary Fund, 14th Annual Jacques Polak Research Conference, November 7–8, 2013; http://www.imf.org/external/np/res/seminars/2013/arc/.

24. "Yet radical redesign of the financial system was largely missing from the conference. After five years of catastrophic macroeconomic performance, 'first steps and early lessons'—to quote the conference title—is not what we should be aiming for. Rather, we should be looking for solutions to the on-going current crisis and strong measures to minimise the chances of anything similar happening again. I worry that the reforms we are focusing on are too small to do that, and that what is needed is a more fundamental rethinking of the design of our financial system and of our frameworks for macroeconomic policy." David Romer at IMF Crises conference.

25. O. Blanchard at IMF Crises conference.

26. George Akerlof, "The Cat in the Tree and Further Observations," *IMF Direct*, May 2013.

27. Akerlof, "The Cat in the Tree and Further Observations."

28. "In sum, we economists did very badly in predicting the crisis. But the economic policies post-crisis have been close to what a good, sensible 'economist-doctor' would have ordered. Those policies have come directly from the Bush and Obama administrations, and from their appointees. They have also been supported by the Congress. The lesson for the future is that good economics and common sense have worked well. We have had trial and success. We must keep this in mind with policy going forward." Joseph Stiglitz, "The Lessons of the North Atlantic Crisis for Economic Theory and Policy," *IMF Direct*, 2013.

29. Stiglitz, "The Lessons of the North Atlantic Crisis."

30. "Standard models had focused on exogenous shocks, and yet it's very clear that a very large fraction of the perturbations to our economy are endogenous. There are not only short run endogenous shocks; there are long run structural transformations and persistent shocks. The models that focussed on exogenous shocks simply misled us – the majority of the really big shocks come from within the economy." Stiglitz, "The Lessons of the North Atlantic Crisis."

31. "In terms of human resources, capital stock, and natural resources, we're roughly at the same levels today that we were before the crisis. Meanwhile, many countries have not regained their pre-crisis GDP levels, to say nothing of a return to the pre-crisis growth paths. In a very fundamental sense, the crisis is still not fully resolved—and there's no good economic theory that explains why that should be the case." Stiglitz, "The Lessons of the North Atlantic Crisis."

32. For him, "Some of this has to do with the issue of the slow pace of de-leveraging. But even as the economy deleverages, there is every reason to believe that it will not return to full employment. . . . This is more than just a balance sheet crisis. There is a deeper cause: The United States and Europe are going through a structural transformation. There is a structural transformation associated with the move from manufacturing to a service sector economy. Additionally, changing comparative advantages requires massive adjustments in the structure of the North Atlantic countries." Stiglitz, "The Lessons of the North Atlantic Crisis."

33. Paul Krugman, *End This Depression Now!* (New York: Norton, 2013), chapter 2.

34. Krugman, *End This Depression Now!*, chapter 2.

35. As Krugman noted, "in the summer of 1940, the US economy went to war. Long before Pearl Harbour, military spending soared as America rushed to replace ships and armaments . . . and army camps were quickly built to house the millions of new recruits…military spending created jobs and family incomes rose . . . as businesses saw their sales growing, they also responded by ramping up spending." Krugman, *End This Depression Now!*

36. Hyman Minsky, "The Financial Instability Hypothesis," Levy Economics Institute Working Paper 74, 1992.

37. Steve Keen, "The Minsky Thesis: Keynesian or Marxian?," in *Financial Keynesianism and Market Instability: The Economic Legacy of Hyman Minsky*, vol. 1, edited by R. Bellofiore and P. Ferri (Cheltenham: Edward Elgar, 2001), 106–20.

38. Recently, Tapia has attempted to synthesize Marx's profit model with a Kalecki-Keen credit model of accumulation. José A. Tapia, "Money and Say's Law: On the Macroeconomic Models of Kalecki, Keen, and Marx," real-world economics review, 70 (February 20, 2015), 110–20, http://www.paecon.net/PAEReview/issue70/Tapia70.pdf.

39. Thus "the Great Recession is not a product of the greed of laisser-faire

capitalism, it is the unintended consequence of very significant inter-
ventions in the operation of the market process: the Fed's expansionary
monetary policy and a set of policies that artificially reduced the costs
and risks of home ownership enabling the creation of highly risky loans
which themselves then lead to even riskier innovations in the financial industry." Robert P. Murphy, "My Reply to Krugman on Austrian
Business-Cycle Theory," *Mises Institute*, 2011, https://mises.org/library/
my-reply-krugman-austrian-business-cycle-theory.

40. "The rate of interest is one of the most important signs of price signals
in any economy. Anything which acts to distort that signal will produce
unintended real economy effects that will eventually have to be corrected by downturn and recession. In the short term, these effects can be
ameliorated or offset by faster growth in credit, but eventually these will
lose traction. Malinvested capital is then exposed and economic activity
turns down as a result." Murphy, "My Reply to Krugman."

41. White admitted that the animal spirits idea has more validity in explaining volatility. But "the Keynesian framework has all its fuzziness and
uncertainties implicit in the principal functional forms being subject to
animal spirits. No wonder, no empirical forecasting by the mainstream
economic bodies can show so much shortcomings." William White,
"Modern Macroeconomics Is on the Wrong Track," *Finance & Development* 46, no. 4 (December 2009).

42. "One tendency that must be resisted is to see this work on imbalances
as related solely to 'financial stability'. In part, this tendency is related
to the misconception that our current problems are limited to those of
a financial crisis." White, "Modern Macroeconomics Is on the Wrong
Track."

43. Michael Kumhof and Romain Rancière, "Leveraging Inequality," *Finance
and Development* (December 2010), 28–31.

44. Joseph. Stiglitz, *The Price of Inequality: How Today's Divided Society
Endangers Our Future* (New York: Norton, 2012).

45. R. Rajan, Faultlines (Princeton, NJ: Princeton University Press, 2010).

46. The varied views on this issue were summed up in a compendium,
ILO, *Income Inequality as a Cause of the Great Recession* (Geneva: ILO,
2011).

47. J. Galbraith, *Inequality and Instability* (New York: Oxford University
Press, 2012).

48. Edward Glaeser, "Does Economic Inequality Cause Crises?," Rappaport
Institute for Greater Boston, December 14, 2010.

49. Roubini, "The Instability of Inequality."

50. R. Reich, *Aftershock* (New York: Vintage, 2011).

51. Kumhof and Rancière, "Leveraging Inequality."

52. So the "bottom group's greater reliance on debt—and the top group's
increase in wealth—generated a higher demand for financial intermediation and the financial sector thus grows rapidly as do the debt-to-in-

come ratios of the middle class relative to the wealthy. The combination of rising middle class debt and stagnant middle class incomes increases instability in financial markets, and the system eventually crashes." Kumhof and Rancière, "Leveraging Inequality."

53. Michael Bordo and Christopher Meissner, "Does Inequality Lead to a Financial Crisis?," NBER Working Paper 17896, 2012.

54. "Using data from a panel of 14 countries for over 120 years, we find strong evidence linking credit booms to banking crises, but no evidence that rising income concentration was a significant determinant of credit booms. Narrative evidence on the US experience in the 1920s, and that of other countries, casts further doubt on the role of rising inequality." Bordo and Meissner, "Does Inequality Lead to a Financial Crisis?"

55. Glaeser, "Does Economic Inequality Cause Crises?"

56. Glaeser refers to Atkinson on this: "Professors Atkinson and Morelli's international data also suggest little regular connection between inequality and crises. Looking at 25 countries over a century, they find ten cases where crises were preceded by rising inequality and seven where crises were preceded by declining inequality." Glaeser, "Does Economic Inequality Cause Crises?"

57. Paolo Lucchino and Salvatore Morelli, "Inequality, Debt and Growth," report, Resolution Foundation (2012).

58. Jonathan D. Ostry, Andrew Berg, and Charalambos G. Tsangarides, "Redistribution, Debt and Growth," IMF Staff Discussion Note 14/02, February 2014, https://www.imf.org/external/pubs/ft/sdn/2014/sdn1402.pdf

59. The IMF paper concluded: "It would . . . be a mistake to focus on growth and let inequality take care of itself, not only because inequality may be ethically undesirable but also because the resulting growth may be low and unsustainable." Ostry, Berg, and Tsangarides, "Redistribution, Debt and Growth."

60. Thomas Piketty and Emmanuel Saez, "Income Inequality in the United States, 1913–1998," Quarterly Journal of Economics 118 (2003), 1–39.

61. See chapter 20 in Roberts, The Great Recession.

62. Engelbert Stockhammer, "Rising Ineqaulity as a Cause of the Present Crisis," Cambridge Journal of Economics, 39 (2013), doi: 10.1093/cje/bet052.

63. In his book, Piketty compared his explanation of growing inequality with Marx's model of recurrent crises (as presented in Marx's nineteenth-century book, the first to be called Capital. Piketty says: "capitalists are concerned to accumulate each year more capital, by will power and perpetuation, or just because their life is already sufficiently high," and then the "return the capital must necessarily be reduced more and more and become infinitely close to zero," otherwise the share of income going to capital would "eventually devour the all of the national income." So there is a "dynamic contradiction pointed to by Marx." So

capitalists must accumulate more to boost productivity "in a desperate attempt to fight against the downward trend in the rate of return." Thomas Piketty, *Capital in the 21st Century* (Cambridge, MA: Harvard Belknap Press, 2014).

64. "Economic activity in a money-making world depends upon factors which affect present or prospective profits." Wesley Mitchell, *Business Cycles* (Berkeley: University of California Press, 1913).

65. 'The engine which drives Enterprise is . . . Profit." J. M. Keynes, *A Treatise on Money* (New York: Harcourt Brace, 1930).

66. J. M. Keynes, *Collected Writings*, vol. 13 (Cambridge: Cambridge University Press, 1978), 343.

67. Minsky, "The Financial Instability Hypothesis."

68. "The financial instability hypothesis incorporates the Kalecki (1965)-Levy (1983) view of profits, in which the structure of aggregate demand determines profits. In the skeletal model, with highly simplified consumption behavior by receivers of profit incomes and wages, in each period aggregate profits equal aggregate investment. In a more complex (though still highly abstract) structure, aggregate profits equal aggregate investment plus the government deficit. Expectations of profits depend upon investment in the future, and realized profits are determined by investment: thus, whether or not liabilities are validated depends upon investment. Investment takes place now because businessmen and their bankers expect investment to take place in the future." Minsky, "The Financial Instability Hypothesis."

69. Paul Krugman, "Fallacies of Immaculate Causation," Conscience of a Liberal, *New York Times*, October 16, 2013, http://krugman.blogs.nytimes.com/2013/10/16/fallacies-of-immaculate-causation/.

70. James Montier, "What Goes Up Must Come Down," GMO White Paper, March 2012.

71. Montier, "What Goes Up Must Come Down."

72. David Levy, Martin Farnham, and Samira Ryan, "Where Profits Come From: Answering the Critical Question that Few Ever Ask," Report, Jerome Levy Forecasting Center, 2008.

73. Cullen Roche, "Budget Deficits Contribute to Corporate Profits, But Don't Matter, Right?," *Pragmatic Capitalism*, October 16, 2013.

74. Roche continues: "but that really shouldn't surprise anyone. After all, when the government pays contractors in Virginia to build planes then those payments get listed as corporate revenues which contribute to the bottom line of corporations. And when you net out investment, household savings, foreign savings and dividends you get the total of corporate profits." Roche, "Budget Deficits Contribute to Corporate Profits."

75. When he said: "public investment should be confined to objects that don't compete with the equipment of private business. Otherwise, the profitability of private investment might be impaired and the effect of

public investment upon employment offset by the negative effect of the decline in private investment." M. Kalecki, "Political Aspects of Full Employment," *Political Quarterly* 14, no. 4 (1943), 322–30.

76. C. Borio and P. White, "Asset Prices, Financial and Monetary Stability: Exploring the Nexus," BIS Working Paper 114, 2002.

77. Robert Skidelsky, *John Maynard Keynes: The Economist as Savior, 1920–1937* (New York: Penguin, 1995), 523.

Chapter 6

1.   Ben Bernanke, *Essays on the Great Depression* (Princeton, NJ: Princeton University Press, 2004).

2.   "Credit accelerates the violent eruptions of this contradiction—crises—and thereby the elements of the disintegration of the old mode of production." Karl Marx, *Capital*, vol. 3 (1895; London: Penguin, 1992), chap. 27.

3.   Marx, *Capital*, vol. 3, chap. 29.

4.   Marx, *Capital*, vol. 3, chap. 29.

5.   "At low levels, debt is good. It is a source of economic growth and stability. But at high levels, public and private debts are bad, increasing volatility and retarding growth. It is in this sense that borrowing can first be beneficial. So long as it is modest. But beyond a certain point, debt becomes dangerous and excessive." S. Cechetti, M. Mohanty, and F. Zampolli, "The Real Effects of Debt," Federal Reserve Bank of Kansas City, 2011.

6.   See E. Thompson and J. Treussard, "The Tulipmania: Fact or Artifact?," UCLA Working Paper, 2002.

7.   Irving Fisher, "The Debt Deflation History of Great Depressions," *Econometrica* 1 (1933), 337–57.

8.   Paul Mattick, *Economic Crisis and Crisis Theory* (Armonk, NY: M. E. Sharpe, 1981), 135.

9.   "In a system of production, where the entire control of the reproduction process rests on credit, a crisis must obviously occur when credit suddenly ceases and cash payments have validity. At first glance therefore, the whole crisis seems to be merely a credit and money crisis." But "what appears to be a crisis on the money market is in reality an expression of abnormal conditions in the very process of production and reproduction." Marx, *Capital*, vol. 3, chap. 27.

10. Marx made it clear that credit and fictitious capital are not the same, but the rise in the measure of global liquidity is a good indicator of the expansion of fictitious capital, too.

11. See the FSB, Defining and Measuring the Shadow Banking System, April 2011.

12. Marx, *Capital*, vol. 3, chap. 27.

13. M. Burke, "The Cash Hoard of Western Companies," *Socialist Economic Bulletin* (October 21, 2013).

14. "In 1995 the investment ratio in the Euro Area was 51.7% and by 2008 it was 53.2%. It fell to 47.1% in 2012. In Britain the investment ratio peaked at 76% in 1975 but by 2008 had fallen to 53%. In 2012 it was just 42.9% (OECD data)." And the cash hoards were up sharply: "The total deposits of NFCs in the Euro Area rose to €1,763bn in July 2013 of which €1,148bn is overnight deposits. This is a rise of €336bn since January 2008, nearly all of which is in overnight deposits, €306bn. In Britain the rise in NFCs bank deposits has been from £76bn at end 2008 to £419bn by July 2013." Burke, "The Cash Hoard of Western Companies."

15. M. Rozworski, "Canada's Profitability Puzzle," Politicalehconomy (blog), December 3, 2013, http://politicalehconomy.wordpress.com/2013/12/03/canadas-profitability-puzzle/.

16. "Because corporations are taking in so much more than they are spending, liquid cash assets in the non-financial corporate sector continue to swell, and now total almost $600 billion." J. Stanford, "Good Time to Rethink Corporate Tax Cuts," *Progressive Economics*, November 14, 2013, http://www.progressive-economics.ca/2013/11/14/good-time-to-rethink-corporate-tax-cuts/.

17. "The ratio of investment to profits has been falling steadily for the past two decades and now sits at just above 60%. Companies are putting less and less of their earnings back into their stock of buildings, machinery and other equipment—the tools they use to produce goods and services. For every dollar earned before tax, only about 60 cents goes back into maintaining and expanding business capital. Compare this to 80 or more cents just a decade ago." Burke, "The Cash Hoard of Western Companies."

18. "We show that this increase is concentrated among firms that do not pay dividends, firms in more recent IPO listing cohorts, and firms in industries that experience the greatest increase in idiosyncratic volatility." T. Bates, K. Kahle, and R. Stulz, "Why Do US Firms Hold so Much More Cash than They Used To?," *Journal of Finance* 64 (2009), 1985–2021.

19. "The greater importance of R&D relative to capital expenditures also has a permanent effect on the cash ratio. Because of lower asset tangibility, R&D investment opportunities are costlier to finance than capital using external capital expenditures. Consequently, greater R&D intensity relative to capital expenditures requires firms to hold a greater cash buffer against future shocks to internally generated cash flow." B. Broadbent, *Costly Capital and the Risk of Rare Disasters* (London: Bloomberg, 2009).

20. "R&D intensive firms require a greater cash buffer against future shocks to internally generated cash flow. In contrast, capital expenditures are more likely to generate assets that can be used as collateral and hence are easier to finance. As a result, capital expenditures may mostly con-

sume cash, which would be consistent with their negative relation with the cash ratio." Broadbent, *Costly Capital.*

21. Broadbent put it: "Yet on a recent Agency visit many companies told me that their hurdle rates of return had risen. Prior to the crisis finance directors would approve new investments that looked likely to pay for themselves (not including depreciation) over a period of six years—equivalent to an expected net rate of return of around 9%. Now, it seems, the payback period has shortened to around four years, a required net rate of return of 14%." He continued: "the investments most vulnerable to such a shift—where you'd expect to find the sharpest increase in required returns— are those that have some element of irreversibility. This will include many projects (spending on intangibles, for example) that are necessary to improve productivity. Thus high risk premia may be inhibiting not just demand but the economy's supply capacity as well . . . Even if the crisis originated in the banking system there is now a higher hurdle for risky investment—a rise in the perceived probability of an extremely bad economic outcome. . . . In reality, many investments involve sunk costs. Big FDI projects, in-firm training, R&D, the adoption of new technologies, even simple managerial reorganisations—these are all things that can improve productivity but have risky returns and cannot be easily reversed after the event." Broadbent, *Costly Capital.*

22. C. Vistesen, "The Big Disconnect between Leverage and Spreads," Seeking Alpha, March 25, 2014, http://seekingalpha.com/article/2107013-the-big-disconnect-between-leverage-and-spreads.

23. "Global debt levels increased rapidly before the global financial crisis. In the decade before 2007, non-financial sector debt to GDP ratios in advanced economies rose by an average of 40 percentage points. Since then, low interest rates have reduced borrowing costs and supported the values of financial and physical assets. Some borrowers have used this period to delever. But low interest rates have also encouraged some private sector borrowers to increase their debt levels. And government debt levels have increased materially. As a result, non-financial sector debt to GDP ratios in advanced economies have risen since 2007, by 55 percentage points on average." Bank of England, *Financial Stability Report* (London: Bank of England, June 2014).

24. Òscar Jordà, Moritz Schularick, and Alan M. Taylor, "Sovereigns versus Banks: Crises, Causes, and Consequences," CEPR Working Paper, 2013. Private credit is aggregate private bank loans to the nonfinancial sector. Public debt is generally consolidated government debt. The average is for seventeen advanced economies: Australia, Belgium, Canada, Denmark, Finland, France, Germany, Italy, Japan, the Netherlands, Norway, Portugal, Spain, Sweden, Switzerland, the United Kingdom, and the United States.

25. Richard Dobbs, Susan Lund, Jonathan Woetzel, and Mina Mutafchie-

va, "Debt and (Not Much) Deleveraging," McKinsey Global Institute, February 2015, http://www.mckinsey.com/insights/economic_studies/debt_and_not_much_deleveraging/.

26. Dobbs, Lund, Woetzel, and Mutafchieva, "Debt and (Not Much) Deleveraging."

27. "The debt we create is basically money we owe to ourselves and the burden it imposes does not involve a real transfer of resources." Paul Krugman, "Debt Is Mostly Money We Owe to Ourselves," Conscience of a Liberal, *New York Times*, December 28, 2011, http://krugman.blogs.nytimes.com/2011/12/28/debt-is-mostly-money-we-owe-to-ourselves/?_r=0.

28. IMF, "Dealing with Household Debt," in *World Economic Outlook: Growth Resuming, Dangers Remain* (Washington, DC: IMF, 2012), 89–124.

29. Gauti Eggertsson and Paul Krugman, "Debt Deleveraging and the Liquidity Trap," Federal Reserve mimeo, November 16, 2010, http://www.princeton.edu/~pkrugman/debt_deleveraging_ge_pk.pdf and "Debt Deleveraging and the Liquidity Trap," Vox EU, November 18, 2010, http://www.voxeu.org/article/debt-deleveraging-and-liquidity-trap-new-model.

30. See my blog posts, "The Cat Is Stuck Up a Tree," Michael Roberts blog, May 10, 2013, https://thenextrecession.wordpress.com/2013/05/10/the-cat-is-stuck-up-a-tree-how-did-it-get-there-and-how-do-you-get-it-down/ and "Revising the Two RRs," April 17, 2013, http://thenextrecession.wordpress.com/2013/04/17/revising-the-two-rrs/.

31. Charles Rosburgh, et al., "Debt and Deleveraging: Uneven Progress on the Path to Growth," Report, McKinsey Global Institute, January 2012.

32. IMF, *World Economic Outlook: Hopes, Realities, Risks* (Washington, DC: IMF, 2013).

33. As John Cochrane put it in his blog, "When I read the review of the 'studies', they are the usual sort of growth regressions or instruments, hardly decisive of causality." In other words, the studies show a correlation between high debt, big budget deficits and recessions, but not the causal direction. J. Cochrane, "The Views of Debt and Stagnation," Grumpy Economist, September 20, 2012, http://johncochrane.blogspot.co.uk.

34. "Debt is the central problem. When debt to income or debt to GDP doubles, triples or quadruples, you have doubled, tripled or quadrupled the amount of future earnings you are using today. That necessarily means you will have less to spend in the future. It's not rocket science." William White, "Modern Macroeconomics Is on the Wrong Track," *Finance & Development* 46, no. 4 (December 2009).

35. The Bank of England explains: "deleveraging in the United States has occurred more quickly than in Europe. Since 2007, the US household debt to GDP ratio has fallen by 15 percentage points, to less than 80%.

And while the US PNFC debt to GDP ratio has risen, it remains lower than in most other advanced economies." Bank of England, *Financial Stability Report.*

36. Societe Generale, "On Our Minds Today: UK SMEs Still in the Doldrums," October 30, 2013.

37. Because "Zombie firms stop workers and money being redeployed to more productive uses, they prevent new, better firms entering the market, they undermine competitiveness, reduce productivity and slow the growth of the whole economy." Societe Generale, "On Our Minds Today."

38. IMF, *Global Financial Stability Report* (Washington, DC: IMF, April 2014), 6.

Chapter 7

1. Paul Mattick, *Business as Usual* (London: Reaktion Books, 2011).

2. David H. Papell and Ruxandra Prodan, "The Statistical Behavior of GDP after Financial Crises and Severe Recessions," University of Houston Research Paper, 2011, http://papers.ssrn.com/sol3/papers.cfm?abstract_id=1933988.

3. IMF World Economic Outlook, April 2015, chapter 1.

4. See Ravi Balakrishnan and Juan Solé, "Close But Not There Yet: Getting to Full Employment in the United States," IMF Direct, April 28, 2015, http://blog-imfdirect.imf.org/2015/04/28/close-but-not-there-yet-getting-to-full-employment-in-the-united-states.

5. See "Strengthening Investment Key to Improving World Economy's B– Grade, Says OECD," March 6, 2015, http://www.oecd.org/economy/strengthening-investment-key-to-improving-world-economy.htm.

6. Catherine Mann, chief economist, press conference, OECD Economic Outlook, June 2015, cited in Financial Times, June 3, 2015, http://www.ft.com/cms/s/0/962772f4-09e0-11e5-a6a8-00144feabdc0.html#axzz3l-WT9r4O2.

7. See World Bank, http://www.worldbank.org/content/dam/Worldbank/GEP/GEP2015a/pdfs/GEP15a_web_full.pdf.

8. World Trade Organization press release, April 14, 2015. Geneva: WTO, https://www.wto.org/english/news_e/pres15_e/pr739_e.htm.

9. WTO press release.

10. See Brad DeLong, "When Do We Start Calling This 'The Greater Depression'?," Washington Center for Equitable Growth, August 28, 2014, http://equitablegrowth.org/2014/08/28/start-calling-greater-depression-early-friday-focus-august-29-2014/.

11. Ben Bernanke, "The Federal Reserve: Looking Back, Looking Forward," speech, Federal Reserve, January 3, 2014.

12. In his speech, Bernanke claimed: "Skeptics have pointed out that the pace of recovery has been disappointingly slow, with inflation-adjusted GDP growth averaging only slightly higher than a 2 percent annual rate

over the past few years and inflation below the Committee's 2 percent longer-term target. However, as I will discuss, the recovery has faced powerful headwinds, suggesting that economic growth might well have been considerably weaker, or even negative, without substantial monetary policy support. For the most part, research supports the conclusion that the combination of forward guidance and large-scale asset purchases has helped promote the recovery. For example, changes in guidance appear to shift interest rate expectations, and the preponderance of studies show that asset purchases push down longer-term interest rates and boost asset prices. These changes in financial conditions in turn appear to have provided material support to the economy." Bernanke, "The Federal Reserve: Looking Back, Looking Forward."

13. Robert Farmer, *Expectations, Employment and Prices* (Oxford: Oxford University Press, 2010).

14. Bernanke admitted this in his speech: "the recovery clearly remains incomplete. At 7 percent, the unemployment rate still is elevated. The number of long-term unemployed remains unusually high, and other measures of labor underutilization, such as the number of people who are working part time for economic reasons, have improved less than the unemployment rate. Labor force participation has continued to decline, and, although some of this decline reflects longer-term trends that were in place prior to the crisis, some of it likely reflects potential workers' discouragement about job prospects." Bernanke, "The Federal Reserve: Looking Back, Looking Forward."

15. See Michael Roberts and Mick Brooks, "It's Time to Take Over the Banks," Fire Brigades Union pamphlet, November 2011.

16. Bob Diamond, BBC Today Business Lecture 2011, http://news.bbc.co.uk/today/hi/today/newsid_9630000/9630673.stm.

17. "When plunder becomes a way of life for a group of men living together in society, they create for themselves in the course of time a legal system that authorises it and a moral code that glorifies it." Frederic Bastiat, *The Law: Selected Essays on Political Economy* (Irvington-on-Hudson, NY: Foundation for Economic Education, 1848).

18. Bill Winters, former head of JP Morgan investment banking: "Banker bashing is a bad thing—if you wake up every morning to be lambasted in the headlines, it is less likely that you will want to work in the field and that reaction will hurt the economy. The UK must stop attacking the industry if it wants to remain a good place for global finance." Bill Winters, "Banker Bashing," *City AM*, February 6, 2013.

19. See Matt Taibi, *Griftopia* (New York: Spiegel and Grau, 2010), for how reckless and fraudulent banking executives have avoided any criminal consequences, even keeping all their ill-gotten gains.

20. As Andy Haldane of the Bank of England pointed out: "There are 400,000 people employed in banking in the UK. The vast majority of those, perhaps even 99%, were not driven by individual greed and were

not professionally negligent. Nor, even in the go-go years, were they trousering skyscraper salaries. It is unfair, as well as inaccurate, to heap the blame on them. For me, the crisis was instead the story of a system with in-built incentives for self-harm: in its structure, its leverage, its governance, the level and form of its remuneration, its (lack of) competition. Avoiding those self-destructive tendencies means changing the incentives and culture of finance, root and branch. This requires a systematic approach, a structural approach, a financial reformation." Andy Haldane, Simon Brennan, and Vasileois Madouros, "The Contribution of the Financial Sector: Miracle or Mirage?," in *The Future of Finance: The LSE Report*, edited by Adair Turner (London: London School of Economics, 2010), pp. 87–120.

21. With caveats: "The combination of financial healing, greater balance in the housing market, less fiscal restraint, and, of course, continued monetary policy accommodation bodes well for U.S. economic growth in coming quarters. But, of course, if the experience of the past few years teaches us anything, it is that we should be cautious in our forecasts." Bernanke, "The Federal Reserve: Looking Back, Looking Forward."

22. See Ryan N. Banerjee, Jonathan Kearns, and Marco Jacopo Lombardi, "(Why) Is Investment Weak?," BIS, March 18, 2015, http://www.bis.org/publ/qtrpdf/r_qt1503g.htm.

23. Paul Krugman, "Profits without Production," op-ed, *New York Times*, June 20, 2013, http://www.nytimes.com/2013/06/21/opinion/krugman-profits-without-production.html.

24. Stewart Lansley, "Wage Led Growth Is an Economic Imperative," New Left Project, September 2, 2013, http://www.newleftproject.org/index.php/site/article_comments/wage_led_growth_is_an_economic_imperative.

25. The United Nations Commission on Trade and Development (UNCTAD), *World Investment Report 2013—Global Value Chains: Investment and Trade for Development* (New York: United Nations, 2013).

26. EU Commission, Winter Economic Forecast (EU Commission, 2014).

27. See Banerjee, Kearns, and Lombardi, "(Why) Is Investment Weak?"

28. JP Morgan, Global Data Watch, April 3, 2015, pp. 13–14.

29. The commission found a "strong negative correlation between changes in investment since the onset of the crisis and pre-crisis debt accumulation, suggesting that the build-up of deleveraging pressures has been an important factor behind investment weakness." EU Commission, Winter Economic Forecast.

30. Richard Dobbs, Susan Lund, Jonathan Woetzel, and Mina Mutafchieva, "Debt and (Not Much) Deleveraging," McKinsey Global Institute, February 2015, http://www.mckinsey.com/insights/economic_studies/debt_and_not_much_deleveraging/.

Chapter 8

1. In Olivier Blanchard et al., "Economic Forum: Policy Responses to the Crises," IMF Economic Forum, video, 1:32.55, November 8, 2013.

2. Doug Short, Advisor Perspectives, 2014, http://www.advisorperspectives.com/dshort/.

3. See Matt Taibi, "The Great American Bubble Machine," *Rolling Stone*, no. 1082 (July 9, 2009).

4. Goldman Sachs, US Economics Analysis, December 2013.

5. Gary Shilling has analyzed this in *The Age of Deleveraging* (New York: Wiley, 2010).

6. Brandon Roberts, Deborah Povich, and Mark Mather, "Low-Income Working Families: The Growing Economic Gap," Policy Brief, Working Poor Families Project, winter 2012–2013, http://www.workingpoorfamilies.org/wp-content/uploads/2013/01/Winter-2012_2013-WPFP-Data-Brief.pdf.

7. Olivier Coibion, Yuriy Gorodnichenko, and Dmitri Koustas, "Amerisclerosis? The Puzzling Rise of US Unemployment Persistence," *Brookings Papers on Economic Activity* 47, no. 2 (2013), 193–260, http://www.brookings.edu/~/media/Projects/BPEA/Fall%202013/2013b_coibion_unemployment_persistence.pdf.

8. OECD report, "Crisis Squeezes Income and Puts Pressure on Inequality and Poverty," http://www.oecd.org/els/soc/OECD2013-Inequality-and-Poverty-8p.pdf.

9. "The State of Working America," 12th ed., Economic Policy Institute, http://www.stateofworkingamerica.org/subjects/overview/?reader.

10. Emmanuel Saez and Gabriel Zucman, "Wealth Inequality in the US Since 1913: Evidence from Capitalized Income Tax Data," NBER Working Paper 20625, October 2014.

11. Claudia Goldin and Lawrence F. Katz, *The Race between Education and Technology* (Cambridge, MA: Harvard University Press, 2008) and National Bureau of Economic Research, May 2009, http://scholar.harvard.edu/files/lkatz/files/the_race_between_education_and_technology_the_evolution_of_u.s._educational_wage_differentials_1890_to_2005_1.pdf.

12. Paul Krugman commented: "So the story has totally shifted; if you want to understand what's happening to income distribution in the 21st century economy, you need to stop talking so much about skills, and *start talking much more about profits and who owns the capital.* Mea culpa: I myself didn't grasp this until recently. But it's really crucial." Paul Krugman, "Human versus Physical Capital," Conscience of a Liberal, *New York Times*, December 11, 2012, http://krugman.blogs.nytimes.com/2012/12/11/human-versus-physical-capital/.

13. Paul Krugman, "The Rise of the Robots," Conscience of a Liberal, *New York Times*, December 8, 2012, http://krugman.blogs.nytimes.com/2012/12/08/rise-of-the-robots/.

Chapter 9

1.   Mick Brooks, "The Crisis of Capitalism and the Euro," Karl Marx net, May 27, 2012, http://www.karlmarx.net/topics/europe/thecrisisofcapitalismandtheeuro.

2.   "During the years that followed the euro's introduction, financial integration proceeded rapidly and markets and governments hailed it as a sign of success. The widespread belief was that it would benefit both south and north—capital was finally able to flow to where it would best be used and foster real convergence. But in fact, a lasting convergence in productivity did not materialize across the European Union. Instead, a competitiveness divide emerged. As the financial crisis gripped the euro area in 2010, these and other problems came to the fore. . . . In fact, there has been little absolute real convergence in the euro area. Those euro area countries that had low per capita incomes in 1999 did not have the highest per capita growth rate." Nemat Shafik, "Convergence, Crisis and Capacity Building in Emerging Europe," IMF Direct, July 27, 2012, http://blog-imfdirect.imf.org/2012/07/27/convergence-crisis-and-capacity-building-in-emerging-europe/.

3.   A report by the Centre for Policy Studies argues that "Estonia proves that a turnaround through swift, sharp austerity is possible for a country provided . . . it is willing to undertake radical supply-side reform alongside curbing spending . . . What is needed are an end to "excessive borrowing, unstable welfare states, high debt burdens, unreformed and illiberal labour markets, excessive regulation etc." Ryan Bourne, "Estonia: A Case Study," CPS, September 2012.

4.   See my post, "Profitability, the Euro Crisis, and Icelandic Myths," Michael Roberts blog, March 27, 2013, at http://thenextrecession. wordpress.com/2013/03/27/profitability-the-euro-crisis-and-icelandic-myths/.

5.   "So is the euro crisis over? No—it's not over until the debt dynamics sing, or perhaps until the debt dynamics sing a duet with internal devaluation. We have yet to see any of the crisis countries reach a point where falling relative wages are generating a clear export-led recovery, or in which austerity is actually paying off in falling debt burdens. But as a europessimist, I do have to admit that it's now possible to see how this could work. The cost—economic, human, and political—will be huge. And the whole thing could still break down. But the ECB's willingness to step up and do its job has given Europe some breathing room." Paul Krugman, "The State of the Euro," Conscience of a Liberal, *New York Times*, January 1, 2014, http://krugman.blogs.nytimes.com/2014/01/01/the-state-of-the-euro-in-one-graph/.

6.   The OECD figures quoted come from OECD, OECD Skills Outlook (Paris: OECD, 2013).

7.   As George Buckley, an economist at Deutsche Bank, points out, up until this point the UK economy has enjoyed a lot of outside help.

"You've got rates at a 300-year low, you've got QE worth almost 25% of GDP, you have the Funding for Lending Scheme . . . [and] the Help to Buy schemes one and two. All of that is a lot of support, and you think to yourself, is that sustainable?" George Buckley, "Bank of England Split," *Daily Telegraph*, February 20, 2013.

8. Michael Burke, "The Cash Hoard of Western Companies," *Socialist Economic Bulletin*, October 21, 2013.

9. See https://flipchartfairytales.wordpress.com/2014/12/17/the-rise-of-the-highly-skilled-but-low-paid-worker/.

10. Michael Roberts, "Argentina, Paul Krugman and the Great Recession," Michael Roberts blog, February 3, 2014, http://thenextrecession.wordpress.com/2014/02/03/argentina-paul-krugman-and-the-great-recession/.

11. Roberts, "Argentina, Paul Krugman and the Great Recession."

12. Michael Roberts, "Eurozone Debt, Monetary Union and Argentina," Michael Roberts blog, May 10, 2012, http://thenextrecession.wordpress.com/2012/05/10/eurozone-debtmonetary-union-and-argentina/.

13. JP Morgan, Eye on the Market, "The Road Less Travelled," May 2, 2012.

14. Global Competitiveness Report 2011–12, World Economic Forum, Geneva (2011). http://www3.weforum.org/docs/WEF_GCR_Report_2011-12.pdf.

15. JP Morgan, Eye on the Market, "The Road Less Travelled."

16. The report is available at http://www.oecd.org/g20/topics/framework-strong-sustainable-balanced-growth/ambitious-reforms-can-create-a-growth-path-that-is-both-strong-and-inclusive.htm.

Chapter 10

1. Paul Krugman, "Japan's Trap," May 1998, http://web.mit.edu/krugman/www/japtrap.html.

2. Paul Krugman, "The Japan Story," Conscience of a Liberal, *New York Times*, February 5, 2013, http://krugman.blogs.nytimes.com/2013/02/05/the-japan-story/.

3. "Here's my take. Japan has pretty much spent the past 20 years in a liquidity trap; as I've been explaining for years, one way to understand such traps is that they happen when, even at a zero real interest rate, the amount that people would want to save at full employment exceeds the amount they would be willing to invest, also at full employment . . . What you need in this situation is a negative real interest rate—which means that you need some expected inflation, because nominal rates face the zero lower bound." Krugman, "The Japan Story."

4. "Oh, and what about the US relevance? We are, for the time being, in the same situation. What I think you can argue is that because we don't share Japan's demographic challenge, our liquidity trap is probably temporary, the product of an episode of deleveraging. So in our case fiscal stimulus is much more likely to serve as a bridge to a revived era

of normal macroeconomics. That said, I welcome efforts by the Fed to modestly raise inflation expectations, and would like to see more. . . . It's a tale of fiscal and monetary policy that have been too cautious, not of stimulus that failed." Krugman, "The Japan Story."

5. Martin Wolf, "Japan Can Put People before Profits," *Financial Times*, February 5, 2013.

6. "The persistent fiscal deficits and deflation are a puzzle. A standard explanation is that they are due to a mistake in monetary policy. If the central bank had avoided deflation, real interest rates could have been negative, making private investment and consumption stronger. I agree that this would have been helpful. But I disagree that deflation is the underlying cause of Japan's ailment." Krugman, "The Japan Story."

7. Wolf "Japan Can Put People before Profits."

8. "The key to a better-balanced economy is taking the vast surplus profits away from a corporate oligopoly that has proved unable to use them. Corporate financial surpluses that end up in vast fiscal liabilities must be trimmed. Let the public enjoy the income instead." Wolf, "Japan Can Put People before Profits."

9. Indeed, he sums up his analysis of Japan in the 2000s as follows: "During the years of 2000–07, Japan grew quite quickly when measured properly (as GDP/working age population), substantially faster than the United States after accounting for demographics. However, during this entire time, it was stuck deep in a liquidity trap, with government spending decreasing and banks and companies deleveraging. Also, Japan did not experience a major improvement in its balance of trade, nor a large currency depreciation, nor an increase in inflation or inflation expectations. Additionally, Japanese services TFP remained flat." He concludes: "I regularly say things like 'Japan confounds macroeconomic analysis.' Now you know what I mean." Noah Smith, "The Koizumi Years: A Macroeconomic Puzzle," Noahopinion (blog), February 9, 2013, http://noahpinionblog.blogspot.co.uk/2013/02/the-koizumi-years-macroeconomic-puzzle.html.

Chapter 11

1. DK Matai, "Can China Save the World?," M2g, August 2, 2011.

2. Although foreign investment was still directed predominantly to other advanced economies.

3. See Michael Roberts, "China's Transition: New Leaders, Old Policies," Michael Roberts blog, November 16, 2012, http://thenextrecession.wordpress.com/2012/11/16/chinas-transition-new-leaders-old-policies/.

4. John Smith, *Imperialism and the Globalisation of Production*, PhD thesis, University of Sheffield, 2010.

5. Jamus Jerome Lim, Sanket Mohapatra, and Marc Stocker, "Tinker, Taper, QE, Bye? The Effect of Quantitative Easing on Financial Flows to De-

veloping Countries," Background paper for Global Economic Prospects 2014, Washington, DC, World Bank.

6.   UNCTAD, World Investment Report (UNCTAD, 2013).

7.   Alejandro Werner, "After a Golden Decade Can Latin America Keep its Luster?," *EconoMonitor*, May 7, 2013, http://www.economonitor.com/blog/2013/05/after-a-golden-decade-can-latin-america-keep-its-luster/.

8.   As the OECD put it in their report on inequality of income in emerging economies: "At one extreme, strong output growth during the past decade went hand-to-hand with declining income inequality in two countries (Brazil and Indonesia). At the other extreme, four countries (China, India, the Russian Federation and South Africa) recorded steep increases in inequality levels during the same period, even though their economies were also expanding strongly." OECD, *Special Focus: Inequality in Emerging Economies* (Paris: OECD, 2011).

9.   Again, as the OECD put it: "This is a particularly serious challenge for South Africa, where geographical divides reflect inequality between races. Although real incomes have been rising for all groups since the end of apartheid, many Africans still live in poverty. At any poverty yardstick, Africans are very much poorer than Coloureds, who are very much poorer than Indians/Asians, themselves poorer than whites." OECD, *Special Focus: Inequality in Emerging Economies*.

10. World Press Freedom Index, 2014, Reporters without Borders, http://rsf.org/index2014/en-middle-east.php.

11. "India's Investment Slowdown," IMF Direct, March 25, 2014, http://blog-imfdirect.imf.org/2014/03/25/indias-investment-slow-down-the-high-cost-of-economic-policy-uncertainty/.

12. OECD, *Special Focus: Inequality in Emerging Economies*.

13. US Bureau of Labor Statistics, "International Comparison of Hourly Compensation Costs" (2011), http://www.bls.gov/fls/#compensation.

14. N. Shafik, "Convergence, Crisis and Capacity Building in Emerging Europe," IMF Direct, July 27, 2013; http://blog-imfdirect.imf.org/2012/07/27/convergence-crisis-and-capacity-building-in-emerging-europe/.

15. John Smith, "Imperialism and the Law of Value," *Global Discourse* 2, no. 1 (2011).

16. Author's calculations from Extended Penn World Tables, August 2011, Adalmir Marquetti, Extended Penn World Tables, Duncan Foley homepage, March 25, 2012, https://sites.google.com/a/newschool.edu/duncan-foley-homepage/home/EPWT.

17. Author's calculations from EU Commisssion, Ameco database, 2014, http://ec.europa.eu/economy_finance/ameco/user/serie/SelectSerie.cfm.

18. World Bank, "China 2030," 2012, http://www.worldbank.org/en/news/2012/02/27/china-2030-executive-summary.

19. John Ross, "China Has Overtaken the US," Key Trends in Globalisation,

September 9, 2013, http://ablog.typepad.com/keytrendsinglobalisation/2013/09/china-has-overtaken-the-us.html.

20. A recent report from the US-China Economic and Security Review Commission provides a balanced and objective review: "The state owned and controlled portion of the Chinese economy is large. Based on reasonable assumptions, it appears that the visible state sector—SOEs and entities directly controlled by SOEs, accounted for more than 40% of China's non-agricultural GDP. If the contributions of indirectly controlled entities, urban collectives and public TVEs are considered, the share of GDP owned and controlled by the state is approximately 50%." Andrew Szamosszegi and Cole Kyle, "An Analysis of State Owned Enterprises and State Capitalism in China," US-China Economic and Security Review Commission, 2011, http://origin.www.uscc.gov/sites/default/files/Research/10_26_11_CapitalTradeSOEStudy.pdf. China Copyright and Media, "CCP Central Committee Resolution Concerning Some Major Issues in Comprehensively Deepening Reform," China Copyright and Media, November 12, 2013, https://chinacopyrightandmedia.wordpress.com/2013/11/15/ccp-central-committee-resolution-concerning-some-major-issues-in-comprehensively-deepening-reform/.

21. Joseph Fan, Randall Morck, and Bernard Yeung, "Capitalizing China," NBER Working Paper 17687, December 2011, http://www.nber.org/papers/w17687.

22. As the paper puts it: "The Chinese Communist Party (CCP), by controlling the career advancement of all senior personnel in all regulatory agencies, all state-owned enterprises (SOEs), and virtually all major financial institutions state-owned enterprises (SOEs) and senior Party positions in all but the smallest non-SOE enterprises, retains sole possession of Lenin's Commanding Heights." China.org, "Third Plenum," 2013, http://wiki.china.org.cn/wiki/index.php/Third_Plenum.

23. As the Fan et al. report says: "The CCP Organization Department manag(es) all senior promotions throughout all major banks, regulators, government ministries and agencies, SOEs, and even many officially designated non-SOE enterprises. The Party promotes people through banks, regulatory agencies, enterprises, governments, and Party organs, handling much of the national economy in one huge human resources management chart. An ambitious young cadre might begin in a government ministry, join middle management in an SOE bank, accept a senior Party position in a listed enterprise, accept promotion into a top regulatory position, accept appointment as a mayor or provincial governor, become CEO of a different SOE bank, and perhaps ultimately rise into upper echelons of the central government or CCP—all by the grace of the CCP OD." Fan, Morck, and Yeung, "Capitalizing China."

24. I did so in Michael Roberts, *The Great Recession* (London: Lulu, 2009), chapter 12. There are other studies that reach slightly different conclu-

sions. Zhang Yu and Zhao Feng, "Rate of Profit in China," 2006, and Mylene Gaulard, "Baisse du taux de profit et croissance chinoise," 2010, http://gesd.free.fr/m6gaulard.pdf, 2010. Also see Esteban Maito, "The Historical Transience of Capital: The Downward Trend in the Rate of Profit since the 19th Century," Working Paper, University of Buenos Aires, Argentina, 2014, http://gesd.free.fr/maito14.pdf.

25. Fung Global Institute, Asian Perspectives, 2014.

26. Typical of these arguments are the comments of James McGregor, *No Ancient Wisdom, No Followers: The Challenges of Chinese Authoritarian Capitalism* (Westport CT: Prospecta Press, 2012). He commented: "China's done well in building infrastructure and getting the nation where it is but state industry is choking off economic growth so they have to re-ignite private industry." James McGregor, January 20, 2014, http://jamesmcgregor-inc.com/.

27. John Ross, "Investment Will Boost China's Economy," Key Trends in Globalisation, November 15, 2013, http://ablog.typepad.com/keytrends-inglobalisation/2012/10/investment-will-boost-chinas-economy.html.

28. Chinag.org, "Third Plenum."

29. China Copyright and Media, "CCP Central Committee Resolution.

30. "On World Bank data China's industrial production in 2007 was only 60% of the US level, whereas by 2011 it was 121%. Therefore in only a six year period China has moved from its industrial production being less than two thirds of the US to overtaking the US by a substantial margin. . . . In six years China's industrial output almost doubled while industrial production in the US, Europe and Japan has not even re-gained pre-crisis levels." Ross, "China Has Overtaken the US."

Chapter 12

1. Karl Marx, *Value Price and Profit* (1864; London: Wildside Press, 2008), chapter 12.

2. N. Kondratiev, *The Long Wave Cycle* (1925; New York: Dutton, 1984).

3. Anwar Shaikh, "The Falling Rate of Profit as the Cause of Long Waves," in *New Findings in Long Wave Research*, edited by A. Kleinknecht, Ernest Mandel, and Immanuel Wallerstein (London: Macmillan, 1992), pp. 174–95, http://gesd.free.fr/shaikh92w.pdf.

4. Noah Smith, "Is the Business Cycle a Cycle?," Noahopinion (blog), February 15, 2013, http://noahpinionblog.blogspot.co.uk/2013/02/is-business-cycle-cycle.html.

5. "There is a new approach in mainstream economics, Hidden Semi-Markov Model, or HSMMs. In an HSMM, there are two 'states' of the economy—a good state, and a bad state. But transitions between these states are abrupt and sudden, rather than smooth as in a harmonic wave. In an HSMM, the likelihood of a transition increases as the time since the last transition increases. In other words, the longer your economy stays in a 'boom' state, the bigger the chances that you're about to suddenly

experience a crash and a transition to a 'bust' state. Again this is not the same as a pure harmonic cycle." Smith, "Is the Business Cycle a Cycle?"

6.   Nate Silver, *The Signal and the Noise: Why Most Predictions Fail—but Some Don't* (New York: Penguin Press, 2012).

7.   Karl Marx, *Capital*, vol. 1 (1867; London: Penguin, 2004), 633.

8.   "I have been telling Moore about a problem with which I have been racking my brains for some time now. However, he thinks it is insoluble, at least pro tempore, because of the many factors involved, factors which for the most part have yet to be discovered. The problem is this: you know about those graphs in which the movements of prices, discount rates, etc. etc., over the year, etc., are shown in rising and falling zigzags. I have variously attempted to analyze crises by calculating these ups and downs as irregular curves and I believed (and still believe it would be possible if the material were sufficiently studied) that I might be able to determine mathematically the principal laws governing crises. As I said, Moore thinks it cannot be done at present and I have resolved to give it up for the time being." Karl Marx, "Letter to Engels," May 31, 1873. *Marx-Engels Werke*, vol. 33, 821.

9.   Karl Marx, *Collected Works* (London: Lawrence and Wishart, 1990), 44:504.

10. Marx, *Collected Works*, 29:105.

11. Marx, *Collected Works*, 40:279–81.

12. Marx, *Collected Works*, 40:282.

13. Karl Marx, *Capital*, vol. 2 (1885; London: Penguin, 1992), 264.

14. Karl Marx, *Capital*, vol. 3 (1895; London: Penguin, 1992), 477n.

15. Shaikh, "The Falling Rate of Profit as the Cause of Long Waves."

16. Minqi Li, Feng Xiao, and Andong Zhu, "Long Waves, Institutional Changes, and Historical Trends," *Journal of World Systems Research* 13 (2007), 33–54, http://gesd.free.fr/lietal.pdf.

17. D. Basu and P. T. Manolakos, "Is There a Tendency for the Rate of Profit to Fall? Econometric Evidence for the US Economy, 1948–2007," *Review of Radical Political Economics* 45 (2012), http://gesd.free.fr/basumano.pdf.

18. Basu and Manolakos, "Is There a Tendency for the Rate of Profit to Fall?," 82.

19. Basu and Manolakos conclude that "under capitalist production or the long-run labor-saving bias of technological change drives the rate of profit to conditionally decline over time. When the counteracting tendencies are strong enough to nullify or even reverse this mechanism, the rate of profit might display an upward movement (as in the period 1982–2000)." Basu and Manolakos, "Is There a Tendency for the Rate of Profit to Fall?"

20. Marx considered the impact of physical destruction on values. "This is most clearly seen in the physical destruction of commodities. This can even happen indirectly in the form of stoppages: Although, in this

respect, time attacks and worsens all means of production (except land), the stoppage would in reality cause far greater damage to the means of production. However, the main effect in this case would be that these means of production would cease to function as such, that their function as means of production would be disturbed for a shorter or longer period." Marx, *Capital*, vol. 3, 362.

21. Claudio Borio, "The Financial Cycle and Macroeconomics: What Have We Learnt?," BIS Working Paper, 2012.

22. Kondratiev, *The Long Wave Cycle*.

23. "Crossing through different stages, capitalism remains capitalism and maintains its basic features and regularities. Otherwise how could these stages be stages of capitalism? . . . I am not aware that the law of value and prices or the law of profit and its conjunctural fluctuations is absolutely different at different stages of capitalist development so as to preclude generalisation." Kondratiev, *The Long Wave Cycle*.

24. Goldstein found that "empirical analysis strongly corroborates long waves in price data both before and after the onset of industrialisation in the late 18th century. Price waves are synchronous among various European countries, reflecting the expansion of the core of the world system and its increasing integration in the industrial era." Joshua Goldstein, "Kondratieff Waves as War Cycles," *International Studies Quarterly* 29 (1985), 411–44.

25. E. Mandel, *Long Waves in Capitalist Development* (New York: Random House, 1995).

26. Joseph Schumpeter, *Business Cycles: A Theoretical, Historical and Statistical Analysis of the Capitalist Process* (New York: McGraw-Hill, 1939).

27. "If the US house price bubble finally burst in 2005, we can expect US house price rises to slip back and fall, at least relative to overall inflation, over the next four years." Michael Roberts, *The Great Recession* (London: Lulu, 2009).

Chapter 13

1. Paul Mattick, *Economic Crisis and Crisis Theory* (London: Merlin Press, 1974).

2. Martin Ford, *The Lights in the Tunnel: Automation, Accelerating Technology and the Economy of the Future* (Acculant, 2009).

3. Jim Davies and Tony Shorrocks, United Nations: Inequality Matters, 2013, http://www.un.org/esa/socdev/documents/reports/Inequality-Matters.pdf and since in Credit Suisse Global Wealth Report (Credit Suisse, 2014).

4. Davies and Shorrocks, Credit Suisse Global Wealth Report.

5. Branco Milanović, "Global Inequality by the Numbers," World Bank Policy Research Working Paper, 2012.

6. Milanović concludes: "Take the whole income of the world and divide

it into two halves: the richest 8% will take one-half and the other 92% of the population will take another half. So, it is a 92-8 world. In the US, the numbers are 78 and 22. Or using Germany, the numbers are 71 and 29. Milanović, "Global Inequality by the Numbers."

7.   "There was a period of more than a century of steady increase in global inequality, followed by perhaps fifty years (between the end of the Second World War and the turn of the 21st century) when global inequality remained on a high plateau, changing very little." Milanović, "Global Inequality by the Numbers."

8.   Olivier Blanchard et al., "Economic Forum: Policy Responses to the Crises," IMF Economic Forum, video, 1:32.55, November 8, 2013.

9.   "Even a great bubble wasn't enough to produce any excess of aggregate demand . . . even with artificial stimulus to demand, coming from all this financial imprudence, you wouldn't see any excess . . . the underlying problem may be there forever." So "we may well need in the years ahead to think about how to manage an economy where the zero nominal interest rate is a chronic and systemic inhibitor of economic activity, holding our economies back below their potential." Blanchard et al., "Policy Responses to the Crisis." Gauti Eggertsson and Neil Mehrotra present a more formal model of secular stagnation, Keynesian-style, based on Alvin Hansen in 1938 toward the end of the Great Depression. Hansen was president of the American Economic Association. He suggested that the Great Depression might just be the start of a new era of ongoing unemployment and economic stagnation without any natural force toward full employment. This idea was called the "secular stagnation" hypothesis. One of the main driving forces of secular stagnation, according to Hansen, was a decline in the population birth rate and an oversupply of savings that was suppressing aggregate demand. Gauti Eggertsson and Neil Mehrotra, "A Model of Secular Stagnation," NBER Working Paper, October 2014.

10.   As Krugman puts it: "What if the world we've been living in for the past five years is the new normal? What if depression-like conditions are on track to persist, not for another year or two, but for decades?" So that "the case for 'secular stagnation'—a persistent state in which a depressed economy is the norm, with episodes of full employment few and far between?" He goes on: "Summers's answer is that we may be an economy that needs bubbles just to achieve something near full employment— that in the absence of bubbles, the economy has a negative natural rate of interest. And this hasn't just been true since the 2008 financial crisis; it has arguably been true, although perhaps with increasing severity, since the 1980s." Paul Krugman, "Secular Stagnation, Coalmines, Bubbles and Larry Summers," Conscience of a Liberal, *New York Times*, November 16, 2013, http://krugman.blogs.nytimes.com/2013/11/16/secular-stagnation-coalmines-bubbles-and-larry-summers.

11.   Paul Krugman, "Secular Stagnation, Coalmines, Bubbles and Larry

Summers," November 16, 2013, *New York Times*, http://krugman.blogs.nytimes.com/2013/11/16/secular-stagnation-coalmines-bubbles-and-larry-summers/?_r=3.

12. Martin Wolf, "Why the Future Looks Sluggish," *Financial Times*, November 20, 2013.

13. Wolf, "Why the Future Looks Sluggish."

14. John Aziz, "On Depressions, the Structure of Production and Fiscal Policy," Noahpinion, October 25, 2013, http://noahpinionblog.blogspot.co.uk/2013/10/on-depressions-structure-of-production.html.

15. "The solution to lowered growth and elevated (and involuntary) *unemployment is relatively simple.* Eventually someone will start using up the idle resources. This will either be the private sector once it independently gets over its slump in animal spirits, or it will be the government." Ah, yes "animal spirits" will return. Or will they? Aziz recognizes that they may not any time soon because "it is perfectly plausible that the economy—as it has done—can remain depressed even with very low rates due to deleveraging pressures, low expectations and low confidence, etc." Aziz, "On Depressions, the Structure of Production and Fiscal Policy."

16. Minqi Li, Feng Xiao, and Andong Zhu, "Long Waves, Institutional Changes, and Historical Trends," *Journal of World Systems Research* 13, no. 1 (2007), 33–54, http://gesd.free.fr/lietal.pdf.

17. Kevin Daly and Ben Broadbent, "The Savings Glut, the Return on Capital and the Rise in Risk Aversion," Global economic paper, Goldman Sachs, May 27, 2009.

18. Esteban Maito, "The Historical Transience of Capital: The Downward Trend in the Rate of Profit since the 19th Century," Working Paper, University of Buenos Aires, Argentina, 2014.

19. Karl Marx, *Capital*, vol. 3 (London: Penguin, 1992), chap. 14.

20. Marx, *Capital*, vol. 3, chap. 15, 367.

21. The UK's right-wing paper *City AM* put it from the perspective of capital: "People, not commodities, land or even capital, are the ultimate resource of an economy, as the US academic Julian Simon famously put it. Without talented, motivated, skilled and educated individuals, nothing is possible; capital itself is a product of labour. Human ingenuity is able to overcome everything. Malthusians who dream of a shrinking population and who reflexively believe that every country is over-populated are wrong. This is always a lesson that nations suffering from shrinking populations relearn at great cost: all the productivity growth in the world is rarely enough to compensate for the psychological and actual effect of a declining population." Allister Heath, "Imagine of the Price of Food Had Gone Up as Fast as Homes," *City AM*, June 14, 2013, http://www.cityam.com/article/imagine-if-price-food-had-gone-fast-homes.

22. George Magnus, *Demographics: From Dividend to Drag, American*

Women, and Abenomics (London: UBS Investment Research, 2013).

23. UN World Population Prospects, 2015 Revision, http://esa.un.org/ unpd/wpp/Publications/Files/Key_Findings_WPP_2015.pdf.

24. John Smith, *Imperialism and the Globalisation of Production*, PhD thesis, University of Sheffield, July 2010.

25. T. Piketty, *Capital in the 21st Century* (Cambridge, MA: Harvard, Belknap Press, 2014).

26. Robert Kurz, "The Apotheosis of Money: The Structural Limits of Capital Valorization, Casino Capitalism and the Global Financial Crisis," 1995, Libcom.org, January 26, 2012, http://libcom.org/library/ apotheosis-money-structural-limits-capital-valorization-casino-capitalism-global-financi.

27. David Graeber, "Of Flying Cars and the Rate of Profit," *Baffler* 19 (2012), http://www.thebaffler.com/salvos/of-flying-cars-and-the-declining-rate-of-profit.

28. "From the internet to nanotech, most of the fundamental advances were funded by government, with businesses moving into the game only once returns were in clear sight. All the radical technologies behind the Iphone were government funded . . . Apple initially received $500,000 from the Small Business Investment Corporation." Mariana Mazzucato, *The Entrepreneurial State: Debunking Private versus Public Sector Myths* (New York: Anthem Press, 2013).

29. Robert J. Gordon, "Is US Economic Growth Over? Faltering Innovation Confronts Six Headwinds," NBER Working Paper 18315, August 2012.

30. Paul Krugman, "Is Growth Over?," *New York Times*, December 26, 2012, http://krugman.blogs.nytimes.com/2012/12/26/is-growth-over/.

31. As Gordon put it in a follow-up paper: "A controversy about the future of U.S. economic growth was ignited by my paper released in late summer 2012. The debate began with my prediction that over some indefinite period of time into the future, perhaps 25 to 40 years, the growth of real per-capita disposable income of the bottom 99% of the U.S. income distribution would average 0.2% per year, compared to 2.0% per year in the century before 2007. This prediction set off a firestorm of controversy with commentary, blogs, and op-eds around the world." Robert J. Gordon, "The Demise of US Economic Growth: Restatement, Rebuttal and Reflections," NBER Working Paper 19895, February 2014.

32. He said, "the primary role of the headwinds in predicting slow future growth escaped notice in the initial round of controversy about innovation." He retorts: "there is no need to forecast that innovation in the future will 'falter,' because the slowdown in the rate of productivity growth over the past 120 years already occurred more than four decades ago. The future forecast assumes that innovations in the next 40 years will be developed at the same pace as the last four decades, but reasons for scepticism are provided for that prediction." Gordon, "Demise of US Economic Growth."

33. Kenneth Rogoff, "Malthus, Marx and Modern Growth," Project Syndi-
    cate, March 4, 2014, http://www.project-syndicate.org/commentary/
    kenneth-rogoff-identifies-several-obstacles-to-keeping-living-stan-
    dards-on-an-upward-trajectory.

34. After all, "so far, every prediction in the modern era that mankind's lot
    will worsen, from Thomas Malthus to Karl Marx, has turned out to be
    spectacularly wrong . . . despite a disconcerting fall in labour's share of
    income in recent decades, the long-run picture still defies Marx's pre-
    diction that capitalism would prove immiserating for workers. Living
    standards around the world continue to rise." Rogoff, "Malthus, Marx
    and Modern Growth."

35. "Will each future generation continue to enjoy a better quality of life
    than its immediate predecessor? In developing countries that have not
    yet reached the technological frontier, the answer is almost certainly yes.
    In advanced economies, though the answer should still be yes, the chal-
    lenges are becoming formidable." Rogoff, "Malthus, Marx and Modern
    Growth."

36. Erik Brynjolfsson and Andrew McAfee, *Race Against the Machine: How
    the Digital Revolution Is Accelerating Innovation* (Lexington, MA: Digi-
    tal Frontier Press, 2011).

37. International Labor Organization, World of Work Report, 2014, http://
    www.ilo.org/global/research/global-reports/world-of-work/2014/lang--
    en/index.htm.

38. Edwin Chan and Nicola Leskie, "Apple to Return MAC Production to
    US in 2013," Reuters, December 7, 2012, http://uk.reuters.com/arti-
    cle/2012/12/07/us-apple-manufacturing-idUSBRE8B50R120121207.

39. Agam Shar, "Lenovo Hopes to Reach US Consumer Faster with Made
    in US Computers," PC World, October 11, 2012, http://www.pcworld.
    com/article/2011590/lenovo-hopes-to-reach-us-customers-faster-with-
    made-in-usa-computers.html.

40. J. Manyika et al., "Manufacturing the Future: The Next Era of Global
    Growth and Innovation," McKinsey Global Institute Report, November
    2012, http://www.mckinsey.com/insights/manufacturing/the_future_of_
    manufacturing.

41. See http://www.theguardian.com/world/2011/aug/01/foxconn-ro-
    bots-replace-chinese-workers.

42. Ford, *The Lights in the Tunnel*.

43. Krugman put it: "The effect of technological progress on wages depends
    on the bias of the progress; if it's capital-biased, workers won't share ful-
    ly in productivity gains, and if it's strongly enough capital-biased, they
    can actually be made worse off. So it's wrong to assume, as many people
    on the right seem to, that gains from technology always trickle down to
    workers; not necessarily. It's also wrong to assume, as some (but not all)
    on the left sometimes seem to that rapid productivity growth is neces-
    sarily jobs- or wage-destroying. It all depends." Krugman, "Technology

and Wages," Conscience of a Liberal, *New York Times*, December 10, 2012, http://krugman.blogs.nytimes.com/?s=the+effect+of+technological+progress+.

44. "Economic Possibilities for Our Grandchildren," "for the first time since his creation man will be faced with his real, his permanent problem—how to use his freedom from pressing economic cares, how to occupy the leisure, which science and compound interest will have won for him, to live wisely and agreeably and well." J. Keynes, *Essays in Persuasion* (New York: Harcourt Brace, 1931).

45. Carl Benedict Frey and Michael A. Osborne, "The Future of Employment," Oxford Martin School, Oxford, September 17, 2013, http://www.oxfordmartin.ox.ac.uk/downloads/academic/The_Future_of_Employment.pdf.

46. Ford, *The Lights in the Tunnel*.

47. "There is no way to envision how the private sector can solve this problem. There is simply no real alternative except for the government to provide some type of income mechanism for consumers." Ford, The Lights in the Tunnel. Ford does not propose socialism, of course, but merely a mechanism to redirect lost wages back to "consumers." Such a scheme would threaten private property and profit.

48. "Multiple economic, social, geopolitical and ecological forces are now converging towards the final demise of the existing world system, the capitalist world economy. All have reached their advanced phases and this demise will take place in front of the eyes within the lifetime of many readers." Minqi Li, *The Rise of China and the Demise of the World Economy* (New York: Monthly Review Press, 2009).

49. "I'm going to argue here that the problem is rooted in the requirements of capitalist reproduction, that large corporations are destroying life on earth, that they can't help themselves, they can't change or change very much, that so long as we live under this system we have little choice but to go along in this destruction, to keep pouring on the gas instead of slamming on the brakes, and that the only alternative—impossible as this may seem right now—is to overthrow this global economic system and all of the governments of the 1% that prop it up, and replace them with a global economic democracy, a radical bottom-up political democracy, an ecosocialist civilization." Richard Smith, "Beyond Growth or Beyond Capitalism," *Truthout*, January 15, 2014, http://www.truthout.org/news/item/21215-beyond-growth-or-beyond-capitalism.

50. IPCC, Fifth Assessment Report (AR5), October 2013, http://www.ipcc.ch/report/ar5/index.shtml.

51. Stocker said: "People always pick 1998 but that was a very special year, because a strong El Niño made it unusually hot, and since then there have been a series of medium-sized volcanic eruptions that have cooled the climate." IPCC, Fifth Assessment Report.

52. Judith Curry, "How People are Reacting to the UN's Climate Change

Report," *Blaze*, September 27, 2013, http://www.theblaze.com/sto-ries/2013/09/27/how-are-climate-change-skeptics-reacting-to-the-u-n-s-climate-report/.

53. Alister Doyle and Simon Johnson, "Scientists More Convinced Mankind Is Main Cause of Warming," *Reuters*, September 27, 2013, http://uk.reuters.com/article/2013/09/27/uk-climate-ipcc-idUKBRE-98Q0A820130927.

54. See http://www.independent.co.uk/environment/climate-change/ipcc-report-the-financial-markets-are-the-only-hope-in-the-race-to-stop-global-warming-8843573.html.

55. John Cook et al., "Quantifying the Consensus on Anthropogen-ic Global Warming in the Scientific Literature," *Environmental Research Letters*, May 15, 2013, http://iopscience.iop.org/arti-cle/10.1088/1748-9326/8/2/024024/pdf.

56. IPCC, Fifth Assessment Report.

57. "As individual capitalists are engaged in production and exchange for the sake of the immediate profit, only the nearest, most immediate results must first be taken into account. As long as the individual man-ufacturer or merchant sells a manufactured or purchased commodity with the usual coveted profit, he is satisfied and does not concern him-self with what afterwards becomes of the commodity and its purchas-ers." F. Engels, *The Dialectics of Nature* (Moscow: Progress Publishers, 1976).

58. "What cared the Spanish planters in Cuba, who burned down forests on the slopes of the mountains and obtained from the ashes sufficient fertilizer for one generation of very highly profitable coffee trees—what cared they that the heavy tropical rainfall afterwards washed away the unprotected upper stratum of the soil, leaving behind only bare rock!" Engels, *The Dialectics of Nature*.

59. Karl Marx, *Das Kapital, The Skeptical Reader Series* (Washington, DC: Regnery Publishing, 2009), 209.

60. José Tapia Granados and Oscar Carpintero, "Dynamics and Economic Aspects of Climate Change," in *Combating Climate Change: An Agri-cultural Perspective*, edited by Manajit S. Kang and Surinder S. Banga (Boca Raton, FL: CRC Press, 2013).

61. As Granados goes onto to say: "However, even in 2009 when the global economy contracted 2.25%, global emissions did not decrease, they just ceased growing to start growing again next year when the world econ-omy somewhat recovered. This shows how dependent on fossil fuels the world economy has become in recent years. In earlier recessions of the global economy—in the mid-1970, early-1980s, early-1990s and late-1990s—emissions not only decreased in many countries, as we have shown, but also worldwide. The notion that economic growth will reduce the carbon intensity of the world economy (the ratio of global emissions to WGDP) is inconsistent with the fact that the carbon inten-

sity of the global economy has increased in recent years. In 2010, after the Great Recession, WGDP grew 5.0%, but emissions grew faster, 5.9%. Furthermore, the average growth of global CO_2 emissions was 3.1% per year in 2000–2011, while it had been 1.0% per year in 1990–2000, and 2.0% per year in 1980–1990." Granados and Carpintero, "Dynamics and Economic Aspects of Climate Change."

62. Doyle and Johnson, "Scientists More Convinced ."
63. Unless a price could be put on carbon emissions that was high enough to force power companies and manufacturers to reduce their fossil-fuel use, there seemed to be little chance of avoiding hugely damaging temperature increases." IPCC, Fifth Assessment Report.
64. In *Wealth of Nations*, Smith explained: "The first and last duty of the sovereign is that of erecting and maintaining those public institutions and those public works, which though they may be in the highest degree advantageous to a great society are, however, of such a nature that the profit could never repay the expense to any individual." And Smith meant by this "good roads, navigable canals, harbours and education." Adam Smith, *The Wealth of Nations* (1776; New York: Barnes and Noble, 2004).
65. R. Smith, "Beyond Growth or Beyond Capitalism," Truthout, January 15, 2014, http://www.truth-out.org/news/item/21215-beyond-growth-or-beyond-capitalism.

Appendix 1

1. Karl Marx, *Capital*, vol. 3 (1895; London: Penguin, 1992), chapter 13.
2. Gérard Duménil and Dominic Lévy, "The Crisis of the 21st Century: A Critical Review of Alternative Interpretations," 2012, http://www.jourdan.ens.fr/levy/dle2011e.pdf.
3. This is a major debate between Andrew Kliman, Michel Husson, and Fred Moseley, see Duménil and Lévy's comments in "The Crisis of the 21st Century."
4. Duménil and Lévy, "The Crisis of the 21st Century."
5. Simon Mohun, "The Present Crisis in Historical Perspective," paper presented at Historical Materialism conference, November 2010.
6. Minqi Li, Feng Xiao, and Andong Zhu, "Long Waves, Institutional Changes, and Historical Trends," *Journal of World Systems Research* 13 (2007), 33–54, http://gesd.free.fr/lietal.pdf.
7. David Kotz, "Accumulation and Crisis in Contemporary US Economy," *Review of Radical Political Economics* 40, no. 2 (2008), 174–88.
8. A. Shaikh, "First Great Depression of the 21st Century," Socialist Register 47 (2011).
9. G. Economakis, A. Anastasiadis, and M. Markaki, "An Empirical Investigation on the US Economic Performance from 1929 to 2008," *Critique: Journal of Socialist Theory* 38, no. 3 (2010), 465–87.
10. E. Bakir and A. Campbell, "Neoliberalism, the Rate of Profit and the

Rate of Accumulation," *Science and Society* (July 2010).

11. Andrew Kliman, "The Persistent Fall in Profitability Underlying the Crisis," *Marxist Humanist Initiative*, March 2010.

Appendix 2

1. As arch-Keynesian Simon Wren-Lewis put it in his blog: "an empirically based aggregate model. You do not find macroeconomic papers like this in the better journals nowadays. Even if papers like this were submitted, I suspect they would be rejected. Why has this style of macro analysis died out? . . . First, such models cannot claim to be internally consistent. Even if each aggregate relationship can be found in some theoretical paper in the literature, we have no reason to believe that these theoretical justifications are consistent with each other. The only way of ensuring consistency is to do the theory within the paper—as a microfounded model does. A second reason this style of modelling has disappeared is a loss of faith in time series econometrics." Simon Wren-Lewis, "Microfoundations—Is There an Alternative?," mainly macro (blog), March 13 2012, http://mainlymacro.blogspot.co.uk/2012/03/microfoundations-is-there-alternative.html.

2. To use Ben Bernanke's recent term; see "Monetary Policy and the Global Economy," speech, Department of Economics and STICERD Public Discussion in Association with the Bankof England, London School of Economics, London, March 25, 2013, http://www.federalreserve.gov/newsevents/speech/bernanke20130325a.htm.

3. "Microfoundations allegedly goes around the Lucas critique by focusing on 'deep' structural, invariant parameters of optimizing individuals' preferences and tastes . . . this is an empty hope without solid empirical or methodological foundation." Lars adds: "The almost quasi-religious insistence that macroeconomics has to have microfoundations—without ever presenting neither ontological nor epistemological justifications for this claim—has put a blind eye to the weakness of the whole enterprise of trying to depict a complex economy based on an all-embracing representative actor equipped with superhuman knowledge, forecasting abilities and forward-looking rational expectation." Lars Syll, "The State of Microfoundations and Macroeconomics," Lars P. Syll blog, March 16, 2012, http://larspsyll.wordpress.com/?s=Microfoundations+allegedly+goes+around+the+Lucas+critique+.

4. As the grand old man of the neoclassical aggregate production function, Robert Solow, commented on DSGE models: "a modern economy is populated by consumers, workers, pensioners, owners, managers, investors, entrepreneurs, bankers, and others, with different and sometimes conflicting desires, information, expectations, capacities, beliefs, and rules of behavior . . . To ignore all this in principle does not seem to qualify as mere abstraction—that is setting aside inessential details. It seems more like the arbitrary suppression of clues merely because they

are inconvenient for cherished preconceptions . . . Friends have remind-
ed me that much effort of 'modern macro' goes into the incorporation
of important deviations from the Panglossian assumptions . . . [But]
a story loses legitimacy and credibility when it is spliced to a simple,
extreme, and on the face of it, irrelevant special case. This is the core of
my objection: adding some realistic frictions does not make it any more
plausible than an observed economy is acting out the desires of a single,
consistent, forward-looking intelligence." Robert Solow, "The State of
Macroeconomics," *Journal of Economic Perspectives* 22, no. 1 (2008),
243–49, quoted in Syll, "The State of Microfoundations and Macroeconomics."

5.   Edward Glaeser, "Does Economic Inequality Cause Crises?," *New York
Times*, December 14, 2010.

6.   Robert J. Gordon, "Is Modern Macro or 1978 Macro More Relevant?,"
paper presented at International Colloquium on the History of Economic Thought, São Paulo, 2009, http://economics.weinberg.northwest-
ern.edu/robert-gordon/GRU_Combined_090909.pdf.

7.   Larry Summers, former adviser to Clinton and Obama and a Harvard
economist, complained: "In four years of reflection and rather intense
involvement with this financial crisis, not a single aspect of dynamic stochastic general equilibrium has seemed worth even a passing
thought." He moaned: "Is macro about—as it was thought before
Keynes, and came to be thought of again—cyclical fluctuations about
a trend determined somewhere else, or about tragic accidents with
millions of people unemployed for years in ways avoidable by better
policies? If we don't think in the second way, we are missing our major
opportunity to engage in human betterment. And inserting another
friction in a DSGE model isn't going to get us there." Larry Summers,
Axel Weber, Mervyn King, Ben Bernanke, and Olivier Blanchard, "'I Do
Not Believe the Long Run Can Be Ceded to the Avatars of Austerity'
Weblogging," Brad DeLong's Grasping Reality, March 25, 2013, http://
delong.typepad.com/sdj/2013/03/mervyn-king-ben-bernanke-olivier-
blanchard-lawrence-summers-axel-weber.html.

8.   Summers advised Obama "not to take ownership of the banks as he has
a healthy skepticism about schemes involving large government action
and an awareness of the possibilities of unintended consequences." John
Cassidy, "Is Larry Summers the New Henry Kissinger?," *New Yorker*,
May 18, 2010, http://www.newyorker.com/rational-irrationality/is-lar-
ry-summers-the-new-henry-kissinger.

Index

About Haymarket Books

Haymarket Books is a nonprofit, progressive book distributor and publisher, a project of the Center for Economic Research and Social Change. We believe that activists need to take ideas, history, and politics into the many struggles for social justice today. Learning the lessons of past victories, as well as defeats, can arm a new generation of fighters for a better world. As Karl Marx said, "The philosophers have merely interpreted the world; the point, however, is to change it."

We take inspiration and courage from our namesakes, the Haymarket Martyrs, who gave their lives fighting for a better world. Their 1886 struggle for the eight-hour day, which gave us May Day, the international workers' holiday, reminds workers around the world that ordinary people can organize and struggle for their own liberation. These struggles continue today across the globe—struggles against oppression, exploitation, hunger, and poverty.

It was August Spies, one of the Martyrs targeted for being an immigrant and an anarchist, who predicted the battles being fought to this day. "If you think that by hanging us you can stamp out the labor movement," Spies told the judge, "then hang us. Here you will tread upon a spark, but here, and there, and behind you, and in front of you, and everywhere, the flames will blaze up. It is a subterranean fire. You cannot put it out. The ground is on fire upon which you stand."

We could not succeed in our publishing efforts without the generous financial support of our readers. Many people contribute to our project through the Haymarket Sustainers program, where donors receive free books in return for their monetary support. If you would like to be a part of this program, please contact us at info@haymarketbooks.org.

Shop our full catalog online at www.haymarketbooks.org or call 773-583-7884.

Also Available from Haymarket Books

A Short History of the U.S. Working Class:
From Colonial Times to the Twenty-First Century
Paul Le Blanc

BRICS: An Anti-capitalist Critique
Edited by Patrick Bond and Ana Garcia

Building Global Labor Solidarity in a Time of Accelerating Globalization
Edited by Kim Scipes

Capitalism's Crisis Deepens: Essays on the Global Economic Meltdown
Richard Wolff

The Capitalist Cycle
Pavel Maksakovsky

Exploring Marx's Capital: Philosophical, Economic and Political
Dimensions
Jacques Bidet

Financialization in Crisis
Edited by Costas Lapavitsas

Marx's Capital Illustrated
David N. Smith

Returns of Marxism: Marxist Theory in a Time of Crisis
Edited by Sara R. Farris

Your Money or Your Life: The Tyranny of Global Finance
Eric Toussaint

Zombie Capitalism: Global Crisis and the Relevance of Marx
Chris Harman

About the Author

Michael Roberts has worked as an economist for more than thirty years in the City of London financial center. He is author of *The Great Recession: A Marxist View*, published in 2009.